商务英语系列课程教材　　　　　　**总主编**　肖云南

商务英语笔译
Business English Translation

边　毅　编著

清华大学出版社
北京交通大学出版社
·北京·

内 容 简 介

本书是《商务英语系列课程教材》之一，共15个单元，分为两部分：前9个单元为英译汉，后6个单元为汉译英。每个单元的基本内容为：佳译赏析（具体学习和分析优秀译作）、他山之石（探讨某些译作中存在的不足）、学生译作分析（点评学生在翻译实践中常见的问题）、翻译技巧介绍（通过实例介绍常用的翻译技巧）、课堂翻译训（供教师课堂安排学生实践之用）、课后练习（供学生课后巩固提高）。

本书可供商务英语等专业的学生使用，也可供具有一定英语水平的自学者学习参考。

本书封面贴有清华大学出版社防伪标签，无标签者不得销售。
版权所有，侵权必究。侵权举报电话：010-62782989　13501256678　13801310933

图书在版编目（CIP）数据

商务英语笔译/边毅编著．—北京：清华大学出版社；北京交通大学出版社，2010.6
（2017.8重印）
（商务英语系列课程教材）
ISBN 978-7-5121-0136-4

Ⅰ.①商… Ⅱ.①边… Ⅲ.①商务-英语-翻译-教材 Ⅳ.①H315.9

中国版本图书馆CIP数据核字（2010）第104562号

商务英语笔译
SHANGWU YINGYU BIYI

责任编辑：张利军　　特邀编辑：易　娜	
出版发行：清华大学出版社　　邮编：100084　电话：010-62776969　http://www.tup.com.cn	
北京交通大学出版社　邮编：100044　电话：010-51686414　http://www.bjtup.com.cn	
印　刷　者：北京鑫海金澳胶印有限公司	
经　　　销：全国新华书店	
开　　　本：185 mm×230 mm　　印张：24.5　　字数：706千字	
版　　　次：2010年6月第1版　　2017年8月第4次印刷	
书　　　号：ISBN 978-7-5121-0136-4/H·202	
印　　　数：6 001～7 000册　　定价：36.00元	

本书如有质量问题，请向北京交通大学出版社质监组反映。对您的意见和批评，我们表示欢迎和感谢。
投诉电话：010-51686043，51686008；传真：010-62225406；E-mail：press@bjtu.edu.cn。

前 言

迈入新世纪和加入WTO，我国正逐步地参与国际竞争，同世界接轨。随着全球经济的发展和市场化的运作，英语作为国际贸易用语变得越来越重要，社会上也越来越迫切地需要既有专业知识又能熟练运用英语的人才。在这一新形势下，一些有条件的院校纷纷开设商务英语专业，商务英语已经进入了很多高校的课程之中。21世纪是一个充满机遇和挑战的时代，它为当前的商务英语教学提出了更新、更高的要求。怎样才能有效地提高学生的实际语言运用能力，培养既有专业知识又能熟练运用英语的人才，使学生所学的知识跟上时代的节奏，符合社会经济生活的实际需求，已成为英语教育工作者的历史责任，也是日益发达的经济和社会发展的需要。

为了适应新的形势，满足高等院校商务英语专业学生和社会上各阶层商务工作者的需求，我们组织编写了这套《商务英语系列课程教材》。目的是帮助商务英语、国际贸易等专业的学生有效地解决学习中出现的问题，让更多的人通过商务英语系列课程的学习，快速提高商务英语听、说、读、写、译等各方面的能力，掌握国际商务领域最新的知识和动态，不断提高自身素质和专业水平，迎接国际竞争的挑战，为祖国的现代化建设服务。

《商务英语系列课程教材》是国家教育部新世纪网络课程建设工程项目之一，本系列教材包括《商务英语听说》（修订本）、《商务英语阅读（精读本）》、《商务英语选读（泛读本）》（第2版）、《商务英语写作》（修订本）、《商务英语笔译》、《商务英语口译》、《国际商务英语综合教程》、《国际商务谈判》（修订本）、《国际贸易实务》、《国际市场营销》、《国际支付与结算》（修订本）、《国际商法》、《国际商务导论》、《国际金融》、《西方经济学导论》、《国际商务礼仪》、《世界贸易组织导论》等。随着国际商务的发展和读者的需要，我们还将不断对这一系列教材进行补充和修订，以期形成受读者欢迎的动态系列教材。本系列教材可作为高等院校商务英语等相关专业的普及教材，也可供社会上从事外贸和商务工作的读者使用。

本系列教材具有以下特色。

1. 本系列教材内容新、全面，专业性、可操作性强。
2. 本系列教材强调专业基础，重视语言运用，各书均配有大量练习，注重全面提高学生运用商务知识和英语的能力。

3. 本系列教材中的部分教材设计有配套的课程软件，便于学生自主学习。操作上可灵活掌握，不仅可供在校生课堂学习，还可以面向全国网络课程的学生和在职人员自学，覆盖面广。

4. 本系列教材的编写者均为从事商务英语教学的一线教师，具有多年丰富的教学经验和极强的事业心和敬业精神。大部分教材由作者根据自身教学经验编写了配套的参考答案，可与同行交流，便于教师授课和辅导学生进行课后实践。如有需要者请与本书作者联系，电子邮件地址为：bian.yi@gmail.com，或与北京交通大学出版社联系，电子邮件地址为：cbszlj@jg.bjtu.edu.cn。

本书是《商务英语系列课程教材》之一，共15个单元，分为两大部分：第1～9单元为英译汉部分，第10～15单元为汉译英部分。每个单元的基本内容为：佳译赏析，具体学习和分析优秀的译作；他山之石，探讨某些译作中存在的不足之处；学生译作分析，点评学生在翻译实践中常见的问题；翻译技巧介绍，通过实例介绍常用的翻译技巧；课堂翻译练习，供教师课堂安排学生实践之用，教师可以随堂点评；课后练习，供学生课后巩固提高之用。

本书具有两大特色：第一，选取的材料一律与商务有关，内容涉及经济、金融、营销、贸易、零售、电子商务和商务礼仪等，而且例句特别丰富，更能体现出商务的特色；第二，书中的"它山之石"和"学生译作分析"两个模块为读者提供了大量的"反面教材"，通过分析和探讨一些有缺陷的译例，帮助读者掌握正确的翻译方法，提高商务英语的翻译水平。

本书可供商务英语等专业的学生使用，也可供其他商务英语自学者学习参考。

由于编著者水平有限，书中不妥之处在所难免，敬请广大读者批评指正。

编　者
2010年6月

学习指导

本书的英文选材全部来自英语国家最新报刊、杂志、网络上所登载的商务文章,内容涉及零售、营销、银行、证券、人力资源、国际贸易、广告等商务领域,所用语言能够反映出当今商务英语的基本特点。中文文章均来自国家权威的刊物。

听、说、读、写、译是英语专业学生必须具备的5个基本技能,但"翻译"这个技能是最难掌握和提高的。翻译不仅要求译者具有一定的英语水平,而且要求译者具有一定的汉语表达能力,而商务英语翻译还要求译者具有一定的商务知识,对各种商务活动有一定的了解。提高翻译水平应该从以下几个方面着手。

(1) 首先应该提高自己的英语水平。英语水平的提高当然不是一朝一夕的事情。除了学习基础的英语课本外,平时应该大量阅读商务方面的英文杂志,熟悉商务英语文体和商务词汇,特别是商务英语的表达习惯和用语。这样,通过日积月累,今后在翻译商务英语文献时就知道用什么对应的汉语来表达。建议学生课后扩大阅读量,上网搜索相关的商务网站寻找阅读资料。

(2) 经常阅读一些商务方面的中文报刊杂志,熟悉经济和商务方面的术语和表达方式,还要注意掌握一些基本的商务知识,如保险、证券、旅游等,因为这些知识对今后的翻译是极有帮助的。另外,经常阅读中文报刊对汉语表达能力的提高也大有益处,因为潜移默化的影响对语言技能的提高作用非常明显。建议学生阅读财经方面的文章,关心时事,阅读经济及财经新闻。

(3) 定期做对比翻译练习是迅速提高翻译水平的有效方法。可以找一篇短文(中英文均可),同时找到该短文的译文,然后自己先将短文翻译出来,反复修改后再对照他人的译文,找出不同之处,这样就可以发现自己译文和他人译文的不同并分出优劣,从而提高自己的翻译水平。这种练习不一定多,但一定要精,也就是说自己翻译时一定要认真和仔细,不可随意,翻译好之后要反复琢磨,仔细推敲,当自己觉得十分满意后再去参阅他人的译文,只有这样才会发现他人译文中的不同特点和处理手法,进而得到迅速提高。选择他人的译文应该注意译文的质量,最好是比较权威的杂志和报刊。学生可以利用本书中所选择的所有文章分段进行此类练习。本书中的"他山之石"和"学生译作分析"更是详尽地分析了一些译作中的优劣之处,学生可以参照这些方法对自己的译作进行分析。

(4) 最后,翻译是一项艰苦而复杂的工作,要真正提高这种技能,反复练习和学习他人的优秀翻译作品是唯一的途径。所以,建议学生多读、多练、多分析,经过一段时间的练习,翻译水平一定能够得到很大的提高。

Contents

Part 1　English-Chinese
英译汉

Unit 1
- 佳译赏析 ··· (2)
  - No Innovation Can Replace Direct Discussions ············· (2)
    创新无法取代直接沟通
- 他山之石 ··· (15)
- 学生译作分析 ·· (17)
- 翻译技巧介绍 ·· (19)
  - 省略（Omission） ·· (19)
- 课堂翻译训练 ·· (23)
- 课后练习 ··· (24)

Unit 2
- 佳译赏析 ··· (26)
  - Growth in Millionaires' Club Slows Sharply ················ (26)
    全球富翁财富增长速度锐减
- 他山之石 ··· (35)
- 学生译作分析 ·· (38)
- 翻译技巧介绍 ·· (40)
  - 数字等的翻译（Translating Figures, etc.） ················· (40)
- 课堂翻译训练 ·· (49)
- 课后练习 ··· (50)

I

Unit 3

- 佳译赏析 ··· (53)
  - Tips for Attire in the Workplace ······················· (53)
  - 工作场所着装有妙招
- 他山之石 ··· (66)
- 学生译作分析 ·· (68)
- 翻译技巧介绍 ·· (70)
  - 词类的转换（Conversion） ······························· (70)
- 课堂翻译训练 ·· (77)
- 课后练习 ··· (78)

Unit 4

- 佳译赏析 ··· (81)
  - A Gold Mine Called Home Shopping ··················· (81)
  - 有座金矿叫"在家购物"
- 他山之石 ··· (88)
- 学生译作分析 ·· (90)
- 翻译技巧介绍 ·· (92)
  - 增译（Amplification） ···································· (92)
- 课堂翻译训练 ·· (102)
- 课后练习 ··· (103)

Unit 5

- 佳译赏析 ··· (105)
  - How Nike Figured Out China ··························· (105)
  - 耐克是如何摸清中国的（I）
- 他山之石 ··· (116)
- 学生译作分析 ·· (119)
- 翻译技巧介绍 ·· (121)
  - 意译（Translating Meaning） ··························· (121)
- 课堂翻译训练 ·· (124)
- 课后练习 ··· (125)

Unit 6

- 佳译赏析 ··· (127)
  - How Nike Figured Out China ································· (127)
  - 耐克是如何摸清中国的(Ⅱ)
- 他山之石 ··· (136)
- 学生译作分析 ··· (138)
- 翻译技巧介绍 ··· (140)
  - 定语从句的翻译(Translating Attributive Clauses) ········· (140)
  - 同位语从句的翻译(Translating Appositive Clauses) ······ (147)
- 课堂翻译训练 ··· (148)
- 课后练习 ··· (149)

Unit 7

- 佳译赏析 ··· (152)
  - Nine Roads to Riches ·· (152)
  - 生财九道
- 他山之石 ··· (167)
- 学生译作分析 ··· (169)
- 翻译技巧介绍 ··· (171)
  - 被动语态的翻译(Translating Passive Voice) ················ (171)
- 课堂翻译训练 ··· (177)
- 课后练习 ··· (178)

Unit 8

- 佳译赏析 ··· (181)
  - 5 Rules for Finding the Next Dell ···························· (181)
  - 如何寻找下一个戴尔?
- 他山之石 ··· (196)
- 学生译作分析 ··· (198)
- 翻译技巧介绍 ··· (199)
  - 长句和复杂句子的翻译(Translating Long and Complex Sentences) ··· (199)
- 课堂翻译训练 ··· (206)
- 课后练习 ··· (207)

Unit 9

- 佳译赏析 ·· (209)
  - The Growth of Direct Marketing and Electronic Business ········ (209)
  - 直接营销和电子商务的发展
- 他山之石 ·· (224)
- 学生译作分析 ·· (225)
- 翻译技巧介绍 ·· (226)
  - 商务词语和术语的翻译（Translating Business Terms）········· (226)
- 课堂翻译训练 ·· (231)
- 课后练习 ·· (232)

综合测试 1 ·· (235)

Part 2 Chinese-English
汉译英

Unit 10

- 佳译赏析 ·· (240)
  - 全球性失衡和高油价双重威胁下的世界经济与中国 ········· (240)
    World Economy and China Threatened by Global Economic Disequilibrium and Surging Oil Prices
- 他山之石 ·· (250)
- 学生译作分析 ·· (252)
- 翻译技巧介绍 ·· (253)
  - 连动式的处理 ··· (253)
- 课堂翻译训练 ·· (258)
- 课后练习 ·· (259)

Unit 11

- 佳译赏析 ·· (261)
  - 外资信用卡不赚钱？ ·· (261)
    Is There Profit in China's Foreign Credit Card Market?
- 他山之石 ·· (275)

学生译作分析 …………………………………………………… (276)
　　翻译技巧介绍 …………………………………………………… (277)
　　　　习语及商务术语的翻译（Translating Idioms and Business Terms）……… (277)
　　课堂翻译训练 …………………………………………………… (281)
　　课后练习 ………………………………………………………… (282)

Unit 12

　　佳译赏析 ………………………………………………………… (284)
　　　　一般货物进口合同 ………………………………………… (284)
　　　　Purchase Contract
　　他山之石 ………………………………………………………… (300)
　　学生译作分析 …………………………………………………… (301)
　　翻译技巧介绍 …………………………………………………… (302)
　　　　商务合同的翻译（Translating Business Contracts）……… (302)
　　课堂翻译训练 …………………………………………………… (309)
　　课后练习 ………………………………………………………… (310)

Unit 13

　　佳译赏析 ………………………………………………………… (312)
　　　　猎头公司瞄准中国公司 …………………………………… (312)
　　　　China's Green Pastures Beckon Headhunters
　　他山之石 ………………………………………………………… (321)
　　学生译作分析 …………………………………………………… (322)
　　翻译技巧介绍 …………………………………………………… (323)
　　　　顺序法、逆序法和变序法 ………………………………… (323)
　　课堂翻译训练 …………………………………………………… (326)
　　课后练习 ………………………………………………………… (327)

Unit 14

　　佳译赏析 ………………………………………………………… (329)
　　　　追求公平 …………………………………………………… (329)
　　　　A Developing Inequity
　　他山之石 ………………………………………………………… (344)

v

学生译作分析 ·· (346)
　　翻译技巧介绍 ·· (347)
　　　　词语的选择 ·· (347)
　　课堂翻译训练 ·· (351)
　　课后练习 ·· (352)

Unit 15
　　佳译赏析 ·· (354)
　　　　广东玩具业：召回事件不是滑铁卢 ···························· (354)
　　　　Back from the Brink
　　他山之石 ·· (364)
　　学生译作分析 ·· (366)
　　翻译技巧介绍 ·· (367)
　　　　重复处理 ·· (367)
　　课堂翻译训练 ·· (375)
　　课后练习 ·· (376)

综合测试 2 ·· (377)

参考文献 ·· (379)

English-Chinese
英译汉

 佳译赏析

"No Innovation Can Replace Direct Discussions"
"创新无法取代直接沟通"

From *Fortune*, July 26, 2004
By Janet Guyon, Richard Tomlinson, Clay Chandler

That's what Samsung[1] CEO[2] Jong-Yong Yun, whose company prizes technology, says about understanding local markets.[3] Going global has always been a tricky business.[4] For many people, the emergence of a global economy has meant unprecedented wealth and unparalleled access to goods and services. A cosmetics brand born in Tennessee can become wildly popular in Shanghai. For those in business, however, globalization has brought unrelenting change and fierce competition. To find out how the best companies manage in a world that's getting smaller and more complicated, we asked two CEOs of Fortune Global 500 companies[5] how they've stayed on the top of the game.[6] Whether based in Europe, the US, or Asia, they've successfully managed global businesses in everything from refrigerators to fragrances.[7] Here's what they had to say.

韩国三星是一家崇尚技术的公司。该公司的首席执行官尹钟龙在谈到如何理解本地市场时说了标题中的这句话。走向全球一直是件难事。对许多人来说，全球化经济的出现意味着前所未有的财富及前所未有的获取产品和服务的方式。一个产于美国田纳西州的化妆品品牌可以在中国上海大受欢迎。然而，对商界人士来说，全球化意味着无情的变革和激烈的竞争。为了探究世界上那些出类拔萃的公司在这样一个日益变小、日趋复杂的世界中是如何进行管理的，我们采访了《财富》杂志"全球500强"中的五家公司的首席执行官，问他们是怎样始终稳居世界领先地位的。无论他们公司的总部设在欧洲、美国，还是亚洲，他们都成功地管理着各种全球性的企业，产品应有尽有，从冰箱到香水各不相同。让我们来听听他们的说法。

Lindsay Owen-Jones
L'Oreal[8]
CEO since 1988
林赛·欧文－琼斯
（自 1988 年开始担任法国欧莱雅公司首席执行官）

ON WHAT MAKES A GLOBAL BRAND[9]: Ultimately it is a question of imagination and intuition in equal parts. It is intuition (when one asks) what do these brands have that just might seduce the world?[10] But also in terms of imagination, what could they become to seduce the world?[11] It took imagination to think that a nice, homey, very basic, user-friendly, popular, and cheap but really not sophisticated make-up line called Maybelline made in Memphis could become the hottest thing for young women in Shanghai.[12] That is why this business is always looking for candidates who not only have basic business disciplines but also an ability to dream. We call them, in French, poetes et paysans.

关于怎样打造国际品牌：从根本上说，打造国际品牌既需要想像力，又需要直觉，两者同样重要。如果有人问公司靠什么才能打造出吸引全球消费者的品牌？答案是直觉。当然，要打造出国际品牌，公司同样离不开想像力。正是因为有了想像力，有人才会想到，产于美国孟菲斯的叫做美宝莲的系列化妆品——有品位、简单、实用、方便、广受欢迎、价格便宜而实际上并非高档的产品——可能会成为上海年轻女士们的最爱。也正是因为这个原因，本企业总是在寻求既具备基本业务素质，又具有想像力的人才。在法语中，我们称这类人才是"诗人加农夫"。

ON RESEARCHING MARKETS: We try to do a major market visit every month. Since the beginning of the year we've been to the US, Japan, Russia, Germany, and Brazil. Typically, the first day we will spend just visiting stores. That's an opportunity not just to look at the stores but to look at what women are wearing and what they've got in their shopping carts. You look at them buying all kinds of other things, not just our products. I usually like to have a quick look at the clothes department if it is a department store, or perhaps cereal or instant coffee if I'm in a supermarket.[13]

关于市场实地考察：我们每个月都争取做一次大型的市场调查。从今年年初到现在，我们已经考察了美国、日本、俄罗斯、德国和巴西。通常，在第一天我们只去商场看看。不只是借此机会考察商场，同时还要留意女士们的穿着，瞧瞧她们的购物车里都装了些什么。你会发现她们不仅买我们的商品，还买其他各种各样的东西。如果去的是百货商店，我一般会去卖服装的地方瞅瞅；如果去的是超级市场，我可能会去卖麦片或速溶咖啡的地方转转。

ON BEAUTY: Understanding what women want anywhere, including your home country, is a major challenge[14], especially in something as personal as beauty. People do not talk honestly of their aspirations. You knock on the door and say, "Do you have a secret aspiration to be a chic French woman?" — they would laugh you out of the door[15]. The key words I would use are observation, cultural understanding, empathy, and intuition. These are probably more important than the traditional scientific marketing-research approaches. I think we are helped by our European heritage. Cultural diversity is an everyday factor of differences.[16] Our success in the US has been heightened by our understanding and awareness of ethnic differences.[17] Every new country you are successful in gives you an added dimension of understanding how the world is different.[18]

关于美：在任何地方——包括你自己的国家——要了解女士们的需求都相当困难，尤其是问她们有关"什么是美"这类个人的问题时。谈到内心的渴望时，人们总是不愿实话实说。如果你去敲人家的门，问："在你心灵深处，是不是很希望成为一位优雅时尚的法国女士？"——她们一定会让你走开。我坚持认为这样几个词语非常关键，即观察、文化上的理解、心领神会和直觉。它们可能比传统的科学的市场调研方法更加重要。我觉得我们的欧洲传统对我们帮助不小。各国市场千差万别，而各国文化上的差异是最根本的。我们在美国的成功很大程度上得益于我们对当地种族差异的理解和认知。你每在一个国家的市场上获得成功，你就会对世界的多样性多一分了解。

ON SETTING AN EXAMPLE: When you have spent a day tramping from morning to evening, and from store to store, eating sandwiches in a minibus as you go from one place to another, you are sending an unwritten message[19] to teams everywhere in the world that the CEO is doing the same thing he expects them to do — which is for all of us to avoid (living) in some sort of ivory tower and to listen to our customers.[20]

关于树立榜样：如果某一天你从早到晚都在商场之间奔波，窝在小公共汽车里从一个地方赶往另一个地方，吃几块三明治充饥，你就是无形中向你在世界各地的员工传递着这样一个信息：他们的首席执行官希望他们做的事，他自己也在身体力行——也就是说我们都不能脱离实际（整天只呆在办公室里），而是应直接去了解顾客的需要。

ON LONG-TERM PLANNING: Everybody who manages a business at L'Oreal has a basic responsibility to the company to do what we (call) "a cow and calves policy".[21] You are responsible not only for managing profitably today's business but also for preparing what will be profitable many years after you have left that particular country or assignment.[22] And you will be judged not only on your ability to produce the numbers now but on the credibility of the plans that will be there when you leave — to create businesses that one day will be the future.[23]

关于长期规划：在欧莱雅，每一位企业管理者都对公司负有一项基本责任，我们称之为"母牛和小牛政策"。你在位时应该使企业创收，而且还必须制定长期规划，以便在你离开那个特定的国家或职位许多年之后，企业仍然能够盈利。这是你的责任。企业对你的评价不仅要看你在位时的创收能力，还要看你在位时所制定的那些长期发展规划在你离职之后能否实施——因为这些规划中（所要创办）的企业将是整个公司的未来。

Charles O. Holliday
DuPont[24]
CEO SINCE 1998
查尔斯·霍利德
（自1998年开始担任杜邦公司首席执行官）

ON GLOBAL EXPANSION: Developing countries are growing more rapidly, but you need to make sure you're bringing in the right products and services at the right time.[25] We have ways of looking at the economy in each country to see if it's ready for agricultural products, automotive products, or construction products. The metric we had going into a developing country was $1,000 GDP[26] per capita, and that's still a general rule of thumb.[27] But averages can be terrible in developing countries because they can be much different in the cities than in the country.[28] You see that in China, where the differences in income are as wide as they can be between the coastal areas and the inner provinces. So we've done regional breakdowns. We look at Jakarta vs. the rest of Indonesia, for example. Jakarta might have a GDP of $1,500 per capita, yet the rest of the country is at $800. We might put in distribution around the major cities if we can't get it into the entire country yet. In China, we sell our Corian countertop material to the upper end. We also bought a producer of solid-surface countertop that's lower end. We're using our branding on it and all our technology to make it an even better lower-end product.

关于全球扩展：发展中国家正在加速发展，但你得保证你是在适当的时候向这些国家输出适当的产品和服务。我们有多种办法观察每个国家的经济状况，看看他们引进农产品、汽车产品或建筑材料的时机是否成熟。什么时候才是进入一个发展中国家市场的时机呢？以前我们是看该国人均国内生产总值是否达到1000美元，现在我们仍然按这个老办法来办理。但是在发展中国家，平均数可能极不可靠，因为城乡差别非常之大。你在中国就能看到这些城乡差别，沿海地区和内陆省份的收入差距就相当悬殊。因此，我们对不同地区的情况做了仔细的分析。比如，我们把雅加达和印度尼西亚的其他地区做了区分。雅加达的人均国内生产总值可能达到了1500美元，可该国其他地区只有800美元。因此，如果我们还无法把市场扩展到整个国家，或许可以先围绕大城市开展销售活动。在中国，我们的"可丽耐"面材就是面向高端用户。我们还收购了一家生产低端产品——实体面材——的生产商，对其产品冠以我们自己的品牌，并完全用我们的技术进行生产，使之成为更好的低端商品。

ON CHINA: We see China as a big logistics and distribution challenge. We build smaller facilities close to our customers to maximize the logistics, as opposed to a big, cost-efficient plant. The other thing about China is they are turning out about 300,000 engineers a year, compared with 62,000 in the US, and they are technically just as good as[29] our crop in the US So we are doing more of our engineering in China.

关于中国：我们认为，在中国进行物流和分销面临着巨大的挑战。为了尽可能地扩大物流，我们在离顾客近的地方设立了比较小的工厂，而不建设成本低而效益高的大工厂。中国的另外一个国情是，他们每年培养出的工程师约30万名，而相比之下美国每年毕业的工程师为6.2万名，而且，论技术水平，他们的技术水平同我们在美国的工程师不相上下。所以，在中国，我们的工程业务更多些。

ON US COMPETIITIVENESS: The real test is if we can go to a higher level of knowledge-content products, which means more research and development around biotechnology and nanotechnology. If we are successful in leading the world in those sciences, then the US is going to be very successful. If we can't, it's more problematic. Let's take genetically modified food[30], which is a big business for us. The US is a world leader today. And the approvals from other parts of the world are starting to come in. Brazil and China are accepting genetically modified soybeans, for instance. It's a great example of how the US is winning.

关于美国的竞争力：真正的考验在于我们能否开发出知识含量更高的产品，这意味着要对生物技术和纳米技术进行更多的研究和开发。如果我们能在这些科学领域里领先世界，那么美国就将非常成功。如果我们做不到，问题就大了。以转基因食品为例，它可是我们的大买卖。目前，美国在这方面走在世界的前面，而其他国家也开始逐渐批准转基因食品的使用，例如巴西和中国也已开始接受转基因大豆。这是美国胜券在握的最好例证。

ON CORPORATE SOCIAL RESPONSIBILITY: You need to pay attention to local customs and practices. In India, we wanted to do something good for a community where we were trying to build a plant. So we decided to put up a free clinic with a nurse and some over-the-counter medicines. We saw that as a big need. We then found that an activist group was pushing against our building the plant. Lo and behold, a local doctor was in the activist group. We weren't thoughtful enough about the fact that we were taking his business away by building a free clinic. How could we be so stupid? We ended up moving the plant to a different town. It's critical to have good people on the ground who know the customers. But we never compromise our ethical standards. We try to think local and resource global.

关于企业的社会责任：你得注意每个地方的风俗和习惯做法。我们曾试图在印度的某处建厂，想为当地的社区谋些福利。于是我们决定开一个免费诊所，配备一名护士，并提供一些非处方药。我们认为当地人很需要这样的诊所。可后来我们发现当地的一个环保激进团体反对我们建设这个工厂。你瞧，原来本地一位医生就在这个组织里。我们考虑不周，没有想到建了免费诊所就等于抢了他的生意。我们怎么会如此愚蠢？最后，我们只能换了个城镇建厂。找一些了解客户的本地人至关重要。但无论怎样，我们都会恪守自己的道德准则。我们要努力做到思维本地化、运筹全球化。

Words and Expressions

prize	v.	to value highly; to esteem or treasure; to appreciate 重视，尊重或珍视
global	a.	of, relating to, or involving the entire earth; worldwide 全球的，有关全球的或涉及全球的，全世界的 global economy 世界经济 global monetary policies 全球金融政策
tricky	a.	difficult because unreliable or uncooperative; having concealed difficulty; difficult, hard, not easy; requiring great physical or mental effort to accomplish or comprehend or endure （工作等）棘手的，复杂的，微妙的
business	n.	an affair or matter 事务，事件 We will proceed no further in this business. 我们在这件事上将不再有什么进展。 a strange business 一件怪事
unrelenting	a.	not diminishing in intensity, pace, or effort 在强度、步伐或努力程度上未减弱的
on the top of the game		(colloq.) ahead of the game; having an advantage; winning （口语）有优势，赢 He tries to stay ahead of the game by keeping up with the new software. 他一直在紧跟软件的更新，试图使自己有竞争优势。
base	v.	to establish or use somewhere as the main place for your business or work 把基地（总部）设在……
fragrance	n.	scent, perfume 香水
seduce	v.	to win over; attract 征服，吸引
intuition	n.	a sense of something not evident or deducible; an impression 直觉（对不明显或不可推断的事物的感觉、印象）
homey	a.	having a feeling of home; comfortable; cozy 家庭般的，舒适的，温暖的，有家的感觉的
user-friendly	a.	(user-friendlier, user-friendliest) easy to use or learn to use 容易（学会）使用的，〈计〉用户界面友好的，用户容易掌握使用的

sophisticated	a.	very complex or complicated 非常复杂精密或尖端的
		the latest and most sophisticated technology 最新最尖端的技术
make-up line		化妆产品
line	n.	merchandise or services of a similar or related nature 系列商品，相关的服务，形式相似或相关的（某一类）商品或服务
		carry a complete line of small tools 包揽了小工具的全部商品
Memphis		a US city of southwest Tennessee on the Mississippi River near the Mississippi border 孟菲斯（美国田纳西州西南部城市，位于密西西河边，接近密西西比州边界）
hot	a.	popular;(*informal*) arousing intense interest, excitement, or controversy 时新的，富于刺激性的，轰动一时的，极风行的，热门的
		a hot new book 一本畅销的新书
		a hot topic 有争议的话题
poetes et paysans		〈法语〉诗人和农夫（=poets and peasants）
cereal	n.	a grass such as wheat, oats, or corn, the starchy grains of which are used as food 谷物（一种如小麦、燕麦或玉米的禾本科植物，其淀粉质谷粒可作为食物）
		a food prepared from any of these plants, especially a breakfast food made from commercially processed grain 荞麦食品（一种用这些作物做成的食品，尤指商业加工过的谷类食物，如早餐吃的麦片粥等）
chic	a.	adopting or setting current fashions and styles; sophisticated 时尚的，采纳或设定当今时尚和风格的，不落俗套的
		chic, well-dressed young executives 穿着考究的年轻经理们
laugh one out of		(*colloq.*) drive one out of; destroy one's credibility in (through ridicule or scorn) 赶走某人，毁坏某人的可信度（通过嘲笑或蔑视）
		They'll laugh you out of court if you file that stupid lawsuit. 如果你提交那起愚蠢的诉讼，他们将把你逐出法庭。
empathy	n.	identification with and understanding of another's situation, feelings, and motives 移情作用，认同和理解别人的处境、感情和动机
heighten	v.	to raise or increase the quantity or degree of; intensify 增加，增强（升高或增加数量或程度）
ethnic	a.	of, relating to, or distinctive of members of such a group 种族风格的（属于、关于或区别于这样一个集团中的成员的）
		ethnic restaurants 民族风味的饭馆
		ethnic art 民族艺术
tramp	vi.	to wander about aimlessly 流浪（毫无目的地四处漂泊）

ivory tower		a place or an attitude of retreat, especially preoccupation with lofty, remote, or intellectual considerations rather than practical everyday life 隐退的地方和态度（尤指致力于崇高的、深邃的或智慧的思考，而不是实际的日常生活），脱离实际的小天地
metric	*n.*	a standard of measurement 度量，衡量标准
GDP	*abbr.*	(Gross Domestic Product) 国内生产总值（一个经济体系在特定时期内生产的所有货品及服务的总值，其中包括消费、政府购买、投资及出口减进口） 对比：Gross National Product(GNP)—the total market value of all the goods and services produced by a nation during a specified period 国民生产总值（指一段特定时期内一国生产的货物和服务的市场总值，相等于国内生产总值加国内人民来自海外投资的收入，减去海外人民在国内赚取的收入）
per capita		per unit of population; per person 每人，人均，按人口计算 In that year, Americans earned $15,304 per capita. Among the states, Connecticut has a high per capita income. 那一年，美国的人均收入为 15 304 美元，在所有州中康涅狄格州的人均收入较高。
rule of thumb		【复数】a useful principle having wide application but not intended to be strictly accurate or reliable in every situation 经验法则（一种可用于许多情况的有用的原则，但并不是放诸四海皆准）
breakdown	*n.*	an analysis, an outline, or a summary consisting of itemized data or essentials 分析，概要（一个包含逐条列出的数据或要素的分析、纲要或总结）
put in		to spend (time) at a location or job 花时间，在某一场所或工作上花费（时间） The inmate had put in six years at hard labor. 犯人已经做了 6 年的苦工。 She put in eight hours behind a desk. 她花了 8 小时办公。
countertop	*n.*	a level surface on a cabinet or display case, as in a kitchen or department store 工作台面（贮藏橱或陈列柜的水平表面）
logistics	*n.*	(used with a sing. or pl. verb) the branch of military operations that deals with procurement, distribution, maintenance, and replacement of materiel and personnel （与单数或复数动词连用）后勤学，后勤，军事后勤学，军事行动的分支（负责物资和人员的获得、分配、维护和补充）
biotechnology	*n.*	the use of microorganisms, such as bacteria or yeasts, or biological substances, such as enzymes, to perform specific industrial or manufacturing processes 生物工艺学（利用微生物，如细菌、酵母或生物物质而进行的具体工业或生产过程）
nanotechnology	*n.*	纳米技术
over-the-counter	*a.*	that can be sold legally without a doctor's prescription 不需处方可以出售的，无医生开的处方也可合法出售的

	over-the-counter drugs	无医生开的处方也可合法出售的药
lo and behold	lo and behold	你瞧（表示惊讶的感叹词）；哟，你瞧！
on the ground	in the actual place where something, especially a war, is happening, rather than in another place where it is being discussed	多用于新闻报道中，指实地报道，这里引申为"在当地"

Notes

1 Samsung 韩国三星电子公司
   总部设在韩国的三星电子集团是世界上最大的电子产品制造商之一。

2 CEO 首席执行官
   A chief executive officer (CEO) or chief executive is the highest-ranking corporate officer or executive officer of a corporation, company, or agency.

3 That's what Samsung CEO Jong-Yong Yun, whose company prizes technology, says about understanding local markets. 韩国三星公司是一家崇尚技术的公司，该公司的首席执行官尹钟龙在谈到如何理解本地市场时说了标题中的这句话。
   该句中的非限制性定语从句"whose company prizes technology"如果就地处理，两头的句子不好处理，因此将其放到句首就更通顺一些。另外，"prizes"在这里译成"崇尚、尊重或者推崇"比译成"重视"或者"珍视"更贴切。这句话也可以译成："韩国三星公司向来崇尚技术。"

4 Going global has always been a tricky business. 走向全球一直是件难事。
   "Going global..."本来是"expand business in the whole world"的意思，也就是全球化的意思。这里将其译成"走向全球"，比译成"全球扩张"、"全球化"或者"在全球范围内扩大业务"更加形象自然。

5 Fortune Global 500 companies 《财富》杂志"全球500强"
   "世界500强"是国人对美国《财富》杂志每年评选的"全球最大五百家公司"排行榜的一种约定俗成的叫法。

6 ... we asked two CEOs of Fortune Global 500 companies how they've stayed on the top of the game.
   这句中的动词"ask"如果直接译成："我们问《财富》杂志'全球500强'中的五家公

司的首席执行官他们是怎样……"，句子则显得过长，因此采取了增词的方式，将句子分开，译成"我们采访了《财富》杂志'全球500强'中的五家公司的首席执行官，问他们……"。这样更符合汉语的表达习惯。这句话还可以译成："……向他们了解他们一直稳居世界领先地位的秘密。"

7　… they've successfully managed global businesses in everything from refrigerators to fragrances.

此句中的介词短语"in everything"修饰"businesses"，等于"… global businesses that manufacture all kinds of products"的意思，所以将其拆译成"……各种全球性的企业，产品应有尽有，从冰箱到香水各不相同"比直接译成前置定语"……他们都成功地管理着全球生产从冰箱到香水等各种产品的企业"更加通顺。

8　L'Oreal　法国欧莱雅公司

法国欧莱雅集团（L'Oreal）是拥有近百年历史的全球最大的化妆品公司，同时也是《财富》杂志评选的全球500强和全球最受赞赏的50家公司之一。

9　ON WHAT MAKES A GLOBAL BRAND　关于怎样打造国际品牌

这里"makes"译得非常地道，因为"打造"比"创立、创建"更具时代感。

10　… might seduce the world?

这里，"the world"可以译成"全球"、"全世界"或者"全球消费者"，但"全球消费者"更加准确。另外，"seduce"这个词一般的词典都只有"诱惑，诱……误入歧途"的意思。根据"Longman Dictionary of Contemporary English"的解释，这个词还有"to make someone want to do something by making it seem very attractive or interesting"的意思，所以这里译成"吸引"或"让全球消费者青睐的"都非常准确自然。

11　It is intuition (when one asks) what do these brands have that just might seduce the world? But also in terms of imagination, what could they become to seduce the world?　如果有人问公司靠什么才能打造出吸引全球消费者的品牌？答案是直觉。当然，要打造出国际品牌，公司同样离不开想像力。

这句中的第一个问句猛地一看很像是英语中的强调句，但仔细一读就不难发现，这个"It is intuition …"实际上是对紧接着的"what do these brands have that just might seduce the world"的回答。但是，如果直译成"（如果有人问，）这些品牌凭借什么去吸引全球的消费者？答案是直觉"，似乎欠妥当，因为"直觉"和"想象力"不是品牌能够具有的，而是打造品牌的人才能有的，所以在翻译时应该将句子中的主语换成具体的人。同样，第二个句子如果译成"同样就想像力来说，为了吸引全球消费者，这些品牌需要怎样自我变革？"，就会让读者感到不知所云，因为"in terms of"直译出来会让读者感到"想像力"与品牌的"自身变革"没有必然的联系。再说，品牌本身也无法"自身变革"。因此，将这两句话译成"如果有人问公司靠什么才能打造出吸引全球消费者的品牌？答案是直觉。当然，要打造出国际品牌，公司同样离不开想像力"，更加忠实于作者的原意，效果也就更好。

12 It took imagination to think that …
如果将此句译成"要有想像力才能想到……"，则似乎不太妥当，因为尽管英语"it"在这里是指后面的不定式短语"to think that …"，但是"it"后面的动词却是过去式，表明这是已经完成的动作。因此，将这句译成"正是因为有了想像力，有人才会想到……可能会成为……"就非常妥当。

13 I usually like to have a quick look at the clothes department if it is a department store, or perhaps cereal or instant coffee if I'm in a supermarket. 如果去的是百货商店，我一般会去卖服装的地方瞅瞅；如果去的是超级市场，我可能会去卖麦片或速溶咖啡的地方转转。因为"have a quick look at"的宾语一个是"clothes department"，而另一个则是"cereal or instant coffee"，不太容易处理。译者将两者都译成地点，而在前面增加前置定语"卖服装的地方"和"卖麦片或速溶咖啡的地方"，并将"have a quick look at"分别译成"瞅瞅"和"转转"，跟前面的"look at"（看看，瞧瞧）正好一致，这样既准确又形象。

14 "challenge"这个词通常被翻译成"挑战"，但有时也应该根据上下文的情况来决定。比如此句如果译成"了解女士们的需求是一项重大的挑战"，就让人觉得费解。根据兰登书屋出版的《韦氏美语学习词典》（Random House Webster's Dictionary of American English）的解释，"challenge"的意思为："something that by its nature is a test or a difficult thing to accomplish"。因此，特将这句译成"要了解女士们的需求相当困难（不容易）"。

15 如果将"they would laugh you out of the door"一句译成："她们可能会大笑，叫你走开"，似不大妥当，所以应将此句译成："……把你赶走"。另外，"would"一词在这里应该表示假设，是"会，就会"的意思，因为前面一句是"要是你去敲别人的门"的虚拟句。因此，这句话还可译成："……她们一定会让你走开。"

16 Cultural diversity is an everyday factor of differences. 各国市场千差万别，而各国文化上的差异是最根本的。
这句很难翻译。如果译为"文化的多样性是各国市场互不相同的最最基本的一个因素"，就会出现两个问题：① 如果把"diversity"译成"多样性"，就应该在该词之前加上"世界"一词，译成"世界文化的多样性"；② 将英语"an everyday factor"直译成"……的因素"过分拘泥原文。如果仔细读原文，就会发现，原文实际上是要表示：各国市场各不相同，但国与国之间文化上的差异是最根本的差异。因此，根据意思将此句译成："各国市场千差万别，而各国文化上的差异是最根本的。"换句话说，就是：各国市场存在很多不同，而首先是文化上的不同。

17 Our success in the US has been heightened by our understanding and awareness of ethnic differences. 我们之所以能在美国市场不断获得成功，就是因为我们对当地各种族文化

有了越来越多的了解和认同。

这句话的英语是"our success"做主语，加之谓语又是被动语态，所以不容易翻译。如果直译成："我们在美国的成功随着我们对当地种族差异的理解和认知的加深而不断加大"，虽然被动改成了主动，但句子仍然显得过长，读起来比较拗口。如果译成："我们在美国的成功很大程度上得益于我们对当地种族差异的理解和认知"，又没有表达出原文"heighten"的含义，而且"在很大程度上"也不准确。因此，应将这句话拆译成"我们之所以能在美国市场不断获得成功，就是因为我们对当地各种族文化有了越来越多的了解和认同"，这样就既将"heighten"的意思译出来了，又表达出了取得这样的成绩是得益于对不同民族文化的深入的了解和认同。

18 Every new country you are successful in gives you an added dimension of understanding how the world is different. 你每在一个国家的市场上获得成功，你就会对世界的多样性多一分了解。

这句话将主语"every new country"转译成状语，而将"you"译成全句的主语，使译文通顺自然。如果直接译成："你所获得成功的每一个国家都会让你对……"就不符合汉语的表达习惯了。

19 将这句中"an unwritten message"译成状语"无形中传递"比译成定语"无形的信息"更好。

20 ... which is for all of us to avoid (living) in some sort of ivory tower and to listen to our customers. ……也就是说我们都不能脱离实际（整天只呆在办公室里），而是应直接去了解顾客的需要。

这句话很容易直译为："……也就是说我们都不能待在某种象牙塔里，而是要多听听顾客的意见。"这样翻译会出现两个问题：① 汉语的"象牙塔"一词本来是"比喻脱离现实生活的文学家和艺术家的小天地"（《现代汉语词典》），现在还多指从事教育的大学或科研机构，因此这里"待在某种象牙塔里"会让人感到费解；② 有些读者可能不知道什么叫"象牙塔"，也就更不明白什么叫"某种象牙塔"了。因此，根据上下文的意思，不如直接将此句译成："也就是说我们都不能脱离实际（整天只呆在办公室里），而是应直接去了解顾客的需要。"，这样既忠实了原文，又让读者容易理解。

21 Everybody who manages a business at L'Oreal has a basic responsibility to the company to do what we (call) "a cow and calves policy". 在欧莱雅，每一位企业管理者都对公司负有一项基本责任，我们称之为"母牛和小牛政策"。

此句不宜将"everybody who manages a business"译为"所有的企业管理人员"，因为制定长远规划的不是所有的企业管理人员，而是决策者，所以应译成"每一位企业管理者"或者"每一位经理"。

22 You are responsible not only for managing profitably today's business but also for preparing what will be profitable many years after you have left that particular country or assignment.

你在位时应该使企业创收，而且还必须制定长期规划，以便在你离开那个特定的国家或职位许多年之后，企业仍然能够盈利。这是你的责任。

此句如果直译为"你不仅要对企业今天的盈利情况负责，还要负责准备好将来你离开那个特定的国家或职位许多年之后企业的盈利内容"，就会显得非常不自然，主要是后面的句子太长，过于拘泥于原文的用词和句式，而且将"prepare"直译成"准备"，翻译的痕迹十分明显。因此，宜拆译成："你在位时应该使企业创收，而且还必须制定长期规划，以便在你离开那个特定的国家或职位许多年之后，企业仍然能够盈利。"这样，就把"prepare"，即"制定未来长期规划"的意思译出来了。

23. And you will be judged not only on your ability to produce the numbers now but on the credibility of the plans that will be there when you leave-to create businesses that one day will be the future. 企业对你的评价不仅要看你在位时的创收能力，还要看你在位时所制定的那些长期发展规划在你离职之后能否实施——因为这些规划中（所要创办）的企业将是整个公司的未来。

此句很容易直译为："企业对你的评价既要看你当前的盈利能力，也要看你离开之后那些有待贯彻的发展计划是否可靠——可以创建代表未来业务走向的业务内容。"这里"那些有待贯彻的发展计划"没有标明是谁制定的，另外最后这句这样翻译实在太生硬，让人难以理解。其实，破折号之后的不定式是"plans"的定语。另外，"credibility"最好不译成"可靠、可信"。

24. DuPont 法国杜邦公司

杜邦公司是一家以科研为基础的全球性企业，提供能提高人类在食物与营养、保健、服装、家居及建筑、电子和交通等生活领域的品质的科学解决之道。

25. ... but you need to make sure you're bringing in the right products and services at the right time.

这句不宜译为："……但你得保证你是在适当的时候引进适当的产品和服务。"此处英语"bring in"实际上指的是企业要把握好向发展中国家推销（expand）其适当产品和服务的时机，所以将"bring in"直接译成"引进"不妥当。因此，应将此句译成："但你得保证你是在适当的时候向这些国家输出适当的产品和服务。"

26. GDP 国内生产总值

A region's gross domestic product, or GDP, is one of several measures of the size of its economy.

国内生产总值（GDP）是指一个国家或地区范围内的所有常住单位，在一定时期内生产最终产品和提供劳务价值的总和。

27. ... and that's still a general rule of thumb.

这句话很难翻译，容易直译成："……而现在这仍然是一条凭经验确定的基本依据。"这样翻译显得非常生硬，因为"一条凭经验确定的基本依据"似乎不大符合汉语的表达习惯。这里要表达的意思是：过去是按这个标准，现在仍然是按这个多年的老办法处理。所以，应将整句译成："什么时候才是进入一个发展中国家市场的时机呢？以前我们是看该国人均国内生产总值是否达到 1000 美元，现在我们仍然按这个老办法来办理。"

28 But averages can be terrible in developing countries because they can be much different in the cities than in the country. 但是在发展中国家，平均数可能极不可靠，因为城乡差别非常之大。

此句中："……因为城乡差别可能相去甚远"的"相去甚远"就是差距大的意思。为了避免重复，这里应将其译成："但是在发展中国家，平均数可能极不可靠，因为城乡差别非常之大。"，或者译成："城乡之间的平均水平相去甚远。"

29 "just as good as" 这里不能译成："与……一样（同样）优秀"，因为原文明显是表示"不比美国的工程师差"的意思，所以应该译成"不相上下"。

30 genetically modified food 转基因食品
转基因食品是通过遗传工程改变植物种子中的脱氧核糖核酸，然后把这些修改过的再复合基因转移到另一些植物种子内，从而获得在自然界中无法自动生长的植物物种。

原文 1：

IBM's performance during the past few years has been dramatically reflected in the price of its stock, which is now selling for only nine times annual earnings. After stock splits are included, the value of a share of IBM has not actually increased since 1968.

原译：

国际商用机器公司过去几年经营成绩的好坏生动地反映在它的股票价格上，现在的价格仅为全年股息收入的九倍。如果把股票分股算在内，国际商用机器公司的每一股的价值实际上从 1968 年以来一直没有增加过。

点评：

① "IBM's performance during the past few years has been dramatically reflected in the price of its stock" 股价反映公司业绩，所以应该倒过来译。
② "stock splits" 是上市公司将高面值的股票折细，一般称为"拆股"。
③ 英语"value"不宜译成"价值"，因为这里是指价格的涨跌。

改译：

国际商用机器公司股票价格过去几年的走势明显地反映出公司业绩的好坏。现在公司股价的市盈率仅为九倍。如果把公司拆股进行复权处理，每一股的价格实际上从1968年以后就再也没有上升。

原文2：

While no one says Pittsburgh, Akron or Detroit is necessarily doomed, the rise of global economic competition and the transportation-and-communication revolution have steadily eroded the strategic advantages on which their growth and wealth were based.

原译：

尽管没有人说匹兹堡、阿克隆或者底特律在劫难逃，全球经济竞争的兴起和交通－通讯革命却已经渐渐削弱了这几座城市赖以发展和致富的战略优势。

点评：

① 将英语中的"the rise of global economic competition"译成"全球经济竞争的兴起"似乎不太合适，因为经济竞争是随着经济活动的出现而存在的，所以这里应该是"日趋激烈"的意思。
② 将"全球经济竞争的兴起和交通－通讯革命"按英语句式译成主语，整个句子稍显过长，不如将其译成动词分句，这样更符合汉语的表达习惯。

改译：

尽管没有人说匹兹堡、阿克隆或者底特律在劫难逃，但全球经济竞争的日趋激烈，交通－通讯革命的兴起，使得这几座城市赖以发展和致富的战略优势逐渐丧失殆尽。

原文3：

That crushing verdict is emphatically not shared by the nation's big-city mayors or by the many millions of Americans who cherish big cities for their beauty, energy, diversity and manifold cultural delights.

原译：

对于这个断然宣称大城市不再需要的结论，美国许多大城市的市长坚决不予认同，成百上千热爱美丽、充满活力、多样化而又有众多文化娱乐的大城市的美国人也坚决不予认同。

点评：

① 此句中的限制性定语从句非常长，如果像原译中这样译成前置定语，定语和主语都太长，显然不符合汉语的表达习惯。因此，可以将定语从句译成表原因的状语放到句子后面。

② 将英语"diversity"译成"多样化",译得太死;将英语"manifold"译成"众多"似乎译得太平。建议将整个句子拆开翻译。

改译:

对于这个断然宣称大城市不再需要的结论,美国许多大城市的市长坚决不予认同,成千上万的美国人也坚决不予认同,因为他们热爱美丽、充满活力和五彩斑斓的大城市,并对大城市丰富多彩的文化娱乐生活情有独钟。

原文 4:

Corporations such as Microsoft, Compaq and Intel are but a few examples of American companies whose early growth was facilitated by venture capital investments.

原译:

像微软、康柏和英特尔这样的公司,仅仅是那些早期发展得益于风险资本投资的美国公司的几个例子而已。

点评:

此句中的英语"a few example of"不太好处理,因此原译只好将其放到句子的最后。但这样翻译似乎太拘泥于原文,因为所谓的几个例子,就是指其中的几个。

改译:

美国很多公司早期发展都曾得益于风险资本投资,微软、康柏和英特尔只不过是其中的几个罢了(而已)。

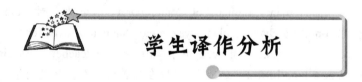

学生译作分析

原文:

Process Management of Contract Approval

Our standard contract routine was introduced in February 2002 with the objective to improve the signing of Customer-Contract. We have made a review recently and the operation of this routine is quite satisfactory. Before signing the contract with customer, internal approval document (IAD) on changing payment terms etc. must be signed by Commercial Director & Finance Director as well as sales contract summary (SCS) by Commercial Director & Processing Director. For very urgent cases, the documents can be e-mailed to the directors & then get their oral confirmation. This will avoid the embarrassing situation to bring up changes with customer later on.

学生原译文：

合同批准管理程序

我们标准的合同程序是于 2002 年 2 月引入的，旨在改善顾客合同的签订。我们最近对我们的程序进行了回顾，对该程序的运作非常满意。在与顾客签订合同之前，国内批准文件，如关于支付方式变化等，必须由贸易主管和金融主管共同签署，同时，贸易合同概要需由贸易主管和处理主管共同签署。在紧急情况下，可以用电子邮件将文件发给这些主管，然后得到他们的口头确认。这将避免日后给顾客带来变化的尴尬局面。

分析：

(1) 标题。一般来说，学生看到英语"process"和"approval"立即想到的就是"程序"和"批准"，因此自然就会将这个标题翻译成"合同批准管理程序"。但如果细读原文，就不难发现，其实这一段文字是关于某公司在对外签订业务合同时必须履行的手续。另外，兰登书屋出版的《韦氏美语学习词典》（Random House Webster's Dictionary of American English）对"process"一词的解释是："to handle (persons , papers , etc.) according to a regular procedure"。因此，一个单位里的"regular procedure"应该就是"规章制度"。至于"approval"一词，译成"批准"不如"审批"更加书面化。

(2) 第一句中有两个词应该注意。一个是"introduce"，另一个是"improve"。学生在原译中分别将这两个词译成"引入"和"改善"，显然没有仔细推敲。《朗文当代英语辞典》（Longman Dictionary of Contemporary English）对"introduce"一词的解释是："to make a change, plan, system etc. happen or exist for the first time：plans to introduce a new system of welfare payments/The teachers' association wanted to introduce a new kind of test."。此外，"旨在改善顾客合同的签订"不通。因此，应该将此句译成："为了完善公司与客户签约的管理制度，2002 年 2 月我们开始试行标准合同管理办法。"

(3) "made a review" 原译为"回顾"，不妥，译成"评估"更加准确。

(4) 原译将"internal approval document（IAD）"译成"国内批准文件"有误，因为"internal"是指"公司内部"；"changing payment terms etc."应译成"支付条款变更等"；"must be signed by"不宜译成"签署"，而应译成"签字批准"；"sales contract summary（SCS）"译成"销售合同概要"不太专业，这里实际上是将销售合同的要点报请领导批准（因为销售合同内容太复杂，全面审阅太费时间）。

(5) "For very urgent cases"仅仅译成"在紧急情况下"读者恐难理解，因此应该增加"一时无法获得有关主管人员的正式签字批复"；"oral confirmation"宜译成"口头批准"或"口头批复"。
(6) 最后一句原译为:"这将避免日后给顾客带来变化的尴尬局面。"这样翻译太拘泥于原文。"to bring up changes with" 不能直接译成"给顾客带来变化",而"…embarrassing situation"是指"让顾客反复修改合同这种让人不愉快的局面",但如果这里将"to bring up changes with customer later on"译成前置定语,又显得拗口,所以可以考虑将此句拆译成:"此举可以避免日后再要求客户修改,给他们带来不便。"

参考译文:

合同报批管理制度(办法)

为了完善公司与客户签约的管理制度,2002年2月我们开始试行标准合同管理办法。最近我们对该办法进行了评估,结果令人十分满意。公司人员对外与客户签约之前,必须先将合同内容呈文报请公司相关部门的主管批准。例如,支付条款变更等事项必须由商务主管和财务主管签字批准,而销售合同方面的事项则应将要点呈文报批,由商务主管和业务主管签字。如果情况紧急,一时无法获得有关主管人员的正式签字批复,也可以将相关批件通过电子邮件呈报给这些主管,并取得他们的口头批准。此举可以避免日后再要求客户修改,给他们带来不便。

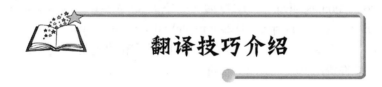

省略
(Omission)

在商务英语翻译中采用省略这一翻译技巧是为了使译文自然通顺。由于英汉两种语言之间存在很大的差异,为了使译文符合汉语语言的规范,让读者读起来感到自然顺畅,在英译汉时应该将英语中的某些词类省略。

1. 人称代词、物主代词的省略

英语中人称代词用得较多,后面往往跟着相应的物主代词,以表示人称的一致性,这是英语的一个特点。但在汉语里,往往将这些人称代词和物主代词省去。例如:

(1) All the statistics tell **us** that Internet shopping is only a tiny percentage of retail sales.

译文：所有的统计数字都显示，网络销售在零售业中所占的比例极小。

（2）It is not rare that either party to a contract may fail to perform **his** duties, or **his** performance is inconsistent with the terms provided on the contract.

译文：合同一方没能履行责任或未按合同履行责任的情况并不少见。

（3）In most cases, bona fides party to an international sales contract will do **his** best to perform **his** duties either as a seller or a buyer.

译文：多数情况下，国际货物买卖合同的当事人，无论卖方或买方，都会尽力履行责任。

（4）Since many banks believe there is a greater risk of a borrower's defaulting on a vacation home, mortgage rates can be higher than **they** would be on a primary residence.

译文：由于很多银行认为买主在购买度假房时更有可能违约，因此抵押贷款率比购买基本住房时要高。

（5）Credit cards enable **their** holders to obtain goods and services on credit.

译文：信用卡能使持卡人通过赊账的方式购买商品，获得服务。

（6）In reality, a commercial bank, as a financial institution, is an enterprise that deals in money with loans being **its** assets and deposits being **its** liabilities.

译文：实际上，一家商业银行，作为一个金融机构，是一个把贷款资金作为资产，把存款资金作为负债的企业。

（7）The global brands such as McDonald's, Coca Cola and Nike are well-known through the millions of dollars spent designing and advertising **them**.

译文：一些全球性品牌，如麦当劳、可口可乐和耐克等，通过在产品外观设计和广告费用上投入数百万美元而得以声名远扬。

2. 冠词的省略

汉语中没有冠词。而在英语中，而冠词却需要经常使用，有时甚至是必不可少的。冠词一般不单独使用，它通常是置于某一名词前或个别起名词作用的形容词前修饰这个名词或形容词，帮助说明该名词或形容词的具体含义。冠词有时还与短语搭配使用，但此时冠词失去其本意，转而具有抽象意义。在英译汉时应注意冠词的意思可以省略还是必须译出。一般的原则是：不定冠词（a, an）除了表示"一"这个数量概念时需要译出外，其他情况通常可以省略；定冠词（the）所修饰的名词或形容词只要译成汉语时，如果是泛指，即不需要加"这、该、那个"等特指的词就能清楚地表明意思，则可以省略。例如：

（1）I get **a** firm offer, and I only accept it if I can get **a** firm buyer, at **a** profit, of course.

译文：我收到实盘后，直到确实有了买主才接受，当然总得有一定的利润。

（2）If you have **a** credit card, you can buy **a** car, eat **a** dinner, take **a** trip, and even get **a** haircut by charging the cost to your account.

译文：有了信用卡，你便能以记账的方式购买汽车、进餐、旅游甚至理发。（省略）

(3) In case of non-delivery, **the** buyer may declare **the** contract avoided. In **a** reasonable manner and within **a** reasonable time, the buyer may claim damage.

译文：在卖方不发货的情况下，买方可以宣布合同无效，在适当的时间，以适当的方式，可以要求索赔。（省略）

(4) The world's rich saw the growth of their fortunes slow sharply last year as the collapse of tech and media stocks wiped out **a** third of new dotcom millionaires, **a** survey showed on Monday.

译文：星期一公布的一项调查结果表明，由于技术和传媒股暴跌，致使三分之一的新网络富翁彻底破产，去年全球富翁的财富增长速度骤然减缓。（不能省略）

(5) With **the** credit card in your wallet or purse, you don't have to carry much cash.

译文：钱包里有了信用卡，你就不必携带许多现金。（省略）

(6) In **the** Middle East, **an** important market for offshore private banking centres such as Switzerland, higher oil prices helped wealth creation and **the** combined value of **the** region's 220,000 high net worth clients surged 18 percent to $1.3 trillion.

译文：中东是国外私立银行中心（如瑞士）的一个重要市场，较高的石油价格促进了中东地区财富的增长。这个地区拥有高额净资产的富翁高达22万，他们的资产总额去年激增了18%，达到了1.3万亿美元。（有的可省略，有的则不能省略）

3. 介词的省略

介词在英语中大量使用，这也是英语的特点之一。在汉译时，部分介词可以省略。这样的情况非常多。一般的原则是：一些表示时间和地点的介词可以省略；一些与动词、名词和形容词搭配使用的介词可以省略。例如：

(1) Shortage of suitable land **in** the urban area has made it necessary to build most new public housing **in** the suburbs.

译文：由于市区缺乏合适的土地，大部分公共房屋必须在郊区兴建。

(2) Another factor **behind** the increase **in** merger activity is the record performance of stock markets.

译文：导致合并不断增加的另一个因素是股票市场的空前繁荣。

(3) **At** about this time, movies actors began running for President, astronauts began flying around the planet to get from on desert to another, and businessmen began renting one-bedroom apartment **for** $2,000 a month.

译文：如今，电影演员开始竞选总统；宇航员在地球周围飞来飞去，从一个沙漠飞到另一个沙漠；商人们开始租用2000美元一月的单卧室公寓。

(4) **On** Oct. 2, three weeks after the World Trade Centre attacks, India National Association of Software & Service Companies took out a full-page ad **in** The New York Times, looking forward to helping (American industry) continue to be competitive.

译文：10月2日，美国世贸中心遭受袭击后3个星期，印度全国软件和服务企业协会（Nasscom）在《纽约时报》用一个整版的篇幅刊出广告，表示"愿意帮助（美国工业）继续保持竞争优势"。

(5) Those **in** marketing or finance did not have to worry **about** technology because they could rest assured that the products they were attempting to finance or sell were superior.

译文：市场营销或财务管理人员其实无须对技术担忧，因为他们尽可放心，他们试图投资或销售的产品一直处于优势地位。

(6) If you live **in** debt, there is no point considering investing in stocks, for paying hefty credit-card charges each month will eat **away** any investment returns you may earn.

译文：如果你靠举债度日，就没有必要考虑投资股票了，因为你每月巨额的信用卡费用就会抵消你可能获得的任何投资收益。

4. 其他省略

除了英语中的一些代词、冠词和介词在译成汉语时可以省略外，还有一些连词、动词不定式符号和语气助词等均可以省略。总之，任何词类或成分在翻译中都可能被省略，但省略一定要依据具体的上下文并符合汉语的表达习惯。例如：

(1) Roche, which has been under pressure from an attempted merger by its Swiss rival Novartis, reiterated it expected full-year **underlying** sales and operating profit to rise by double-digit percentage rates.

译文：罗氏一直受到本国竞争对手诺华兼并计划的压力。罗氏重申，预计集团全年的销售额和营业利润都会以两位数的速度增长。（省译形容词）

(2) Once broadband becomes mainstream, it will open up new opportunities like using high-quality video, but there is also the cost **implication** of developing such materials.

译文：一旦宽带成为主流，它将创造许多新机会，比如使用高质量电视等。但开发这类设备还需要经费。（省译名词）

(3) **On condition that** you sign this receipt, I will pay the balance.

译文：你在收据上签字，我就付款。（省译介词短语）

(4) Such is human nature, **that** a great many people are often willing to sacrifice higher pay for the privilege of becoming white collar workers.

译文：许多人为了得到白领工作者的地位常常愿意放弃较高的薪水。人的本性竟然如此。（省译结果或程度状语从句的连词）

(5) **It** is these documents that enable the importing customs to assess consignments as the

correct rate of duty.

译文：进口国海关就是凭这些单据按正确的税率对货物估价征税。（省译非人称代词 "it"）

（6）Should, for certain reasons, it become necessary for the Buyer to replace the named vessel with another one, or should the named vessel arrive at the port of shipment earlier or later than the date of arrival as previously notified to the Seller, the Buyer or its shipping agent shall advise the Seller **to this effect** in due time.

译文：如买方因故需要变更船只或者船只比预先通知卖方的日期提前或推迟到达装运港口，买方或其船运代理人应及时通知卖方。（省译介词短语 "to this effect"）

（7）The Seller shall advise by cable or telex in time the Buyer of the result **thereof**.

译文：卖方应将联系结果通过电报或电传及时报告买方。（省译副词 "thereof"）

（8）It is not surprising, then, that the world **saw** a return to floating exchange rate system. Central banks were no longer required to support their own currencies.

译文：在这种情况下，世界各国又恢复浮动汇率就不足为奇了。各国中央银行也就无须维持本币的汇价了。（省译动词）

课堂翻译训练

将下列句子译成汉语。

1. This is part of the data collected by the International Labor Office on hourly rates in forty-one occupations and consumer prices for a sample of household items in about 100 countries.
2. Please notify the beneficiary that this letter of credit is transferable and any transfer must be effected through you. However the transfer does not become operative until you have informed us of the name of the transferee and the name has been approved by us as not being contrary to US government regulations and we have informed you accordingly.
3. At first, the new business plan seemed counterintuitive — if not a quick route to bankruptcy.
4. Its beginnings obscured by unemployment caused by the world economic slow-down, the new technological unemployment may emerge as the great socio-economic challenge of the end of the 20th century.
5. Hybrid malls（混合购物中心）pick up on the growing popularity of village-style shopping, with its connections to real communities.

6. We have a sales force at present of twenty-four salesmen on the road, each with his own territory.
7. These papers are critical for maintaining good relations with your banker. They also will present a complete picture of your total business operation which will benefit you as well.
8. It may take you a bit of time and effort to analyze the company check-book, take inventory, review bank statements and, in general, just catch up on your paperwork.

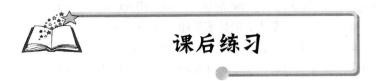

将下列短文译成英语,注意运用本单元所学的翻译技巧。

1.

Northern Europe and key East Asian countries and regions are the most competitive economies in the world, retaining their positions in the top 10 of a survey released Wednesday by the World Economic Forum.

For the third straight year, Finland has the most competitive economy, followed by the United States, according to a survey of almost 11,000 business leaders in the "Global Competitiveness Report."

The success of the Nordics is based on their "very healthy macroeconomic environments and public institutions that are highly transparent and efficient," said Augusto Lopez-Claros, chief economist and director of the Geneva-based institute's global competitiveness program.

China dropped for the second straight year to No. 49 from No. 44 in 2003, as the survey said it continues "to suffer from institutional weaknesses which, unless addressed, are likely to slow down their ascension to the top tier of the most competitive economies in the world."

The aim of the survey, the World Economic Forum says, is to examine the range of factors that can affect an economy's business environment and development — including the levels of judicial independence, protection of property rights, government favoritism and corruption.

Finland, home of mobile phone giant Nokia Corp., topped the study because of its swiftness in adapting to new technology and the quality of its public institutions, the report said.

The United States ranked second because it "demonstrates overall technological supremacy, with a very powerful culture of innovation," the World Economic Forum said. But it suggested the United States might have been kept from the top spot because of its low scores for contractual law and macroeconomic management.

2.

Top talent has never been more valuable, nor the competition for it fiercer. On these pages, we profile 12 leaders who are one step from superstardom. They're not CEOs yet, but they're on deck—at the biggest companies on the planet. Learn from them.

An unprecedented war for top talent is raging in the world economy. Meet the people who love it rather than fear it. The enviable men and women on the following pages occupy the absolute best place to be in that war: not on one side or the other, but right in the middle—they're the treasure being fought over.

We've identified a dozen standout executives you may not know now but probably will. Poised on the verge of superstardom, with top headhunters and board directors watching their every move, they aren't CEOs yet but most likely will be—some of them fairly soon. When you see how Ellen Kullman is igniting new growth at 200-year-old DuPont, or how Greg Brown is helping turn around Motorola, or how Mary Minnick is fixing the world's most storied brand, Coca-Cola, you realize you've been overlooking some awesomely talented people. Or consider David Calhoun, who would already be a famous CEO if the $40 billion of businesses he oversees didn't happen to be part of the even huger General Electric. Then look at what's driving these men and women to the top, their creativity, irreverence, boundless energy, and relentless determination—and apply those lessons to your own career.

It'll pay to do so, because today—after 500 years or so—the scarcest, most valuable resource in business is no longer financial capital. It's talent. If you doubt that, just watch how hard companies are battling for the best people. Google hires a top Microsoft executive—not an unusual event in the tech world—and Microsoft files a mammoth lawsuit. Nortel Networks hires a former Motorola executive as president, and Motorola declares courtroom war. Yahoo hires a group of computer engineers from a small software firm, which immediately sues. The stakes are getting higher. Why now? After all, the law of markets says that prices go down when supply goes up, and the supply of talent is emphatically rising. U.S. business schools turn out more MBAs every year—about 130,000 in 2005. More broadly, the global talent supply is exploding as China, India, Russia, and other places wholeheartedly join the world economy. With two billion or three billion new participants in global capitalism, how could top business talent possibly be scarcer and more valuable than ever? The answer is that even amid today's massive new supplies of talent, there isn't nearly enough of the very best stuff.

 佳译赏析

Growth in Millionaires' Club[1] Slows Sharply
全球富翁财富增长速度锐减

From *Reuters Business Report*, May 14, 2001
By Elif Kaban, European Private Banking Correspondent

LONDON, May 14 (Reuters) —The world's rich saw the growth of their fortunes slow sharply last year as the collapse of tech and media stocks wiped out a third of new dotcom millionaires[2], a survey showed on Monday.
伦敦5月14日（路透社）——星期一公布的一项调查结果表明，由于技术和传媒股暴跌，三分之一的新网络富翁彻底破产，去年全球富翁的财富增长速度骤然减缓。

The personal wealth of the world's millionaires rose by six percent in 2000 after an 18 percent surge in 1999, although this came against the background of a 375 percent surge since 1986, the report by US bank Merrill Lynch[4] and consultants Cap Gemini Ernst & Young[5] said.[3] Some 80,000 of the 260,000 dotcom millionaires created[6] last year lost their fortunes, however, after tech and media stocks went into sharp decline from March, according to the annual *World Wealth Report*.[7]
由美国美林银行、凯捷永安咨询公司联合所作的调查报告指出，虽然全球富翁的个人财富1986年以来猛增了375%，但是在此基础上自1999年增长18%后2000年又增长了6%。但是，据年度《全球财富报告》披露，在去年新出现的26万网络富翁中，约有8万人在经历了从3月份开始的技术和传媒股暴跌后财产损失殆尽。

Despite the plunge in equity markets[8], the total wealth of high net worth individuals—defined as people worth more than $1 million each, excluding real estate—around the world grew 6 percent to $27 trillion in 2000, from $25.5 trillion a year earlier. "Despite the turmoil, despite the difficult markets that we saw for the last 12 months, wealth around the world has not decreased[9]," Winthrop H. Smith Jr., chairman of Merrill Lynch International and president of the firm's International Private Client Group, said at a news conference in New York. The total wealth held by these individuals is more than twice as large as the global pensions market and three times the size of the global mutual fund industry.

尽管股市大幅跳水,但全球拥有高额净资产(指除不动产外个人资产超过100万美元)的个人的财富总和比一年前增长了6%,由25.5万亿美元增加到2000年的27万亿美元。美林国际集团董事长及公司国际个人客户集团总裁温思罗普·H·史明思在纽约举行的一次记者招待会上说:"尽管去年世界局势动荡不安,全球市场连续12个月危机不断,但全球的财富并未因此而减少。"全球拥有高额净资产个人所拥有的财富总和为全球养老金市场总资产的两倍多,是全球共同基金投资资产的三倍。

The report said the number of high net worth individuals worldwide grew 2.9 percent to 7.2 million in 2000. The number of ultra-high net worth individuals with investible assets of more than $30 million apiece rose three percent to 57,000. Their wealth expanded by six percent to $8.37 trillion.

《全球财富报告》称,2000年全世界拥有高额净资产的人数增加了2.9%,达到了720万人。此外,拥有巨额净资产(即个人可供投资的资产超过3 000万美元)的人数增加了3%。达到5.7万人。他们的财富增加了6%,达到了8.37万亿美元。

In London, Christopher Humphry, Cap Gemini Ernst & Young Vice President, told a news conference that the survey lowered its forecast for growth for the high net worth market over the next five years to 8 percent annually from 12 percent.[10] Total asset for the group is expected to reach $39.7 trillion by 2005. Tim Taylor, Merrill Lynch chief marketing officer for private clients in Europe, Middle East and Africa, said rich clients suffered less than other investors in the market downturn because of diversification and higher exposure to hedge funds[11] and other alternative investments[12].

卡普·杰米尼和凯捷永安咨询公司副总裁克里斯托弗·汉弗莱在伦敦举行的一次记者招待会上说,公司的调查报告降低了对今后5年高额净资产增长趋势的预期,将原来每年增长12%调低为8%。到2005年,全球拥有高额净资产个人所拥有的资产总和预计将达到39.7万亿美元。美林国际集团负责欧洲、中东及非洲地区个人客户的营销总经理提姆·泰勒说,虽然市场持续走低,但资金雄厚的客户所遭受的损失却比一般客户要小,因为他们的投资多元化,更有实力参与对冲基金并选择其他的投资品种进行投资。

"Our research indicates that most high net worth clients had well diversified portfolios and took measures to preserve that wealth[13]," Taylor said. US, EUROPE, MIDDLE EAST FORTUNES GROW, ASIA CRUSHED. Europe produced the highest growth in 2000 in the number of millionaires[14], up six percent to 2.3 million. The dollar value of their fortunes grew by 7.5 percent to $7.2 trillion.

泰勒在记者招待会上说:"我们的调查表明,大多数拥有高额净资产的客户都是通过极为分散的投资并采取其他多种措施避免其资产受损。"美国、欧洲、中东财富增长,亚洲财富损失惨重。2000年欧洲富翁人数增长最快,增长了6%,达到了230万人。以美元计算,他们的财富增长了7.5%,达到了7.2万亿。

US and European banking giants have locked horns in Europe to win a bigger share of onshore markets, led by Germany and Britain that have produced double-digit client asset growth.[15] Merrill Lynch and Cap Gemini said the wealth held by western European millionaires had risen 440 percent since 1986 and was forecast to grow 46 percent to $10.5 trillion by the end of 2005. The combined wealth of high net worth individuals in North America rose 9 percent to $8.8 trillion despite volatile US stocks. The number of millionaires rose 2.4 percent to 2.5 million people.

美国和欧洲的银行业巨头在欧洲竞争以期赢得较大份额的欧陆市场,其中德国和英国的银行巨头实现了两位数的客户资产增长,居领先地位。美林银行和凯捷的调查报告说,自1986年以来,西欧富翁的财富增长了440%,预计2005年底会再增长46%,达到10.5万亿美元。尽管美国股市动荡,北美拥有高额净值资产富翁的财富总额还是增长了9%,达到8.8万亿美元,富翁的人数也增长了2.4%,达到250万人。

Latin America's 200,000 millionaires also fared slightly above global averages, registering growth of 6.5 percent. Latin American millionaires held a staggering 12.3 percent of total global wealth, suggesting an average Latin American client portfolio of more than $15 million —over four times the average North American portfolio.[16]

拉美的20万富翁的财富增长情况也略好于全球的平均水平,达到6.5%。拉美富翁的财富令人难以置信,竟占全球财富总额的12.3%,这表明平均每个拉美富翁的投资金额超过1 500万美元,是北美富翁平均投资金额的4倍还多。

In the Middle East, an important market for offshore private banking centres such as Switzerland, higher oil prices helped wealth creation and the combined value of the region's 220,000 high net worth clients surged 18 percent to $1.3 trillion. The wealth of Middle Eastern millionaires has increased 216 percent since 1986 and is forecast to rise 54 percent to $2 trillion by the end of 2005, Merrill Lynch and Cap Gemini said.

中东是境外私立银行中心（如瑞士）的一个重要市场。较高的石油价格促进了中东地区财富的增长。这个地区拥有高额净资产的富翁高达22万，他们的资产总值去年激增了18%，达到1.3万亿美元。美林银行和凯捷的调查报告说，1986年以来中东地区富翁的财富增长了216%，预计到2005年底将再增长54%，达到2万亿美元。

But Asia's 1.7 million high net worth individuals, whose wealth had grown by 22 percent in 1999, saw fortunes fall by more than nine percent in 2000, most of it in Japan due to its stagnant economic growth and a 26 percent fall in the Nikkei. [17]
亚洲拥有高额净资产的富翁有170万，虽然1999年他们的财富增长了22%，但是2000年却减少了9%以上，这主要发生在日本，是日本经济不景气和日经股指下跌26%所致。

Growth in High Net Worth Wealth by Region

Region	Rise since 1999	Rise since 1986	Market share
Africa	steady	166 percent	1.9 percent
Asia	-9 percent	600 percent	18.2 percent
Europe	7.5 percent	440 percent	26.8 percent
Latin America	6.5 percent	275 percent	12.3 percent
Middle East	18 percent	216 percent	4.8 percent
North America	9 percent	313 percent	32.7 percent

全球富翁高额净资产增长情况

地区	1999年以来	1986年以来	市场份额
非洲	持平	166%	1.9%
亚洲	-9%	600%	18.2%
欧洲	7.5%	440%	26.8%
拉丁美洲	6.5%	275%	12.3%
中东	18%	216%	4.8%
北美	9%	313%	32.7%

Words and Expressions

club	n.	a group of people organized for a common purpose, especially a group that meets regularly　为了共同目的组织起来的一群人，尤指定期聚会的一群人

Reuters	n.	（英国）路透社
collapse	v.	to fall or decline suddenly, as in value 崩盘，（市场价格）崩溃，猛烈下跌
		The foreign exchange market collapsed and investors lost big money. 外汇市场崩盘，投资者损失惨重。
tech and media stocks		科技网络股
wipe out		to eliminate completely and without a trace; to cause someone to lose or spend all their money 勾销，抹掉（债等）
		My neighbor was totally wiped out by the last recession. 刚刚过去的经济萧条让我的邻居彻底破产。
		A night out with Paul and Michelle just about wiped us out. 与保罗和米歇尔在外玩了一晚上把我们累死了。
		The five-year bear market in China wiped out the fortunes of lots of investors. 中国股市持续5年的熊市让众多投资者的投资损失殆尽。
World Wealth Report		a report, which is compiled annually by Merrill Lynch and Capgemini, on individuals with a net worth of at least $1 million in financial assets 《全球财富报告》
dotcom	n.	a company that embraces the Internet as the key component in its business 网络公司，网站
surge	v.	to increase suddenly 猛增，突然增加
		As favorable reviews came out, interest in the software surged. 由于评估报告出来很有利，人们对该软件的兴趣陡增。
plunge	n./v.	a steep and rapid fall; drop steeply 猛跌，持续下跌
		The stock market plunged. 股票市场持续下跌。
equity market		股本市场，股票市场，产权市场
net worth		Net worth (sometimes "net assets") is the total assets minus total liabilities of an individual or company. For a company, this is called shareholders' equity or net assets. 资本净值，净值
real estate		land, including all the natural resources and permanent buildings on it; property consisting of houses and land 不动产（土地，包括土地上的所有自然资源和永久性建筑）
turmoil	n.	a state of extreme confusion or agitation; commotion or tumult 动乱（完全混乱或极端骚动的状态），骚乱
		a country in turmoil over labor strikes 处于工人罢工造成的动乱中的国家
mutual fund		an investment company that continually offers new shares and buys existing shares back on demand and uses its capital to invest in diversified securities of other companies; a regulated investment company with a pool of assets that regularly sells and redeems its shares ＜美＞共有基金（或称共同基金，一种投资公司，其不断发行新股票并且一经要求即可买回现存股票，并且用其资金投资于其他公司的多种证券上）
investible	a.	可供投资的
apiece	ad.	to or for each one; each 各，每，各个，就每个而论

		There is enough bread for everyone to have two slices apiece. 面包足够每个人吃两片。
downturn	n.	a tendency downward, especially in business or economic activity　衰退，下降趋势（尤指商业或经济活动的下降趋势），低迷时期
diversification	n.	the act of introducing variety（especially in investments or in the variety of goods and services offered）　多样化，经营多样化 My broker recommended a greater diversification of my investments. 经纪人给了我一个更加多样化的投资建议。 He limited his losses by diversification of his product line. 他通过经营各种产品来减少损失。
exposure	n.	an act of subjecting or an instance of being subjected to an action or an influence　受影响（受到某种行为或影响支配的行为或事例） She wanted to work on television, but she had no exposure to the TV industry. 她想去电视台工作，但却很难有机会接触到电视行业。
portfolio	n.	the securities, etc., held by a private investor, investment company, or financial institution　个人、投资公司或者金融机构所持有的有价证券等 an investment portfolio　一组投资组合
lock horns		(*colloq.*) to become embroiled in conflict; be in a dispute（with one another），fight or contend（with one another）彼此处于争议中，彼此争斗或竞争 The governor and the legislature have locked horns on this issue before. 政府和议会过去曾因这个议题争论过。
onshore	a. / ad.	on or toward the land　陆上的，在岸上的，向岸的；向岸，在岸上，沿岸 They were living onshore.　他们家住在海边。
offshore	a. / ad.	from shore; away from land　向海的，离岸的，近海的；向海，离岸 cruising three miles offshore　在离海岸3英里的地方巡逻
double-digit	a.	being between 10 and 99 percent　两位数的，介于10%和99%之间的 double-digit inflation　两位数的通货膨胀
volatile	a.	tending to vary often or widely, as in price　易波动的，不稳定的，易于经常或大幅度变化的（如价格） the ups and downs of volatile stocks　股价跌宕起伏，波动很大
fare	v.	proceed or get along　遭遇，进展，进步，经营，过活
register	v.	to attain or achieve　获得，取得，完成或达到 register a new high in sales　达到一个新的销售记录
staggering	a.	causing great astonishment, amazement, or dismay; overwhelming　令人大为吃惊、惊讶或沮丧的，使束手无策的 a staggering achievement　惊人的成就 a staggering defeat　全军覆没
stagnant	a.	showing little or no sign of activity or advancement; not developing or progressing; inactive　不景气的，不发展和停滞的或没有前进或活动迹象的，不发展或前进的

		a stagnant economy　停滞的经济
Nikkei	n.	a trademark used for an index of the relative price of selected stocks listed on the Tokyo Stock Exchange　日经指数［日本东京证交所所编制的股价指数，是国际投资人在研究日本股市时一个重要的参考指数。日经指数亦有许多不同的系列指数，如最为人所熟知的日经 225（Nikkei 225）即涵盖了东京证交所里最具代表性的 225 只股票，这项指数自 1945 年 5 月 16 日编制至今，历史悠久。］

1　如果将"Millionaires' Club"译成"百万富翁俱乐部"就不太合适，因为那样会让读者觉得世界上真有个什么"百万富翁俱乐部"。所以，译者将其译成"富翁"，既准确，又易懂。

2　The world's rich saw the growth of their fortunes slow sharply last year as the collapse of tech and media stocks wiped out a third of new dotcom millionaires …

此句中的谓语"saw"和后面的宾语补足语是英语中常见的表达方式，如果直接将其译成"世界富人看见（着）自己财富的增长骤然减速……"就不通顺，意思也不准确。这里译者将"as"引导的表因果的状语从句放在前面，后面的句子中省去动词"saw"，句子就非常通顺了。

3　The personal wealth of the world's millionaires rose by six percent in 2000 after an 18 percent surge in 1999, although this came against the background of a 375 percent surge since 1986 …

这个句子是典型的英语句式，如果直接翻译，"although this came against the background of"就很难处理，因为：①"this"指代前面的"rose by six percent"，如果译出，就必须重复；②"came against the background of"如果译成"基于……之上"又不通顺；③"although"这个让步从句摆在句尾不大符合汉语的句式要求。因此，译者采取"词类转换"和"逆序法"将让步从句中的名词"surge"转译成动词，使其作为"The personal wealth of the world's millionaires"的谓语，变成汉语的动宾结构，并将整个句子倒过来翻译，解决了直接翻译的困难，使译文准确、通顺。

4　Merrill Lynch　美林国际

It is an investment banking and stock brokerage company. As one of the world's largest financial management and advisory companies, it has one of the more recognizable names in the world of finance. The company once occupied most of the 34 stories in 4 World Financial Center.
美林国际是世界领先的金融管理与咨询公司之一，在 36 个国家建立了分支机构，管理的资产达 1.1 万亿美元。

5　Cap Gemini Ernst & Young　凯捷安永集团
2000 年 5 月由法国凯捷集团和永安咨询公司合并而成，是全球最大的咨询、技术和外包服务公司之一。

6　这个过去分词"created"不是很好翻译，如果译成"创造"，就不通顺，因为这些富翁不是股市创造的。查查字典，发现"create"有"to give rise to"，即"产生"的意思，所以这里将这个"created"译成"新出现"或"产生"再恰当不过了。

7　Some 80,000 of the 260,000 dotcom millionaires created last year lost their fortunes, however, after tech and media stocks went into sharp decline from March, according to the annual *World Wealth Report*.　但是，据年度《全球财富报告》披露，在去年新出现的 26 万网络富翁中，约有 8 万人在经历了从 3 月份开始的技术和传媒股暴跌后财产损失殆尽。
这个英语句子的原主语是"dotcom millionaires"，谓语动词是"lost"，介词"after"后是状语。如果直接翻译成"……，约有 8 万人在从 3 月份开始的技术和传媒股暴跌后损失了财产（破产、遭受了损失）"，就无法准确地将"损失"的程度表达出来，而且句子读起来也不是很通顺。为了使译文更加符合汉语的表达习惯，译文在状语中增加了动词"经历"，然后将主语转换成"财产"，译成汉语的动宾结构，这样就可以准确地表达原文的意思：三分之一的暴发户经历了短短几个月的股市大跌，其财产便损失得差不多了。

8　Despite the plunge in equity markets...
英语"plunge"一词用得非常形象，股市中常用这个词表示股价猛烈下跌。要是将这句话译成"尽管产权市场不景气"就无法表达"股市短期内凌厉下跌，造成巨大财产损失"这一层意思。因此，将其译成"股票市场价格大幅跳水"，这样既形象又专业。

9　Despite the turmoil, despite the difficult markets that we saw for the last 12 months, wealth around the world has not decreased...　尽管去年世界局势动荡不安，全球市场连续 12 个月危机不断，但全球的财富并未因此而减少……
此句中的两个介词短语"despite the turmoil, despite the difficult markets that we saw for the last 12 months"在翻译时应该进行增词和词类转换。"the turmoil"前增加"世界局势"，将"the turmoil"转译成动词"动荡"即可。但后面这个句子比较难办，既不能把"the difficult markets"译成"困难的市场"，又不能将定语从句"that we saw for the last 12 months"译成汉语的偏正结构，只好将"we saw"省略，把"连续 12 个月"的意思译

出，并将"difficult"转译成"危机不断"。

10 ... that the survey lowered its forecast for growth for the high net worth market over the next five years to eight percent annually from 12 percent.
本句中的"market"不能译成"市场"，否则这句话就变成了"调查报告对今后5年的高额净值资产市场增长趋势的预测作了修订"。这样读者很难理解什么是"高额净值资产市场"。其实，"market"在这里就是指"走向、趋势"，所以这句话宜翻译成："公司的调查报告降低了对今后5年高额净资产增长趋势的预期，将原来每年增长12%调低至8%。"

11 hedge fund 对冲基金
基金有两种，分别是传统基金和对冲基金。

12 ... rich clients suffered less than other investors in the market downturn because of diversification and higher exposure to hedge funds and other alternative investments. ……
虽然市场持续走低，但资金雄厚的客户所遭受的损失比普通客户要小，因为他们的投资多元化，更有实力参与对冲基金并选择合适的投资品种进行投资。
这句话中的"rich"和"other"不能简单地译成"富有的"和"其他的"，而应该分别译成"资金雄厚的"和"普通的"。另外，"exposure"一词最不好处理，如果直接译成"更容易加入"或者"有更多的机会加入"，读者就很难理解：为什么他们就更有机会呢？由于对冲基金这一类的投资公司只接受少量的资金大户（a small number of large investors, usually the minimum investment is ＄1 million），所以翻译时应该具体一些，表明他们更有实力。英语中有些词汇比较抽象和模糊，因此在选择汉语对等的词语时，应该更加具体一些，否则难以表达出原文的含义。

13 Our research indicates that most high net worth clients had well diversified portfolios and took measures to preserve that wealth ... 我们的调查表明，大多数拥有高额净资产的客户都是通过极为分散的投资并采取其他多种措施避免其资产受损……
这个句子中的两个谓语动词"had"和"took ... to preserve"很容易译成汉语的"拥有良好的多样化投资组合"和"采取了……保护自己的财产"。这样翻译虽然意思还算明白，但句子过于拘泥原文。另外，"well diversified portfolios"中的"well"并不是"良好的"意思，而是用来修饰"diversified"的，表示"多样化"的程度。

14 Europe produced the highest growth in 2000 in the number of millionaires ... 2000年欧洲富翁人数增长最快……
这句话不能照英语句式直接翻译。译文将两个介词"in"省略，将"number"译成主语，将"欧洲"译成定语，将"growth"转译成动词，再将"highest"译成状语，使句子完全符合汉语的表达习惯，既通顺又自然。

15 US and European banking giants have locked horns in Europe to win a bigger share of onshore markets, led by Germany and Britain that have produced double-digit client asset

growth. 美国和欧洲的银行业巨头在欧洲竞争以期赢得较大份额的欧陆市场，其中德国和英国的银行巨头实现了两位数的客户资产增长，居领先地位。

本句将过去分词短语拆译：将介词"by"的宾语"Germany and Britain"译成主语，将定语"that have produced double-digit client asset growth"译成谓语，将"led"被动变主动，译成汉语的独立分句，表示结果。这样翻译就完全符合汉语的表达习惯。

16 Latin American millionaires held a staggering 12.3 percent of total global wealth, suggesting an average Latin American client portfolio of more than \$15 million—over four times the average North American portfolio. 拉美富翁的财富令人难以置信，竟占全球财富总额的12.3%，这表明平均每个拉美富翁的投资金额超过1500万美元，是北美富翁平均投资金额的4倍还多。

这句话中的"staggering"本来是形容词，作定语，译成汉语"令人难以置信"比译成定语更通顺。另外，句中的两个"portfolio"不宜直接译成投资组合，因为这里明显是指富翁们用于投资的资金额度，所以还是译成"金额"更恰当。

17 But Asia's 1.7 million high net worth individuals, whose wealth had grown by 22 percent in 1999, saw fortunes fall by more than nine percent in 2000, most of it in Japan due to its stagnant economic growth and a 26 percent fall in the Nikkei. 亚洲拥有高额净资产的富翁有170万，虽然1999年他们的财富增长了22%，但是2000年却减少了9%以上，这主要发生在日本，是日本经济不景气和日经股指下跌26%所致。

句中的"most of it"指前句中财产的减少。虽然不是完整的句子，但翻译时应该把省略的内容译出。另外，"its stagnant economic growth"可直译为"经济增长停滞不前"，但译成"不景气"更加简练。

他山之石

原文1：

The \$36 billion US computer industry has for months been anxiously awaiting the entry of International Business Machines into the hot new market for personal computers. Said Garland Asher, director of financial planning for Tandy Corp., one of the leading sellers of the television set-size machines: "Some people were convinced that IBM would be unveiling a new Holy Grail." Last week IBM finally showed off its product. Priced between \$1,565 and \$6,300, the desk-top computer can store documents that once would have required a roomful of filing cabinets;

it can also produce graphs in four colors, receive information over phone lines from remot data banks or libraries and even play popular new computer games.

原译：

生意达 360 亿美元的美国计算机工业好几个月来一直焦急地等待着国际通用机器公司进入个人计算机这个热门的新市场。这种像电视机一样大小的机器的几家最大的销售商之一，坦迪公司的财务计划经理加兰·阿谢尔说："有些人相信国际商用机器公司会展出一个新的圣杯。"上星期，国际商用机器公司终于端出了它的产品。定价从 1 565 美元至 6 300 美元，这种放在桌头的计算机能储存一度曾需要满房子的文件柜才放得下的文件；它还能描出四种颜色的图表，通过电话线路接收来自远处数据库或图书馆的信息，甚至于还能在它上面玩流行的新的计算机游戏。

点评：

① 将 "$36 billion" 译成 "生意" 既不准确也不专业。反映某行业物质生产部门在一定时期内生产的货物和服务价值总和（生产经营活动总成果）的计算单位应该是 "总产值"。

② "industry" 译成 "行业" 更加贴切。

③ "one of the leading..." 这一句的译文太长，连续三个 "的" 使句子读起来非常别扭。虽然英语的这个同位语无动词分句是对前面 "Tandy Corp." 的补充说明，但译成汉语时应考虑将其拆译成汉语的其他结构。

④ "a new Holy Grail" 如果直接译成 "一个新的圣杯"，很多读者就难以理解，因此不如根据上下文将其译成 "人们期待已久的新机型"。

⑤ "showed off" 译成 "亮出" 更加妥当，带有 "胜券在握" 的意思。

⑥ "Priced between $1,565 and $6,300" 这个过去分词短语如果按英语的句式翻译成状语，就不符合汉语的表达习惯。

⑦ "that once would have required a roomful of filing cabinets" 这个定语从句虽然是限制性的，但如此直译显得句子冗长拗口。

⑧ "even play popular new computer games" 译成 "在它上面玩流行的新的……" 不如译成 "用它来玩流行的新游戏"。

改译：

美国计算机行业的总产值为 360 亿美元。几个月来，这个行业一直迫切地期待着国际通用机器公司（IBM）能涉足个人计算机这个热门的新市场。坦迪公司是这种电视机一般大小机器的主要经销商之一。该公司的财务计划经理加兰·阿谢尔说："有些人认为国际商用机器公司一定会很快推出一款人们期待已久的新机型。"上星期，国际商用机器公司终于亮出了它的产品。这种台式电脑的价格从 1 565 美元至 6 300 美元不等，能储存过去需要一屋子文件柜才能装下的文件，还能绘出四种颜色的图表，通过电话线路接收来自远处数据库或图书馆的信息,甚至还能用它玩流行的新游戏。

原文 2:

IBM was also the go-go stock of Wall Street's go-go years in the '60s, selling in 1968 for a stunning 66 times annual earnings.

原译:

国际商用机器公司也是六十年代华尔街生意兴旺时期的畅销股票,1968 年股票价格令人眩晕地卖到全年股息收入的 66 倍。

点评:

① 英语 "go-go" 的意思是 "characterized by the fast growth and development that invites speculative investment"。这里含有投机和过度炒作的意思。因此,第一个 "go-go" 可以译成 "大黑马"、"抢手货" 或者 "大牛股"、"热门股";第二个 "go-go" 是形容股市持续上涨,牛气冲天,投机气氛浓厚,因此可译成 "暴涨"。

② "stunning" 这个形容词不很好翻译,"令人眩晕地" 译得太生硬,无非就是想表达涨得太高吗,所以干脆就译成 "狂炒"、"狂涨"。

③ 将 "66 times annual earnings" 译成 "卖到全年股息收入的 66 倍",意思有误。这里的 "earnings" 指的是公司每年的盈利,也就是股价与公司盈利之比,即市盈率(PE)。因此,应该译成 "市盈率高达 66 倍"。

改译:

国际商用机器公司也是六十年代华尔街股市兴旺时期的大牛股,1968 年该股股价狂涨至最高点,市盈率高达 66 倍。

原文 3:

First popular in California, credit cards spread throughout the United States and most of Western Europe during the late 1960s. Although credit cards are becoming a more acceptable part of the financial scene, they are still regarded with suspicion by many as being a major part of the "live now, pay later" syndrome.

原译:

信用卡最初流行于加利福尼亚,后来在 60 年代后期推广到整个美国和西欧的大多数国家。虽然信用卡正成为金融业更能接受的付款方式,但是许多人仍然心存疑虑,把信用卡看成是 "寅吃卯粮" 生活方式的主要表现。

点评:

① 这里将 "the financial scene" 译成 "金融业" 不太妥当。因为根据兰登书屋出版的《韦氏美语学习词典》(Random House Webster's Dictionary of American English)的解

释,"scene"的意思是"an area of activity, interest, etc.: the fashion scene",而不能说是一种行业。这里可以省译。

② 把"becoming a more acceptable part"译成"正在成为更能接受的……"也不符合汉语的习惯,而英语"acceptable"应该是"受欢迎"的意思。

③ 相对于"最初"、"60年代后期",这里宜增加"今天",以示区别。因此,建议将此句译成:"今天,作为一种付款方式,信用卡受到越来越多的人的欢迎(青睐),但……"或译成:"今天,尽管信用卡逐渐成为了一种更受欢迎的支付方式,但……"。

改译:

(1) 今天,作为一种付款方式,信用卡受到越来越多的人的欢迎(青睐),但是许多人仍然心存疑虑,把信用卡看成是"寅吃卯粮"生活方式的主要表现。

(2) 今天,信用卡已逐渐成为一种更受欢迎的支付方式,但不少人仍心存疑虑,认为信用卡消费是"寅吃卯粮"生活方式的主要表现。

学生译作分析

原文:

Courtesy begins with introductions. If an introduction is mismanaged, there is a strong possibility that the emerging business relationship will also be subject to problems. That is why you must start right away to build a strong foundation for your new business relationships.

It probably comes as no surprise to you to learn that the initial phase of a business relationship can have extraordinary effects on careers — and on whole organizations. But who hasn't felt at least a little awkward during a business introduction? Fortunately, a few simple principles can have a dramatic, positive effect on the way you meet and greet new business associates.

学生原译文:

随着经人介绍与陌生人相识,礼仪便开始了。如果介绍处理不当,很可能随之出现的业务关系就会困难重重。所以,从一开始你就必须为你的新业务关系建立牢固的基础。

你也许非常清楚,业务关系的建立能对某个人的生涯——甚至整个组织的前途产生特别的影响。但是,谁在结识新业务关系时不会感到至少一点儿尴尬呢?幸好,一些简单的原则可以让你在与业务关系打交道时产生戏剧性和肯定的效果。

分析:

(1) "introduction"有"介绍互相认识"之意,如果非要将"介绍"翻译出来,句子就显得别扭，其实这里就是"与别人初次打交道"、"刚刚认识"的意思，翻译时可以不把"介绍"译出来，否则后面的那个"introduction"也不好处理。

(2) 将"emerging"译成"随之出现的"不妥，译成"新建立的"更确切一些。初学翻译的学生容易犯这类错误，就是看到"introduction"就再也摆脱不了"介绍"的意思，看到"emerge"就总是想着"出现，涌现"。"emerging"虽然是"随之出现"的意思，但汉语通常不说"业务关系随之出现"。又如："emerging nations"（新兴国家）、"emerging growth businesses"（新型成长性企业）。

(3) "to be subject to problems"意译成"困难重重"稍微重了一点，再说"业务关系"会"困难重重"也不通顺。译成"难免不出问题"或者"很可能会碰到麻烦"更贴切一些。

(4) "从一开始你就……"这句话读起来很顺口，但细读原文则发现这里并没有"从一开始"的意思。作者这里是建议你赶快行动起来，掌握一些基本的礼仪知识，以便将来处理好与新客户的关系。因此，还是要把"you must start right away"直译出来。

(5) "为你的新业务关系建立牢固的基础"让读者难以明白，这样翻译主要是"foundation"后面的那个"for"引导的介词短语没有处理好。所以，不能直接译成"为你的新业务关系"，而要增加"发展"一词，这样才能将原意准确地表达出来。

(6) 将"It probably comes as no surprise to you to learn …"译成"你也许非常清楚"不如译成"你或许不难理解"。后面"that"引导的宾语从句中的主语是"the initial phase of a business relationship"，译文将其译成"业务关系的建立"不是很准确。这里不是强调建立业务关系的重要性，而是强调业务关系建立之初的重要性。另外，将"careers"译成"某个人的生涯"也不够具体。"careers"指"某人工作经历或事业上取得成就的总的过程或进程"，这里显然是指某人的经商过程，翻译时可稍微引申一下。

(7) 将"awkward"译成"尴尬"不妥。不能看到"awkward"就理解成"尴尬"，这样翻译读者就不容易理解，怎么在刚建立业务关系就会感到至少一点儿尴尬呢？查查词典就会发现"awkward"有"requiring great tact, ingenuity, skill, and discretion"（棘手的，难处理的）的意思。

(8) "you meet and greet new business associates"译成"结识新客户"比"与新业务关系打交道"更加自然、准确。另外，这句话中虽然"a few simple principles"是主语，但不宜按英语句式直译。还有，"a dramatic, positive effect"不要译得太生硬。

参考译文：

与人初次相识就得讲究礼仪。如果这个头没开好，那你刚刚开始的业务关系以后就难免不出问题。因此，你必须立即着手为将来发展你的新业务关系打好基础。

你或许不难理解，建立新业务关系时能否开个好头对你个人今后的业务发展——甚至整个公司的前途能产生重大的影响。但是，在建立新业务关系之初，谁又没有碰到过一些难以应付的局面呢？幸运的是，在结识新客户时，你完全可以遵循一些简单的原则，以取得显著而良好的效果。

翻译技巧介绍

数字等的翻译
（Tanslating Figures, etc.）

商务英语离不开数据、百分比、倍数、分数及与数字有关的对比表达方式。这些数字和对比方式有时与汉语的表达习惯并不完全一样，如果翻译不好，出现误译，轻则误导读者，重则还有可能造成经济上的损失。因此，在翻译与数据有关的资料时，必须谨慎而小心，尽量避免出错。例如"Since reform began in 1978, an average growth rate of almost 10% a year has seen China's GNP nearly quadruple."（自 1978 年经济改革以来，中国经济以年均近 10%的速度增长，使其国民生产总值几乎增长了 3 倍）。注意，这句话的最后一个词"quadruple"翻译时就必须小心，千万不能译成"增长了 4 倍"或"翻了 4 番"，但可以译成"翻了 2 番"、"是 1978 年的 4 倍"或"增长了 3 倍"。

1. 普通数字的翻译

遇到普通的数字（包括数量词、习惯短语等），直译即可，但注意要将相应的量词和单位翻译出来，而且千万不可将数字和量词写错或译错（如 million、billion 和 trillion 等）。

（1）This is part of the data collected by the International Labor Office on hourly rates in **forty-one** occupations and consumer prices for a sample of household items in about **100** countries.

译文：这个资料是国际劳工局所收集的数据的一部分，该局在大约 100 个国家里收集了 41 种职业的计时工资率，并进行了一次家用消费品价格的抽样调查。

（2）The so-called leading indicator, a forward-looking index the OECD compiles, showed a readout of **131.0** for the US in May after **129.4** in April. For the Euro zone the leading indicator rose to **119.3** from **118.7**.

译文：这个由 OECD 编制的前瞻性"先行指数"显示，美国的数据从四月份的

129.4 点提高到五月份的 131.0 点，而欧元区的这一先行指数则从 118.7 点上升到了 119.8 点。

(3) Losing an average of **$1,227** on every vehicle sold during the first six months of 2005, GM's North American operations piled up **$2.5 billion** in losses.

译文：在 2005 年上半年，平均每售出一辆汽车就亏损 **1 227 美元**，通用汽车公司的北美业务亏损总额累计高达 **25 亿美元**。

(4) It says that since 2000, it has increased its workforce in the Asia Pacific region by **100 staff to about 750**.

译文：该行说，自 2000 年以来，它在亚太地区的员工已增加了 **100 名**，总数增至**约 750 名**。

(5) To be sure, the stock market remains one of the best places for **millions of** Americans to invest for the long term in diversified portfolios. After all, returns from stock funds over the long run handily beat risk-free havens like bank certificates of deposits.

译文：可以肯定的是，华尔街的股票市场仍然是**数以百万计**的美国人进行多样化长线投资组合最为合适的场所之一。毕竟，长期的股票收益轻而易举就可超过银行存款等零风险投资方式的收益。

(6) Customer satisfaction "is not about spending **squillions** of dollars, it's about looking after the customer".

译文：令顾客满意"并不是要花费'**不计其数**'的钱，而是要好好关照顾客"。

(7) Noting that **seven of the largest 20 mutual funds** in the US hold one or more gambling stocks, Anita Green, the director of social research at Pax World Fund suggests that investors pick a fund that has sworn to avoid them-namely, her own.

译文：阿妮塔·格林是派克斯世界基金的社会研究经理，她注意到美国最大的 **20 个共同基金中的 7 个**拥有 1 个或多个博彩类股票，于是呼吁投资者选择那些发誓不买博彩股的基金——也就是她自己所任职的基金公司的基金。

(8) **Of 10 toy segments, there are only two**, arts and crafts, and dolls, have generated sales growth over a recent 12-month period, according to investment frim Harris Nesbitt.

译文：根据投资公司 Harris Nesbitt 公司的报告，在最近 12 个月的销售中，**在 10 个玩具细分市场中，出现销售增长的只有两种**，一是艺术和手工类玩具，二是洋娃娃玩偶类。

(9) In a Boston Consulting survey of 250 senior executives, nearly **seven out of ten** cited innovation as a top priority and said they plan to hike R&D spending.

译文：在波士顿咨询公司对 250 名高级主管进行的调查中，**有近 7 成的人**称研发的地位最为重要，并表示计划加大这方面的投入。

(10) I don't think consumers have the ability to continue to perform this feat of spending

rapidly while their energy bills grow **at a double-digit rate.**

译文：我觉得消费者没有能力在他们的能源账款**以两位数率**增长的同时继续如此快速地消费。

(11) No banks provide a geographic break-out for the financial performance of their private banking arms. But most claim they have been enjoying **double digit growth** in assets under management and net income in Asia.

译文：没有哪家银行对其私人银行业分支机构的理财业绩提出地域上的硬性要求，但大都宣称，它们在亚洲管理的资产及其净收入一直在**以两位数**增长。

2. 百分比的翻译

碰到百分比时，可以将其译成"（的）百分之……"或使用"％"，也可视情况将其译成"……倍"、"……百分点"或"……成"。

(1) France has historically been the world's favourite tourist destinations and last year 77 million foreign visitors generated €100 bn — **7 per cent** of France's GDP.

译文：历史上，法国一直是全世界游客最爱去的地方。去年7 700万外国游客在这里花费了1 000亿欧元，相当于法国国内生产总值的**7％**。

(2) In 1977, the sum total of Chinese imports and exports was less that 15 billion, putting China's share of world trade at **0.6 percent**.

译文：在1977年，中国进出口总额还不到150亿美元，仅占世界贸易总额的**0.6％**。

(3) It's easy to understand the business case for MTV Networks' world tour. It reaches **87.6 million homes** in America, but outside the United States, it's in more than **331 million homes**, in **164 countries and territories**, broadcast in **18 languages.** Despite MTV Networks' huge global presence already, the US arm accounts for fully **80 percent of overall revenue of ＄5.2 billion.**

译文：很容易理解MTV音乐电视网世界之旅这一商业案例。在美国它进入了**8760万户家庭**，而在美国之外，它进入了**164个国家和地区超过3.31亿户家庭**，用**18种语言进行广播**。尽管音乐电视网在全球已广泛存在，在美国的公司仍足足占据了**52亿美元总收入的80％**。

(4) Year on year, the newspaper has seen sales fall **5％**, which is in line with an overall **6％** dip in red-top sales.

译文：年复一年，《太阳报》的销量已下滑了**5％**，与通俗小报整体销量下跌的**6％**保持一致。

(5) The company's furious addition of new stores fuels its booming bottom line and caffeinated stock price, **up 1,500 percent** in the past decade.

译文：迅猛增加的新店刺激该公司利润迅速上升和仿佛添加了咖啡因的股票价格飞涨——公司的股价在过去的 10 年中**涨了 1 500％（15 倍）**。

(6) Half a gallon of soy milk typically sells for **$2.79** to **$3.99**—a **50 to 100 percent** premium over cow's milk.

译文：半加仑豆奶的一般售价为 **2.79 至 3.99 美元**，比牛奶高出 **50％～100％**。

(7) During the 1990s, relative mobility—that is, the share of Americans changing income quintiles in any direction, up or down—slipped **by two percentage points**, to **62％**.

译文：在 20 世纪 90 年代，相对的地位变迁率——即收入档次提高和下降的美国人占人口总数之百分比——下降了两个百分点，降至 **62％**。

(8) CEO pay has risen **866 percent** over the past 15 years to an average of more than **$10 million**, while worker pay has risen only about **63 percent** in the same period.

译文：在过去的 15 年里，CEO 的报酬上涨了 **866％**，平均年薪超过 **1 000 万美元**，而一般员工同期只涨了约 **63％**。

(9) SG Private Banking, which serves clients with financial assets of **$250,000 or more**, says its net asset under management rose **100 percent** in 2000 and **35 percent** last year. The company is on track for **30–35 per cent** growth again this year.

译文：服务于金融资产**至少为 25 万美元**客户的"法国兴业私人银行业务"表明，它所管理的净资产在 2000 年增长了 **100％**，去年为 **35％**。今年公司正再次迈上 **30％～35％**的增长轨道。

(10) Citigroup Private Bank, whose target market is people with **$5m** in net assets and above, claims a compound annual growth rate for net assets under management over the past five years of **more than 25 per cent**.

译文："花旗私人银行"的目标市场是净资产**不低于 500 万美元**的客户，该行称，过去 5 年来，其管理的净资产的年综合增长率超过了 **25％**。

(11) Roche, which has been under pressure from an attempted merger by its Swiss rival Novartis, reiterated it expected full-year underlying sales and operating profit to rise by **double-digit percentage rates**.

译文：罗氏一直受到本国竞争对手诺华兼并计划的压力。罗氏重申，预计集团全年的销售额和运营利润都会**以两位数的速度**增长。

3. 倍数的翻译

倍数必须特别小心，因为英语和汉语的表达方式有所不同。特别要注意 double、treble 和 quadruple 等词的译法。

(1) Analysts expect cable TV viewership to **double** to 8 million this year, while Net shopping could surge **fourfold** to $8.5 billion by 2005.

译文：分析家预计，有线电视的观众人数今年将**翻一番**，达到 800 万；而网上购物总额到 2005 年可能猛增至原来的 **4 倍**，达到 85 亿美元。

(2) In 1970, the value of two-way trade was equal to just 13% of the US economy. Last year, that figure, at 28%, was **more than twice as high**.

译文：1970 年双边贸易额只占美国经济的 13%，而去年已上升到 28%，比 1970 年**增加了一倍多**。

(3) The Argentine economy is expected to grow 9 per cent this year after an 11 per cent decline in 2002. The dollar value of its stock market is **up 100 per cent** this year—the largest increase of any major market in the world.

译文：在 2002 年出现 11% 的负增长之后，今年阿根廷经济可望增长 9%。以美元计价的股票市值今年**上涨了一倍**，是全世界主要股票市场中增长最快的。

(4) In Taiwan, long known for churning out me-too electronics products, R&D spending has leapt **fivefold**, to $7.5 billion, since 1990.

译文：长期以来以生产仿制电子产品闻名的中国台湾地区，自 1990 年以来投入的研发资金已激增了 **5 倍**，达到了 75 亿美元。

(5) Tata said its offer is **nine times** Corus's earnings before interest, taxes, depreciation and amortization, or Ebitda, based on the British steel maker's earnings in the 12 months ended Sept. 30. Mittal's offer for Arcelor was **4.46 times** the Luxembourg-based company's earnings.

译文：塔塔说，公司的出价是抗力斯集团这家英国钢铁制造商到 9 月 30 日为止 12 个月的总收入——息税折旧摊销前赢利（Ebitda）——的 **9 倍**。而米塔尔钢铁集团为国际钢厂阿塞勒提出的收购价仅为这家总部设在里斯本的国际钢铁公司收入的 **4.46 倍**。

(6) The acquisition will push Tata's consolidated debt to **4.2 times** its equity in the year ending March 31, requiring the company to sell new shares.

译文：这场并购将使塔塔钢铁公司的合并债务提高到其截止至今年 3 月 31 日资产净值的 **4.2 倍**，这需要公司卖掉一些新的股份。

(7) Consumers bought nearly a billion cell phones last year, **10 times** the number of iPods in circulation. Break off just 1% of that, and you can buy yourself a lot of black turtlenecks.

译文：去年，消费者购买了将近 10 亿个手机，**10 倍**于 iPod 的销售量。将其 1% 的份额拿出来，你就能为自己买许多黑色高领套衫。

(8) It has been five years since the iPod launched, 30 years since Jobs co-founded Apple (with Stephen Wozniak) and 10 since he returned there after having been fired, during which decade, Apple's stock has gone up **more than 1,500%**.

译文：5 年前，iPod 问世；30 年前，乔布斯与人（斯蒂芬·沃兹尼克）共同创建了苹果公司；从他被解雇又回到这里也已经 10 年了。在这 10 年间，苹果公司的股票上涨**超过了 15 倍**。

(9) South Koreans, for example, charged 331 trillion won ($252 billion) in the first nine months of 2001, **treble** the amount from the year before. Hong Kong had 9,151 personal bankruptcies last year, about **double** the prior year's total.

译文：例如韩国，2001 年头 9 个月便贷出 331 万亿韩元（2 520 美元），比上一年**多了两倍**。香港去年有 9 151 起个人破产案，约为上一年的**两倍**。

(10) Now, Britons average nearly two credit cards per person, and consumer debt has **quadrupled** in the past eight years.

译文：目前英国人平均每人约有两张信用卡，在过去的 8 年里消费贷款已增加了 **3 倍**。

(11) A survey at the National University of Singapore showed there were 69 entrepreneurs in the class of 2002, **more than 2.5 times** the number in 2001. At Nanyang Technological University, it was 10 in 2002, **doubled** the number from a year before.

译文：在新加坡国立大学进行的一项调查表明，在 2002 级毕业生中有 69 人创办了自己的企业，比 2001 级**增长了 2.5 倍**。南洋理工大学 2002 级毕业生中自办企业的有 10 人，也比上一年**增加了 1 倍**。

(12) The past 50 years have seen an exceptional growth in world trade. Merchandise exports grew on average by 6% annually and total trade in 1997 was **14 times** the level of 1950.

译文：在过去的 50 年里，世界贸易有了惊人的增长，商品出口平均每年增长 6%。1997 年贸易额是 1950 年的 **14 倍**。

(13) It has had scant success: Seiyu's share price has fallen by **three-quarters** since Wal-Mart invested, thanks to the same inefficiencies that afflict most Japanese retailers.

译文：到目前为止，沃尔玛尚未取得多少成功。沃尔玛投资以来，西友公司的股价下跌了 **3/4**，幸亏大多数日本零售商也同样承受着低效率的折磨。

(14) The company now has assets of NZ$20 to $25 million, and a turnover of NZ$16 million a year—**a 10-fold** increase over the last five years.

译文：现在，公司拥有 2 000 至 2 500 万新西兰元的资产，每年有 1 600 万新元的营业收入——在过去 5 年里增长了 **10 倍**。

4. 分数和序数词的翻译

英语的分数表达方式与汉语不同，汉语可写成"……分之……"或用阿拉伯数字表示，还可译成百分数。翻译时应特别注意 quarter 等词，不可将其与"季度"混淆。翻译序数词时别忘记后面的量词。

（1）The Fed last cut interest rates **by a modest quarter percentage point** at the policy meeting in June, taking the federal funds rate to a 45-year low of 1 per cent.

译文：美联储上一次以**四分之一个百分点**的幅度温和降息是在六月份的政策会议上，这使得联邦基金利率45年来首次降至1%。

（2）As the decade progressed, Nokia advanced its multinational interests and expanded its work force, becoming the engine of Finland's economy, representing **two-thirds** of the stock market's value and **a fifth** of the country's total export.

译文：在过去10年中，诺基亚通过不断扩展其跨国公司业务和扩大员工队伍，一跃成为芬兰经济的发动机，其股票市值占该国整个股市市值的**三分之二**，出口量占到了芬兰出口总值的**五分之一**。

（3）Although the Internet bubble has burst and Nokia's share price is only **around a third** of its record highs in 2000, the company's influence on Finnish society is the clearest example of broader collision of values within Europe's welfare states.

译文：虽然因特网经济的泡沫已经破灭，诺基亚的股价现在也只有它2000年创下的最高价的**三分之一左右**，但就欧洲福利国家内价值观越来越大的冲突来说，诺基亚对芬兰社会的影响是这一冲突最明显的例子。

（4）The acquisition will form a company with revenue of $24.4 billion, with **two-third** of its sales in Europe, and lift Tata **to fifth from 56th** in global steel rankings.

译文：此项并购将产生一家年收入244亿美元、**三分之二**的销售额在欧洲完成的大公司，这将使塔塔在全球钢铁生产商中的排名从**第56位上升至第5位**。

（5）The most populous country in the world, China ranked a distant **30th** among exporting nations.

译文：世界上人口最多的中国在出口国中排名靠后，仅为**第30位**。

（6）We think we have **one-tenth** the number of people running these lines, compared with rivals in Mexico or China, and the savings make the company's commercial motors, in the $40-to-$60 range, competitive with models produced manually offshore.

译文：我们认为我们操作这些生产线只需**1/10**的人员。此种节约使公司价格在40～60美元之间的商用电机与海外手工生产的型号相比颇具竞争力。

（7）Start with Pepsi's share of the US carbonated soft-drink market, including brands like Montain Dew and Slice：**up two-tenths** of a percentage point to 31.6% last year, Beverage Digest reports. Coke brands, including Diet Coke and Sprite, still lead easily with a 43.7% share—but that's **down four-tenths of a point**.

译文：首先是百事可乐在美国碳酸软饮料市场上的份额，包括像Montain Dew 和Slice这些品牌：据《饮料文摘》报道，去年上升了**0.2个百分点**而达到了31.6%。虽然可口可乐的品牌，包括健怡可乐和雪碧，仍然以43.7%的份额轻松领先，却已**下滑了 0.4 个（百分）点**。

(8) Swiss healthcare group Roche has reported a fall in first-half net profits **by almost a quarter** but it saved itself from a share sell-off by announcing strong growth in key drugs and offering a solid outlook.

译文：瑞士罗氏医药集团报告，上半年公司净利润减少**近四分之一**。不过，由于宣布主产药品强劲增长，前途稳固，从而避免了公司股票被抛售的厄运。

(9) Seiyu, a Japanese discount retailer, this week forecast its **sixth straight annual loss**.

译文：本周，日本折扣零售商西友百货预测该公司将连续**第 6 年亏损**。

(10) The Chinese government has poured large amounts of money into meeting this challenge, doubling its expenditure on research and development as a percentage of GDP from 1995 to 2005—when it reached $30 billion—to become **the sixth-largest spender in the world**.

译文：为应对这一挑战，中国政府投入了大量资金。1995 年至 2005 年，中国的研发经费占国内生产总值的比例增加了 1 倍，达到 300 亿美元，**位居世界第六**。

5. 比较级和最高级的翻译

翻译比较级时应特别注意比较的对象，避免让读者产生误解。另外，有时英语中虽然没有用比较级，但却表达了比较的意思，应该将这层意思翻译出来。当然，翻译时还应注意英语中的一些比较级和最高级的习惯表达方式（如用比较级形式表示最高级的意思及用形容词的比较级表示"较……"的意思等）。

(1) Soy milk sales reached a high of about $700 million last year. But that's **minuscule compared with** soft drinks' $63 billion, milk's $10 billion and bottled water's $8 billion in retail sales.

译文：去年豆奶销售额高达 7 亿美元。但与软饮料的 630 亿、牛奶的 100 亿和瓶装水的 80 亿零售额**相比还是微不足道的**。

(2) We Britain rely **more than any other major economy** on the goods and services that we export, the investment that we attract and we make abroad.

译文：英国对商品和服务出口及投资和引资的依赖**超过了世界上其他经济大国**。

(3) As for performance, the 80 "socially responsible" mutual funds tracked by Morningstar Inc., the Chicago research company, returned 15 percent a year on average in the five years through October. That **compares** to an 18 percent return for all US stock funds, and 26 percent for the Standard & Poor's 500 Index during the same period.

译文：据芝加哥的一家调研公司——晨星股份有限公司的跟踪调查，就业绩来讲，80 家"对社会负责"的共同基金在直至 10 月份的过去 5 年的平均收益是 15%。**与之相比**，同阶段美国所有的证券基金的平均收益是 18%，标准普尔500指数的平均收益是26%。

(4) As of August 1, 2005, Taobao was reaching 15,800 out of every 1 million Internet users, **compared with** just under 10,000 for eBay China. The number of page views per user—a measure of interest in the site—was 10.7 for Taobao **vs.** 7.4 for eBay.

译文：截止到2005年8月1日，每100万因特网用户中就有1.58万人是淘宝的用户，**而** eBay 中国的用户只有不到1万人。按照每个用户浏览页面的次数（一种测量用户对某一网站的兴趣程度的方法）来看，淘宝是10.7次，**而** eBay 是7.4次。

(5) Sales of SUVs and other light trucks dropped 7.7 percent, **while** sales of passenger cars—which had fallen to **less than half of** all vehicles sold—rebounded by 0.5 percent.

译文：运动型多功能汽车和其他轻型货车的销售量下降了7.7%，**而**轿车的销售量（曾一度跌至**不到**所有售出车辆数目的**一半**）反弹了0.5%。

(6) We ourselves (British) attract **more** foreign investment **than** any country **but** the US; **more** US investment **than** in the whole pacific region.

译文：我们所吸引的外资**仅次于**美国，居世界第二，而美国在英投资**高于**其在整个太平洋地区的投资总和。

(7) The US Department of Commerce on Friday said total US e-commerce sales reached $12.5 billion in the second quarter, which is a **28 per cent gain over** sales for the same period in 2002. However, the growth **placed in comparison with** the 26 per cent quarterly leap reported in the first quarter of 2003.

译文：美国商务部在星期五宣布，第二季度全美电子商务销售额达到125亿美元，这个数字比2002年同期**增长了28%**。但是，同2003年第一季度26%的暴涨相比，第二季度的增长速度就黯然失色了。

(8) **A more efficient** factory, even with **fewer workers** is **better than** the alternative.

译文：一个生产效率**较高**的工厂，即使工人较少，也**比**一个有较多工人的低效率工厂好。

(9) The unemployment rate is at 6.2 per cent, just **off an eight-year high**, and capacity utilization levels are **near 20-year lows**.

译文：现在的失业率为6.2%，**几乎是八年来的最高点**，而生产能力利用率也**接近20年来的最低点**。

(10) Since the manufacturing sector tipped into recession in mid-2000, it has shed 2.1 million jobs, leaving **fewer** industrial workers in the US **than** at any time since the early 1960s.

译文：自美国制造业2000年中期陷入衰退以来，已裁减了210万个工作岗位，这是自20世纪60年代初以来美国产业工人在册数量**最少的一次**。

(11) Far from being deterred by last year's global economic downturn, Asia's wealthiest are

turning to private bankers to manage their fortunes **in ever greater numbers**.

译文：去年的全球经济衰退远远未能挡住亚洲巨富们的脚步，他们正**以空前的数量**需求私人银行家为其管理财富。

（12）Although Japan's inward FDI double between 2000 and 2005, it still amounted to only 2.4% of national output, **far less than** in other big economies. In America the comparable figure is 15%, and in Germany, France and Britain it is between 30% and $40%, which means that foreign firms' share of the economy is **far smaller than** in other countries.

译文：尽管进入日本的外国直接投资在2000年到2005年之间翻了一倍，但也只占国民产出的2.4%，**远远低于**其他经济大国。在美国，相应的比率为15%，而德国、法国及英国则在30%至40%之间。这就意味着外国公司在日本经济中的份额**远远少于**其他国家。

（13）Since 2000, China has **ranked behind only** the United States in the number of scientific researchers, and in 2005 they published **more** scientific papers **than** their colleagues anywhere except in the US, Britain, Germany, and Japan.

译文：自2000年以来，中国的科研人员数量**仅次于**美国，2005年，他们发表的科研论文数量**比**美国、英国、德国和日本以外所有国家的同行都**多**。

课堂翻译训练

将下列句子译成汉语。

1. Today we have about 15% of the global market, which is 40% more than our closest competitor. When we began we were a $3.5 billion company; we'll end this year with more than $13 billion in revenue.

2. Currently 83% of our sales are derived through exports, and we operate approximately 100 offices for production, sales, distribution, and R&D in 50 countries throughout the world.

3. Starting Tuesday, prices for Hong Kong residents will be slashed by HK$50 (US$6.40) per ticket — a reduction of about 20 percent.

4. On October 19, the Dow Jones industrial average dropped 508 points, which was 22.6 percent and nearly twice the largest one-day decline during the 1929 crash.

5. Web search leader Google Inc. on Tuesday posted a sharply higher quarterly profit as revenue

doubled with a net income shot up more than seven times from a year earlier, blowing away Wall Street expectations when shares in Google jumped 9 percent.

6. Berkshire's loss in net worth during 2001 was $3.77 billion, which decreased the per-share book value of both our Class A and Class B stock by 6.2%. Over the last 37 years (that is, since present management took over) per-share book value has grown from $19 to $37,920, a rate of 22.6% compounded annually.

7. Domestic automakers'market share slipped to 53.3 percent in April, down 3 percentage points from a year earlier. Toyota's market share hit 15.2 percent—eclipsing that of Chrysler for the first time ever. Right now, automakers sell about 200,000 small cars in the United States, barely 1 percent of the roughly 17 million new cars purchased each year.

8. Tata's bid on Dec. 10 of 500 pence was to be financed by about $7.2 billion of loans, almost eight times last year's profit. Tata said it would pay for the higher offer using additional debt and its own cash.

9. The advantage of plastic notes are considerable. They cost about twice as much as paper notes but last four to five times as long—Australia's $10 paper note had an average life of eight months but plastic lasts at least 30 months.

10. eBay's gross-merchandise volume (GMV)—the total dollar value of the deals done on a given website—in Britain, France and Italy all increased 100% or more in 2004. Consider that in 2000, eBay's international revenue totaled $29 million. By 2004, that figure was $1 billion.

课后练习

将下列短文译成英语,注意运用本单元所学的翻译技巧。

1.

In the USA Forbes magazine has published its annual list of the richest people in the world. Bill Gates of Microsoft is the richest man again for the eleventh successive year with a fortune of 44 billion dollars.

There are a record 691 dollar billionaires, according to Forbes magazine. Between them they have a fortune of 2.2 trillion dollars. That figure is slightly more than the annual value of all goods and services produced in China and India, the two most populous countries. The highest concentration of the ultra-rich is in New York, followed by Moscow and San Francisco and then

London and Los Angeles. But in total the very wealthy live in 47 different nations, with Iceland, Kazakstan, Ukraine and Poland entering the list for the first time this year.

Laksmi Mittal, an Indian born steel tycoon, enjoyed the biggest increase in personal fortune. His net worth has quadrupled to 13 billion dollars making him the world's third richest man. Ingvar Kamprad, founder of the Swedish furniture chain Ikea, also saw a big increase in wealth taking him to the sixth place. Developing countries make more of a showing than in past years - there are for example three Russians and four Indians in the top sixty richest people, though surprisingly perhaps none from China, excluding Hong Kong. Asian wealth is probably under-represented as its usually spread among families, whereas Forbes looks at individuals.

Relatively few women feature in the list — among them is JK Rowling, author of the Harry Potter novels, ranked 620th with a fortune of 519 million dollars. New entrants to the list include the founders of the internet search group Google Sergie Brin and Larry Page, each worth more than 7 billion dollars after their company's recent stock market debut. The richest Italian is the prime minister Silvio Berlusconi, ranked number 25 in the global wealth league.

2.

"Sex" was the keyword most frequently searched by Internet users on Google in Egypt, India and Turkey, the search engine giant said a couple of months ago.

But on the Chinese mainland, it was money and technology that took the honors last year, according to a list released by Google China on Tuesday.

Four of the top six were wealth-related: Three banks and "stock".

China Merchants Bank, Industrial and Commercial Bank of China and China Construction Bank, ranked second, third and sixth, all having listed in 2006 and proving a big draw for investors.

Fourth on the list was "stock", not surprising with Shanghai shares having risen 97 percent last year after doubling the previous year. At number 1 was "QQ", a Chinese instant message service and a brand of car.

The others were: "game" (5th), "Google Earth" (7th), download tool "Thunder" (8th), the anti-virus software "Kaspersky" (9th), and "MSN" (10th).

But when it comes to Chinese, food can't be far behind. The most googled dish was sweet-and-sour ribs, followed by fish-flavored shredded pork, home-style braised pork and braised eggplant.

And for unexplained reasons, the most googled English word was "wire mesh", followed by "crystal", "china", "mushroom" and "ballast".

Among entertainment stars, Taiwan R&B star Jay Chou was No 1 followed by Chen Chusheng, the champion of the television contest Happy Boy last year.

In another list of "seeking knowledge", "what is a blue chip" and "how to invest in the stock market" were the most searched questions on Google in China, while "what is love" and "how to kiss" ranked top of the global list.

3.

After a year of record mortgage foreclosures and slumping home prices, Americans are more determined to shape up their flabby finances in 2008 than their bodies, according to a study released by Countrywide Bank on Tuesday.

Some 67 percent of the 1,002 adults surveyed nationwide said that becoming financially fit is a top New Year's resolution, while 57 percent are committed to becoming physically fit in 2008.

"The results of the survey are an indicator that people are finally putting financial health on a par with physical health," said clinical psychologist Dr. Melody Alderman in a statement from Countrywide.

By gender, women are more insecure about their finances, with 37 percent saying they are financially fit, compared with 55 percent for men. Dads are more confident about finances than moms, and single people feel more secure than the married.

Geographically, US Northeasterners felt better about their money, with 52 percent saying they are financially fit. The Midwest and South were tied at the bottom with 43 percent feeling secure about finances.

Countrywide Bank is part of Countrywide Financial Corp, the largest mortgage lender in the United States with a big stake in the troubled subprime mortgage market. It has been battered by escalating loan defaults.

Unit 3

佳译赏析

Tips for Attire in the Workplace
工作场所着装有妙招

From *Business Etiquette —101 Ways to Conduct Business with Charm & Savvy*
By Ann Marie Sabath

"I have heard with admiring submission[1] the experience of the lady who declared that the sense of being perfectly well-dressed gives a feeling of inward tranquility which religion is powerless to bestow."

—Ralph Waldo Emerson[2]

"某女士关于衣着的体会曾让我心悦诚服。她告诉人们说,那种穿着极为得体的感受能让人内心产生宁静——宗教也无法带来的宁静。"

——拉尔夫·瓦尔多·爱默生

Emerson was probably right—but the opposite is also true. Being less than perfectly well-dressed in a business setting can result in a feeling of profound discomfort that may well require therapy to dispel![3] And the sad truth is that "clothing mismatches" on the job can ruin the day of the person who's wearing the inappropriate attire—and the people with whom he or she comes in contact![4]

爱默生可能是对的——但这话反过来说也有道理。生意场上衣着极不得体就会让人感到浑身不自在,而这种郁闷的心情应该通过一番治疗来消除!可惜事实上有人往往因工作时"衣装搭配不当"弄得自己和与之接触的人整天不自在!

What can go wrong when it comes to professional attire? Plenty. The following are some to-the-point advice on handling the most important issues related to workplace attire. As you'll soon learn, even "casual day"[5] wardrobe selections that carry potentially dire implications on the job can be avoided with just a minimal investment of time, care, and attention.[6]

那么工作时着装会出什么差错呢？多着呢。以下一些中肯的建议能使你处理好工作着装方面最要紧的问题。你很快就会明白，你只需花点儿工夫，留点儿神并稍加注意，就可以远离那些可能给你工作时的形象造成恶劣影响的"便装日"休闲服饰了。

Tip #1   Know when to dress up—or dress down
妙招一   分清何时着工作装——何时着便装

Offices vary when it comes to dress codes. Some businesses have very high standards for their employees and set strict guidelines for office attire, while others maintain a more relaxed attitude. However, it is always important to remember that no matter what your company's attitude is regarding what you wear, you are working in a business environment and you should dress accordingly. This applies not only to business casual wear but to more formal business attire, as well. Certain items may be more appropriate for evening wear than for a business meeting, just as shorts and a T-shirt are better suited for the beach than for an office environment.[7]

说到着装的规矩，各公司要求不同。有些公司对员工上班时的着装要求很高，制度也很严格，而有些公司在这方面却相对宽松一些。但是，你可千万别忘了，你从事的是商务工作，不管贵公司对你上班时的穿着持什么态度，你的着装都应该与你所从事的工作相称，商务休闲装和较正式的工作装都如此。有些服饰更适合做晚礼服，却不能在开商务会议时穿，正像体恤短裤在海滩上穿比较合适，穿着去上班就不大得体。

Your attire should reflect both your environment and your position. A senior vice president has a different image to maintain than that of a secretary or sales assistant.
你的穿着既要与你的工作环境相称，又要能显示出你的身份。公司一位资深的副总裁应该让自己的形象有别于一个秘书或销售助理。

Like it or not, you can and will be judged by your personal appearance!
不管你喜不喜欢，人们可能还是要以貌取人的！

This is never more apparent than on "dress-down days", when what you wear can say more about you than any business suit ever could. In fact, people will pay more attention to what you wear on dress-down days than on "business professional" days! Thus, when dressing in "business casual" clothes, try to put some flair into your wardrobe choices[8]; recognize that the "real" definition of business casual is to dress just one notch down from[9] what you would normally wear on business-professional attire days. Avoid jeans, worn, wrinkled polo shirts, sneakers, scuffed shoes, halter tops[10], and revealing blouses. For men, try wearing a neat pair of pants and a buttoned shirt with long or short sleeves that has more color or texture in the fabric. For women, wear skirts or tailored pants with blouses, blazers, and accessories that mean business yet convey a more casual look than your standard business attire.[11]

这一点在"便装日"尤为明显,这一天你的穿着比你平时所穿的任何工作装更能说明问题。其实,人们更加关注你"便装日"的衣着!所以,当你选择"商务休闲"服饰时,应该在独特的风格和品味上下点工夫。要知道,"商务休闲"的"真正"定义就是:你的着装只需比平时"着装日"正规的职业装略为随意一点儿。不要穿牛仔服、破旧皱巴的套头运动衫、胶底运动鞋、家用平底拖鞋、三角背心和暴露的衬衣。男士可以尝试穿一条整洁的长裤和一件有纽扣的长袖或短袖衬衣,衣料的质地精美,颜色多样。女士则可穿裙子或朴素的长裤,上身穿衬衫或颜色鲜艳的运动上衣,再配上具有商务特色的提包、手套等小配件,这样看起来比穿正规的职业装更加随意。

One simple, never-to-be-violated rule that applies to both men and women: Avoid wearing clothes that reveal too much or leave little to the imagination! For example, men who wear shorts to the office—even on Saturdays—may unintentionally signal to others that they don't recognize standards for[12] appropriate business casual dress. The same rule holds true for women who wear skirts that are tighter and shorter than "business professional" skirts. Why risk the chance of not being taken seriously by managers and colleagues?

不论男女,都可以遵循这样一条简单而永不为过的原则:太暴露或者缺乏想像力的服装坚决不穿!比如,某些男士穿着短裤上办公室(即使是星期六),某些女士的裙子比其"职业装"更紧更短,那他们也许无意中在告诉别人:他们不懂规矩,不知道什么是得体的商务休闲装。何必要冒险让老板和同事瞧不起呢?

Remember, there are boundaries between your career and your social life. You should dress one way for play and another way when you mean business.

别忘了,你的工作有别于你的社交活动。因此,你工作和休闲时的穿着也应该有所不同。

Always ask yourself where you're going and how other people will be dressed when you get there. Is the final destination the opera, the beach, or the office? Dress accordingly, and you will discover the truth in the axiom that clothes make the man—and the woman! When in doubt, always err on the side of dressing slightly more conservatively than the situation demand. Remember, you can always remove a jacket, but you can't put one on if you didn't think to take it with you!

随时随地你都得问问自己去的是什么地方,到了那里别的人会怎样穿着,你要去的地方是剧场、海滩还是办公室。然后根据不同的场合调整自己的衣着,这样你就会明白"人靠衣装"

这句话的真谛！要是你拿不准，就这样做好了：宁可稍微保守一点儿也不要穿得太随便。记住，你可以随时把夹克衫脱掉，但你要是压根儿就没想带上一件，需要穿的时候你就没辙了！

Tip #2　Avoid overaccessorizing
妙招二　服饰配件不宜过多

Whether you are a man or a woman, the way in which you use accessories reveals a great deal about you. [13] Accessories can communicate who and what you are as a person, in the way you are presenting yourself and in your attention to detail.

不管你是男是女，服饰配件的使用都能让别人充分地了解你。也就是说，人们往往可以通过你所选用的服饰配件——你展现自己的方式和你对细节的关注——得知你的身份和职业。

The most common opportunity for overaccessorizing is probably to be found in jewelry. In this case, the basic rule of thumb in a business environment is that less is more. [14] Earrings on men are strictly taboo; women should choose earrings that are simple yet elegant and should wear no more than one pair. Pins provide nice accents to a business ensemble, yet they need not be the main attention-grabber. Be tuned into your organization's culture to decide whether or not you can wear multiple-bangle bracelets; in some workplaces they are considered inappropriate. For both sexes, "appropriate" in a professional setting means wearing a maximum of one ring on each hand, worn on either the ring finger or the pinkie.

人们最容易滥用的服饰配件大概是珠宝首饰。因此，根据经验，在商务活动中，最基本的原则是：宁少勿滥。男士绝对禁止戴耳环；女士则应该选择式样简洁而雅致的耳环，但只能佩戴一付。着商务套装时佩戴胸针可为你增色，但决不能太抢眼，以免喧宾夺主。至于环饰多样的手镯则应视具体的企业文化而定，因为在有的工作场合戴手镯被认为是不妥当的。戒指"得体的"佩戴方法是：无论男女，每只手最多戴一枚，戴在无名指或小指上。

Tip #3　Skip the cheap accessories
妙招三　不用便宜的配饰

Make sure that (for instance) the business pen you carry portrays a positive professional image. When dressed professionally, avoid carrying a plastic pen, just as you would avoid wearing a Power Rangers[15] watch[16] with a plastic band.

你所配备的商务用笔（比方说）一定要展示出你良好的职业形象。如果你身着职业装，就不要佩带塑料钢笔，就像你决不会身着职业装而佩戴一只塑料表带的"恐龙突击队"卡通手表一样。

While you're investing in a decent-looking pen, you should also take note of your briefcase, luggage, and umbrella. Are they as well-maintained as they can possibly be? Do they look sharp? Or can they stand to be replaced? If a "maybe" even popped into your mind[17], get out there and invest in some new stuff that will pay big dividends for your career.

当你去买一支像样的钢笔时，你也应该注意一下你所使用的公文包、手提箱和雨伞。这些东西是否仍旧完好无损？看上去是否还时髦？是不是该换新的了？只要当时你脑子里闪过"也许该换了"的念头，就应该立即付诸行动购买新的，这些东西将给你的工作带来不少好处。

Tip #4   If you're an employer, clarify "business casual attire"
妙招四   如果你是老板，向雇员讲明什么是"商务便装"

Some companies set up a "dress-down day" policy, then forget to tell the employees exactly what they mean by "dress-down". Unpleasant sartorial surprises sometimes arise as a result!

一些公司设立了"便装工作日"，却忘了告诉员工"便装"具体指的是什么，导致公司里令人不快的员工"着装意外事件"时有发生！

If you are the person responsible for creating a policy and procedure manual—or at the very least, a detailed memo—that describes specifically what you do and don't want to see on business casual days. By doing this, you'll give your people guidelines and help them plan that (often tricky) "third wardrobe[18]".

如果你是公司的负责人，你就应该制定相关的规章、职工行为守则或至少一个详细的备忘录，具体说明你希望员工"便装日"怎样穿着。这样你就会使员工有章可依并利于他们筹备这种（常常难办的）"第三类服饰"。

Remember to mention the basics: If you want men to wear shoes and socks instead of open-toed sandals and women to wear hosiery with dresses, even if they have a great tan, say so. By taking a few simple steps to formalize the boundaries of business casual day, you can clarify what is and isn't acceptable, keep your working environment professional, and avoid the strange looks from important visitors when your work force as a whole looks like it just returned from Schlockville, USA.[19]

别忘了讲明你的基本要求：比如你希望男员工上班穿鞋袜，不穿凉鞋；女员工即使有晒得健康的肤色也得在穿套装时穿长筒袜，你就对他们说好了。另外，你还可以采取一些简单的措施将"便装日"该如何着装具体化。明确告诉员工什么能穿，什么不能穿，以保证公司的工作环境具有行业特色，免得来公司的贵宾对员工们的穿着感到诧异，以为这些员工刚从美国乡下归来。

Tip #5   Refer to "the Book" to solve attire problems among subordinates
妙招五   依"法"解决下属的着装问题

Recently, I received a call from a personnel director who wanted to know how to approach a woman who wore sleeveless blouses to work (whose bra and slip straps always seemed to show). The caller wanted to know how she could get this person to change the way she dressed, without shattering her ego?

最近某公司人事经理打电话给我，问我怎样处理她公司里一位穿无袖衫上班的女士（她的乳罩和滑动的吊带总是隐约可见）。该经理想知道如何才能让这位女士改变着装，同时又不致伤害她的自尊心。

I suggested that she appropriately update the organization's procedure manual to include a business casual code and that she depersonalize the exchange[20] by taking a "rules are rules" approach during a private (and low-key) meeting. It worked!

我建议那位人事经理适当修改一下公司的员工守则，增加关于商务便装的规章，然后以一种"公事公办"的态度找该女士私下（低调）心平气和地谈谈。这招真灵！

There's a very good chance that today's managers will have to contend with fashion statements that send the wrong message—loudly—to colleagues, visiting clients, and last but not least, The Big Boss. In cases where you're looking at major provocations, rather than minor misunderstandings of the company dress code on casual day, your best bet is to pull the person aside, find a place for a private discussion, and explain the nature of the problem sensitively yet directly.[21] Your causes will be considerably easier if you have a written dress code that outlines exactly what is and is not acceptable on casual day. Begin by telling the person that he or she is a valued employee. Then explain—without making accusations or casting aspersions on the other person's style—that casual day is a tricky thing and that the way the company has attempted to avoid confusion[22] is by stating what it considers appropriate in its handouts and printed materials[23]. Let the offender know that the company needs his or her assistance now—that it's time to go home to change into *business* casual attire, rather than the "casual" and inappropriate garment(s) he or she is currently wearing. Specify exactly what's "over the line": a halter top, a see-through blouse, Bermuda shorts, a miniskirt. Be specific, rather than assuming that the person can read your mind. Whether the person lives 10 minutes from work or an hour, you should take this action. Why? It will set the necessary precedent, relaying to other employees that rules are meant to be followed and if they are not, changes will have to be made.[24]

如今的公司经理们很可能不得不行动起来抵制那些公然误导他人的时尚观点，其受影响者往往是他们的同事、来访的客户，以及那些大老板们。如果"便装日"公司有人不按公司的有关规章着装，又不是因为小小误解所致，而是明知故犯，那么最有效的解决办法是：把这个人拽到一旁，找个适合私下交谈的地方，认真而坦率地把问题的性质谈一谈。要是你手头上有一份书面的公司"便装日"着装条例，事情就好办多了，上面清楚地写着"便装日"

什么能穿什么不能穿。谈话一开始先表明他或她是个不错的职员，然后让他或她明白——用不着指责或诋毁他或她服装的款式——"便装日"该怎样着装本来是一件需慎重对待的事，因此，为了防止各行其是，公司特地作了明文规定，而且是白纸黑字。接着，告诉这个违规者，现在公司需要他或她配合一下——回家脱掉身上这套"休闲"和不得体的服装，换一套商务便装再来。明确指出他或她什么地方"出格"了：三角背心、透明的衬衫、百慕大短裤或者超短裙。一定要具体，不要以为你不说对方就明白你的意思。不管对方回家往返需要多少时间，十分钟或者一个小时，你都必须这样做。为什么？杀一儆百。让其他员工都明白：规章制度人人都必须遵守，谁做不到，谁就得回家换衣服。

Tip #6 Make sure your casual dress says that you mean business
妙招六 休闲装一定要穿出商务特色

How casual is your organization's business casual day?[25] The answer varies from company to company, of course, and, alas, not all companies develop formal written guidelines for the benefit of employees. One thing is for certain, though. You will never get in trouble for being too underdressed on business casual days if you follow this simple rule: Change your regular professional attire by only a single garment.

你们公司的"便装日"究竟允许你穿着随便到什么程度呢？当然，各个公司的回答不尽相同，何况并非所有的公司都有明文规定供员工们遵照执行，但有一点却是肯定的。只要你牢记这个简单的原则，你就永远不会因"便装日"穿得太随便而招来麻烦：脱掉平时穿的职业装，换上一件普通的外套即可。

For example, men, if your organization's culture requires that you wear a suit on "business professional days", wear a sport coat on business casual days. And for women, swap that conservative blouse you wear on most days with a knit top that is compatible with your blazer.

比如，如果公司要求男士们在"着装日"穿西装，那你在"便装日"就换上一件运动衫好了；而女士们则可脱下几乎天天穿着的老式罩衫，换上一件针织外套和相称的运动夹克。

By following this simple (and, yes, conservative) rule when dressing business casual, you'll still be able to go to a last-minute client meeting on a moment's notice—without having to apologize for how you look. I've been asked many times whether it's acceptable for women to wear slacks on dress-down days in professional environments where this would otherwise be considered inappropriate. The (frustrating) answer is: It depends on the culture of the organization for which you work. The safest standard is probably to keep an eye on what the highest-ranking woman in your organization does and follow her example.

着商务便装的时候按这条简单（而且稳妥）的原则行事，你就仍能够接到通知马上从容地去会见一位突然来访的客户——而无须为自己的装束向对方道歉。经常有人问我，女士在"便装日"上班时是否可以穿宽松的休闲裤，因为有人也认为这是不得体的。（令其失望的）回答是：可以根据你们公司的具体做法而定。或许留意并效仿你公司最上层女士的做法最保险。

Words and Expressions

tip	n.	a helpful hint 提示，技巧
attire	n.	clothing or array; apparel 服装，衣着，盛装，服饰
etiquette	n.	the practices and forms prescribed by social convention or by authority 礼节（由社会习俗或权威所规定的常规或惯例）
savvy	n.	practical understanding or shrewdness 实际知识或才智
		a banker known for financial savvy 以金融技能著称的银行家
less than		not at all 根本不
		He had a less than favorable view of the matter. 他对那种事情根本不抱好感。
dispel	v.	to rid one's mind of; to drive away or off by or as if by scattering 消除，驱散
on the job		while working; at work 工作中的
to-the-point	a.	concerning or with relevance to the matter at hand 切题的，切中的
wardrobe	n.	garments considered as a group, especially all the articles of clothing that belong to one person 全部服装，服装的总称（尤指属于一个人的全部服装）
dire	a.	warning of or having dreadful or terrible consequences; calamitous 可怕的，灾难的
		a dire economic forecast 紧急经济预报
		dire threats 严重威胁
dress up		to wear formal or fancy clothes 盛装，穿正式的或精选的服装
		They dressed up and went to the official opening of the joint venture. 他们盛装去参加那个合资企业的开业典礼。
dress down		to wear informal clothes, befitting an occasion or location 穿平常的衣服，穿非正式服装以适应场合或地点
		I dressed down for such a casual occasion. 在这样非正式的场合，我穿着随便。
code	n.	a systematic collection of regulations and rules of procedure or conduct 法规
		a traffic code 交通法规
dress code		a set of rules specifying the correct manner of dress while on the premises of the institution (or specifying what manner of dress is prohibited) 着装要求
		When working in this company, you have to follow the company's white-shirt black-tie dress code. 在这个公司工作，你就必须遵守公司的着装规定：白衬衣，黑领带。

evening wear		formal wear (more often in the United States) or formal dress (in the United Kingdom), also called evening wear or evening dress, is a general fashion term used to describe clothing suitable for formal events, including weddings, debutante（初次参加社交活动的）cotillions（一种正式的舞会，尤指姑娘被介绍入社交界的舞会），balls, etc.　晚礼服
flair	n.	distinctive and stylish elegance; a sense of style　特别的风雅或风格 She dressed with flair.　她在穿着打扮方面有个人独特的风格。
notch	n.	a level or degree　水平或程度，等级 a notch or two higher in quality　质量上一个层次或再高两个层次 This one is a notch better than the other.　这一个要比那一个高一等。
polo shirt		a pullover sport shirt of knitted cotton　马球衬衫（一种棉质编织的套头运动衫）
scuff	n.	a flat, backless house slipper　家用平底拖鞋
halter	n.	a bodice for women that ties behind the neck and across the back, leaving the arms, shoulders, and back bare　三角背心
tailored	a.	simple, trim, or severe in line or design　在线条或设计上简单、合身或朴素的 a neat, tailored dress　一件干净而朴素的衣服 tailored curtains　简单朴素的窗帘
blazer	n.	a lightweight, often striped or brightly colored sports jacket having pockets and notched lapels　运动夹克（一种质量轻、常有条纹或色彩鲜艳的运动夹克，有衣袋和V字形翻领），运动上衣
accessory	n.	clothing that is worn or carried, but not part of your main clothing　[复]妇女全套衣饰中的小配件（如提包、手套等）
accessorize	v.	to furnish with accessories　装饰，用饰品装饰
axiom	n.	a self-evident or universally recognized truth; a maxim　公理，自明之理，不言而喻的或普遍被认定的真理，格言，规则 "It is an economic axiom as old as the hills that goods and services can be paid for only with goods and services."—Albert Jay Nock "只有用商品和服务才能换来商品和服务，这是和山一样古老的经济原理。"——艾伯特·杰·诺克
err	vi.	to make an error or a mistake　犯错误，出差错 To err is human.　人都会犯错误。 It is better to err on the side of mercy.　宁可失之过于怜悯。
taboo	n./a.	excluded or forbidden from use, approach, or mention　忌讳的，不能或禁止使用、接近或提到的 a taboo subject　一个忌讳的话题 Alcohol is (a) taboo in this tribe.　在这个部落酒是禁忌品。

accent	n.	a distinctive feature or quality, such as a feature that accentuates or complements a decorative style 特点，特征，特色（区别性特征或性质，如强调或补充一种装饰风格的特征）
ensemble	n.	a coordinated outfit (set of clothing); the entire costume of an individual, esp. when the parts are in harmony （妇女的）套装 She wore a beautiful ensemble at the opening ceremony of the company. 在公司的开业典礼上她身着美丽的套装。
bangle	n.	an ornament that hangs from a bracelet or necklace 环饰（挂在手镯或项链上的装饰物）
ring finger		the third finger of the left hand 无名指
pinkie	n.	the little finger （手的）小指
sharp	a.	attractive or stylish 时髦的，漂亮的 a sharp jacket 一件时髦的夹克
pop	v.	to move quickly or unexpectedly; appear abruptly 突然出现
maybe	n.	a possibility and uncertainty 不确定性 There are so many maybes involved in playing the stock market. 股票交易市场中牵涉到这么多的不定因素。
sartorial	a.	of or relating to a tailor, tailoring, or tailored clothing 裁缝的或缝纫的 sartorial elegance 服饰优雅
schlock	n.	something, such as merchandise or literature, that is inferior or shoddy 伪劣品，次品
hosiery	n.	socks and stockings; hose 短袜和长筒袜
tan	n.	the brown color that sun rays impart to the skin 古铜色（光照射后使皮肤具有的褐色）
ego	n.	appropriate pride in oneself; self-esteem 自尊心（适度的自我骄傲）
depersonalize	v.	to render impersonal 使不受个人感情影响 depersonalize an interview 客观地进行采访
bet	n.	a plan or an option considered with regard to its probable consequence 可能性 Your best bet is to make reservations ahead of time. 最好的方法是你提前预订。
last but not least		in addition to all the foregoing 最后一点也很重要
aspersion	n.	an unfavorable or damaging remark; slander 中伤，诽谤或中伤的话，造谣 Don't cast aspersions on my honesty. 不要对我的诚实诽谤中伤。
Bermuda shorts		short pants that end slightly above the knee 百慕大短裤
underdress	v.	to dress too informally for the occasion 穿着太随便
concern oneself with		to engage the attention of; involve 参与，集中注意力于……，卷入 We concerned ourselves with accomplishing the task at hand. 我们参与了手边的这项任务。

swap	v.	to exchange (one thing) for another 以……（一物）换……（另一物），交换，用……做交易
last-minute	a.	just before a deadline; at the last minute 最后的，紧急关头的，最后关头的 last-minute arrangements 最后的安排
on a moment's notice		at or on short or a moment's notice: with very little advance warning 一接到通知马上就……
slacks	n.	casual trousers that are not part of a suit 宽松的裤子，休闲裤（非套装的一部分）

Notes

1 "with admiring submission" 这个介词短语不很容易翻译，因为英语中的一些形容词与后面所修饰的名词的搭配跟汉语不一样，所以无法直接翻译成汉语对等的词组。将这个介词短语翻译成 "赞赏的屈服" 就不通顺。如果译成 "我曾恭敬顺从地听过一位女士的经验之谈"，意思又不够准确。这种情况在翻译时经常出现，千万不可死译硬译，而必须找到对应的汉语词组将原意翻译出来。这里用汉语的四字句 "心悦诚服" 将英语里作状语的介词短语转译成汉语的兼语式，既准确地表达了原意，又符合汉语的表达习惯。

2 Ralph Waldo Emerson 拉尔夫·瓦尔多·爱默生
Ralph Waldo Emerson（1803－1882）is US essayist, lecturer, and poet.

3 Being less than perfectly well-dressed in a business setting can result in a feeling of profound discomfort that may well require therapy to dispel! 生意场上衣着极不得体就会让人感到浑身不自在，而这种郁闷的心情应该通过一番治疗来消除！
拆译这个限制性定语从句比译成汉语的前置定语更加合适。

4 And the sad truth is that "clothing mismatches" on the job can ruin the day of the person who's wearing the inappropriate attire—and the people with whom he or she comes in contact! 可惜事实上有人往往因工作时 "衣装搭配不当" 弄得自己和与之接触的人整天不自在！
这句话中 "that" 引导的表语从句里的主语是 "clothing mismatches"，如果按照英语句式翻译，修饰宾语 "the day" 的定语就不好摆放，所以翻译时将主语转译成 "有人"，并将 "clothing mismatches" 转译成其他成分，这样句子就通顺了。

5 casual day 便装日
Casual Friday（also known as dress-down Friday or simply casual day）is an American business custom.

6　As you'll soon learn, even "casual day" wardrobe selections that carry potentially dire implications on the job can be avoided with just a minimal investment of time, care, and attention.　你很快就会明白，你只需花点儿工夫，留点儿神并稍加注意，就可以远离那些可能给你工作时的形象造成恶劣影响的"休闲服饰"。

将这句话中的被动语态转译成主动语态，使"你"成为动作的发出者，并把介词宾语"a minimal investment of time, care, and attention"全部转译成动词，使汉语句子通畅自如。

7　Certain items may be more appropriate for evening wear than for a business meeting, just as shorts and a T-shirt are better suited for the beach than for an office environment.　有些服饰更适合做晚礼服，却不能在开商务会议时穿，正像体恤短裤在海滩上穿比较合适，穿着去上班就不大得体。

这个句子英语并不难懂，但翻译成汉语时会碰到英语中的两个比较级。如果直接译成"比……更合适"，"than"和后面的介词短语"for a business meeting"和"for an office environment"就很难处理。如果要说清楚，用"比……更合适"的句型又显过长，所以只好拆开翻译。

8　"try to put some flair into your wardrobe choices"中的"flair"作不可数名词时是"a sense of style"的意思，因此这里将其译成"独特的风格和品味"。

9　"one notch down from"本来是"低一个档次"的意思，但这里不宜直译，而应该将"略为随意一点儿"的含义译出。

10　halter top　三角背心，露背装

Halter top refers to a type of women's clothing with one strap around the back of the neck instead of two over the shoulders.

11　For women, wear skirts or tailored pants with blouses, blazers, and accessories that mean business yet convey a more casual look than your standard business attire.　女士则可穿裙子或朴素的长裤，上身穿衬衫或颜色鲜艳的运动上衣，再配上具有商务特色的提包、手套等小配件，这样看起来比穿正规的职业装更加随意。

翻译时应将这句话中的介词"with"转译成动词"上身穿"和"再配上"，并将"that"引导的限制性定语从句拆译成汉语的状语分句。

12　"don't recognize standards for"中的"recognize"究竟是"承认，认同"的意思，还是指"认识，明白"呢？从上下文看，这里更像是"明白，懂得"的意思，所以将其译成"懂……规矩"。

13　Whether you are a man or a woman, the way in which you use accessories reveals a great deal about you.　不管你是男是女，你所使用的服饰配件都能让别人充分地了解你。

这句话如果按英语句式译成"不管是男是女，你使用服饰配件的方法都会向人们好好展示一下你自己"，就会显得很别扭，因此将"服饰配件"译成主语更恰当，然后将"reveals"转译成"让别人……了解……"，也可译成"……都能让你得到充分的展示"。

14 ... that less is more.

这句英语是"少即是多"的意思。但从上下文来看,好像有"宁少勿滥"的含义,所以这句话也可翻译成"越少越好"、"少即是多"或者"求质不求量"。

15 Power Rangers 《金刚突击队》(电视动画片名)

16 "avoid wearing a Power Rangers watch"中的"Power Rangers"很容易被误认为是一种名贵的手表,因为名表配塑料表带也不得体。其实,"Power Rangers"是日本的动画片,所以翻译时应该增译"卡通"二字,以便于读者理解。

17 "If a 'maybe' even popped into your mind ..."中的"maybe"翻译时较难处理。尽管它是对上文中的"Or can they stand to be replaced?"一句的回答,但又不好直接翻译成"只要你有这种念头"。所以,为了忠实原文,还是将其译成"只要当时你脑子里闪过'也许该换了'的念头"。另外,"get out"在句中所表达的意思是:立即说出这个念头,所以意译为"立即付诸行动购买新的"。

18 "third wardrobe"的意思是"a set of clothes with a style that lies between formal business attire and casual wear"。这里为了简洁,将其直译成"第三类服饰",也可译成"另类服饰"。

19 "... just returned from Schlockville, USA."中的"Schlockville"应该是作者杜撰的一个地名,目的是讽刺穿着不得体的员工。所以,这里将其译成"刚从美国乡下归来"。

20 "depersonalize the exchange"是指"使……不受个人感情影响",可以将这个动词转译成汉语的副词"开诚布公地"或"心平气和地",然后将"exchange"转译成动词"谈话,谈谈"。

21 In cases where you're looking at major provocations, rather than minor misunderstandings of the company dress code on casual day, your best bet is to pull the person aside, find a place for a private discussion, and explain the nature of the problem sensitively yet directly. 如果"便装日"公司有人不按公司的有关规章着装,又不是因为小小误解所致,而是明知故犯,那么最有效的解决办法是:把这个人拽到一旁,找个适合私下交谈的地方,认真而坦率地把问题的性质谈一谈。

原文中的"major provocations"不好处理。直译为"挑衅"或者"公然冒犯"似乎语气太重,所以转译成动词"明知故犯",这样比译成"如果哪天你遇到了别人实质性的挑战"更恰当。

22 如果将"to avoid confusion"译成"为了防止混乱",容易让读者产生误解,所以"各行其是"更能准确地表达"乱穿一通"之意。

23 将"it considers appropriate in its handouts and printed materials"译成"公司特地作了明文规定,而且是白纸黑字"比直译成"公司在宣传材料和印刷品上……"更符合汉语的表达习惯。

24 It will set the necessary precedent, relaying to other employees that rules are meant to be followed and if they are not, changes will have to be made. 杀一儆百。让其他员工都明白:规章制度人人都必须遵守,谁做不到,谁就得回家换衣服。

"set a precedent for"是"为……创先例"的意思。这里就是要为全公司职工创一个先例，实际上就是"杀一儆百"的意思。后面一句中的"changes will have to be made"是指规章"应该修改"还是指"应该回家换衣裳"呢？英语"change"这个词作动词时有"to put on other clothing"（换衣服）的意思，如："We changed for dinner. 我们换了衣服去吃饭。"；作名词用时也有"a different or fresh set of clothing"的意思。

25 How casual is your organization's business casual day? 你公司的"便装日"究竟允许你穿着随便到什么程度呢？

这个句子不能直接译成"你公司的'便装日'究竟有多随便？"翻译时可采取"增词法"，将第一个形容词"casual"的含义译出来，因为这句话不仅表达：你们公司的员工在"便装日"能够穿得多随便，还包含了"公司在这一天规定你们如何穿着"的含义。

他山之石

原文 1：

Despite its troubles, Coke has seen its stock jump 19% since Jan. 31, after languishing near a six-year low for most of 2001. Behind the move is an improving overall outlook at Coke, including healthier bottlers that presumably will be more aggressive with holidays and supermarket promotions—key tasks that fall to them.

原译：

尽管有麻烦，可口可乐的股票在2001年在6年最低点附近徘徊了大半年之后，自1月31日起跃升了19%。这一动态的背后是对可口可乐整体前景的改善，包括运营较好的装瓶厂可能在假日促销和超市促销——它们担负的重要任务中干劲更足。

点评：

① "despite its troubles"中的"troubles"是复数，因此为了与后面股票仍然上涨的事实形成对比，最好译成"尽管麻烦不少"或"麻烦不少"。

② 英语"languish"的意思是"to remain unattended or be neglected"（被冷落，未被注意或被忽视），所以如果仅仅译成"徘徊"，就只描述了股价的走势，并没有把"备受冷落"之意译出来。

③ 将"Behind the move is an improving overall outlook at Coke"译成"这一动态的背后是对可口可乐整体前景的改善"，汉语似乎有语病。"背后是对……的改善"讲不通，而且读者也不容易理解。不如将这句话译成"股价的这种走势反映了可口可乐

公司总的前景转好（有所改观）"。

④ "including..." 一句译得太长，读起来很别扭，主要是过分拘泥原文的句式所致。"healthy" 应该指的是"装瓶能力更强的"，而 "key tasks that fall to them" 则是前面句子的同位语。

改译：

尽管麻烦不少，但可口可乐公司的股票价格自今年1月31日至今已飙升了19%，而2001年几乎一年的时间股价都在6年来的最低点附近盘整，无人问津。股价的这种走势反映了可口可乐公司总的前景转好（有所好转），其中本来就占有优势的公司罐瓶厂承担了假日促销和超市促销的关键业务，其竞争能力应该将大大提高。

原文 2：

We must therefore define a market as any area over which buyers and sellers are in such close touch with one another, either directly or through dealers, that the prices obtainable in one part of the market affect the prices paid in other parts.

原译：

因此，我们说市场的定义是指一个地区，在这个地区买卖双方或者直接，或者通过代理人彼此密切联系，以致在这个市场的一个部分所卖出得到的价格会影响这个市场别的部分所买进付出的价格。

点评：

① 将 "We must define a market as any area" 译成 "我们说市场的定义是指一个地区"，漏译了 "must" 一词，应该译成 "我们可以这样给市场下定义：市场是……" 或者 "我们可以将市场定义为……"。

② "such...that" 状语从句的后半部分翻译过于拘泥原文。两个形容词 "obtainable" 和 "paid" 也处理得不很妥当。所谓 "the prices obtainable" 和 "prices paid" 就是商品的买价和卖价。

改译：

因此，我们可以将市场定义为一个区域，在此区域中，买卖双方直接或通过其代理保持密切联系，这样，这个区域中某处的商品买价就会影响区域中另外一处商品的售价。

原文 3：

Also, the use of stolen, lost, or counterfeit credit cards by criminals has become a big headache for the credit card company that is responsible for the goods and services illegally charged to its customers' account.

原译：

而且，还有犯罪分子使用盗得失主的或伪造的信用卡的问题，这些事情真叫信用卡公司大伤脑筋，因为在客户的账目中如记有非分内的商品和劳务支出，公司就得承担全部责任。

点评：

① "lost"在这里分明是指客户遗失的信用卡，将其译成"失主的"不妥。

② 由于"use"在句中是名词，所以译者只好在句尾增译了"的问题"，然后再用"这些事情"，这样译显得句子不够简洁，不如将"使用……的问题"改成汉语的连动词组做主语，后面那个"这些事情"就可省略。

③ "that"引导的定语从句中的"the goods and services illegally charged to its customers' account"译得不够准确，不宜将"illegally charged"译成"记有非分内的"。

改译：

而且，犯罪分子用盗得、拾得或伪造的信用卡进行消费已经让信用卡公司大伤脑筋，因为客户信用卡账户中这些由犯罪分子非法开支的商品和服务费用都必须由公司承担。

学生译作分析

原文 1：

If the customers get the feeling you really care them, they'll respond to that. They'll actually become reluctant not to buy from you.

学生原译文：

（1）如果顾客觉得你确实关心他们，他们便会做出反应。他们就不会不愿意从你手上买产品。

（2）假如客户感到你真的在乎他们，他们就会对此有所表示，就不好意思不从你这里购买产品和服务。

（3）要是顾客认为你的确关心他们，他们就会予以回报，就会很愿意买你的商品和服务。

分析：

（1）"respond to"译成"做出反应"、"有所反应"、"有所回应"和"有所表示"意思都没错，而"予以回报"语气稍重了些，但这些都表示顾客会做出积极的反应。在实际生活中，卖主如果真想顾客之所想，处处为顾客考虑，顾客一般会受感动，因此有时可能碍着情面买下某商品，但却不一定肯定会做出这种反应。所以，将

"they'll respond to that"这个肯定句反过来翻译成"不会无动于衷"更能准确地表达这一层意思。

(2) "They'll actually become reluctant not to buy from you."一句不太好处理，直接翻译是"他们实际上会变得不愿意（情愿）不从你这里买东西。"因此，原译（3）就干脆将其译成了"会很愿意买"。这样翻译显然是不准确的，因为要是这样，作者为什么不直接说"They'll actually become willing to buy from you."呢？英语"reluctant"一词有"勉强"之意，所以在翻译这句话时最好能把"顾客感动，因此为了表示感激而购买"这层意思表达出来。

参考译文：

顾客如果感到你确实关心他们，就不会无动于衷，就不好不买你的产品而一走了之。

原文 2：

Two important criteria may be isolated in attempting to evaluate a country's development: the level of scientific endeavor, and the extent to which the economy is based on modern technology.

学生原译文：

(1) 两条重要标准在尝试评价某个国家的发展时或许可以独立地使用，也就是这个国家的科研投入水平及经济对现代技术的依赖程度。

(2) 在试图评价一个国家的发展时，可仅仅从以下两条重要标准来考虑：科学技术水平和经济建立在现代化技术上的程度。

分析：

(1) 英语"isolated"是学生在翻译这句话时感到最头疼的，加上这句话是被动句，所以感觉不容易处理。原译（1）将"isolated"译成"可以独立地使用"，这样译读者还是不太明白。另外，整个句子仍然是个被动句，主语是"两条重要标准"，只不过将"使用"一词之前的"被"字省去了而已。原译（2）将这句译成"仅仅从以下两条重要标准来考虑"，"isolated"完全没有译出来，所以意思不够准确。

(2) "development"过于抽象，所以英译汉时宜增加范畴词"情况，状况"。

(3) "level of scientific endeavor"一词原译（1）译成"科研投入水平"，原译（2）译成"科学技术水平"。"endeavor"本是"a strong effort, attempt"的意思，汉语为"尽力，力图"，所以译成"科研投入水平"比"科学技术水平"更加忠实原文。但"投入水平"指能表明国家所投入的人力、财力和物力的数量，无法表达出投入之后的结果，因此将其译成"科研水平"或"科研工作水平"效果应该更好。

(4) 将"the extent ... is based on ..."译成"对……依赖程度"显然意思有误，还是按原译（2）将其直译成"建立在……上的程度"更妥切。

参考译文：

在试图对一个国家的发展情况进行评价时，或许可分别采用以下两条重要标准：科研工作水平,以及该国经济建立在现代化技术上的程度。

翻译技巧介绍

词类的转换
(Conversion)

由于英汉两种语言在表达方式上有所不同,所以在商务英语英译汉时常遇到一些句子无法按原文的词性译成汉语,即使勉强译成了汉语,也不通顺,或根本不符合汉语表达的习惯。为了使译文在句子结构及语法上更符合汉语习惯,在翻译时就有必要改变词性。一般说来,翻译时词类的转换是没有限制的,也就是说,只要不违背原文意思,有助于译文的通顺流畅,就可能将原文中某一词类译成汉语中的其他词类。尽管如此,由于英汉两种语言某些固有的表达特点,在大量商务翻译实践中,也可发现一些规律性的东西,因此为了教学方便,特将词类转换分成若干类型,如名词转换成动词、形容词转换成动词、副词转换成形容词和介词转换成动词,等等。

一、转译成动词

汉语中动词使用得比较多,因此英译汉时可将英语的很多词类转译成汉语的动词。

1. 名词转译成动词

英语中具有动作意义或由动词转化而来的名词可转译成汉语动词。

1) 动作名词转译成动词(act, cut, walk, sight, wash 等)

(1) The personal wealth of the world's millionaires rose by six percent in 2000 after an 18 percent **surge** in 1999, although this came against the background of a 375 percent **surge** since 1986.

译文:虽然全球富翁的个人财富 1986 年以来**猛增**了 375%,但是在此基础上自 1999 年**增长** 18% 后 2000 年又增长了 6%。

(2) When money is in short **supply** many businesses fail.

译文:银根**吃紧**时,许多企业会倒闭。

(3) This is **compelling evidence** that market liberalization is compatible with a wide range of economic, social and political preferences.

译文：这强有力地证明了市场自由化与广泛的经济、社会和政治倾向是相融的。

(4) If major problems exist and goals are not being achieved, then **changes** need to be made in the company's organizational or managerial structure.

译文：如果存在较大的问题，而且目标没有完成，那么就需要**改变**公司的组织结构或者管理结构。

(5) The **repeal** of the Corn Laws by Great Britain in 1846 ended Britain's long-standing policy of protectionism.

译文：1846年英国**废除**《谷物法》，结束了英国长期存在的贸易保护主义政策。

2) 派生的名词转译成动词

(1) Rich clients suffered less than other investors in the market **downturn** because of diversification and higher **exposure** to hedge funds and other alternative investment.

译文：虽然市场**持续走低**，但资金雄厚的客户所遭受的损失却比一般客户要小，因为他们的投资多元化，更有实力**参与**对冲基金并选择其他投资品种进行投资。

(2) Documentation means an act of **furnishing** or **authentication** of documents.

译文：所谓制单，就是**提供**或**证实**各种单据的一种行为。

(3) A **commonplace criticism** of American culture is its **excessive preoccupation** with material goods and **corresponding neglect** of the human spirit.

译文：人们**普遍批评**美国文化过于**强调**对于物质产品的占有而**相应地过于忽视**人们的精神生活。

3) 后缀为-er 或-or 的名词转译成动词

后缀-er 或-or 的名词，在句中如果不表示身份和职业，而动作意味强时，宜转译成动词。

(1) To be a success **manager** of a hotel, one must have the true love of service.

译文：要**管理**好饭店，你就必须真正热爱服务这一行。

(2) Motorola is the pre-eminent **supplier** of equipment to a global industry with some 100 million users.

译文：摩托罗拉公司向一个拥有近一亿用户的全球性行业**提供**装备，业绩十分突出。

(3) The **holder** of an MBA from the University of Chicago, he has spent his entire 32-year career at the company.

译文：他**获有**芝加哥大学的工商管理硕士学位，在这个公司一干就是整整32年。

(4) The **maker** of Pantene and Head and Shoulders shampoo could not bear the idea of an important former employee working for a rival.

译文：**生产**潘婷和海飞丝洗发香波的宝洁公司，无法容忍一名重要的前雇员为它的竞争对手工作的想法。

（5）Though seldom a **leader** in technology, Sony built a superlative marketing and service organization.

译文：尽管索尼公司很少在技术上**领先**，但其销售和服务体系却是一流的。

4）惯用语主体名词转译成动词

（1）You must take pricing strategy into **consideration** before developing an overall marketing strategy.

译文：在全面推行市场策略之前，你必须**考虑**定价策略。

（2）But what is the best way to advertise, and is there a technique for making the best **use** of advertising?

译文：但做广告的最佳方式是什么，是否有一种最有效地**利用**广告的技巧？

（3）Just as advertising money should be spent in **relation** to the highs and lows of the business, merchandise should be promoted in **proportion** to what it contributes to the turnover.

译文：正如广告费的支出应与生意的高低峰**相联系**那样，推销某种商品的广告费也应与该商品对营业额的贡献**成比例**。

5）一般抽象名词转译成动词

（1）There is considerable **debate** about how best and how much to reduce income inequality.

译文：至于如何有效地缩小收入方面的分配不均，以及把这种分配不均缩小到什么程度，目前还**众说纷纭**。

（2）The board of directors will hold a **consultation** about the matter.

译文：董事会将**商议**此事。

（3）This firm has a large business **connection**.

译文：这家公司**交易**很广。

（4）There is a large **attendance** at the Fair.

译文：**出席**交易会的人很多。

（5）A tricky question in investing is how much of a role ethics should play in your stock **selections**.

译文：道德规范在你**选择**股票时应该占多大分量，这是你投资时需要慎重考虑的一个问题。

（6）"Hybrid malls" are an **attempt** to conjoin large enclosed malls with an outdoor urban streetscape retail/entertainment component.

译文："综合购物中心"**试图**将室内购物中心与室外城市街道店铺或娱乐设施结合起来。

（7）There's also growing **angst** among Americans that the rapid advance of Chinese, Indian, and Russian science is imperiling US global economic leadership.

译文：美国人还愈发**担心**，中国、印度及俄罗斯在科学上的飞速进步正渐渐威胁美国在全球经济中的领导地位。

2. 形容词转译成动词

可译成汉语动词的英语形容词大多是表达知觉、情感和欲望的形容词。

（1）Procter & Gamble itself knows the risks and the company's attempts to build a wall around its Cincinatti headquarters, dubbed the Kremlin by its detractors, are **legendary**.

译文：宝洁公司自身也意识到间谍活动的危险性，**传说**公司试图在其辛辛那提总部建一堵围墙——诋毁者将其戏称为克里姆林宫。

（2）The developed countries **are rich in** skilled work force and capital resources, so they can concentrate on producing many technology-intensive products such as computers and aircrafts.

译文：发达国家**拥有大量的**熟练劳动力和资本，所以它们能集中生产很多技术密集型的产品，比如计算机和飞机。

（3）Demand for business travel has proved far more elastic than previously thought. That is because companies are getting used to **tighter budgets**.

译文：商业性旅行的需求比预算的有更大的伸缩性，这是因为各公司正在逐步**压缩**预算。

（4）We are especially **grateful** to you for arranging the meeting for us with the Machinery Trading Delegation at such short notice.

译文：我们特别**感谢**你们在时间那么短促的情况下安排我们同机械交易团的成员们会面。

（5）The company was not adequately **prepared** for this model's success, and so deliveries were sometimes **delayed** for three or four years, angering customers.

译文：公司完全没**想到**这种机型会走俏，以致交货期有时**推迟**3、4年之久，使客户极为不满。

（6）However, one of the major hurdles is finding ways to reassure customers their credit card integrity is **secure** when details are sent on to a worldwide net.

译文：然而最大的障碍之一是想办法让顾客放心，在将详细资料输进国际互联网时，**确保**他们信用卡的安全。

（7）He is expected to appeal for **increased** American technology sales.

译文：估计他将呼吁美国**增加**技术销售。

（8）The company's legal problems are far from over, but a furious fightback has left many observers **skeptical** that the government will ever succeed in breaking up Microsoft.

译文：微软的诉讼案还远未结束，但微软发起的猛烈回击使许多观察家们**怀疑**政府究竟能否成功地将其分解。

（9）**Falling** wages, **reduced** benefits and rising job insecurity seem to be increasingly entrenched features of the job scene across most parts of the developed world.

译文：工资**下降**，福利**减少**，工作岗位越来越不稳定，似乎日益成为大多数发达国家劳动就业固有的特点。

3. 介词转译成动词

英语中的介词都具有很强的动词性能，有时可表动态，有时表静态或状态，因此可以将某些介词或介词短语转译成动词。

（1）We have decided to place a trial order for the following **on** the terms stated in your letter.

译文：**根据**来函条款，我公司决定试订下列货物。

（2）These are centres **without** actual automobiles, but computer-stimulated versions of the latest model cars for sale.

译文：这些中心里并**没有**真正的汽车，销售的是电脑模拟版的最新款式汽车。

（3）In big cities, advertisements are painted on buildings, and sometimes one can even find people walking with advertisements **on** their bodies.

译文：在大城市里，楼房上涂着广告，有时甚至有些行人的身上也**挂着**广告。

（4）**With** the credit card in your wallet or purse, you don't have to carry much cash.

译文：钱包里**有**了信用卡，你就不必携带许多现金。

（5）One nation can sell some items **at** a lower cost than other countries.

译文：有的国家可以**以（按）**低于其他国家的成本销售某些商品。

（6）The on-campus interview lets you meet recruiters **with** job openings.

译文：校园面试使你有机会见到可**提供**空缺职位的公司招聘人员。

4. 副词和动词互相转译

跟在系动词后做表语的副词及复合宾语中作宾语补足语的副词大多可以转译成动词。而且，英语中有些动词译成汉语时转译成副词更符合汉语的表达习惯。

（1）Most economists reckon that by the end of 2005 the US deficit might be **down** to ＄650 billion.

译文：多数经济学家估计，到 2005 年底，美国的贸易赤字可能会**降**到 6 500 亿美元。（副词转译成动词）

（2）Companies should **strive** to convince consumers that the benefits of an online data-collection program outweigh its intrusiveness.

译文：公司应当**努力**让客户相信，在线数据收集程序的好处要大于它的干扰所带来的麻烦。（动词转译成副词）

二、转译成名词

1. 动词转译成名词

英语中有些动词的概念很难直接用汉语的动词来表达，这时可将这类动词转译成名词。

（1）Our import policy **is aimed at** acquiring capital that embodies the modern technology needed to develop China's economy.

译文：我们进口政策的直接**目的**是为了获得资本，以便发展中国经济急需的现代技术。

（2）Monster first began **eyeing** the Chinese market in 2001 but owing to official policy at the time, had to defer its plans.

译文：早在2001年，Monster就**把目光投向**了中国市场，但由于当时政策的限制，Monster延缓了其在中国的收购计划。

（3）When nations **export** more than they **import**, they are said to have a favorable balance of trade. When they **import** more than they **export**, an unfavorable balance of trade exists.

译文：当一国的**出口量**大于**进口量**，就称之为贸易顺差；当**进口量**大于**出口量**时，贸易逆差便产生了。

2. 形容词转译成名词

英语形容词做表语，说明主语的特征、属性，可译成汉语名词。

（1）The new contract would be **good** for 5 years.

译文：这个新合同的**有效期**为5年。

（2）The **increasing** number of unemployed people poses many new problems for the society.

译文：失业人数的**增加**给社会带来了许多新问题。

（3）I believe that his report was an important one because it spurred greater **public** awareness of the company's practices.

译文：我认为他的报道十分重要，因为它让**公众**更多地关注公司的这种做法。

（4）So what's **new** in the brand-name explosion this spring?

译文：那么今春的品牌大战又有何**新招**呢？

（5）Nowadays, however, national currencies are considered to be **as strong as** the national economies which support them.

译文：然而，现今美国的货币被认为同支撑它的国家经济具**有同等的力量**。

（6）American firms did not have to worry about their technological competitiveness because they were **superior**.

译文：美国公司因为处于**优势地位**而不必担忧什么技术竞争。

3. 副词转译成名词

（1）No wonder the multinational corporations have been growing **fantastically** and now dominate many sections of the international market.

译文：难怪跨国公司一直**以惊人的速度**发展并控制着国际市场的许多领域。

（2）Some employees may have strong interpersonal skills, another may be very good **analytically**, and yet another may be very good at seeing long-range possibilities.

译文：有些员工也许具备较强的交际技能，有些也许非常擅长**分析**，而另一些员工也许擅长预见公司长远的发展前景。

三、转译成形容词

1. 副词转译成形容词

（1）Everything has **greatly** changed in banking accounting system.

译文：银行结算系统全都发生了**巨大的**变化。

（2）Companies should **adequately** compensate consumers who are willing to contribute to their increasingly valuable market research services.

译文：对那些愿意帮助公司进行市场调研的客户，公司应该支付**足够**的补偿，因为这种调研越来越有价值。

2. 名词转译成形容词

（1）The APEC meeting in Shanghai was a great **success**.

译文：在上海召开的亚太经合组织会议非常**成功**。

（2）Inflation could flare up, too, since Japanese and German manufacturers will eventually pass along price **hikes** — and US companies might follow suit to increase their profit margins.

译文：因为日本和德国厂商最终会将**大幅上涨**的价格转嫁出去，美国公司也可能这么做，提高其利润幅度，从而使通货膨胀再次爆发。

（3）Just think of the **convenience** of getting rid of cash and checks and even eliminating loose change by using credit cards.

译文：试想，用信用卡而不用现金和支票**多么便利**，连找零钱付费的麻烦也省去了。

（4）There's also growing angst among Americans that the rapid advance of Chinese, Indian, and Russian **science** is imperiling US global economic leadership.

译文：美国人还愈发担心，中国、印度及俄罗斯**在科学上**的飞速进步正渐渐威胁美国在全球经济中的领导地位。

课堂翻译训练

将下列句子译成汉语。

1. The survey says that national forecasts of West European countries suggest that West European growth this year will not be more than three percent. It draws attention to the risks of a further recession following a short recovery, or a prolonged stagnation.
2. Weak loan demand and low interest rates at home have prompted a scramble among Japanese banks to foist credit on Asian (especially Chinese) borrowers.
3. Hybrid malls pick up on the growing popularity of village-style shopping, with its connections to real communications.
4. The fabricating service of our company is based on abundant experience accumulated in over 100 years of designing and manufacturing complete process plants or unit process equipment for the chemical and petroleum industries.
5. Thirteen years after launching its quality campaign, Motorola regains a model of how to use TQM (Total Quality Management) to reinvigorate a corporation.
6. Advances in office communication are occurring so rapidly that what is on the design board this morning is fact this afternoon and becomes obsolescent tomorrow.
7. Our unique concept was a response to buyer needs, bringing greater reliability, higher-quality output, exceptional user-friendliness and operational ease.
8. Banks originated as places to which people took their valuables for safe-keeping, but today the great banks of the world have many functions in addition to acting as guardians of valuable private possessions.
9. And, finally, if a plummeting dollar leads to a rise in interest rates, the stock market rally could stall.
10. American hopes that pressure from the US will force Japan to suddenly dismantle its trade barriers are almost certain to evaporate in disappointment.

课后练习

将下列短文译成英语，注意运用本单元所学的翻译技巧。

1.

Tom McKillop

CEO of AstraZeneca since 1999

Pharmacopia AstraZeneca's 2003 sales：＄18.9 billion

US	46%
Europe	36%
Japan	6%
Rest of world	12%

　　ON INDUSTRY CONSOLIDATION. There is no sign that getting bigger leads to a better-quality business. GlaxoSmithKline is a product of a series of mergers, and there's no real evidence that it is a better-quality company. Our merger between Astra and Zeneca was different, because we were two medium-sized companies and we needed to get bigger for sales and marketing. We were totally committed to research and development. We've had an excellent flow of new products, and we've got a good pipeline. Our merger was not about cost cutting.

　　ON THE COST OF R&D. R&D has been getting more expensive, and you do need to be big enough to afford the different technologies that will keep you competitive. But beyond a certain point you risk running a less efficient R&D business. You need speed and creativity. Those aren't attributes that you normally associate with big companies.

　　ON GENERICS. There is a synergy, or symbiosis, between the generics industry and the innovative industry. Our industry depends fundamentally on intellectual property that is respected and protected. Otherwise people will not invest. At the end of the patent period it is natural that other competitors can come in, and that will bring the cost down dramatically to create economic headroom for innovation. What is worrying is if there is a premature attack on intellectually protected product. Then you take away the incentive for innovation.

　　ON THE GRAY MARKET FOR CHEAP DRUGS. In Europe we have a single economic unit with free movement of goods between countries, which arbitrarily change and set prices. That has led to a downward pricing of drugs, which has been extremely negative for the industry and for R&D in Europe. And that has led to the US being the big economic winner. Many European politicians realize this is crazy, because historically the pharmaceutical industry was the most successful industry in Europe. But it's been dramatically losing competitiveness to the US. In Canada we've had an artificial market, with high generic prices, while not rewarding companies for their innovative drugs. If US legislation is passed insisting on product availability through Canada, then no company could afford to launch a new product.

ON THE SAFETY OF DRUGS BOUGHT ON THE INTERNET. The FDA has done a study in which it ordered products from Internet sites. Eighty percent of the products had something wrong with them, or were mislabled or improperly stored. Companies are legally liable for their products. But if we don't know where the product has been, how can we be liable? We are heading into very dangerous waters here. The flow of product that has been counterfeited with no active ingredient is increasing. Very loose distribution systems are highly dangerous.

2.

There is a second myth: that China would benefit from letting its exchange rate float freely, letting market forces set the price. No market economy has foresworn intervening in the exchange rate. More to the point, no market economy has foresworn macroeconomic interventions. Governments intervene regularly in financial markets, for instance, setting interest rates. Some market fundamentalists claim that governments should do none of this. But today, no country and few respectable economists subscribe to these views. The question, then, is what is the best set of interventions in the market? There is a high cost to exchange rate volatility, and countries where governments have intervened judiciously to stabilize their exchange rate have, by and large, done better than those that have not.

Exchange rate risks impose huge costs on companies; it is costly and often impossible to divest themselves of this risk, especially in developing countries. The question of exchange rate management brings up a broader issue: the role of the state in managing the economy. Today, almost everyone recognizes that countries can suffer from too little government intervention just as they can suffer from too much. China has been rebalancing and, over the past two decades, markets have become more important, the government less so. But the government still plays a critical role. China's particular blend has served the Chinese well. It is not just that incomes have been rising at an amazing 9 per cent annually, and that high rates have been sustained for more than two decades, but the fruits of that growth have been widely shared. From 1981 to 2001, 422m Chinese have moved out of poverty.

The US economy is growing at a third the pace of China's. Poverty is rising and median household incomes are, in real terms, declining. America's total net savings are much less than China's. China produces far more of the engineers and scientists that are necessary to compete in the global economy than the US, while America is cutting its expenditures on basic research as it increases military spending. Meanwhile, as America's debt continues to balloon, its president wants to make tax cuts for the richest people permanent. With all this in mind, China's leaders may not feel they need to seek advice from the US on how to manage either the exchange rate or the economy.

佳译赏析

A Gold Mine Called Home Shopping
有座金矿叫"在家购物"

LG's[1] 24-hour channel is a smash[2], but rivals are moving in.
LG 的全天销售频道一炮打响,但对手们也尾随而至。

From *Business Week*, November 5, 2001
By Moon Ihlwan

At first, the new business plan seemed counterintuitive—if not a quick route to bankruptcy. Koreans who ordered products from LG Home Shopping, a television shopping channel hawking everything from jewelry to cookware, could return them no questions asked[3] and get a refund even before the items were collected from their home. All deliveries were free. And the new plan was launched in the depths of the Asian financial crisis in 1998.

最初,这个新的商业计划即使不是通向破产的捷径,看上去也有些违背常理。那些从"LG 在家购物"——一个从珠宝到厨房用品无所不售的电视购物频道——上订购商品的韩国人可在商家不问任何问题的情况下退货,甚至在所购商品从他们家里搬走之前就可拿到退款。所有商品都免费送货。而这个新的商业计划是在 1998 年亚洲金融危机最严重的时候启动的。

Little wonder that everyone including his staff thought LG Home Shopping Inc. Chief Executive Choi Yung Jae had a screw loose. Even as Choi offered one of the best bargains in Korea[4], he refused to sacrifice quality. One day, he appeared at a Seoul warehouse for a spot inspection[5]—and canceled orders from nearly 70% of LG's suppliers. "Customer trust will make or break our business[6]," he declared. Not long after, Choi set up a fax line in his office to handle customer complaints directly. Complaints poured in. "But then," says LG manager Shin Hyung Bum, "six months later he started getting complimentary faxes."

难怪所有的人，包括"LG 在家购物公司"的工作人员都认为，总裁崔永才的脑子有问题。崔永才即使卖的也是韩国最畅销的商品，但拒绝牺牲质量。有一天，他到汉城一家货栈做现场调研，当场就取消了将近 70% 的 LG 供货商的订单。他说："顾客的信任可以成就我们的事业，也可断送我们的事业。"不久后，崔永才在他的办公室开通了一条热线传真，直接受理顾客投诉。大量投诉如潮涌入。"不过"，LG 的经理申衡范说，"6 个月后，他便开始收到表扬的传真了。"

Choi is still getting them.[7] In 1998, LG Home Shopping earned its first profit as sales tripled, to ＄169 million. The channel, which airs around the clock and prices items up to one-third cheaper than department stores, has thrived ever since.[8] Despite the global slowdown, the company predicts sales of ＄779 million this year, up 68% from 2000. Executives are confident sales will jump another 50% next year. Says Chief Financial Officer Choi Jong Sam: "We want to be the no-store retail king."

崔永才现在仍然收到来自顾客的各种传真。1998 年，当"LG 在家购物"的销售额增加了两倍、达到 1.69 亿美元时，它首次实现了盈利。从此之后，这个全天 24 小时播放、商品定价比百货公司低 1/3 的电视购物频道便火暴起来。尽管全球经济衰退，该公司预计今年的销售额仍将达到 7.79 亿美元，比 2000 年增加 68%。公司的主管人员对明年销售额再增长 50% 充满信心。财务总监崔正三说："我们要当无店零售的大王。"

WEB LEVERAGE[9]. To help fulfill that goal, the company launched a cybermall in May, 2000. This year, LG expects the online site to do about ＄77 million in business. LG's goal next year is to pass Samsung Corp. as Korea's top e-tailer—though that means increasing online sales 150%.[10] The Web site is leveraging the channel, luring online shoppers with slick TV footage of its latest products that can be downloaded via the nation's broadband connections.[11] Complemented by its mail-order business, the retail unit of LG Group aims at shoppers who want goods delivered to their homes.

网络的力量。为了确保实现这个目标，公司在 2000 年 5 月创办了网上购物中心。今年，LG 期望该网点的成交额能达到 7 700 万美元左右。公司来年的奋斗目标是超越三星公司成为韩国网上零售的龙头老大——尽管这意味着其网上销售额需要增加 150%。该网点正在影响电视购物频道。它把最新的产品拍成精彩的电视画面，通过与国家宽带连接下载来吸引网上消费者。LG 集团的零售部门以邮购业务为补充，将目标用户定为希望送货上门的顾客。

LG takes advantage of Korean demographics. Knowing that most middle-class women are

homemakers, it has focused its marketing on females in their 30s and 40s. And delivery costs are minimal because nearly half of Korea's 14. 3 million families reside in apartment blocks.
LG 充分利用韩国的人口统计资料。在得知绝大多数中产阶级女性都是家庭主妇时，LG 遂将营销重点集中在 30 多岁和 40 多岁的女性身上。而且，送货的费用也极低，因为在韩国的 1 430 万家庭中，有将近半数住在公寓大楼里。

The operation is also resolutely up-market, in contrast to similar US channels.[12] Because most cable-TV subscribers in Korea are well-to-do, LG sells no item for less than $23, which it figures is the minimum it can charge and still make a 4% margin after covering delivery. On average, LG shoppers spend $110 per order, triple what US TV shoppers spend.
此外，LG 销售的是绝对的高档产品，这与美国同类销售频道有所不同。由于韩国大多数有线电视用户都是有钱人，LG 从不销售价格低于 23 美元的商品，这个价格是他们能收取的最低价，除去送货费用，仍可有 4% 的利润。LG 的顾客每次订货的平均消费是 110 美元，为美国电视购物者每次消费额的 3 倍。

Rivals acknowledge Choi's contribution to electronic shopping, which has gobbled 3% of Korea's $90 billion retail market.[13] "The whole industry is indebted to Choi's pioneering campaign[14]," says Samsung Vice-President Suh Kang Ho, who heads the chaebol's[15] Internet shopping division[16]. "The big question is if LG can keep its momentum in the face of tougher competition."
竞争对手都承认崔永才对电子购物做出了巨大贡献，因为电子购物已占韩国 900 亿美元零售市场的 3%。"整个行业都感激崔永才的开创之举"，三星副总裁、"大家族" 互联网购物部门的领军人物隋江浩说，"关键是 LG 能否在日益激烈的竞争中保持其发展势头。"

The field is getting crowded. Already, LG's market share has slipped to 57%, from 60% last year, as rival CJ39 Shopping has stepped up its marketing campaign after being taken over by Korea's largest food company, Cheil Jedang. In March, the government awarded three more shopping channel licenses. Two companies—Woori Home Shopping and Nongsusan TV—are already operating. The third, to be run by retail giant Hyundai Department Store, aims to launch in November. "Rivals will quickly copy LG's strategies," says Chang Mihwara, retail analyst at Tongyang Securities Co. "Unless it keeps moving ahead, its market share and margins will keep shrinking."
这个领域正变得越来越人满为患。LG 的市场份额已从去年的 60% 下滑到 57%，因为它的竞争对手 "CJ39 购物" 在被韩国最大的食品公司 "铁再东" 兼并后，已经加快了它的营销活动。3 月份，政府又给另外 3 家公司颁发了电视购物频道经营许可证。其中两家公司——"我们在家购物" 和 "农秀山 TV" ——已经开始营业，第三家将由零售业巨头 "现代百货公司"经营，它打算于 11 月开始营业。东洋证券公司的零售分析家张美花说："对手们将很快照搬 LG 的营销战略。除非 LG 不断创新，否则，它的市场份额和利润将持续减少。"

For the short term, however, industry fundamentals should give LG plenty of room to expand. Analysts expect cable TV viewership to double to 8 million this year, while Net shopping could surge fourfold to ＄8.5 billion by 2005. If he can dominate this new industry, this retail king may yet be crowned emperor.

然而，就短期而言，企业坚实的基础将为 LG 提供足够的扩展空间。分析家预计，有线电视的观众人数今年将翻一番，达到 800 万；而网上购物到 2005 年可能猛增至原来的 4 倍，达到 85 亿美元。如果他能主宰这个新兴行业，那这个零售业大王就可成为加冕的皇帝了。

Words and Expressions

smash	n.	(*informal*) a resounding success; a conspicuous success　巨大成功 The test-market was a smash on the Chinese market. 在中国进行的试销取得了巨大的成功。
move in	v.	to begin to occupy a residence or place of business　搬进，开始占据一个住宅地或商业场所，进军某个行业
counterintuitive	a.	contrary to what common sense would suggest; not reasonable; not showing good judgment　违反直觉的，违背常理的
hawk	v.	to peddle goods aggressively, especially by calling out　叫卖（尤指通过吆喝的方式积极主动地兜售货物）
cookware	n.	cooking utensils　烹饪用具
refund	n.	a repayment of funds　资金偿还，退款
item	n.	商品目录中所列出的商品
have a screw loose	v.	(*slang*) to behave in an eccentric manner　出故障，出毛病
bargain	n.	something offered or acquired at a price advantageous to the buyer　廉价货（以对买者有利的价格出售货物）
complimentary	a.	expressing, using, or resembling a compliment　表达、运用或类似赞美方式的
air	v.	to broadcast on television or radio　播送（在电视或无线电里播送）
around the clock		without stopping　不断地，不停地
triple	v.	to be or become three times as great in number or amount　增至三倍，成三倍
price	v.	to fix or establish a price for　定价，给……定价或建立价格 shoes that are priced at nine dollars　价格为九美元的鞋子
thrive	v.	to make steady progress; prosper　繁荣稳定地发展，繁荣

slowdown	n.	the act or process of slowing down; a slackening of pace 减速,减慢(慢下来的行动或过程),速度的减慢
a production slowdown		生产速度的下降
leverage	n.	positional advantage; power to act effectively 优势,力量(位置上的优势),有效的行动,影响
cybermall	n.	a shopping mall on the Internet 网上购物中心
e-(re)tailer	n.	an online retailer who leverages the efficiency of the Internet to improve a customer's buying experience 网络零售商
slick	a.	superficially attractive or plausible but lacking depth or soundness; glib 华而不实的(表面上有吸引力或似乎合理但缺乏深度和合理性的)
footage	n.	a shot or series of shots of a specified nature or subject 连续镜头(一个特别性质或题目的一个镜头或一系列镜头)
demographics	n.	the characteristics of human populations and population segments, especially when used to identify consumer markets 人口统计状况(人口及其细分,尤其用作标识消费者市场的状况)
demographic	a.	of or relating to demography 人口统计的,与人口统计有关的
homemaker	n.	one who manages a household 持家者,管理家务的人,主妇
up-market	a./ad.	高档的(地),高档消费的(地)
margin	n.	the difference between the cost and the selling price of securities or commodities 盈余(证券或商品的成本与销售价之间的差额)
gobble	v.	to take greedily; grab 吞并,贪婪地攫取
chaebol	n.	a conglomerate of businesses, usually owned by a single family, especially in Korea 大企业,财阀,集团公司(尤指韩国)
momentum	n.	impetus of a nonphysical process, such as an idea or a course of events 势头,非物质发展的动力(如思想或事物的进程) The soaring rise in interest rates finally appeared to be losing momentum. 利率飞速上涨的势头终于减弱了。
slip	v.	to decline from a former or standard level; fall off 下跌,滑落(从以前的或正常的水平下降),跌落
step up	v.	to raise by degrees; to increase, especially in stages 增加(尤指逐步增加) Pepsi has stepped up its efforts to promote its new products in China. 百事可乐公司加倍努力改进在中国的产品。
viewership	n.	a television audience, especially of a particular kind or extent 电视观众(特别是特定种类或者范围的电视观众)

Notes

1. 韩国的 LG 集团是领导世界产业发展的国际性企业集团，目前在 171 个国家与地区建立了 300 多家海外办事机构，事业领域覆盖化学能源、电机电子、机械金融、贸易服务等。
2. "a smash" 本来表示"巨大的成功"，这里译成"一炮打响"，把 LG 公司一涉足电子商务行业就大获成功的意思完全表达出来了。
3. 将 "could return them no questions asked" 中的介词短语 "(with) no questions asked" 增译成"商家不问任何问题的情况下"，使整个句子的语意完整准确，符合汉语的表达习惯。
4. "Even as Choi offered one of the best bargains in Korea" 中的 "one of the best bargains" 不太容易直接处理，所以将其译成"卖的也是"，这样就把"其中之一"的意思表达出来了。
5. "inspection" 一词通常会翻译成"检查，视察"，尽管意思没错，但"调研"却更能表达"下基层进行实地考察"的工作作风。
6. Customer trust will make or break our business… 顾客的信任可以成就我们的事业，也可断送我们的事业……
   翻译英语 "make" 和 "break" 这一类比较模糊的词时，一定要选准汉语中对应的词汇，否则难以准确地表达原文的意思。这里因为后面是 "business"，所以将这两个词分别译成"成就"和"断送"，并将 "business" 译成"事业"，处理得恰到好处。
7. "Choi is still getting them." 这句话中的 "them" 可以指投诉传真、表扬传真、投诉传真+表扬传真或各种其他传真。从上下文看，这里的意思应该是指这条传真热线仍然是开通的，所以译成"来自顾客的各种传真"比较合适。
8. The channel, which airs around the clock and prices items up to one-third cheaper than department stores, has thrived ever since. 从此之后，这个全天 24 小时播放、商品定价比百货公司低 1/3 的电视购物频道的生意便火暴起来。
   将非限制性定语从句译成前置定语，译得非常自然。另外，将 "thrive" 译成"生意火暴起来"，把生意红火的场面展现在读者的面前，比译成"繁荣"更加形象。
9. WEB LEVERAGE 网络的力量
   将 "web leverage" 译成"网的杠杆作用"显得太生硬，其实就是利用互联网推销产品，所以译成"网络的力量"或"网络的影响"更贴切。
10. LG's goal next year is to pass Samsung Corp. as Korea's top e-tailer—though that means

increasing online sales 150%. 公司来年的奋斗目标是超越三星公司成为韩国网上零售的龙头老大——尽管这意味着其网上销售额需要增加150%。

将"top e-tailer"译成"网上零售的龙头老大",颇具时代气息。

11. The Web site is leveraging the channel, luring online shoppers with slick TV footage of its latest products that can be downloaded via the nation's broadband connections. 该网点正在影响电视购物频道。它把最新的产品拍成精彩的电视画面,通过与国家宽带连接下载来吸引网上消费者。

此句很长,主句之后又跟了一个现在分词短语,里面还有一个限制性定语从句。如果按顺序连起来翻译,句子不容易摆顺。所以,将句子断开,采取逆序法,将分词短语放到最后。这样,句子便通顺自然了。注意,中间的定语从句"that can be downloaded via the nation's broadband connections"没有译成定语,而是译成了汉语的方式状语,修饰分词短语"吸引网上消费者"。

12. The operation is also resolutely up-market, in contrast to similar US channels. 此外,LG销售的是绝对的高档产品,这与美国同类销售频道有所不同。

这个句子紧接上一段,所以"also"一词可以译成"此外",以便与上文相连。较难处理的是"operation"一词。如果将这个句子译成"与美国的同类销售频道相比,LG的运作绝对是高质量的",就很难表达出原文中"LG卖的是不低于23美元的高档产品,而美国的类似频道不是"这个意思。所以,这里的"operation"不宜直译成"运作",而应译成"经营、销售"。

13. Rivals acknowledge Choi's contribution to electronic shopping, which has gobbled 3% of Korea's $90 billion retail market. 竞争对手都承认崔永才对电子购物做出了巨大贡献,因为电子购物已占韩国900亿美元零售市场的3%。

非限制性定语从句中的先行词"which"虽然是指代前面的"electronic shopping",但因为前句讲的是崔永才对电子购物的贡献,所以为了使两句话在逻辑上能够连起来,还是将定语从句译成表因果的状语比较合适。

14. The whole industry is indebted to Choi's pioneering campaign... 整个行业都感激崔永才的开创之举……

将"pioneering campaign"译成"开创之举"比译成"创建活动"更加自然。

15. chaebol 韩国综合企业财团

或译成"财阀",韩国多元化经营的企业集团的通称。

16. 将"who heads the chaebol's Internet shopping division"这个非限制性定语从句中的"who heads"转译成"领军人物",译得很有时代感。

原文 1：

Avoid following the herd and buying into the latest fashionable initial public offering. News takes a long time to filter down to the guy in the street and chances are that any hot tip is past its sell-by date.

原译：

不要随波逐流，去买进一些最新公开买卖的时髦证券。对普通人来讲，信息需要很长时间方能传到他们的耳中，往往等得知那些热门的内部消息时，早已错过了合适的买进时机。

点评：

① 将"follow the herd"译成"随波逐流"不如译成"跟风"。在股票市场的语境下，使用投资者常用的语言，读者会感到更加容易理解。
② 英语"avoid"之后是两个并列的动名词短语。也就是说这两个动作都是应该"避免"的。因此，将"and"译成"去"，就等于把前面的"随波逐流"变成了副词，修饰动作"去买"。这不符合原意。
③ 将"the latest fashionable initial public offering"译成"最新公开买卖的时髦证券"不符合股票市场的语境，宜译成"刚刚发行上市的热门股票"。
④ "the guy in the street"是指华尔街的股票经纪人，而不是"普通人"。"the street"就是指华尔街。
⑤ "chances are"是"很可能"之意，不能漏掉。
⑥ 不能将"sell-by date"译成"合适的买进时机"，因为"hot tips"不一定是只利于买进某股票，也可以利于卖出某股票。这里是指利用"内部消息"获利的最佳时机。

改译：

投资股票切忌跟风，也不要去碰刚刚发行上市的热门股票。情况往往是，当股市中的内部消息传到你的经纪人耳中时，任何获利的机会可能已经消失。

原文 2：

A good relationship can help you to do business more easily and it's more rewarding to deal with people you know than with strangers.

原译：

好的关系能帮你更容易地做生意，跟认识的人打交道比跟不熟悉的人打交道更能得到回报。

点评：

① "a good relationship" 译成"好的关系"太抽象，究竟是指社会关系，还是指业务关系，还是指人缘关系，翻译时应该根据上下文翻译得具体一些。

② 将"help"一词直译成"帮"没有错，但汉语里如果"help"的动作发出者是非生命的事物，这个动词一般不说"帮"，而用"让利于，便于"。

③ "more easily"译成"轻松地、自如地"更贴切。

④ 将"more rewarding"直译成"更能得到回报"意思有误，难道与熟悉的人打交道是为了获得回报？其实，"rewarding"在此是"providing personal satisfaction"的意思。

⑤ 将"people you know"译成"认识的人"不如译成"熟人"准确。

改译：

人缘关系不错你就能轻松做生意，与熟人来往比跟生人打交道让你更开心。

原文 3：

Although we discussed the advantages and disadvantages of bringing forward our delivery date, it was agreed that this might result in lower standards of quality.

原译：

我们讨论了将我们的发货期提前的优缺点，但大家一致认为这可能会导致质量标准下降。

点评：

译文符合原意，没有错误，但翻译得太"执著"，基本上是逐字逐句对译，读起来很生硬。

改译：

我们分析了提前发货的利弊，最后一致认为这样做可能会降低产品的质量。

原文 4：

Today, venture capital investing represents a significant focus of most institutional or corporate investment portfolios, and many of the largest venture funds are operated by major financial institutions, or by subsidiaries specifically designed for private equity investment.

原译：

今天，风险资本投资则是大多数机构投资证券组合或公司投资证券组合的一个重要的投资焦点，而且许多最大的风险基金是由主要的金融机构或专门从事私募投资的子公司运作的。

点评：

① 将"a significant focus"直译成"一个重要的投资焦点"过于生硬，其实就是"投资重点"的意思。另外，这个句子译得过长。

② "financial institutions"不宜译成"金融机构"，因为中国的金融机构包括银行、保险

及证券等国家机构,而国外的"financial institutions"则指的是"an institution (public or private) that collects funds (from the public or other institutions) and invests them in financial assets"。

③ "major"译成"大型的"更加合适。

④ 将"private equity investment"译成"私募投资"意思有误,正确的译法是"私人股权投资"。这种投资并不是指"私募",与"私募基金"的筹集方式并无关系。进行这类投资的基金通常被称为"private equity fund",即"私人股权投资基金"。之所以得名,正是因其主要投资于私人股权(Private Equity),也就是非上市公司股权,与国内所谓"私募基金"正好完全相反。

改译:

今天,大多数机构投资者都将风险资本作为重点纳入自己的投资组合,而且大型的融资机构及其专门从事私人股权投资的子公司还掌管着全球许多最大的风险投资基金。

学生译作分析

原文:

Interview Q & A with the Department Head

Q: What's the mission of IPD (IP Division)? Why has this BD (business division) been created?

A: To answer these questions, let's, first of all, review the market and its evolution. As we all know, after two years of decline, the market in 2004 is still filled with uncertainties and there is not any positive sign we are all expecting. Alcatel has made a series of adjustments and is planning an organizational restructuring, which we hope will enable us to focus our strengths on leveraging the considerable resources across the whole organization. As to the mission of IPD, IPD will help put carriers, which is our customers on the right track that is sure to make their business successful and profitable.

学生原译文:

和部门主管访谈的"问"和"答"

问:网际协议部门的使命是什么?成立这个商业部门的原因是什么?

答:要回答这个问题,首先让我们回顾一下这个市场和它的演变。我们都知道,在经过

2 年的萎缩后，2004 年这个市场依然充满了不确定性，没有任何我们期望的积极迹象出现。阿尔卡特已经进行了一系列的调整，并正在计划一次重组，我们希望这次重组能使我们集中力量把整个机构的可观资源进行调节。至于网际协议部门的任务，它会帮助发送信号，这是我们的顾客所希望的，这会使他们的生意成功，有利可图。

分析：

(1) 将"IP"译成"网际协议"读者不太容易理解。其实，很多大的电信公司都有自己的 IP 事业部（IP Devision），IP 是 "internet protocal" 的缩写。这里可将"IP Devision"翻译成"互联网事业部、网络事业部、电信事业部"。所以，翻译英语中的缩写词时，一定要仔细查字典，或上网搜寻，还要结合上下文来判断，否则译文就不准确。

(2) "mission"一词在修饰部门或组织时，还是译成"任务"比较好。

(3) "business division" 应该译成"业务部门"。

(4) "evolution" 因为是修饰"市场"，所以还是译成"发展"更贴切。

(5) "decline"一词宜译成"衰退"或者"低迷"。

(6) "uncertainties" 是复数，可以增译范畴词将复数译出，意思更加具体。

(7) "restructuring" 是"改组"，不是"重组"。

(8) "leveraging" 这个词很难译准确，因为它有"像杠杆一样进行补充、调解、影响"等意思。那么，在这里应该是指对公司内部的资源进行调配并合理使用。

(9) 定语从句"which is our customers"是修饰前面的"carriers"，因此将其译成"这是我们的顾客所希望的"显然意思有误。而且，"carriers"指的是"运营商"。原文实际上是说："This IP Division will help put our customers — carriers — on the right track, which will surely make their business successful and profitable."，而"put/get someone on the right track"是"doing something correctly or well"的意思，在这里不太容易处理，所以可以采取意译。

参考译文：

对 IP 事业部经理的访谈

问：IP 事业部的任务是什么？当初为什么成立这个业务部门？

答：回答这个问题之前，我们先来回顾一下这个市场和及其发展情况。我们都知道，这个市场经过 2 年的低迷，到 2004 年仍然充满许多不确定因素，我们至今仍看不到有任何改观的迹象。阿尔卡特公司已经完成了一系列的调整，目前正计划进行一次公司机构改组。希望通过此次改组，我们能集中力量对全公司丰富的资源进行调配，并使其得到合理使用。至于 IP 事业部的任务，它将有利于我们的电信客户运营畅通无误，从而确保他们业务兴旺，创利不断。

翻译技巧介绍

增译
(Amplification)

在商务英语的翻译过程中，由于英汉两种语言表达方式的不同，很难做到字词上的完全对应。翻译时既可能要进行词类的转换，又可能要在词句上加以增减，也就是按照词义、修辞和句法的需要，在译文中适当增添一些虽无其词而有其意的词或句子，使译文与原文达到意义上一致，以便更忠实通顺地表达原文的思想内容。增译时必须权衡语气的轻重，分清意思的主次，理解原文的寓意，考虑修辞的效果并符合具体商务专业的用词特点和习惯。为了便于教学，根据增译的特点，可将其分为以下几类。

一、名词或名词词组前后的增译

1. 增译动词

汉译时，为了使译文鲜明，可以在名词或名词词组前增译动词，形成汉语的动宾结构，在名词后加上动词，形成汉语的主谓结构，或增加动词，形成动补结构等。这样，不仅意思明确，而且读起来通顺自然。

1) 在名词或名词词组前增译动词

(1) When there's blood in the street, I'd suggest **global blue chips.** With internationally strong companies, you don't have to worry that they won't turn around next year.
译文：当市场华尔街的股票市场出现"割肉"行情时，我主张**选购**全球性的蓝筹股。拥有国际一流公司的股票，你就不愁来年他们不会有突出的表现。

(2) The manager spoke hopefully of the **success** of the trade fair this fall.
译文：这位公司经理满怀希望地谈到今年秋交会会**取得**成功。

(3) By making a note of all your assets, you can work out what sort of investment suits you and **over what time frame.**
译文：对你所有的财产做一个记录，你就能搞清楚适合你的投资类型，并**选择**投资的时段。

(4) Eager to boost profits and brand-name recognition, US companies such as Citigroup are setting up partnerships with foreign banks or going solo with expensive **ad-campaigns**.

译文：由于渴望增加利润和提高品牌知名度，花旗集团等美国公司纷纷与外国银行合作或独自斥巨资**开展**广告宣传活动。

(5) Stick to **your plan**, even if your investment seems to be floundering.

译文：坚持**执行**你自己的计划，哪怕你的投资看起来有些糟糕。

(6) At worst, debt could be this decade's **analogue to 1970s-style inflation**: a **scourge** of consumers and a **damper** on growth.

译文：在最坏的情况下，借贷能使眼下这 10 年**出现** 20 世纪 70 年代类型的通货膨胀：给消费者**带来**苦难，给经济增长**造成**阻滞。

(7) Worldwide innovation networks are the new keys to R&D **vitality**—and **competitiveness**.

译文：全球创新网络是**保持**研发活力——以及**增强**竞争力——的新要诀。

2) 在名词后增译动词

(1) By this schedule, the recession which started almost a year ago must nearly be over. Time for **recovery**.

译文：根据以上模式，约一年之前开始的经济衰退应该已接近尾声。经济复苏的时刻**该到了**。

(2) In the event of **damage at sea**, the company that has arranged insurance will get a decided advantage.

译文：如果海损**发生**，给货物投了保的公司就会获得决定性优势。

(3) While that is far from the 2001 US mark of close to 1 million, Hongkong's rapid increase frightens banking authorities, who are chopping credit limits to head off **further trouble.**

译文：虽然这远低于 2001 年美国近 100 万的数字，但香港这种增长速度令银行管理部门十分恐惧，他们在大幅降低贷款限额以防止进一步的麻烦**出现**。

(4) He said that their supply had no organization, but depended on irregular **purchase.**

译文：他说他们的供应渠道组织不善，只靠不定期的收购来**解决**。

(5) On the other hand, Wal-Mart is well known for the cold, calculated way it wrings **low prices** from suppliers.

译文：另一方面，沃尔玛还以其不讲情面、斤斤计较的方式从供应商那里以最低的价格**进货**。

(6) The success of McDonald's strategy has encouraged many **imitators**.

译文：麦当劳快餐连锁店经营策略的成功已促使很多餐饮店**步其后尘**。

2. 增译形容词

1) 在名词前增译形容词

(1) For the short term, however, industry **fundamentals** should give BP Global plenty of

room to expand.

译文：然而，就短期而言，企业**坚实的**基础将为英国 BP 公司提供足够的扩展空间。

（2）As a result of these innovative management practices, Sony is an intensely lively, feisty organization that prides itself on personal **ability** as much as traditional company loyalty, on individual creativity as much as group effort.

译文：由于索尼公司采用了这些富于革新精神的管理办法，使得它成为一个极为活跃蒸蒸日上的企业。对成员本人的**卓越**才干及他们忠于公司的传统，对个人创造性及对集体力量，索尼公司通通一样引以为骄傲。

（3）However, the Penny Arcades show another side of the Commerce Bancorp strategy: spend **money** to get results.

译文：然而这些"投币自动换票机"显示了商业银行经营策略的另外一个方面：为了取得成效，不惜花费**重**金。

（4）Rivals acknowledge his **contribution** to electronic shopping, which has gobbled 3% of Korea's ＄90 billion retail market.

译文：竞争对手都承认他对电子购物做出了**巨大**贡献，因为电子购物已占韩国 900 亿美元零售市场的 3%。

（5）We regret to say that the delivery may not be made within 2 months due to the **snow** and **rain** that are seldom seen in our district.

译文：很抱歉，我们无法在两个月内交货，因为这里出现了罕见的**大**雪和**暴**雨。

2）在名词后增译形容词

（1）Wal-Mart calls employees "associates", a practice now widely copied by competitors. The associates work as partners, become deeply involved in operations, and share rewards for its **performance**.

译文：沃尔玛将其雇员称为"合作人"。这一做法现已被其对手们广泛效仿。作为合作人，沃尔玛的雇员与商店的运作息息相关并且根据业绩**好坏**分别获得奖励。

（2）Some commodities, however, like tea and wool and certain spices, can not be accurately graded because the quality varies from year to year and from **consignment** to consignment.

译文：但是，有些商品，如茶叶、羊毛和某些香料却不能精确地分级，因为品质逐年变化，每批不同。

（3）We finally decided to buy those Chinese gooseberry in spite of their **looks**.

译文：尽管外表**差**，我们最终还是决定买下那些猕猴桃。

（4）Service is what often differentiates one **hotel** from another in the minds of consumers. It's impossible to underestimate the importance of service to guest satisfaction, repeat business, and a hotel's reputation.

译文：在消费者看来，饭店的**好坏**完全在于服务的质量。因此，任何饭店决不会忽视服务的重要性，因为这关系到客人是否满意、会不会再度光顾及饭店的声誉。

3. 在名词后增译范畴词

（1）I tend to be tolerant of most vices in life, and also in **investing**.

译文：我倾向于容忍生活中的大部分不道德行为，在投资**方面**也是如此。

（2）Credit cards are an empowering device and would simply replace some of these other kinds of **debts**.

译文：信用卡是一种授权方法，并将完全取代诸如此类的一些借贷**形式**。

（3）Only 1.47 percent of the Nokia's total **sales** occur in Finland, and more than 90 percent of its shares are held by people outside the country, particularly Americans, who clamor for higher valuations.

译文：在诺基亚的总销售**额**中，只有1.47%是在芬兰本土创造的，并且该公司超过90%的股份由境外投资者持有，特别是美国的投资者，他们强烈要求更高的资产估值。

（4）There's also growing angst among Americans that the rapid advance of Chinese, Indian, and Russian science is imperiling US global economic **leadership**.

译文：美国人还愈发担心，中国、印度及俄罗斯在科学上的飞速进步正渐渐威胁美国在全球经济中的领导**地位**。

（5）Subway is the only fast food outlet in the United States to be showing any real **growth**.

译文：赛百味是美国唯一一家真正显示出增长**势头**的快餐企业。

（6）Analysts expect cable TV **viewership** to double to 8 million this year, while **Net shopping** could surge fourfold to \$8.5 billion by 2005.

译文：分析家预计，有线电视的观众**人数**今年将翻一番，达到800万；而网上购物**总额**到2005年可能猛增至原来的4倍，达到85亿美元。

4. 在名词前后增译概括性的词

（1）Every **spring** and **fall**, the Guangzhou Commodities Fair is held in China.

译文：每年春秋**两季**，中国都要举办广州商品交易会。

（2）Where the payment term offered by **the respective party** causes conflict, it is essential to negotiate with the customer and not just give in.

译文：双方**各自**提出的付款条件产生矛盾时，重要的是同客户进行谈判，而不是单纯地服从。

（3）This transaction involves **you**, Lenovo and an British trader.

译文：这笔买卖涉及到你公司、联想集团和一家英国贸易公司**这三方**。

（4）The purpose of health insurance is to protect individuals from **losses** of income and to cover the **expenses** of hospitalization and some of its associated **costs**.

译文：健康保险的目的在于使个人免遭**种种**收入损失，并能支付住院治疗和因患病支出的**各种**费用。

5. 在名词前增译量词

英语没有个体量词，可数名词前可以直接加数词。因此，根据汉语表达习惯，在翻译时需要增译个体量词。

（1）**Every bill of lading** is printed with the phrase "shipped, in apparent good order and condition, by ... for delivery ...".

译文：**每一份**提单上都应有"货物表面状况良好，由……交给……"字样。

（2）Normally four copies of a bill of lading are issued, **two** will be signed by the ship's master or his agent, **two** remaining unsigned.

译文：提单一般签发四张。两**张**由船长或其代理签字，两**张**不签字。

6. 在形容词后增译名词

（1）The deal to supply frozen bread, muffins and cookies to Australasia, Asia and the Pacific is **very lucrative**.

译文：把冷冻的面团、松饼和小甜饼出售给大洋洲及南太平洋群岛和亚太地区是个利润丰厚的**买卖**。

（2）But if you're looking for alternatives, you might be **better off** with more traditional companies, FPL Group, for example, one of the biggest producers of wind power in the nation.

译文：但是如果你在找石油替代品的话，传统一点的公司可能是不错的**选择**，如美国最大的风能生产者之一的佛罗里达电器照明集团公司。

二、动词前后的增译

1. 在不及物动词后面增译名词

在翻译英语中很多不及物动词时，可以在这些动词后增译一些汉语对应的名词，以便使语义更加明确和完整。

（1）Consumers spent by skimping on savings, **borrowing** heavily or cashing in stock profits.

译文：消费者通过提取储蓄存款，大肆举**债**，或抛出获利的股票来进行消费。

（2）But for years, even during the 1990s boom, much of Corporate America had already embraced Wal-Mart-like stratagems to control labor cost, such as hiring temps and part-timers, fighting unions, dismantling internal career ladders and **outsourcing** to lower-paying contractor at home and abroad.

译文：但多年来，即使在经济迅速发展的 20 世纪 90 年代，企业文化盛行的美国社会早已普遍在控制劳动力成本方面引入了沃尔玛式的策略，诸如雇用临时工和兼职人员、同工会斗争、消除内部晋升机制及向国内外人力成本较低的承包商外包**制造环节**。

2. 增译表示时态的词

英语的动词有时态变化，如过去时、现在时、将来时等。汉语的动词不用词形变化来表示时间，而用时态助词或一般表示时间的副词来表达。已完成的动作用"曾、已经、过、了"等；正在进行的动作用"在、正在"等；将要发生的动作用"将、就、要、会"等。因此，在翻译时应该酌情将英语中的一些动词时态形式通过增译变成符合汉语的表达方式，从而使读者准确理解原文中动作发生的时间。

1) 翻译具体时态时增译

（1）Please understand that we **did make our utmost** getting supplies from other manufacturers, although in vain.

译文：请理解，虽然我们没有从别的厂商那里获得货源，但我们确**曾**竭尽全力。

（2）If one product **is slipping** in popularity, you need to have something else in the pipeline.

译文：如果一种产品的流行**正在**走下坡路，你就需要让另一些产品进入流通渠道。

（3）Arlene Levy, who along with a brother and sister, **runs** A. Messe & Sons, a Chicago industrial plumbing and heating supple company their father bought 30 years ago, says the siblings **had** plenty of ideas for change under their father, but those notions **weren't** always welcomed by their father, who **was still running** it with an iron fist when he die in 1991.

译文：阿林·莱维和她的兄妹一起经营**着** A·梅西和索斯公司，这是其父亲 30 年前盘下的一家芝加哥工业水暖供热公司。她说，兄妹们在父亲掌管公司时就**曾**有许多变革的想法，但这些想法**当时**并不总是受到父亲的欢迎。父亲在 1991 年去世前一直对公司实行着铁腕管理。

2) 强调时间上的对比时增译

（1）According to our record your corporation **bought** substantial quantity of chemicals from us. Unfortunately the business between us **has been interrupted** in the last few years.

译文：根据我们的记录，你公司**过去**买我们化工产品的数量相当大，可是近几年**来**

业务中断了。

（2）Once the big boys had used their muscle to introduce the concept of sweet, fruity, slightly alcoholic drinks, other upstarts **came** on the scene.

译文：一旦这两个大公司用它们的影响力推出这种甜甜的水果味低酒精概念的饮料，其他类似的竞争者**就会立即跟进**。

三、增译使语义完整

英语里有许多句子或者是省略句，或者是省去了某些词。汉译时应将省略部分加上去，使结构完整、意义确切。

（1）The Sony's great secret is its ability to satisfy **unvoiced desires**.

译文：索尼公司最大的秘诀就是它有本事满足**人们心中**还未说出来的愿望。

（2）This is because advertising maximizes **the interest** in the goods which sell well.

译文：这是因为做广告可最大限度地增加**人们**对热销商品的兴趣。

（3）Despite the global **slowdown**, the company predicts sales of ＄779 million this year, up 68％ from 2000.

译文：尽管全球**经济**衰退，该公司预计今年的销售额仍将达到7.79亿美元，比2000年增加68％。

（4）Rivals will quickly copy Sony's **strategies**.

译文：对手们将很快照搬索尼的**营销**战略。

（5）**But the right merchandise at the right price** isn't the only key to Wal-Mart's success, Wal-Mart also produces outstanding service to make sure that customers are satisfied with their goods and services.

译文：但是，以适当的价格**卖掉**适当的产品并不是沃尔玛成功的唯一一把金钥匙。沃尔玛还提供优良的服务，以确保产品和服务满足顾客需求。

（6）Manufactured articles, just like raw materials and produce, can either be sold on a sample basis, or according to **a standard specification**.

译文：制成品（就好像原料和农产品一样）可以按样品出售，或按标准规格**出售**。

（7）We entrust **SINOCHART** with chartering.

译文：我们委托**中国船租公司**租船。

（在英语里，介绍某种产品时，常只给出其型号，而不给其名称。翻译时，应将名称增译上去，以使译文明确。）

（8）With the purchase of two **Boeing-747** the country's volume of trade with the United States has reached an all time high.

译文：由于购买了两架**波音**747**飞机**，该国与美国的贸易额达到历年最高水平。

另外，在翻译过程中译者还必须特别注意原文中的一些背景信息，因为这些信息对于用译入语进行阅读的读者来说也许是陌生的。如果译者自身不了解这些信息，就必须在动手翻译前设法获取这些信息，只有这样，译文的意义才能够完整，才能让读者了解原文中所涉及事件的前因后果，从而准确无误地理解原文。例如：

（1）原文：Brin and Page are products of **Montessori schools** and credit the **system** with developing their individuality and entrepreneurship.

译文：布林和佩奇都曾在蒙特梭利幼儿学校接受学前教育，他们的个性和企业家风范正是通过**学校那种发展儿童潜能的教育方法**培养出来的。

点评：Wikipedia 百科对 Montessori 一词的解释是："The Montessori method is an educational method for children, based on theories of child development originated by Italian educator Maria Montessori in the late 19th and early 20th century. It is applied primarily in preschool and elementary school settings, though some Montessori high schools exist. The method is characterized by an emphasis on self-directed activity on the part of the child and clinical observation on the part of the teacher (often called a 'director', 'directress', or 'guide'). It stresses the importance of adapting the child's learning environment to his developmental level, and of the role of physical activity in absorbing academic concepts and practical skills."

由此可以得知，蒙特梭利幼儿学校是采用了**发展儿童潜能的教育方法**来培养学生的，所以在译文中应该将其译出。

（2）原文：Instead, viewers would see the same products every week, cleverly woven into the plot throughout **the season**, and characters would discuss the brands—a bit like a 13-week ad campaign.

译文：与此相反，观众每星期都会在剧中看到同样的商品，这些商品被巧妙地编织到从每年9月上旬到第二年4月下旬**电视系列剧"映季"**期间播放的电视剧剧情中，而且剧中人物会讨论这些品牌产品——有些像长达13个星期的广告宣传活动。

点评：通过查找相关信息，可以得知：美国很多电视节目都是按季播出，其中最典型的就是电视系列剧、真人秀类型的节目，如我们熟悉的《老友记》、《绝望的主妇》、《幸存者》、《学徒》等，播放的进度都是以"季"来计算的。通常情况下，这种类型的电视节目都有所谓"映季"之说，电视系列剧"映季"的时间一般是从每年的9月上旬到第二年的4月下旬，而真人秀节目的播出季节则在每年的三四月份。因此，可以在译文中增译这一内容，以便读者了解。

汉译英时也是如此。

（1）原文：中西部地区大开发，是党中央贯彻邓小平关于我国现代化建设"**两个大局**"

战略思想，面向新世纪所作出的重大决策。

译文：The large-scale development of the central and western regions of the country is a major policy decision made by the CPC for the new century. The move is in accordance with Deng Xiaoping's strategy for the country's modernization, which encompasses **the development of both coastal areas and the interior**.

点评：原文中出现了"两个大局"这一概念。通过查找相关资料，可以了解到：20世纪80年代，邓小平对全国经济的协调发展进行过深入的考虑，并提出了"两个大局"的思想，即：(1) 沿海地区要加快对外开放，使这个拥有2亿人口的广大地带较快地先发展起来，从而带动内地更好地发展，这是一个事关大局的问题，内地要顾全这个大局；(2) 反过来，发展到一定的时候，又要求沿海拿出更多力量来帮助内地发展，这也是个大局，那时沿海也要服从这个大局。其目的是逐步缩小全国各地区之间的发展差距，实现全国经济社会的协调发展和最终达到全国人民的共同富裕。

了解了这一背景信息之后，翻译时就可以将"两个大局"概括地翻译成"Deng Xiaoping's strategy, which encompasses the development of both coastal areas and the interior"，而不是直接翻译成"Deng Xiaoping's two main strategies"或"the strategic thought of Deng Xiao-ping's two overall situations"，那样，英语读者就无法理解原文的含义了。

(2) **原文**：银行体制改革有较大的动作：首先是实行**人民币汇率并轨**，这为使人民币逐步成为可兑换的目标，迈出了决定性的一步。

译文：There will be rather big movement in the reform of the banking system: first, there was the unification of the dual exchange rates of Renminbi, **a fixed official exchange rate and a parallel exchange rate for trade settlements**, into a single floating rate, which will be a decisive step for gradually changing Renminbi into a convertible currency.

点评："人民币汇率并轨"指的是自1988年起，我国实行**官方牌价与外汇市场调剂价并行**的汇率双轨制，并对两种汇率都采取了有管理的浮动方式进行调整。后因人民币汇价波动频繁，对经济生活产生了一些不良影响，于1997年实现多轨合并。因此，翻译时增译"a fixed official exchange rate and a parallel exchange rate for trade settlements"。

当然，如果条件允许，也可以通过加注的方法来补充一些译文中无法译出的背景信息。

(1) The new Chevy Aveo coming out this summer was designed in Detroit and at **GM's Daewoo*** subsidiary in South Korea.

译文：今夏新推出的学府蓝乐驰是在通用公司总部底特律和它在韩国的通用大宇分公司设计出来的。

注：韩国大宇汽车公司曾是韩国第二大汽车生产企业，2000年宣布破产。2000年通用汽车收购了大宇公司的主要资产，成立了通用大宇汽车科技公司（简称通用大宇）。

（2）You don't need to alter your lifestyle much to help protect baby seals or punish Kathie Lee* for supporting sweatshops, but you might need to suffer inconveniences—like higher gas prices, energy-conservation efforts and new taxes for alternative-fuel research—if better energy policies were adopted.

译文：如果（政府）采取了更好的能源政策，你不需要太多改变自己的生活方式就可以帮助保护海豹幼子或者惩罚凯西·李维持血汗工厂的罪行，但你可能得忍受一些不方便——如更高的天然气价格、能源保护措施和为研究替代燃料征收的新税。

注：凯西·李·吉福德，美国电视明星，2000年4月，她在洪都拉斯和美国本土血汗工厂建立服装生产线一事被媒体曝光，同时对凯西·李的表演拥有所有权的迪斯尼公司也被查出利用血汗工厂的劳工为其动画片中的角色制作服装，此事引发诉讼，在美国轰动一时。

四、增译使结构完整

在英语的许多句子中，分词短语和介词短语用得很多，为了使汉语的结构完整，不妨增加一些连接词语，使汉语译文流畅自然。

（1）The category was created by wine manufacturers, **looking for** an alternative to beer to offer young drinkers.

译文：这类产品是由葡萄酒生产商开发的，**目的是**向爱喝酒的年轻人提供一种啤酒的替代品。

（2）Sobered by the lessons of five years ago, the region's once free-wheeling investors have become focused on preventing the same destruction of their wealth from occurring again.

译文：5年前的教训使该地区曾经随心所欲的投资者们冷静下来，**于是**他们开始集中精力防止他们的财富再度遭受这样的浩劫。

（3）By mobilizing global R&D teams around the clock, nimble companies can accelerate development cycles, **bringing** new technologies to consumers and industry faster, cheaper, and in more varieties.

译文：通过动员全球的研发团队昼夜不停地工作，运作敏捷的公司能够缩短研发周期，**从而**把新技术更快、更实惠，也更多样化地提供给消费者和这个产业。

（4）**With the reforms in place**, Wall Street was again "an environment where honest business and honest risk-taking will be encouraged and rewarded".

译文：随着各项改革一一到位，华尔街再度成为"一个鼓励和回报诚实的经营和诚实的风险投资的环境"。

(5) The ranks of individual investors who still believe in stock-picking as a quick route to riches appear to be growing again, **given** the rising popularity of hedge funds and renewed interest in some tech stocks.

译文：随着对冲基金越来越受欢迎，以及对某些科技股的关注再度升温，那些依然相信选对了股票便可以迅速致富的投资者的队伍似乎又在逐渐壮大。

课堂翻译训练

将下列句子译成汉语。

1. The prediction accords with research on beef production and consumption in China that has underscored AFFCO's own move, one the company hails as part of its "internationalization"—a plan to source, process and supply product all-the-year round.

2. Another factor behind the increase in merger activity is the record performance of stock markets, which has enabled companies to finance major acquisitions on the strength of their inflated share prices.

3. As the decade progressed, Nokia advanced its multinational interests and expanded its work force, becoming the engine of Finland's economy, representing two-thirds of the stock market's value and a fifth of the country's total export.

4. Stores may have more sales if they accept cards, but the added cost to the store when credit cards are accepted instead of cash is actually passed on to all consumers in higher prices.

5. Add imagination, grinding hard work, fiercely motivated managers and innovative engineers and designers, and the company seems almost impossible to beat.

6. Besides inspired use of its scientific talent and know-how, Procter & Gamble is backed by highly innovative management.

7. On the other hand, advertisements and commercials do many important things for society: they convey business information and market situations, facilitate communication between the individual businessmen and the public, and help keep the business world moving.

8. By mobilizing global R&D teams around the clock, nimble companies can accelerate development cycles, bringing new technologies to consumers and industry faster, cheaper,

and in more varieties.
9. As you will have realized from the catalogue we sent you in August, our blanket is a perfect combination of durability, warmth, softness, and easy care.
10. Commerce Bankcorp's colorful approach to the normally grey business of selling bank services appears to be paying dividends.

课后练习

将下列短文译成英语，注意运用本单元所学的翻译技巧。

1.

Move Beyond Deadlines

A deadline should mean more than the due date of a project. Before committing to a deadline, consider what it means to your schedule. If everyone in your workplace followed the rule, "The Proper Time To Do Something Is Before It Needs To Be Done," no one would ever be late with or for anything. In addition, we all might feel less frazzled, have more time, and many egos would be spared. If you haven't already found a way to be in control of deadlines and your time—rather than letting them control you—here are some ideas to keep in mind:

- The secret to never being late for an appointment or sending something later than you've promised is to commit to take action at an appropriate point before the deadline. Write down when the promised item needs to leave your hands in order for it to be received on time, and put that appointment date on your calendar.
- For an appointment, rather than focusing on the time you have to be at your destination, write down or commit to the time that you have to leave in order to get there, say, 5 to 10 minutes early.
- Underpromise and overdeliver. Try to build in a "buffer" that allows you enough time to resolve last-minute problems.

Delivering materials on time and showing up on time will help you shine professionally. So use deadlines and start times as beginning points, rather than as calendar entries.

2.

In America and Europe magazine publishers have a common lament: total circulation is either flat or declining slightly as people devote more time to the internet, and an ever greater share of advertising spending is going online. Magazine units are mostly a drag on growth for their parents. Time Inc, the world's biggest magazine company, has to fend off rumours that its parent, Time Warner, will sell it. People in the industry expect that Time Warner will soon sell IPC Media, its British magazine subsidiary. In Germany publishers reckon that Bertelsmann, a media conglomerate, may sell Grner + Jahr, its magazine unit, when its new chief executive takes over in January 2008.

"It's a long, slow sunset for ink-on-paper magazines," says Felix Dennis, a publishing entrepreneur, "but sunsets can produce vast sums of money." He recently sold his firm's American arm, which publishes Maxim, a racy men's magazine, to Quadrangle Capital Partners, a private-equity business, for a reported $240 m.

The business model for consumer magazines is under pressure from several directions at once, both online and off. Magazines have become more expensive to launch, and the cost of attracting and keeping new subscribers has risen. In America newsstand sales have been worryingly weak, partly because supermarkets dominate distribution and shelf-space is in short supply.

The internet's popularity has hit men's titles the hardest. FHM, Emap's flagship "lads" magazine, for instance, lost a quarter of its circulation in the year to June, its lingerie-clad lovelies finding it hard to compete with online porn. Not long ago consumer magazines were Emap's prize asset, but slowing growth from the division contributed to the company's decision to put itself up for sale. Men's magazines are in trouble in most developed world markets. In France, America and Italy, the three biggest magazine markets for Lagardere Active, part of Lagardere, a French conglomerate, men have quickly switched from magazines to online services, says Carlo d'Asaro Biondo, the division's head of international operations. "We have solved the problem in the automotive sector with new web services," he says, "but no magazine publisher has cracked the problem as a whole yet."

Unit 5

佳译赏析

How Nike[1] Figured Out China[2]
耐克是如何摸清中国的（I）

From *Time*, October 25, 2004
By Matthew Forney

The China market is finally for real.[3] To the country's new consumers, Western products mean one thing: status. They can't get enough of those Air Jordans.[4]
中国市场终成现实。对这个国家新的消费者而言，西方产品有一种含义：地位。再多的飞人乔丹篮球鞋他们也不嫌多。

Nike swung into action[5] even before most Chinese knew they had a new hero. The moment hurdler Liu Xiang became the country's first Olympic medalist in a short-distance speed event—he claimed the gold with a new Olympic record in the 110-m hurdles on Aug. 28—Nike launched a television advertisement in China showing Liu destroying the field and superimposed a series of questions designed to set nationalistic teeth on edge.[6] "Asians lack muscle?" asked one. "Asians lack the will to win?" Then came the kicker, as Liu raised his arms above the trademark Swoosh on his shoulder: "Stereotypes are made to be broken." It was an instant success. "Nike understands why Chinese are proud,[7]" says Li Yao, a weekend player at Swoosh-bedecked basketball courts near Beijing's Tiananmen Square.
在大多数中国人知道他们出了个新英雄之前，耐克公司就已经开始积极行动了。跨栏选手刘翔刚成为中国首位赢得奥运短跑项目奖牌的选手——8月28日他刷新了110米栏奥运纪录并一举夺得金牌——耐克就在中国播放了刘翔征服田径赛场的电视广告，并且在画面上增加了一连串旨在触动爱国人士神经的问题。"亚洲人缺乏强壮的肌肉吗？"是问题之一。另一个问题是"亚洲人缺乏必胜的信念?"紧接着,只见刘翔高举双臂,露出肩上的耐克闪电注册商标(Swoosh),同时广告词话锋一转:"定律是用来被打破的。"这支广告一炮而红。"耐克明白中国人为什么会感到自豪",每周末都到北京天安门广场附近那些用耐克闪电注册商标(Swoosh)装饰的篮球场打球的李耀(译音)说。

Such clever marketing tactics have helped make Nike the icon for the new China. [8] According to a recent Hill & Knowlton[9] survey, Chinese consider Nike the Middle Kingdom's "coolest brand". Just as a new Flying Pigeon bicycle defined success when reforms began in the 1980s and a washing machine that could also scrub potatoes became the status symbol a decade later, so the Air Jordan — or any number of[10] Nike products turned out in factories across Asia — has become the symbol of success for China's new middle class[11]. Sales rose 66% last year, to an estimated $300 million, and Nike is opening an average of 1.5 new stores a day in China. Yes, a day. The goal is to migrate inland from China's richer east-coast towns in time for the outpouring of interest in sports that will accompany the 2008 Summer Olympics in Beijing. [12] How did Nike build such a booming business? For starters, the company promoted the right sports and launched a series of inspired ad campaigns. [13] But the story of how Nike cracked the China code has as much to do with the rise of China's new middle class, which is hungry for Western gear and individualism, and Nike's ability to tap into that hunger. [14]

这类精明的营销策略已经将耐克打造成对外开放之后中国人心目中的偶像品牌。伟达公关公司最近的一份调查显示,中国人把耐克看成中国"最酷的品牌"。正如上世纪80年代改革开放初期一辆新的飞鸽牌自行车代表着成功、90年代一台可兼洗马铃薯的洗衣机象征着地位一样,如今乔丹篮球鞋——或者在亚洲各地工厂生产的许多其他耐克产品——已经成为中国新生中产阶级成功的标志。耐克去年在中国的销售额增长了66%,估计达到了3亿美元,而且在中国平均每天开1.5家新店。没错,每天。其目标是迅速从中国较富裕的东海沿岸城镇向内地市场进军,以便赶上随着2008年北京夏季奥运会的召开而掀起的运动热潮。耐克是如何将生意做得如此红火的呢?首先,耐克开发了恰当的运动产品,并且推出一系列创意十足的广告宣传。但是,耐克之所以能够攻克中国市场,主要归功于中国新生中产阶级的崛起——这个阶级渴望享用西方产品、追求西方的个性张扬——以及耐克充分利用这种需求的能力。

Americans have dreamed of penetrating the elusive China market since traders began peddling opium to Chinese addicts in exchange for tea and spices in the 19th century. War kept the Chinese poor and Westerners out. But with the rise of a newly affluent class and the rapid growth of the country's economy, the China market has become the fastest growing for almost any American company you can think of. [15] Although Washington runs a huge trade deficit with Beijing[16], exports to China have risen 76% in the past three years. According to a survey by the American

Chamber of Commerce, 3 out of 4 US companies say their China operations are profitable; most say their margins are higher in China than elsewhere in the world. "For companies selling consumer items, a presence here is essential[17]" says Jim Gradoville, chairman of the American Chamber in China.

从 19 世纪商人们开始向中国吸毒者贩卖鸦片以换取茶叶和香料起，美国人就一直梦想占领难以捉摸的中国市场。连年的战争造成中国持续贫穷并将西方人拒之国门之外。但是，随着近年来富裕人口的壮大和中国经济的迅猛发展，几乎所有你能想到的美国公司都认为中国已经成为世界上发展最快的市场。虽然美国对中国贸易逆差巨大，但是过去 3 年来美国对中国的出口仍增长了 76%。根据美国商会的一项调查，3/4 的美国公司表示它们在中国开展业务有利可图；大多数都说它们在中国的利润超过其在世界其他地方的投资。美国在华商会主席基姆·格拉多维尔表示："经营消费品的公司要想在中国销售自己的产品，就必须首先在这个市场上占有一席之地。"

For Chinese consumers, Western goods mean one thing: status. Chinese-made Lenovo (formerly Legend) computers used to outsell foreign competitors 2 to 1[18]; now more expensive Dells are closing the gap. Foreign-made refrigerators are displacing Haier as the favorite in China's kitchens. Chinese dress in their baggiest jeans to sit at Starbucks, which has opened 100 outlets and plans hundreds more. China's biggest seller of athletic shoes, Li Ning, recently surrendered its top position to Nike, even though Nike's shoes — upwards of $100 a pair — cost twice as much. The new middle class "seeks Western culture," says Zhang Wanli, a social scientist at the Chinese Academy of Social Sciences. "Nike was smart because it didn't enter China selling usefulness, but selling status.[19]"

对中国消费者来说，西方产品有一种含义：地位。过去，中国联想电脑（Lenovo，以前为 Legend）的销售量曾是外国品牌销量的 2 倍。如今，价格更高的戴尔电脑在逐渐缩小这个差距。外国生产的冰箱逐渐取代海尔，成为中国家庭厨房的最爱。中国人身穿极为宽松的牛仔裤，坐在星巴克里——一家已经在中国开了一百家分店，并且计划再开数百家的咖啡馆。中国最大的运动鞋销售商李宁公司最近将自己全国第一的宝座让给了耐克，尽管耐克鞋的售价——每双 100 美元以上——比李宁鞋高出一倍。新生的中产阶级"追求西方文化"，中国社会科学院的社会科学家张万利（译音）表示，"耐克很精明，因为它在中国出售的是地位，而不是产品的实用性。"

The quest for cool hooked Zhang Han early. An art student in a loose Donald Duck T shirt and Carhartt work pants, Zhang, 20, has gone from occasional basketball player to All-Star consumer. He pries open his bedroom closet to reveal 19 pairs of Air Jordans, a full line of Dunks and signature shoes of NBA stars like Vince Carter — more than 60 pairs costing $6,000. Zhang began gathering Nikes in the 1990s after a cousin sent some from Japan; his businessman father bankrolls his acquisitions. "Most Chinese can't afford this stuff," Zhang says, "but I know people with hundreds of pairs." Then he climbs into his jeep to drive his girlfriend to McDonald's.

张晗（译音）很早就迷上了追求酷。他，20岁，美术专业的学生，身穿宽松的唐老鸭T恤衫和卡哈特牌工装裤。开始他只是偶尔打打篮球，现在他已经成了全明星产品的消费者。他使劲打开卧室的衣橱，向我们展示他的19双耐克飞人乔丹篮球鞋，全套耐克扣篮系列球鞋，以及文思·卡特等NBA球星的签名鞋——总共超过60双、价值6 000美元。上世纪90年代，他的一位表兄从日本给他寄了几双耐克鞋。从那以后，张晗开始收集耐克鞋，而买鞋的钱是他经商的父亲资助的。张晗说："大多数中国人都买不起这玩意儿，不过我知道有人有好几百双。"说完，他登上自己的吉普车，带他的女朋友去麦当劳。

Zhang hadn't yet been born when Nike founder Phil Knight first traveled to China in 1980, before Beijing could even ship to US ports; the country was just emerging from the turmoil of the Cultural Revolution. By the mid-'80s, Knight had moved much of his production to China from South Korea. But he saw China as more than a workshop. "There are 2 billion feet out there" former Nike executives recall his saying. "Go get them!"[20]

耐克创始人菲尔·奈特1980年首次来到中国时，张晗还没出生。当时北京直达美国的航运尚未开通；中国刚从"文化大革命"的动乱中走出来。到了上世纪80年代中期，奈特已经把许多工厂从韩国迁到了中国内地。但是他并没有把中国仅仅看成一个生产基地。耐克公司以前的管理人员记得奈特当时曾这样说："那里有二十亿只脚，别让他们跑啦！"

Phase 1, getting the Swoosh recognized, proved relatively easy.[21] Nike outfitted top Chinese athletes and sponsored all the teams in China's new pro basketball league in 1995. But the company had its share of horror stories too[22], struggling with production problems (gray sneakers instead of white), rampant knock-offs, then criticism that it was exploiting Chinese labor. Cracking the market in a big way seemed impossible. Why would the Chinese consumer spend so much — twice the average monthly salary back in the late 1990s — on a pair of sneakers?

后来证明，耐克的第一步——让人们认识耐克的闪电注册商标（Swoosh）——相对容易。耐克为一流的中国运动员提供全套服装，并在1995年为中国新的职业篮球联赛的所有球队提供赞助。但是，耐克公司也曾有过极为不快的经历，如艰难地应付生产问题（白球鞋被做成灰色）、猖獗的仿冒，还有指责它剥削中国工人的批评之声。当时要大规模地打开中国市场似乎不大可能。中国消费者为什么要花这么多钱——上世纪90年代末平均两个月的工资——去买一双球鞋？

Sports simply wasn't a factor in a country where, since the days of Confucius, education levels and test scores dictated success.[23] So Nike executives set themselves a potentially quixotic challenge: to change China's culture.[24] Recalls Terry Rhoads, then director of sports marketing for Nike in China: "We thought, 'We won't get anything if they don't play sports.'" A Chinese speaker, Rhoads saw basketball as Nike's ticket. He donated equipment to Shanghai's high schools and paid them to open their basketball courts to the public after hours. He put together three-on-three tournaments and founded the city's first high school basketball league, the Nike League, which has spread to 17 cities. At games, Rhoads blasted the recorded sound of cheering to encourage straitlaced fans to loosen up[25], and he arranged for the state-run television network to broadcast the finals nationally. The Chinese responded: sales through the 1990s picked up 60% a year. "Our goal was to hook kids into Nike early and hold them for life," says Rhoads, who now runs a Shanghai-based sports marketing company, Zou Marketing. Nike also hitched its wagon to the NBA (which had begun televising games in China), bringing players like Michael Jordan for visits. Slowly but surely, in-the-know Chinese came to call sneakers "Nai-ke".[26]

从孔子时代起中国人的成功就一直取决于其受教育的程度和考试成绩，因此参不参加体育活动根本无关紧要。所以，耐克的管理者们向自己提出了一个近乎异想天开的挑战：改变中国文化。当时负责耐克中国地区运动系列产品销售的泰瑞·罗德回忆说："当时我们想，'要是中国人不开展体育运动，我们将一无所获。'"会说汉语的罗德认为篮球是耐克进入中国市场的入场券。他向上海的一些中学捐赠了运动器材，并让他们放学后将篮球场向公众开放，费用由他支付。他还组织了 3 对 3 比赛，并且举办了上海第一个中学篮球联赛——耐克篮球联赛，该项赛事现已扩展到全国 17 个城市。比赛时，罗德播放事先录制好的加油声，带动拘谨的球迷，让他们活跃起来。此外，他还安排国营电视网向全国转播联赛的决赛实况。对于这些努力，中国人作出了回应：20 世纪 90 年代耐克的销售量每年递增 60%。罗德表示"我们要让孩子们从小就迷上耐克，并终身使用耐克"。他目前在上海经营"前锐（上海）商务咨询有限公司"——一家从事体育运动品牌营销的公司。耐克还借助 NBA 开展宣传（当时中国已开始电视转播 NBA 赛事），安排迈克尔·乔丹等球员访问中国。进展虽然缓慢，但认识了耐克的中国人确实开始将这种穿着打篮球的球鞋称为"Nai-ke"。

Words and Expressions

figure out		(*informal*) to find the solution to (a problem or question) or understand the meaning of; to discover or decide 算出，了解
for real		(*slang*) truly so in fact or actuality; actually or truly, often said in reaction to what someone else says 真正地，确实地，事实或现实确实如此地
swing	*v.*	to move along with an easy, swaying gait 顺利且迅速地开始，轻快地开始走或走动

event	n.	(sports) a contest or an item in a sports program （体育运动）比赛项目
hurdler	n.	an athlete who runs the hurdles 跳栏比赛选手
superimpose	v.	to add as a distinct feature, element, or quality 添加（添声加色，使形象、某因素或性质更加清楚）
nationalistic	a.	devotion to the interests or culture of a particular nation including promoting the interests of one country over those of others 国家主义的
set sb.'s teeth on edge		to cause a disagreeable tingling sensation in the teeth, as by bringing acids into contact with them; to produce a disagreeable or unpleasant sensation; to annoy or repel, often used of sounds, such as the screeching of the subway train wheels （酸味、噪音等）使人有不快之感，感到刺耳
kicker	n.	a sudden, surprising turn of events or ending; a twist 意外转折，突然的、令人吃惊的转折或结局，突然的变化
Swoosh		Swoosh（意为"嗖的一声"）是 NIKE 的标志。
bedeck	v.	to adorn or ornament in a showy fashion 过分装饰，过分点缀
migrate	v.	to move from one country or region and settle in another 移居，迁徙
crack	v.	to discover the solution to, especially after considerable effort 解决（尤指在经过大量努力后发现……的解决方法） crack a code 破译密码
gear	n.	clothing and accessories 衣服和装饰品 the latest gear for teenagers 最新的青少年服饰
tap into		① to establish a connection with; have access to 建立联系，接近 tapped into a new market for their products 将产品打入新市场 ② to take advantage of 利用 tapped into their enthusiasm to improve the school 利用他们的热情来改进学校
the Middle Kingdom	n.	an old name for China "中国"的旧称
for starters		(*informal*) to begin with; initially 首先，起初
penetrate	v.	to enter and gain a share of (a market) 进入，进入（市场）或取得（市场）分额 penetrated the home-computer market with an affordable new model 以大众可承受的新机型打入家用电脑市场
elusive	a.	be difficult to detect or grasp by the mind; subtle 难捉摸的
peddle	v.	sell or offer for sale from place to place; to engage in the illicit sale of (narcotics) 从事毒品的非法售卖
outsell	v.	to outdo (another) in selling; sell more than others 比……更会推销 a salesperson who outsold her colleagues 比其同事更会推销的推销员

displace	v.	to take the place of; supplant 取代……的位置，替代
baggy	a.	bulging or hanging loosely 宽松的，膨胀的或宽松下垂的
outlet	n.	a store that sells the goods of a particular manufacturer or wholesaler 商店（出售特定制造商或批发商的货物的商店）
seller	n.	an item that sells in a certain way 销售物，以某种方式出售的产品 This washing machine has been an excellent seller. 这种洗衣机的销路极好。
upward of		more than; above 超过，多于
quest for		go in search of or hunt for; quest after, go after, pursue 追求，探索
hook	v.	to cause to become addicted 钩住，沉迷，上瘾
Carhartt		Carhartt is a US based clothing line specializing in work clothes. The company was founded in 1889. 美国潮牌休闲服（该厂家已有111年的历史）
pry	v.	to move or force, especially in an effort to get something open 用力打开，弄开
bankroll	v.	to underwrite the expense of (a business venture, for example) 为……提供资金
acquisition	n.	something acquired or gained 获得物
outfit	v.	to provide with necessary equipment 配备
horror	n.	intense aversion; intense dislike; abhorrence 极端讨厌，痛恨
rampant	a.	occurring without restraint and frequently, widely, or menacingly; rife 猖獗的，盛行的
knock off		(*informal*) to copy or imitate, especially without permission【非正式用语】翻印，复印或模仿（尤指在未经允许的情况下） knocking off someone else's ideas 抄袭别人的构想
quixotic	a.	caught up in the romance of noble deeds and the pursuit of unreachable goals; idealistic without regard to practicality 堂吉诃德式的，沉湎于传奇故事中崇高业绩并追求无法实现的目标的，不考虑到实际的观念的
after hours		not during regular hours 办公时间以后，营业时间过后，闭市后，放学后
tournament	n.	a series of contests in which a number of contestants compete and the one that prevails through the final round or that finishes with the best record is declared the winner 锦标赛，联赛
blast	v.	to play or sound loudly 尖响，发出或制造尖响的声音 The referees blasted their whistle. 裁判高声吹哨。
straitlaced	a.	exaggeratedly proper 严格的，固执的，刻板的
pick up		(*informal*) to improve in condition or activity【非正式用语】有起色，改善 Sales picked up last fall. 去年的销售有起色。
hitch	v.	(*informal*) to hitchhike 免费乘车，搭便车
hitch your wagon to sb./sth.		to try to become successful by becoming involved with someone or something that is already successful or has a good chance of becoming successful 试图通过结交某成功人士而获得成功

> He wisely decided to hitch his wagon to the environmentalist movement, which was then gaining support throughout the country. 他打定主意要利用一下这次环境学者的活动，因为这个活动在该国获得了广泛的支持。
> She hitched her wagon to a rising young star on the music scene.
> 她攀上了音乐界的一个新星。
>
> in-the-know　　　　a.　(*informal*) possessing special or secret information　知内情的，熟悉内情的

Notes

1. Nike　耐克

   耐克公司成立于1964年，由一位会计师菲尔·奈特（Phil Knight）和一位运动教练比尔·鲍尔曼（Bill Bowerman）共同创立，在1980年股票公开上市，凭借优良的产品设计和卓越的营销手法，建立了一流的品牌形象，超越了竞争对手锐步（Reebok）和阿迪达斯（Adidas），成为领导性的品牌。

2. How Nike Figured Out China　耐克是如何摸清中国的

   这句话直译就是"耐克是如何摸清中国的"。"figure out"这个词很不好处理，Longman Dictionary of Contemporary English 对该词的解释是："to figure sth. out: to think about a problem or situation until you find the answer or understand what hs happened"。译成"摸清、搞清、弄清"好像有点儿口语化，但如果按文章的意思译成"耐克走进中国之路"又很难将"figure out"的味道译出。

3. The China market is finally for real.　中国市场终成现实。

   英语"for real"的意思是"真的，事实"。如果将此句译成"中国市场终于玩真的了"，意思表达得不够清楚，因为这里是想表达：经过多年努力，耐克终于打造了中国市场。

4. They can't get enough of those Air Jordans.　再多的飞人乔丹篮球鞋他们也不嫌多。

   英语"enough"作为代词在这类句型中往往是"对某物厌倦"的意思，所以这句话如果意译成"他们对飞人乔丹鞋的需求是无限的"似乎很难表达出"他们对……永不会感到厌倦"这层意思。另外，"Air Jordans"是以乔丹的名字命名的"篮球鞋"，即打篮球的专用鞋，而不是某种品牌的普通球鞋（汉语中，普通意义的球鞋指的是跑鞋、运动鞋等），因此译成"飞人乔丹篮球鞋"能让不懂乔丹鞋的读者更能理解。

5. Nike swung into action...　……耐克公司就已经开始积极行动了。

   将这句话译成"耐克公司就行动起来了"和"耐克就已经展开行动了"都没有将英语"swing"的意思译出，"swing into action"在这里含有"顺利、迅速地开始"之意，所以宜将其译成"开始积极行动"。

6 ... Nike launched a television advertisement in China showing Liu destroying the field and superimposed a series of questions designed to set nationalistic teeth on edge.　……耐克就在中国播放了刘翔征服田径赛场的电视广告，并且在画面上增加了一连串旨在触动爱国人士神经的问题。

这句话中的"set nationalistic teeth on edge"不太容易处理。如果译成"煽起中国人民的爱国情怀的"，好像不符合"set one's teeth on edge"这个短语的意思；如果译成"引起民族伤感的"，语气又稍显过重，而且这个短语也没有"伤感"之意。另外，"nationalist"是指那些自认为自己民族优于其他民族的人，就是"民族主义者"，并不是所有中国人。所以译成"触动爱国人士神经的"比较合适，读者可以自己去理解和体会。

7 Nike understands why Chinese are proud ...　耐克明白中国人为什么会感到自豪……

这句话不能译成"耐克明白中国人为什么而自豪"，因为这样会让人理解成"for what they are proud"，因此译成"……中国人为什么会自豪（骄傲）"比较妥切。

8 Such clever marketing tactics have helped make Nike the icon for the new China.　这类精明的营销策略已经将耐克打造成对外开放之后中国人心目中的偶像品牌。

句中的"new China"不宜直译成"新中国"，因为容易与解放后的中国混淆。从上下文分析，这里的"新中国"理应指改革开放之后的中国。另外，"icon"到底是指"标志"还是指人们崇拜的"偶像"呢。从上下文分析，说"耐克成为新中国的标志"好像不大准确，所以应该是表示：耐克已成了人们心中想拥有的东西。

9 Hill & Knowlton　伟达公关公司

Hill & Knowlton is one of the world's five largest public relations firms.

10 "any number of"是"许多"的意思，不宜译成"任何一款"。

11 "new middle class"不宜直接译成"新中产阶级"因为这样会让读者理解成中国曾有一个旧中产阶级。所以，这里可以增译成"新生的中产阶级"或"新兴的中产阶级"。

12 The goal is to migrate inland from China's richer east-coast towns in time for the outpouring of interest in sports that will accompany the 2008 Summer Olympics in Beijing.　其目标是迅速从中国较富裕的东海沿岸城镇向内地市场进军，以便赶上随着2008年北京夏季奥运会的召开而掀起的运动热潮。

英语"migrate"有迅速迁移之意，所以应增加"迅速"一词。此外，"accompany"一词如果直译成"伴随"，则后面的句子不容易摆，所以将其拆开，译成"随着……而掀起的……"。

13 For starters, the company promoted the right sports and launched a series of inspired ad campaigns.　首先，耐克开发了恰当的运动产品，并且推出一系列创意十足的广告宣传。

"promote"后面接的是"the right sports"，如果译成"推销了体育项目"，汉语似乎搭配不当，所以译成"开发了恰当的运动产品"比较合适。"inspired"本意为"有灵感的"，这里按广告的语境译成"创意十足"非常妥当。

14. But the story of how Nike cracked the China code has as much to do with the rise of China's new middle class, which is hungry for Western gear and individualism, and Nike's ability to tap into that hunger. 但是，耐克之所以能够攻克中国市场，主要归功于中国新生中产阶级的崛起——这个阶级渴望享用西方产品、追求西方的个性张扬——以及耐克充分利用这种需求的能力。

如果将"cracked the China code"直译成"破解中国密码"就显得太拘泥于原文，这里原文无非就是要表达"耐克成功地占领了中国市场"，所以译成"攻克（攻占）中国市场"比较合适。另外，"which is hungry for Western gear and individualism"中的"individualism"很不好处理，因为"渴望西方产品"讲得通，但"渴望西方的个人主义"就不大通顺，所以翻译时将其拆开，增加动词，译成"渴望享用西方产品、追求西方的个性张扬"，这样句子就通顺了。

15. ... the China market has become the fastest growing for almost any American company you can think of. ……几乎所有你能想到的美国公司都认为中国已经成为世界上发展最快的市场。

这句话如果按英语的句式直译，即译成"中国已成为你所能想到的几乎任何一家美国公司增长最快的市场"，中间的两个定语"你所能想到的"和"几乎任何一家美国公司"显得非常长，而且后面的意思表达得不清楚，到底是美国公司增长最快还是美国公司认为中国市场发展最快呢？因此，这里将美国公司译成句子的主语，将中国译成宾语，从而解决了定语过长、含混不清的问题。

16. Although Washington runs a huge trade deficit with Beijing ... 虽然美国对中国贸易逆差巨大……

华盛顿和北京代表的是中美两国，不是两个城市，所以应该意译成"中美两国"。

17. For companies selling consumer items, a presence here is essential ... 经营消费品的公司要想在中国销售自己的产品，就必须首先在这个市场上占有一席之地……

如果将"a presence here is essential"译成"这里是必争之地"，意思与原文有出入。如果译成"在中国市场占有一席之地至关重要"，又没有将"essential"的意思表达准确，因为"essential"的意思是"basic or indispensable; necessary"（基本的，必需的，不可缺少的，绝对必要的），所以译成"首先必须"才能准确地表达这层意思。

18. Chinese-made Lenovo (formerly Legend) computers used to outsell foreign competitors 2 to 1 ... 过去，中国联想电脑（Lenovo，以前为Legend）的销售量曾是外国品牌销量的2倍……

"competitors"在这里应理解成"同类产品的外国品牌"，因为前面的主语是"电脑的销售量"而不是"人"。另外，"outsell ... 2 to 1"是"以2比1的比例销售，即外国品牌卖出1台，联想则卖出2台。"换句话说，就是联想的销售量是外国品牌销售量的两倍。

19. Nike was smart because it didn't enter China selling usefulness, but selling status. 耐克很精明，因为它在中国出售的是地位，而不是产品的实用性。

这句话中的"usefulness"应该是指产品的实用性,因此翻译时应该增译为"产品的实用性"。另外,为了强调耐克卖的是地位,译者采取了逆序法,将"selling status"放到前面的"因为"之后。

20 Go get them! 别让他们跑啦!
奈特的这句话很难翻译。意思虽然明了,但味道却难表达。翻译时的几种选择是:① 给我统统拿下!② 让他们都穿上耐克!③ 抓住这个市场!④ 别让他们跑啦!"穿上耐克"和"抓住市场"意思没错,但翻译得太直白,味道尽失。"给我拿下"中却不见了"20亿只脚",而且有点像黑社会老大的口气。"别让他们跑啦!"跟脚联系上了,但又少了一点商业味道。

21 Phase 1, getting the Swoosh recognized, proved relatively easy. 后来证明,耐克的第一步——让人们认识耐克的闪电注册商标(Swoosh)——相对容易。
英语"proved"是"被证实"的意思,翻译时如果还是放在后面做谓语,就会变成汉语的被动语态:耐克的第一步——让人们认识耐克的闪电注册商标(Swoosh)——后来证明相对容易。因此,不如将动词"prove"提前,这样更符合汉语的表达习惯。另外,"recognized"在这里译成"认识"比"认可"好,因为推销某品牌必须先让消费者认识这个品牌的标志,用习惯了,觉得好,才会认可。

22 But the company had its share of horror stories too... 但是,耐克公司也曾有过许多极为不快的经历……
这句话中的"horror stories"不宜译成"许多惊险故事",因为:① 英语"horror"只有"惊骇,恐怖"的意思,并没有"惊险"之意;② 即使有"惊险"之意,后面句子所表达的内容也没有什么惊险之处。所以,将"horror stories"译成"许多极为不快的经历"更加妥当,因为:① 英语"horror"有"intense dislike; abhorrence"(极端讨厌,痛恨)的意思;② 英语"story"有"经历"的意思。

23 Sports simply wasn't a factor in a country where, since the days of Confucius, education levels and test scores dictated success. 从孔子时代起中国人的成功就一直取决于其所受教育的程度和考试成绩,因此参不参加体育活动根本无关紧要。
英语"level"在这里是复数形式,表示某人获得的教育等级,即所受教育的程度,因此不宜直译成"教育水平"。"sports"表示"参加体育活动"。"dictate"是"决定"的意思。句子如果按英语句式翻译,后面的定语从句就只能译成汉语的地点状语"在……国家里",这样译句就显得过长。因此,将句子拆开,定语从句译成主句,将英语的主句"Sports simply wasn't a factor"译成结果状语,这样句子就通顺了。

24 So Nike executives set themselves a potentially quixotic challenge: to change China's culture. 所以,耐克的管理者们向自己提出了一个近乎异想天开的挑战:改变中国文化。
"quixotic"是"空想的,不切实际的,易冲动的"的意思,这里没必要将"堂吉诃德式的"译出,因为有些读者并不一定知道堂吉诃德的故事。再说,"改变中国文化"不说是一种狂想，至少也可以说是"异想天开"吧。

25　At games, Rhoads blasted the recorded sound of cheering to encourage straitlaced fans to loosen up... 比赛时，罗德播放事先录制好的加油声，带动拘谨的球迷，让他们活跃起来……
英语"encourage"不宜直译成"鼓励"，因为汉语"鼓励某人活跃或放松"讲不通，所以将"encourage"拆译就比较合适。

26　Slowly but surely, in-the-know Chinese came to call sneakers "Nai-ke". 进展虽然缓慢，但认识了耐克的中国人确实开始将这种穿着打篮球的球鞋称为"Nai-ke"。
句中"Slowly but surely"不大好处理，只好将其拆开，"slowly"表示耐克的发展并未能一蹴而就，"surely"表示的确功夫没有白花，已开始初见成效。

他山之石

原文1：

Although more and more businesses are coming to the capital markets to raise funds, majority business still remain heavily dependent on commercial banks.

原译：

虽然越来越多的商业正进入资本市场以获得资金，但大部分商业仍然是主要依靠商业银行获得资金。

点评：

① "businesses"是"a person or corporation that buys and sells goods"的意思，不能译成"商业"。另外，"商业正进入资本市场"也不通。

② "raise funds"译成"获得资金"虽然意思没错，但不是专业术语，应该译成"融资"。

③ 最后一句虽然主语还是"businesses"，但谓语"still remain heavily dependent on"不大好直译，所以不妨将主语转译成"企业的资金"，这样句子摆起来就可避免重复，也很自然。

改译：

尽管越来越多的商业企业开始进入资本市场进行融资，但大部分企业的资金仍主要来自商业银行。

原文 2：

Fifty-three million American households, either directly or indirectly, once owned stocks in the corporations who share the trade on the major US exchanges. Today that number has dwindled to about thirty eight million. Increasingly investors turn to the fixed interest rate government bonds and bank certificates of deposits. Other investors have put their money into their homes in the form of improvement and additions. A second reason for the fall-off share trading is a widely held perception of the small investors' being at disadvantage to the large pension fund institutional investors who account for over half of all market trading value. Therefore, before their stocks appear in the primary market, most issuers will have them presented to authoritative institutions for appraising their credit standing grades, which will be often adjusted in line with their behaviors in the market later on.

原译：

曾有 5 300 万美国家庭直接或间接地购买公司股票。这些公司在美国主要证券交易所做股票交易。现在拥有股票的家庭已减少到 3 800 万户左右。越来越多的投资者转向有固定利息的国家债券和银行存款。其他投资者则把钱投放在家中增置资产。购买股票者减少的第二个原因是，大家普遍认为，大投资者占了股票市场一半以上的贸易额，相比之下，小投资者处于不利地位。因此，在股票上市前，多数股票发行人要请权威性信评机构进行资信级别的评估。上市以后，股票的等级也要按其表现不断进行调整。

点评：

① 将限制性定语从句 "who share the trade on the major US exchanges" 译成 "这些公司在美国主要证券交易所做股票交易"，读者就会理解成：5 300 万美国家庭购买上市公司的股票，而这些上市公司又从事股票交易。这显然是不合法的行为，因为上市公司不可能天天炒股票，也不可能投资自己的股票。这里应该是指：美国家庭购买的各公司的股票每天都在交易所进行交易。

② "put their money into their homes in the form of improvement and additions" 不宜译成 "把钱投放在家中增置资产"，因为 "put money into" 是 "投资于" 的意思，而 "homes" 在此应该指 "住宅"。另外 "improvement" 和 "additions" 应该是 "房屋的改造和扩建"。

③ 仅仅将 "the large pension fund institutional investors" 译成 "大投资者" 不够准确，应该是 "大型养老金机构投资者"。

④ "market trading value" 不是 "贸易额"，而是 "交易额"。

⑤ "before their stocks appear in the primary market" 中的 "primary market" 是指 "股票发行市场"，也叫 "初次市场（即证券发行机构）"，而 "上市" 是指股票发行之后

再到二级市场进行交易。所以,这句不能简单地翻译成"在股票上市前",而应该译成"股票发行之前"。

⑥ 将"appraising their credit standing grades"译成"进行资信级别的评估"不够完整。这里应该将"appraising"拆译成"进行资信评估并且定级"意思才完整。

⑦ "behaviors"可以译成"表现",也可以译成"走势",但最好在前面加上"二级市场",这样就更加地道了。

改译:

美国曾有5 300万家庭直接或间接地在美国主要证券交易所买卖上市公司的股票。现在拥有股票的家庭已减少到3 800万户左右。越来越多的投资者转向有固定利息的国库券和银行存款。其他投资者则将资金用于改造和添置家业。购买股票者减少的第二个原因是,大家普遍认为,由于大型养金机构投资者占了股票市场交易额的一半以上,相比之下,小投资者处于不利地位。因此,在发行股票之前,多数股票发行人要请权威机构对其股票进行资信评估并且定级。上市以后,股票的等级还要根据其在二级市场上的表现经常进行调整。

原文3:

No review of the achievements of the WTO would be completed without mentioning the Dispute Settlement System, in many ways the central pillar of the multilateral trading system and the WTO's most individual contribution to the stability of the global economy. The new WTO is at once stronger, more automatic and more credible than its GATT predecessor.

原译:

提到世界贸易组织就不能不提及争端协调体系,在许多方面争端协调体系是多边贸易体系的中心支柱,也是世界贸易组织对全球经济稳定做出的贡献。新的世界贸易组织比其前身关贸总协定更强大,更自觉,也更值得信赖。

点评:

① 将"No review of the achievements of the WTO would be completed"译成"提到世界贸易组织"过于简单,而是应该将"就无法对世贸组织所做出的成绩进行全面的评价"这层意思完整地表达出来。

② "Dispute Settlement System"通常翻译成"争端解决机制"。

③ "individual"不能省,要译出来。

④ 将"the new WTO"译成"新的世界贸易组织"容易使读者误以为曾有个"旧的世界贸易组织"。这篇文章是1997年发表的,而世界贸易组织是1995年成立的,所以可以将"the new WTO"译成"刚刚成立不久的世界贸易组织"或者"不久前建立的世界贸易组织"。

⑤ 三个形容词"stronger, more automatic and more credible"不容易翻译。"强大、自

觉"可否改为"得力、高效"?

改译:

要对世界贸易组织所做出的成绩进行全面的评价,就必须提及世界贸易组织的争端解决机制。这个机制在许多方面是多边贸易体系的中心支柱,也是世界贸易组织对全球经济稳定做出的独特贡献。刚刚成立不久的世界贸易组织比其前身关贸总协定更加得力、高效和值得信赖。

学生译作分析

原文 1:

One of the main disadvantages of a long, complex sentence, which may still be found in some business correspondence despite the progress that has been made in recent years towards simplifying business writing styles in the English-speaking world, is that the reader is likely to find it more difficult to understand than a series of shorter sentences, which in turn may lead to frustration and misunderstanding, particularly if the reader is a busy person who has more important things to do.

学生原译文:

尽管近年来,在英语世界里,商务写作风格已经在向简化方向发展,但长而复杂的句子还是在某些商务书信中可以看到。这类句子的一个主要缺点是:读者,尤其是忙于做更重要的事情的读者,可能会觉得一个复杂的长句比一串短句读起来更费劲,结果也许会令其产生挫败感和错误理解。

分析:

(1) 这个句子非常长,其中含有 4 个定语从句。原译通过运用逆序和转译等翻译技巧将 4 个定语从句译出,处理得恰到好处。

(2) 将"in the English-speaking world"译成"在英语世界里"太模糊。"English-speaking countries"意思是"说英语的国家",这里自然不能译成"说英语的世界"。但是,仔细读原文就不难发现,这一段讲的是"商务写作",所以不妨变通一下,将"business writing styles in the English-speaking world"合起来译成"人们在用英语书写商务信函时"。

(3) "difficult to understand"译成"难懂一些"或"难理解"比"更加费解"或"更费劲"好,因为"更……"很容易理解成"读短句费解,读长句更加费解"。汉语中一般用了"比"字，后面通常不再使用"更"字。
(4) "frustration" 一词在此不宜译成"挫败感"，因为汉语通常不这样表达。原文是想表达：长句没时间细读，也很难懂，而读不懂就会感到灰心丧气，甚至可能把意思理解错，所以还是译成"灰心"更自然贴切。
(5) 最后，整个译文虽然忠实通顺，但如果遣词造句上能够更加精准简洁一些就会更好。

参考译文：

近年来，人们在用英语书写商务信函时已明显趋向简洁的风格，但长而复杂的句子或许仍时而可见。这类句子的一个主要缺点是：读者，尤其是那些有其他要务在身的读者，可能会觉得复杂的长句比一串短句难懂一些，甚至可能使他们感到灰心并产生错误的理解。

原文 2：

The US stock markets suffered from the worst one-day crash in modern history on October 19th, 1987, the day which has come to be known as Black Monday.

学生原译文：

美国股票市场曾遭受了现代历史上最惨重的"一天暴跌"。事情发生在1987年10月19日这一天，后来人们称之为"黑色星期一"。

分析：

(1) 将"worst one-day crash"译成"最惨重的'一天暴跌'"不通顺，因为：① "遭受……暴跌"不符合汉语的表达习惯，一般说"经历……暴跌"；② "最惨重的暴跌"搭配上也有问题；③ "一天暴跌"不是行话，应该译成"单日最大跌幅"。
(2) "in modern history"不能直接译成"现代历史上"，因为股票市场的历史非常短，不能分成古代、近代和现代。这里讲的"in modern history"其实就指"自有股市以来"。Wikipedia 中对"黑色星期一"的解释非常清楚："Black Monday, 19 October 1987—the largest one-day decline in recorded stock market history." 注意，是"in recorded stock market history"。这一天道琼斯平均工业指数下跌了22.6%。
(3) 翻译同位语"the day"及修饰它的定语从句时，完全没有必要拆译成"事情发生在1987年10月19日这一天，后来……"，因为英语中经常将时间状语放到句尾，这里只需将"October 19th, 1987"放到句首，后面顺着译即可。

参考译文：

1987年10月19日，美国股票市场遭受了自有股市以来最大的单日跌幅。后来人们称这一天为"黑色星期一"。

原文 3：

Railroads justify rate discrimination against captive shippers on the grounds that in the long run it reduces everyone's cost.

学生原译文：

（1）从长远来看，受目光短浅货主歧视的铁路部门其收费合理可以降低大多数人的成本。

（2）铁路部门证实：对特定的托运人实行区别费率制是合理的，最后的结果是减少了每个人的成本。

分析：

（1）第一种译文问题比较大，主要是将"discrimination against captive shippers"译成了"Railroads"的定语"受目光短浅货主歧视的铁路部门"，这显然是对原文的错误理解。另外，将整个句子的主语译成"收费合理"也不对。从句子结构上分析，这句话中"Railroads"是主语，"justify"是谓语，"rate discrimination"是宾语，"against captive shippers"是定语，"on the grounds that in the long run it reduces everyone's cost"是状语。

（2）第二种译文意思基本正确，但"justify"不能直接译成"证实"，而且"on the grounds that"译成"结果"也不妥。

参考译文：

铁路运输公司都认为对这一特定的托运人实行区别收费是合理的，因为（理由是），长期来看，这样做可以降低每个（所有）托运人的运输成本。

翻译技巧介绍

意译
(Translating Meaning)

英、汉语的结构有相同的一面，汉译时可照译，即所谓的"直译"——既忠实原文内容，又符合原文的结构形式。但这两种语言之间还有许多差别，若完全照译，势必出现"英化汉语"，这时就需要"意译"——在忠实原文内容的前提下，摆脱原文结构的束缚，使译文符合汉语的规范。只有在正确理解原文的基础上，运用相应的翻译方法调整原文结构，用规范的汉语加以表达，才能真正做到"意译"。翻译实践证明，大量英语句子的汉译都要采取"意译法"。一般来说，在翻译过程中，完全用直译或完全用意译的情况不多见。通常的做法是，能直译的地方就直译，不能直译的地方就采用意译。换言之，能直译尽量直译。直译的好处在于既能表达原文的意思，又能尽量保持原文的语言风格。

(1) Customers are starting to **vote with their feet** and go to other businesses when they find a particular company rude, or uncaring, or basically unaware of the customer's need.
译文：如果顾客发现某公司对待顾客粗鲁、冷漠，或是对顾客的需要根本一无所知，他们就会**拔腿**走向其他的商家。（用脚投票）

(2) Commerce has been built on the belief that **selling bank accounts and loans** is little different from offloading fresh fruit and breakfast cereal.
译文：商业银行的经营就是基于这样的信念：**银行吸引存贷**也同超市搞新鲜水果、早餐谷物类食品促销非常相像。

(3) Service Excellence: Leading the Way to **Wow**!
译文：卓越服务：令人叫绝！

(4) Here, Commerce students learn how to **wow** their customers.
译文：在这所大学里，学员们学习如何**博得**客户的**赞赏**。

(5) The future of the world economy is of particular interest to my country because **we have such a huge stake in it**.
译文：世界经济的未来与我国**休戚相关**，所以我们格外关注。

(6) China's rapid emergence as a **major world actor** is a tribute to the drive and entrepreneurial spirit of her people, and more particularly to the fundamental economic reforms she has pursued over the past two decades.
译文：中国迅速崛起，成为世界上发挥重要作用的**国家**，这应归功于中国人民的努力和进取精神，尤其是过去20年里中国所进行的根本性的经济改革。

(7) The question is whether Commerce can continue to **dazzle** its customers and Wall Street when it becomes the biggest bank on the block.
译文：这儿的未知数是：当商业银行成为华尔街上最大的银行时，它能否继续使客户和华尔街**为之倾倒**。

(8) A credit card thief may be **sitting on a potential goldmine**, particularly if there is a delay in reporting the loss of the card.
译文：信用卡盗贼可能会**大发横财**——尤其是在失主没有能及时报失的情况下。

(9) The government blames its poor export performance on the slump in the price for its main export—cotton—its **lack of influence** over the World Trade Organisation regime.
译文：政府将出口业绩不佳归咎于占其出口大宗的棉花价格暴跌，以及它在世贸组织体制中的**人微言轻**。

(10) But for banks, personal, unsecured loans represent one of the **most profitable niches**.
译文：但是，对银行而言，个人的、无担保的贷款是**最好的一种摇钱树**。

(11) It's the first time in this egalitarian society that some people got rich quickly, so there is a lot of envy, resentment of **this money**.

译文：一些人很快富了起来，在这个平等主义的社会里这是前所未有的事，因此对于这种**有钱人**，社会上存在着许多嫉妒和愤恨。

（12） His book would be the **bible** for the unhappy customers.

译文：他的书也就会成为心情不悦的顾客的**金科玉律**。

（13） Besides **inspired use** of its scientific talent and know-how, Sony is backed by highly innovative management.

译文：索尼公司除了**鬼使神差般巧妙地发挥**其科技人才与技术知识的作用之外，还以有高度创新精神的经营管理体系作为其后盾。

（14） Clearing and forwarding agents handle all the **details** of transporting cargo: packing, weighing and marking, making customs entries, and the many dock services entailed in loading and unloading.

译文：清关发货代理人经管货物运输方面的**一切杂务**，如包装、过磅、刷唛、报关及与装卸有关的许多必不可少的码头事务。

（15） Real communications **occurs** when we listen with understanding. It means to see the expressed idea and attitude from the other person's point of view, to sense **how it feels to be him**, to achieve his frame of reference in regard to the thing he is talking about.

译文：真正的交流**需要会心**的倾听，就是要根据对方的观点来了解对方的想法和态度，**体会对方的感受**并理解对方对所谈问题的看法。

（16） Marketers and advertisers who want to be successful on the Net should be **playing to its strength, not its weakness**.

译文：想在网上有所作为的营销公司和广告公司应当**扬长避短**。

（17） Service is **what** often differentiates one hotel from another in the minds of consumers. It's impossible to underestimate the importance of service to guest **satisfaction, repeat business, and a hotel's reputation.**

译文：在消费者看来，服务质量是区分饭店好坏的**关键**。因此，任何饭店绝不可能忽视服务的重要性，因为这关系到**客人是否满意、会不会再度光顾及饭店声誉的好坏**。

（18） Yes, it can seem like there's a Starbucks on every corner, but Howard Schultz says his company is just **warming up**.

译文：不错，我们现在似乎可以在任何角落见到星巴克，但是霍华德·舒尔茨却认为他的公司才**刚刚起步**。

（19） America's latest cultural export is the **buy-now, pay-later** shopping habit.

译文：美国最新文化输出是"**先购物，后付款**"的购物习惯。

（20） In Italy, many consumers prefer cash to credit to **hide transactions from** tax authorities.

译文：在意大利，许多消费者宁愿用现金而不用信用卡，目的是**避免税务当局扣税**。

(21) However, he believes that many of Commerce's rivals will fail because they are too big and **unfocused**.

译文：然而，他还是相信商业银行的许多竞争对手会失败，因为他们过于庞大和**缺乏特色**。

(22) The EEC's Common Agricultural Policy（农业共同政策）is a **dinosaur** which is adding 13.50 a week to the food bill of the average British family.

译文：欧洲经济共同体的农业共同政策早已**不合时宜**，它使英国家庭平均每周在食品开销上多支出13.50英镑。

(23) For western businesses who have already exhausted opportunities in mature markets such as America and Europe, cracking China in a major way is **something of a holy grail**.

译文：对于在美洲、欧洲这样的成熟市场中已经难觅商机的西方商家来说，全力开启中国市场的大门正是他们**梦寐以求的**。

(24) OPEC is still **skating on thin ice**.

译文：欧佩克现在仍**如履薄冰**，尚未走出险境。

(25) Once you have a core position, look around for satellite investments that may **spice up your portfolio**.

译文：有了主导的投资品种，打量着再做一些附属投资，这可能给你的投资组合带来更大的胜算。

课堂翻译训练

将下列句子译成汉语。

1. Hotels are many things. They are businesses in a very competitive industry, and this affects how they need to be managed.

2. In almost all guest experiences, the employee can make the difference between a satisfied guest and a dissatisfied guest. The employee can also turn satisfaction to wow.

3. There is more to their life than political and social economic problems; more than transient everydayness.

4. If you can't stomach 50 percent losses in your stock portfolio, get out now and save yourself a

heart attack. You may not buy that mansion in Spain, but you'll live to see your granddaughter's graduation.

5. Starbuck's unconventional approach to real estate goes back to an impulse decision by its chairman more than 15 years ago.
6. Both companies' flagship colas, which together account for 1 of every 3 sodas sold in the US, lost share last year.
7. I'm eyeing at least one nuclear-power stock, and am favorably disposed toward gambling stocks.
8. Finally, excellent hotel managers must know how to make profits when times are good and occupancies and revenues are high and also when times are bad and costs must be controlled closely.
9. It's so easy for people to walk away from a business after a good experience with a good story to tell others, not a bad story.

课后练习

将下列短文译成英语，注意运用本单元所学的翻译技巧。

1.
In addition to history being made, much of the world's work takes place in hotels. Great conferences on the most pressing issues of our time are held in hotels. Physicians meet seeking cures for diseases, scientists gather to discuss the origins of the universe, diplomats huddle to plan relief for flood victims, and financiers negotiate billion dollar corporate takeovers. As one hotel executive put it, "The hotel business is bringing people together to solve the world's problems." That surrounds hotels. Of course, history is made at the local and county level as well. So whether it's a meeting to pick a candidate for county commissioner, a strategy session to choose a Supreme Court justice, or delicate negotiations to end hostilities between two warring nations, history is always being made in hotels. The world's problems are both large and small and many of them are solved in hotels. That's a lot more exciting than thinking of hotels as a place where heads are put on beds.

2.

Global financial markets provide a brutal but life-giving therapy to sick economies. The latest turnaround is Argentina. Once its peso was allowed to float freely, it fell to levels that made the country irresistible to investors. The Argentine economy is expected to grow 9 percent this year after an 11 per cent decline in 2002. The dollar value of its stock market is up 100 per cent this year—the largest increase of any major market in the world.

The countries that are faring worst, not surprisingly, are those that resist the forces of globalization. Politicians in France and Germany talk about reform of their rigid labor markets. But reducing the conservative power of labor unions in those countries may require a new generation that prefers change and growth to stasis.

The biggest cloud on the global economic horizon is the United States. US politicians continue to think they can balloon trade and budget deficits, ignoring the economic rules that globalization imposes on everyone else. Even Brazil's President Luza da Silva has learned better. One can only hope that President Bush and Congress will get the message of globalization before it imposes a severe penalty on the United States.

Unit 6

佳译赏析

How Nike Figured Out China
耐克是如何摸清中国的（II）

From *Time*, October 25, 2004
By Matthew Forney

And those sneakers brought with them a lot more than just basketball.[1] Nike gambled[2] that the new middle class, now some 40 million people who make an average of ＄8,500 a year for a family of three, was developing a whole new set of values, centered on individualism. Nike unabashedly[3] made American culture its selling point, with ads that challenge China's traditional, group-oriented ethos. This year the company released Internet teaser clips showing a faceless but Asian-looking high school basketball player shaking-and-baking his way through a defense. It was timed to coincide with Nike tournaments around the country and concluded with the question: "Is this you?" The viral advertisement drew 5 million e-mails.[4] Nike then aired TV spots contrasting Chinese-style team-oriented play with a more individualistic American style[5], complete with a theme song blending traditional Chinese music and hip-hop[6].

这些耐克球鞋带给消费者的绝不只是篮球运动。耐克确信，在中国投资这个险值得冒，因为中国约4 000万人口的富裕阶层——平均年收入8 500美元的三口之家群体——正在形成一套以发扬个性为中心的全新价值观。这样，耐克便大胆把美国文化作为产品的卖点，推出了挑战中国传统的集体主义道德观的广告。今年，耐克又在网上发布了一些优惠广告短片，只见一个外形像亚洲人但没有露出脸部的中学篮球选手一路左闪右突、终于突破了对方的防守。这些广告特意选在全国耐克篮球联赛举办之际发布，并以"这是你吗？"这个问题结束全片。其传播力和感染力之强，竟吸引了五百万封电子回信。接着耐克又在电视上插播广告，使观众领略了强调集体配合的中式球风和提倡单打独斗的美式球风，广告还配上了一首融合了传统中国音乐与嘻哈（hip-hop）音乐的主题曲。

Starting in 2001, Nike coined a new phrase for its China marketing, borrowing from American black street culture: "Hip Hoop". The idea is to "connect Nike with a creative lifestyle," says Frank Pan, Nike's current director of sports marketing for China. The hip-hop message "connects the disparate elements of black cool culture and associates it with Nike,"[7] says Edward Bell, director of planning for Ogilvy & Mather[8] in Hong Kong. "But black culture can be aggressive, and Nike softens it to make it more acceptable to Chinese.[9]" At a recent store opening in Shanghai, Nike flew in a streetball team from Beijing.

从2001年起，为了在中国销售产品，耐克公司根据美国街头黑人文化创造了一个新词：Hip Hoop（嘻哈篮筐，由 Hip Hop "嘻哈音乐"及 hoop "篮筐"改造而成）。这样做是为了"把耐克与富于创意的生活联系到一起"，现任耐克中国运动器材销售经理弗兰克·潘表示。这种通过嘻哈音乐传递的信息"综合了黑人酷文化中的各种不同的元素，并且将这种文化与耐克联系在起来"，香港奥美广告计划经理艾德华·贝尔说，"但是黑人文化有时具有挑衅性，耐克为了让中国人容易接受，把这种音乐改编得温和悦耳。"最近上海的一家耐克新店开张，耐克就从北京空运来一支街头球队。

Thanks in part to Nike's promotions[10], urban hip-hop culture is all the rage among young Chinese. One of Beijing's leading DJs, Gu Yu, credits Nike with "making me the person I am". Handsome and tall under a mop of shoulder-length hair, Gu got hooked on hip-hop after hearing rapper Black Rob rhyme praises to Nike in a television ad. Gu learned more on Nike's Internet page and persuaded overseas friends to send him music. Now they send something else too: limited-edition Nikes unavailable in China. Gu and his partner sell them in their shop, Upward, to Beijing's several hundred "sneaker friends" and wear them while spinning tunes in Beijing's top clubs.

由于耐克在某种程度上的宣传，城市嘻哈文化在中国年轻人中风靡一时。北京一位重要的节目主持人顾宇（译音）认为耐克打造了"今天的我"。顾宇又高又帅、长发披肩。自从他听到饶舌歌手布莱克·罗布在电视广告中通过歌声赞美耐克之后，他就迷上了嘻哈音乐。然后顾宇又通过耐克的网站进一步了解了这种音乐，并且请国外的朋友给他寄这种音乐。现在，这些朋友还给他邮寄另一种东西：中国买不到的限量发行的耐克球鞋。接着顾宇和合伙人在他们北京的鞋店"UPWARD"向数以百计的北京"鞋友"出售这种球鞋。他们还穿着这些鞋子到北京最火的夜总会做节目。

The Nike phenomenon is challenging Confucian-style deference to elders too. At the Nike shop in a ritzy Shanghai shopping mall, Zhen Zhiye, 22, a dental hygienist in a miniskirt, persuades her elderly aunt, who has worn only cheap sneakers that she says "make my feet stink", to drop $60 on a new pair. Zhen explains the "fragrant possibilities" of higher-quality shoes and chides her aunt for her dowdy ways. Her aunt settles on a cross trainer. For most of China's history, this exchange would have been unthinkable.[11] "In our tradition, elders pass culture to youth," says researcher Zhang. "Now it's a great reversal, with parents and grandparents eating and clothing themselves like children."

耐克现象也向中国儒家顺从长辈的传统发起了挑战。上海一家豪华购物中心的耐克店里,身着超短裙的22岁的口腔医师甄芝烨(译音)就劝她年老的姑妈花60美元买双新球鞋,她姑妈从前只穿便宜的球鞋,还说穿便宜的鞋子"脚臭"。甄小姐告诉她姑妈,质量好的鞋子"不臭脚",并且责怪她姑妈不爱卫生。最后,她姑妈决定买一双跑步和打球两用软运动鞋。在中国,从古到今晚辈很少有这样跟长辈说话的。张万利研究员说:"长辈将文化传给晚辈是我们的传统。现在完全颠倒了,爸爸妈妈和爷爷奶奶吃饭穿衣反而要效仿他们的晚辈。"

Success aside, Nike has had its stumbles. When it began outfitting Chinese professional soccer teams in the mid-1990s, its ill-fitting cleats caused heel sores so painful that Nike had to let its athletes wear Adidas (with black tape over the trademark). In 1997, Nike ramped up production just before the Asian banking crisis[12] killed demand, then flooded the market with cheap shoes, undercutting its own retailers and driving many into the arms of Adidas.[13] Two years later, the company created a $15 Swoosh-bearing canvas sneaker designed for poor Chinese. The "World Shoe" flopped so badly that Nike killed it.

耐克在中国有成功之处,但也曾经历过挫折。20世纪90年代中期,耐克开始为中国职业足球队提供服装。因为耐克提供的足球鞋不合脚,运动员感到脚跟酸痛,耐克不得不让运动员穿阿迪达斯的球鞋(用黑胶带遮住商标)。1997年,耐克刚刚提高产量,亚洲金融危机的爆发便使需求量急剧下降,耐克只好以低廉的价格大量出售自己的鞋子,使自己的零售商损失惨重,逼得很大一部分投入了阿迪达斯的怀抱。两年之后,耐克公司又专为并不富裕的中国消费者开发了一款价值15美元、带有耐克闪电商标的帆布球鞋。这款"世界鞋"销售情况太差,耐克只好停止销售。

Yet all that amounts to a frayed shoelace compared with losing China's most famous living human.[14] Yao Ming had worn Nike since Rhoads discovered him as a skinny kid with a sweet jumper — and brought him some size 18s made for NBA All-Star Alonzo Mourning. In 1999 he signed Yao to a four-year contract worth $200,000. But Nike let his contract expire last year. Yao defected to Reebok for an estimated $100 million. The failure leaves Nike executives visibly dejected.[15] "The only thing I know is, we lost Yao Ming," says a Shanghai executive who negotiated with the star.

然而,这些遭遇加起来也只不过相当于一条磨破的鞋带而已,因为耐克最大的损失莫过于失去中国当今最有名气的人。姚明被罗德发现时还只是一个穿着汗衫的单瘦孩子,当时罗德还给了他几双 NBA 全明星球员阿朗佐·莫宁专用的 18 号篮球鞋。从此姚明便穿起了耐克鞋。1999 年,罗德与姚明签了为期 4 年价值约 20 万美元的合同。但耐克去年在该合同到期时却没有续约,结果姚明转而与锐步公司签订了价值约为 1 亿美元的合同。这一失败显然让耐克的管理者非常沮丧。耐克在上海的一位曾与姚明谈判的经理说:"我只知道我们失去了姚明。"

Nike is determined not to repeat the mistake. It has already signed China's next NBA prospect[16], the 7-ft. Yi Jianlian, 18, who plays for the Guangdong Tigers. And the company has resolved problems that dogged it a few years ago. Nike has cleaned up its shop floors. [17] It cut its footwear suppliers in China from 40 to 16, and 15 of those sell only to Nike, allowing the company to monitor conditions more easily. At Shoetown in the southern city of Guangzhou, 10,000 mostly female laborers work legal hours stitching shoes for $95 a month — more than minimum wage. "They've made huge progress," says Li Qiang, director of New York City-based China Labor Watch.

耐克决心不再重犯这种错误。它已经与中国下一个有望去 NBA 打球的球员易建联签订了合同。易建联今年 18 岁、身高 213 公分,目前效力于广东宏远队。耐克还解决了几年前困扰过它的一些问题,重新调整了生产能力,将中国的鞋类供应商从 40 个削减至 16 个,其中 15 个只为耐克供货,使公司比较容易监控各种情况。在中国南方城市广州的"鞋城",有 1 万名工人为耐克缝制球鞋,他们大多数是女性,工作时间合法,月薪 95 美元——高于当地最低工资标准。总部设在纽约的"中国劳动观察组织"执行董事李强(译音)表示,"他们进步非常大。"

In China, Nike is hardly viewed as the ugly imperialist. In fact, the company's celebration of American culture is totally in synch with the Chinese as they hurtle into a freer time. [18] In July, at a Nike three-on-three competition in the capital, a Chinese DJ named Jo Eli played songs like I'll Be Damned off his Dell computer. "Nike says play hip-hop because that's what blacks listen to," he says. "The government doesn't exactly promote these things. But we can all expose ourselves to something new." That sounds pretty close to a Chinese translation of "Just Do It". [19]

在中国,几乎没有人把耐克视为险恶的帝国主义者。事实上,随着中国进一步对外开放,人们的生活更加丰富多彩,耐克公司对美国文化的颂扬完全顺应了这一趋势。今年 7 月,耐克在北京举办了 3 对 3 篮球对抗赛,一个名叫乔爱理(译音)的中国节目主持人用他的戴尔计算机播放《真想不到》这类歌曲。他说,"耐克说要放嘻哈,因为黑人就听这个。政府并没有大力提倡这类东西,但我们完全可以自己去接触一些新事物。"这句话正是耐克那句经典广告词所要表达的内涵——"Just Do It"——只管去做!

Words and Expressions

gamble	v.	to take a risk in the hope of gaining an advantage or a benefit 投机，冒险（为获得好处或利益而冒险）
unabashed	a.	not concealed or disguised; obvious 不加掩饰的，明显的
selling point	n.	an aspect of a product or service that is stressed in advertising or marketing; or a characteristic of something that is up for sale that makes it attractive to potential customers 卖点
ethos	n.	the disposition, character, or fundamental values peculiar to a specific person, people, culture, or movement 社会精神特质（一种特定的人、民族、文化或社会活动所特有的性情、气质、个性或基本的价值），气质，道义，民族精神，社会思潮，风气
teaser	n.	an advertisement that attracts customers by offering something extra or free 优惠广告（通过提供额外的或免费的东西来吸引顾客的广告）
clip	n.	a short extract from a film or videotape 剪辑（从电影胶片或录像带剪出的片断）
faceless	a.	without a face or identity 无特性的，没有个性的，无法辨认的，不知名的
defense	n.	(sports) the team or those players on the team attempting to stop the opposition from scoring 【体育运动】防守队员（试图阻止对方进球的球队或球队队员们）
coincide	v.	to happen at the same time or during the same period 同时发生
viral	a.	of, relating to, or caused by a virus 病毒的，关于病毒的或由病毒引起的
hip-hop	n.	希普霍普（由快板歌、涂墙艺术、霹雳舞等构成的亚文化），嘻哈音乐
coin	v.	to devise (a new word or phrase) 杜撰，设计（新单词或短语）
hoop	n.	the basket 篮筐
disparate	a.	fundamentally distinct or different in kind; entirely dissimilar 全异的，异类的，完全不同的，根本不同的
streetball	n.	an urban form of basketball, played in playgrounds and imitated in gymnasiums across the world 街头篮球队
design	n.	(often designs) a secretive plot or scheme （常作 designs）阴谋 He has designs on my job. 他在打我工作的主意。
all the rage		very fashionable or stylish; a current, eagerly adopted fashion; a fad or craze 风行一时，时尚，流行，时兴的东西 when torn jeans were all the rage 当撕破的牛仔裤非常流行的时候 DVDs are all the rage, and several movie companies have started releasing titles in this format. 数字化视频光盘非常流行，所以几家电影公司已经开始发行这类电影。 Flared slacks and low heels are the latest rage in women's fashion. 女装的流行款式是休闲裤和低跟鞋。
DJ	abbr.	（广播电台）流行音乐播音员，流行音乐节目主持人（disc jockey）

mop	n.	a loosely tangled bunch or mass 拖把状物
		a mop of unruly hair 乱蓬蓬的杂乱的头发
rapper	n.	one who performs rap 说唱艺人
rap	n.	a form of popular music characterized by spoken or chanted rhyming lyrics with a syncopated, repetitive rhythmic accompaniment 敲击音乐（一种流行音乐形式，以其中的大量说唱或配有同步重复的伴奏韵律的押韵抒情文章而著称）
rhyme	v.	to put into rhyme or compose with rhymes 使成押韵，使成韵或用韵律构作
spin	v.	to play (records), especially as a disc jockey 播放（录音）
deference	n.	courteous respect 敬重，尊敬
ritzy	a.	elegant; fancy 豪华的，时髦的，漂亮的，高级的
drop	v.	(informal) to spend, especially lavishly or rashly 花费（尤指挥霍无度地）
		dropping $50,000 in an Atlantic City casino 在大西洋城赌场花掉5万美元
chide	v.	to scold mildly so as to correct or improve; reprimand 为了以纠正或改进而温和地责备，训斥
		chided the boy for his sloppiness 责怪这男孩粗心
dowdy	a.	lacking stylishness or neatness; shabby; old-fashioned; antiquated 不整洁的或衣着过时的，邋遢的，老式的，过时的
cross-trainer	n.	an athletic shoe designed for cross-training, as for running and court sports 跑步和打球两用软运动鞋
reversal	n.	the act or an instance of reversing 倒转，颠倒，颠倒或翻转的行为或实例
stumble	n.	a mistake or blunder 错误，过失
cleat	n.	a projecting piece of metal or hard rubber attached to the underside of a shoe to provide traction 耐磨钉（在鞋底防止磨损的一块金属或硬橡胶的凸出物）
ramp up		bolster or strengthen 增加，提高
flood	v.	to fill with an abundance or an excess 充斥（以丰富或过多的东西充满）
		flood the market with cheap foreign goods 市场上充斥着廉价的外国货
undercut	v.	to diminish or destroy the province or effectiveness of; undermine 削弱（减弱或毁灭……的范围或效力）
flop	v.	(informal) to fail utterly 【非正式用语】彻底失败
fray	v.	to wear away (the edges of fabric, for example) by rubbing 磨损
skinny	a.	very thin 极瘦的
jumper	n.	a shot made by a player at the highest point of a jump (also called "jump shot") 跳投（一种投篮方式，球员跳跃至最高点时投篮）
defect	v.	to abandon a position or an association, often to join an opposing group 背叛
		defected from the party over the issue of free trade 在自由贸易的问题上背叛了自己的政党
dejected	a.	being in low spirits; depressed 垂头丧气，情绪低落的，沮丧的

dog	*v.*	to track or trail persistently	跟随，尾随
clean up		to make clean or orderly	清理，使清洁或有秩序
stitch	*v.*	to fasten or join with or as if with stitches	缝
celebrate	*v.*	to extol or praise	歌颂或赞扬
synch	*n.*	harmony; accord	同时，同步
		in sync with today's fashions	符合当今时尚潮流
hurtle	*v.*	to move with or as if with great speed and a rushing noise	呼啸而过
promote	*v.*	to urge the adoption of; advocate	促进，助长，倡议

Notes

1. And those sneakers brought with them a lot more than just basketball. 这些耐克球鞋带给消费者的绝不只是篮球运动。
"basketball" 容易直译成"篮球"，这里还是译成"篮球运动"比较合适，因为前面已经介绍过，耐克公司是通过开展公共篮球活动这一策略来推销球鞋的。

2. "gamble" 一词不太容易处理。翻译时有几种选择：① 直译成"打赌"；② 意译成"大胆假定"；③ 意译成"确信"；④ 意译成"耐克确信，在中国投资这个险值得冒"。由于 "gamble" 含有 "take a risk in the hope of a favorable outcome" 的意思，所以为了将"甘冒风险"这层意思译出，还是选择第 4 种译文比较妥当。

3. 将 "unabashedly" 译成"公然"不大合适。这个词含贬义，既然是商业活动，还是用"大胆"比较好，而且还可以与前面的"冒险"相呼应。另外，"its selling point" 不宜直译成"它的卖点"，应该译成"耐克产品的卖点"。

4. The viral advertisement drew 5 million e-mails. 其传播力和感染力之强，竟吸引了五百万封电子回信。
如果将 "viral advertisement" 这个词译成"病毒营销式广告"，那么不懂"病毒式网络营销"的读者也可能会理解成：广告是采用病毒文件发布的，只要用户的电脑感染，就会自动播放。其实"病毒式网络营销"的定义是："Viral marketing and viral advertising refer to marketing techniques that seek to exploit pre-existing social networks to produce exponential increases in brand awareness, through viral processes similar to the spread of an epidemic. It is word-of-mouth delivered and enhanced online; it harnesses the network effect of the Internet and can be very useful in reaching a large number of people rapidly."。因此，

可以根据"病毒式网络营销"的含义将这句话译成："其传播力和感染力之强，竟吸引了五百万封电子回信。"

5 Nike then aired TV spots contrasting Chinese-style team-oriented play with a more individualistic American style…   接着耐克又在电视上插播广告，使观众领略了强调集体配合的中式球风和提倡单打独斗的美式球风……

这句话中"team-oriented"和"more individualistic"很棘手。如果译成"团队为导向的"和"更加个人主义的"就感到很别扭，所以将其分别译成"强调集体配合的中式球风"和"提倡单打独斗的美式球风"比较符合汉语的表达习惯，因为我们常说"要发扬集体主义（团队）精神"，而"individualistic"在篮球比赛中正好表现为"单打独斗"。

6 hip-hop 嘻哈

嘻哈文化源于上世纪70年代美国黑人的一种街头说唱文化，英文中hip意指臀部，hop指单脚跳，hip-hop则是轻扭摆臀的意思。

7 The hip-hop message "connects the disparate elements of black cool culture and associates it with Nike"…   这种通过嘻哈音乐传递的信息"综合了黑人酷文化中的各种不同的元素，并且将这种文化与耐克联系在一起"……

最好将"the hip-hop message"意译成"这种通过嘻哈音乐传递的信息"。

8 Ogilvy & Mather   奥美广告公司

奥美是世界上最大的市场传播机构之一，与其他代理商相比，它服务于更多名列世界500强的客户，遍布5个以上的国家。

9 …and Nike softens it to make it more acceptable to Chinese.   ……耐克为了让中国人容易接受，把这种音乐改编得温和悦耳。

英语"soften"这个词不太好处理。考虑到hip-hop节奏感很强，比较刺耳，所以将"soften"意译为"把这种音乐改编得温和悦耳"。

10 Thanks in part to Nike's promotions…   由于耐克在某种程度上的大力宣传……

如果将"in part"和"thanks to"连起来译成"部分归功于"总觉得别扭，所以还是将"thanks to"译成"由于"或者"多亏"。另外，"promotions"是复数，因此翻译时加上了"大力"。

11 For most of China's history, this exchange would have been unthinkable.   在中国，从古到今晚辈很少有这样跟长辈说话的。

"For most of China's history"如果译成"中国历史上大部分时间"就不通顺，所以不如在后半句中用"很少"反过来表达"大部分"的含义。

12 the Asian banking crisis 亚洲金融危机

亚洲金融危机发生于1997年7月，由泰国开始，之后进一步影响了邻近亚洲国家的货币、股票市场和其他的资产价值。此危机的另一名称是"亚洲金融风暴"（常见于香港）。

13 In 1997, Nike ramped up production just before the Asian banking crisis killed demand, then

flooded the market with cheap shoes, undercutting its own retailers and driving many into the arms of Adidas. 1997年，耐克刚刚提高产量，亚洲金融危机的爆发就使需求量急剧下降，耐克只好以低廉的价格大量出售自己的鞋子，使自己的零售商损失惨重，逼得很大一部分投入了阿迪达斯的怀抱。

英语"just before the Asian banking crisis killed demand"不宜译成"亚洲金融危机严重降低需求之前"，而应该倒过来译成"耐克刚刚提高产量，亚洲金融危机的爆发就使需求量急剧下降"，这样才更加符合汉语的表达习惯。接下来再说"耐克只好……，使得……，逼得……"，更加表明"亚洲金融危机"的突然性。

14. Yet all that amounts to a frayed shoelace compared with losing China's most famous living human. 然而，这些遭遇加起来也只不过相当于一条磨破的鞋带而已，因为耐克遭受的最大的损失莫过于失去中国当今最有名气的人。

这个句子如果译成"而这一切加起来与失去中国当前最有名气的人相比只不过是（不啻为）一根破烂的鞋带"就显得过长，所以拆开翻译效果似乎好一些。

15. The failure leaves Nike executives visibly dejected. 这一失败显然让耐克的管理者非常沮丧。

英语"leave"是"to cause or allow to be or remain in a specified state"的意思，译成汉语的"让"非常贴切。"visibly"一词留在原处不好处理，将其提前修饰"让"就通顺了。

16. "signed"是"to hire or engage by obtaining a signature on a contract"（签约）的意思。"next NBA prospect"不能译成"下一个NBA希望之星"，这里只表明易建联可能成为下一个到NBA打球的球员，并不一定能成为NBA的明星球员。

17. Nike has cleaned up its shop floors. 耐克调整了生产能力。

"shop floors"是"工厂，车间"的意思。这里不能译成"打扫了车间"。根据上下文，应该理解成：金融危机爆发时，耐克的产量太大，所以供大于求，现在耐克根据市场需求调整了生产能力。

18. In fact, the company's celebration of American culture is totally in synch with the Chinese as they hurtle into a freer time. 事实上，随着中国进一步对外开放，人们的生活更加丰富多彩，耐克公司对美国文化的颂扬完全顺应了这一趋势。

这个句子中的"as they hurtle into a freer time"应该意译，因为"freer time"不容易理解，所以翻译时增加"随着中国进一步对外开放，人们的生活更加丰富多彩"，这样读者更好理解一些。

19. That sounds pretty close to a Chinese translation of "Just Do It". 这正是耐克那句经典广告词所要表达的内涵——"Just Do It"——只管去做！

"Just Do It"是耐克的广告词，为了让读者能够理解，翻译时必须增加对它的解释，所以将"pretty close to a Chinese translation of"意译成"正是耐克那句经典广告词所要表达的内涵"。

他山之石

原文 1：

Today the company (Starbucks) that weaned us away from the free mud in the office kitchen and hooked us on $3 tall double caramel machiatos (with nonfat milk, please) has 5,945 stores in the United States and 2,392 more overseas and in Canada.

原译：

而今，这家使我们抛弃办公室厨房里泥浆般的免费劣质咖啡，转而迷上它所提供的美味饮料——比如3美元一中杯加双份焦糖玛奇朵（请再加上脱脂奶）——的公司在美国拥有5 945家连锁店，在加拿大和其他国家还有2 392家店。

点评：

① 将"that"引导的定语从句译得过长，让人读起来喘不过气来。如果将定语从句拆译，不译成汉语的偏正结构，效果会好得多，比如放到主句后面。

② 英语"weaned us away"和"hooked us on"如果一定要对应地译成汉语的使动句，就会感到很别扭，因为两个动词都很难改动，只能译成"（星巴克）使我们抛弃了……，让我们迷上了……"。因此，能否考虑改换一个句式，将这层意思表达出来呢？

③ 将"free mud in the office kitchen"译成"办公室厨房里泥浆般的免费劣质咖啡"太模糊，几个形容词堆在一起，表达就会含混不清，所以应该在有些词前面增译一些动词或将某些词转换成别的词来解决这个问题。

改译：

如今，这家公司在美国拥有5 945家连锁店，在加拿大和其他国家还有2 392家。有了它，我们就不必天天免费饮用办公室厨房制作的泥浆般的劣质咖啡，而是时时想着星巴克提供的咖啡饮料——一中杯双份焦糖玛奇朵（再请加上脱脂奶）。

原文 2：

In managing risk, the most effective measure is to allocate resources reasonably. In case a loss does happen, people still can get repayments from other ways. Before doing so, people need to have enough data to support their decision. They need to know the level of overall risk to which people are routinely exposed and the level of safety that might be achieved through efforts before they determine what levels of risks are socially and economically tolerable. But people's ability to manage risk is often limited by a lack of adequate data and effective analyses.

原译：

在风险管理中，最有效的措施就是合理地分配资源。万一有一处发生损失，人们仍然可以从其他方面获得补偿。在这样做之前，人们需要获得足够的信息以证实他们所做的决定。在决定什么风险水平对社会和经济方面的影响是可以接受的之前，他们需要了解人们日常所面对的整个风险的水平和通过努力所能达到的安全水平。但人们管理风险的能力常常受到缺乏充分的信息和有效的分析的限制。

点评：

① "In case a loss does happen" 有强调的意味，译成"即便"比"万一"更准确。
② "Before doing so" 应该是指"合理地分配资源"。为了让读者便于理解，不能仅仅译成"在这样做之前"，应该更具体一些。
③ "need" 是"必须"的意思，不能译成"需要"。
④ "support their decision" 不是"证实他们所做的决定"，而是"帮他们做出正确的决定"。
⑤ "They need to know the level ... tolerable." 这句话很长。翻译时首先不能按英语的句式将"before"所引导的状语直接译成汉语的"在……之前"，而应该译成"必须先……，然后……"。
⑥ 三个"level"都译成"水平"，句子读起来相当别扭，而且意思也很抽象，能否译得具体一些呢？
⑦ 最后一句译成汉语的被动式"受到……限制"太拘泥原文的句式，不符合汉语的表达习惯。

改译：

风险管理最有效的措施是合理地分配资源。即便人们在某个方面遭受损失，他们还可以从其他方面得到补偿。但首先他们必须掌握足够的信息，以便他们进行决策。他们应该先了解人们通常容易遇到哪些风险，通过努力可以获得多少安全，然后据此判断出社会和经济能够承受多大的风险。然而，由于信息不足和缺乏有效的分析，人们管理风险的能力常常是有限的。

原文 3：

In addition, the need to produce goods and services at quality levels previously thought impossible to obtain in mass production and the spreading use of participatory management techniques will require a work force with much higher levels of education and skills.

原译：

另外，以前认为不可能在批量生产方式中获得的对优质产品和服务的需求及参与大型管理技巧的广泛使用，将会要求劳动力具有更高层次的教育和更高水平的技能。

点评：

① "need" 不能译成"需求"，因为在这里是"必要"、"必须"之意。
② "mass production" 译成"大规模流水作业"更加合适。
③ "a work force" 不宜译成"劳动力"，而要译成"工人们"。
④ "much higher levels" 同时修饰 "education" 和"技能"，译成汉语时搭配要恰当。
⑤ 过去分词 "previously thought…" 这一后置定语不宜译成汉语的偏正结构，因为这样使整个句子长而难懂，应该拆译成其他分句。
⑥ 如果整个句子的主语是 "need" 和 "the spreading use of"，那么译文除去定语就应该是"……需求及参与大型管理技巧的广泛使用，将会……"，中间的逗号用得不妥。

改译：

另外，人们从前认为，大规模流水化作业无法生产出优质产品和提供一流的服务，但企业要实现这一目标并且要采取流行的民主参与的方式进行管理，就必须提高工人们的教育水平和技术能力。

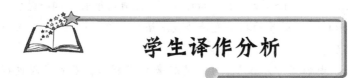

学生译作分析

原文 1：

We are part of one of the fastest growing markets that's ever existed, so it's very satisfying to see how we have been able to be successful in that environment and to see the way in which we are helping to change the nature of communications in the future, and I think that's both very exciting and very satisfying.

学生原译文：

我们处身于有史以来发展得最快的市场当中，看到我们在那样的外部环境中能获得成功并且我们的努力能给未来的信息通讯带来实质性变化，这是非常令人高兴的，我觉得这令人既激动又高兴。

分析：

(1) "the fastest growing markets that's ever existed" 中的"市场"应该是指"世界市场"，但如果按英语原句式将其译成汉语的偏正句，会感觉定语过长，因此可以考虑将"市场"作为句子的主语，这样句子就好译了。

(2) "very satisfying" 后的两个不定式 "to see" 不容易处理，如果译出来，哪怕只译一个，"看到"后面的句子就会很长，读起来较费劲，而且与后面的"这是……"

也无法搭配。怎么办？有两个办法：① 顺序译，省掉"to see"，将后面的"have been able to be successful"和"are helping to change the nature of communications"与前面的"身处"并列，最后仍用使动句并将两个"satisfying"合为一个；② 逆序译，把最后的感受提前，然后说明原因。

(3) "in that environment"就是指"in the fastest growing markets that's ever existed"，所以可以译成"发展中"，而不一定要译成"在那样的（外部）环境中"。

(4) "helping to change the nature of"的字面意思是"（帮助）改变……性质"，其实就是指"革命"。另外，"communications"指"通讯"，没有必要加上"信息"（information）。

(5) 因为是口头谈话，所以出现了"it's very satisfying"和"that's both very exciting and very satisfying"，二者不妨合二为一。

参考译文：

(1) 世界市场正以前所未有的速度发展，身处其中，我们获得了成功，并正努力促进未来通讯业的革命，这真让我倍感振奋和欣慰。

(2) 世界市场正以前所未有的速度发展，置身其中，我感到无比振奋和欣慰，因为我们在发展中取得了成绩，并正在为未来通讯业的革命发挥自己的作用。

原文 2：

Whether you are a supervisor, manager, or team leader, you lead people who must grow, and that growth can be managed! It is important to understand that you do not get paid for what *you* do; you get paid for what *your people* do. The performance appraisal provides you with the opportunity to direct your employees' attention to the things that really matter. You're judged on the results you're able to achieve, but these results must be achieved through others.

学生原译文：

无论你是高级管理阶层，还是一般管理人员或团队领导，带领的团队必须成长发展，而这种团队的发展是可以操纵的。作为管理阶层的你，你得到的酬劳并不是因为你做了什么具体工作。而是因为你的下属做出了一定的成绩所获，要明白这一点非常重要。业绩评估使你有机会调整评估你的雇员对重大事情的态度，对你所获取的成果进行评判。但这些成果必须通过他人实现。

分析：

(1) "a supervisor, manager, or team leader"有层次，从高到低，可以更具体一些。

(2) 绩效评估往往是针对个人，所以将"people who must grow"译成"队员"或者"下属"比"团队"更贴切。既然是个人，"grow"就可以译成"成长"或者"进步"，而且"must"译成"必须"不通顺，译成"必然"才符合汉语的习惯。

(3) "… and that growth can be managed!"这个被动态强调某种性质，后面用的又是感

叹号，所以可以将其译成汉语中的"是……的"句型，但"manage"不宜译成"操纵"；因为汉语一般不说"操纵某人的成长、进步或发展"。

(4) "It is important to understand" 在这段文字中还是放在句首比较合适，因为这样可以与上文自然地对接。如果放到句尾，句子之间的连贯性就比较差。

(5) 注意"for what you do"和"for what your people do"中的"you"和"your people"都是斜体，这里是强调，所以翻译时应该把语气译出来。

(6) "direct"应该译成"引导"，而不是"调整"，译文"调整评估你的雇员对重大事情的态度，对你所获取的成果进行评判"显然让读者不知所云。这里的意思是：通过绩效评估正确引导员工，让他们明白工作中什么是最重要的。英语句子中的主语是"the performance appraisal"，译成汉语时不宜用原句式。

(7) 最后一句"You're judged on the results you're able to achieve, but these results must be achieved through others."似乎与上面的句子关联不大，但实际上还是在强调你的工作业绩与员工工作的好坏有着密切的联系。翻译时应该保持整个段落意思的完整，避免读者误解。

参考译文：

不论你的职位是公司领导、部门经理还是业务主管，你的下属都必然要进步和成长，而这种进步和成长是能够进行管理的！重要的是你应该明白，你得到酬劳并不是因为你自己具体做了什么，而是因为你下属的工作成绩突出。你可以通过业绩评估引导员工把握工作中的重点。因此，尽管人们可以根据你的工作业绩来评价你，但这些成绩却离不开员工的表现。

翻译技巧介绍

定语从句的翻译
(Translating Attributive Clauses)

一、前置

1. 短句

英语中的定语从句分限制性和非限制性两种，在句子中有的修饰某个词，有的修饰某个句子。定语从句有短有长，短的定语从句（无论限制性还是非限制性）比较好处理，因为其结构跟汉语基本相同，只是位置不同，翻译时可以将它放在它所修饰的名词前面。

(1) Many developing countries continue to export the traditional commodities **for which**

they have always been known, like copper from Zambia, tea from India and Sri Lanka, tin from Malaysia and Indonesia, bananas from Central America.

译文：许多发展中国家继续在出口**一向闻名的**传统产品，如赞比亚的紫铜、印度和斯里兰卡的茶、马来西亚和印尼的锡、中美洲的香蕉。

（2）Customers faced with many unknown factors on the wide-ranging Internet look for products **which have credibility** and for retail names **which will provide them with security of purchase**.

译文：由于互联网信息繁杂，未知因素太多，所以购物者自然要寻找信得过的产品和**让人放心的**零售商。

（3）Gasoline has also jumped higher after the massive electricity blackouts in the US, closed production at seven refineries, hurting supplies, **which are already thin**.

译文：汽油价格也在美国大停电以后攀升，那次停电使7家炼油厂停产，打击了**本来就已经紧张的**汽油供给。

（4）In those comments, Finns heard an executive **whom they feared** may be ready to bull out of the country, jeopardizing the tax base **that supports the state's extensive welfare benefits**.

译文：芬兰人从那些话语中听出，他们**所敬畏的**一位总经理可能准备努力在国外求得发展，此举会危及**支撑这个国家巨额福利金的**税收基础。

（5）In nations **where failure to pay debts confers personal shame**, the bankrupt often lose the will to work, scrimp, or plan.

译文：在**那些因无法偿还债务会带来个人耻辱的**国家，破产往往使人失去工作、节俭和制定计划的意愿。

（6）A lot of shops advertise goods **that are not selling well**.

译文：许多商家为**销路不畅的**产品做广告。

（7）Shops cater for the do-it-yourself craze not only by running special advisory services for novices, but by offering consumers bits and pieces **which they can assemble at home**.

译文：为了迎合这种"自己动手热"，商店不仅专门为新手开设了咨询服务，而且还为顾客提供**可以在家里进行装备的**各种零件。

2. 长句

英语中有些定语从句可能很长，但与前面所修饰的部分结合得很紧，如果拆开翻译就会影响整个句子的意思。这类定语从句也可以直接译成汉语的偏正结构，将定语放置在所修饰的部分前面。

（1）It is easy enough for a director to retire, but the likelihood is that he will want to cash in on his shares **which have accumulated some value over the period of his** participation in the business.

译文:一个董事退休很容易,但他可能希望卖掉他在公司任职期间已升值的股份。

(2) The convention provides that damages for breach of contract consist of a sum equal to the loss, including loss of profit suffered by the injured party as a consequence of the breach, and the damages may not exceed the loss **which the party in breach foresaw or ought to have foreseen at the time of the conclusion of the contract**, in the light of the facts and matters of **which he then knew or ought to have known**.

译文:"公约"规定,违约的赔偿金额应等同于另一方当事人因违约所遭受的包括利润在内的损失金额,而且,守约方得到的损失赔偿,不得超出**违约方在订立合同时,按照他当时已知或理应知道的情况对违约预料到或理应预料到的**可能损失。

(3) The customer can gain goods or services by showing his card to a store, a hotel or a restaurant **that has pre-arrangement with the issuing bank to accept credit cards**.

译文:客户可凭此卡到**与发卡银行签订接受信用卡协定的**商店、宾馆或餐馆购物或获取服务。

(4) In reality, a commercial bank, as a financial institution, is an enterprise **that deals in money with loans being its assets and deposits being its liabilities**.

译文:实际上,一家商业银行,作为一个金融机构,是一个**把贷款资金作为资产,把存款资金作为负债的**企业。

(5) Corporation universities (CU) can be described as institutional mechanisms **that tie together the strategic development of organization with the development of its human resources**.

译文:公司大学(CU)可以被描述为**将公司的战略发展与其人力资源的发展结合起来的**具有公共机构特征的组织。

(6) Both companies' flagship colas, **which together account for 1 of every 3 sodas sold in the US** lost share last year.

译文:**占美国苏打水销售量1/3 的**两家公司的拳头品牌可乐,去年都失去了一些市场份额。

(7) Even Japan, **whose economy has been stagnant for a decade**, has seen its Morgan Stanley stock index rise 2,166% in the same period.

译文:即使**在10年来经济一直停滞不前的**日本,其摩根斯坦利股票指数同期涨幅也达到了2 160%。

(8) Current weakness in the US dollar is partly to blame as well as the SARS virus, **which also dampened sales in Asia of Gucci's glamorous bags, fashion goods and perfumes**.

译文:这部分归罪于美元目前的疲软走势,还有使古奇公司迷人的手包、时尚用品和香水的销量在亚洲市场受挫的非典病毒。

二、后置

1. 短句

有些定语从句虽然很短,而且从形式上看也多属于限制性的定语从句,但与前面所修饰的部分结合得并不很紧,往往是对前面的词或者句子补充说明。这类定语从句译成汉语时可以用并列谓语或并列分句顺着往下说,或者另起一句。

(1) The desire that men feel to increase their income is quite as much a desire for success as for the extra comforts **that a higher income can obtain**.

译文:人们希望增加收入的愿望,同他们希望获得成功、希望**高收入能带来**特别舒适的愿望非常相似。

(2) After dinner, the four key negotiators resumed their business talks **which continued well into the night**.

译文:饭后,四个主要谈判人继续进行贸易谈判,**一直谈到深夜**。

(3) The mission of marketers is to provide people with the products and services **that give them the means to fulfill needs at every level**.

译文:营销人员的任务就是为人们提供产品和服务,**使其满足人们各个层次的生活需求**。

(4) Also in June last year, Chinese government took firm measures to stop the unusual and dangerous increase in stock market, and avoided a more severe crisis, **which shows the power of the government in dealing with risks**.

译文:去年6月,中国政府采取果断措施阻止了股票市场中不正常且危险的上涨,从而避免了一场更严重的危机,**这表明了政府在风险管理方面所具有的能力**。

(5) If you feel your budget, worked out as 3% of turnover, is too small for large impact advertising, you could decide on a size **which gives you good frequency**.

译文:如果你觉得占营业额3%的广告预算太小,无法起到巨大的宣传作用,你可以在广告的篇幅上做文章,**提高广告的频率**。

(6) Last year it brought out Diet Coke with lemon, **which has done reasonably well**, and the company is now gearing up to launch Vanilla Coke.

译文:去年它推出了含柠檬的健怡可乐,**成绩相当不错**,现在公司正加紧推出香草可乐。

(7) Most international sales contracts contain a claim clause **in which the principles, time and applicable law of remedy are provided**.

译文:多数国际货物买卖合同都包含索赔条款,**其中规定了补救的原则、时间和适用的法规**。

2. 长句

有些定语从句很长，形式上既有限制性的，也有非限制性的，而且有些从句中又包含了一个或几个定语从句，翻译这类定语从句时一般可就地处理，多采用重复前面的先行词，省掉关系代词或关系副词，甚至译成汉语的连动式。

(1) It was always the case that a company could not acquire its own share, because in doing so it was obtaining ownership of itself, **which is contrary to the most fundamental legal principles surrounding the nature and existence of companies.**

译文：总存在这样的情况：一个公司不能买自身的股份，因为这样做是取得自身的所有权，**这样做违背有关公司性质和存在的最根本的法律原则**。

(2) This will be particularly true since energy pinch will make it difficult to continue agriculture in the high-energy American fashion **that makes it possible to combine few farmers with high yields.**

译文：这种困境将是确定无疑的，因为能源的匮乏使农业无法以高能消耗这种美国耕作方式继续下去，**而这种耕作方式可以投入少数农民就获得高产**。

(3) The international business community has high hopes that staging the games will be a catalyst, **which will open up the market in the same way the Seoul and Korea games did.**

译文：国际商界殷切期望这次奥运会的筹办过程能**成为启动市场的催化剂，就像汉城奥运会一样**。

(4) This is particularly true of the countries of the commonwealth, **who see Britain's membership of the Community a guarantee** that the policies of the community will take their interests into account.

译文：英联邦各国尤其如此，**它们认为英国加入欧共体**将能保证欧共体的政策照顾到它们的利益。

(5) BA says it will impose the controversial electronic clocking-in system, **which was the reason behind the unofficial walk-out on Friday which lead to five days of chaos for thousands of travelers.**

译文：英航声称它将引入备受争议的电子打卡系统，这正是导致星期五非正式罢工的内在原因，那次事件造成的五天混乱影响了成千上万的旅客。

(6) For the conservative investor, a good option is a fund-of-funds such as the Momentum All Weather Fund, **which invests in nearly 30 hedge funds that follow different strategies and operate in various markets.**

译文：对保守的投资者来说，一个不错的选择是像"动量多头空头基金"这样的雨伞基金，它投资于近 30 种对冲基金，这 30 种基金运用不同的策略在不同的市场进行运作。

（7）A giant department store chain in America always promotes garden plants and house paint in Spring **when customers are about to tidy up the garden for summer and renovate their houses**. The same chain store advertises its tents in June, **when people will be going camping for the summer holiday**.

译文：美国的大百货连锁店总是**在春天顾客即将为夏天的到来收拾花园、修整房子时**，推销园艺植物和刷房涂料；在六月份**人们要去野营度假时**，为帐篷做广告。

（8）Trade friction is channeled into the WTO's dispute settlement process **where the focus is on interpreting agreements and commitments, and how to ensure that countries' trade policies conform with them**.

译文：贸易摩擦由世界贸易组织协调解决，**主要是解释签订的协议和应尽的义务，并且确保成员国遵守相应的贸易政策**。

三、融合

有时一个句子中可能连续出现两个或者两个以上的定语从句，这时如果一个定语从句既不能前置，又不容易原地处理，就不妨打乱句子的顺序，将修饰作用强、意思联系较紧的译成前置，将补充说明一类的译成后置；有时甚至改变原句子的结构，将某个定语从句提前，以便后面的句子容易安排；还可以采用词类转换法，将有的定语从译成其他成分；甚至可以将其中一个定语从句译成另一个单独的句子。

（1）McDonald's, the American fastfood giant **which imports beef for the hamburgers which it is selling in a growing number of Chinese outlets**, is also interested in this New Zealand meat company.

译文：麦当劳是美国的快餐业巨头，**随着它设在中国的分销店日益增多，这家靠进口牛肉制作汉堡销售的饮食企业**也瞄上了这家新西兰肉品生产商。

（2）One of the main disadvantages of a long, complex sentence, **which may still be found in some business correspondence** despite the progress **that has been made in recent years** towards simplifying business writing styles in the English-speaking world, is that the reader is likely to find it more difficult to understand than a series of shorter sentences, **which in turn may lead to frustration and misunderstanding**, particularly if the reader is a busy person **who has more important things to do**.

译文：近年来，人们在用英语书写商务信函时已**基本趋向简明的风格**，但长而复杂的句子**仍然时而可见**。这类句子的一个主要缺点是：读者，尤其是**其他要务缠身**的读者，可能会觉得复杂的长句比一串短句更加费解，**很容易使他们感到灰心并产生错误的理解**。

(3) Tax cuts planned for next year, **which had been welcomed by consumers** will result in an extra shortfall of 15 billion Euros **which the Bundesbank say must be met by cuts in Government spending**.

译文：计划明年实施的减税**受到消费者的欢迎**，但会带来 150 亿欧元的额外亏空。德国央行说，**这必须靠削减政府开支来弥补**。

(4) Some policies also carry disability provisions, **which will pay insured individuals should they be unable to work because of extended illness or permanent physical disability**.

译文：某些保单还载明失去工作能力的条款，只要投保人因长期患病或永久性残废而失去了工作能力，保险公司将负责赔偿。

四、译成汉语的状语

为了行文流畅，符合汉语的表达习惯，翻译时可以根据上下文将英语中的很多定语从句译成汉语的状语分句，用来表示谓语动作发生的原因、目的、条件、让步、方式和结果等。

(1) If you are using newspaper advertising, rather than take out just one full page advertisement **which your advertising budget affords for the year**, you could decide to buy four quarter page advertisements or eight one-eight pages.

译文：如果是在报纸上做广告，你可以买 1/4 广告版或 1/8 广告版，而不是把整个广告版都买下，**尽管你的全年广告预算负担得起**。（表示让步）

(2) The Levis jeans, **which are quite out of fashion**, are still selling well in this area.

译文：利维斯牛仔裤**虽然已完全过时**，但在这个地区仍然畅销。（表示让步）

(3) Once you have a core position, look around for satellite investments **that may spice up your portfolio**.

译文：有了主导的投资品种，打量着再做一些附属投资，**就可能给你的投资组合带来更大的胜算**。（表示结果）

(4) If there are more purchases than sales on it, **which render its price up**, it is called "Bull Market".

译文：一旦某股票（商品）的买盘大于卖盘，（从而）**使该股票（商品）的价格上升**，就被称为"牛市"。（表示结果）

(5) Many borrowers wish to raise funds by way of bond issuance, especially those **who seek for funds in international security centers, where lots of capital are aggregated**. In such a case, it is generally characterized by the borrower's selling of bonds to buyers outside his country and the selection of a currency **in which the buyers (bond investors) purchase the bonds and the borrower repays his debt under the bonds**.

译文：许多借款人希望通过发行债券筹措资金，尤其是**希望在国际债券交易中心**

发行，因为大量的资金聚集在那里。在那里发行债券，一般以借款人向国外的债券买主出售债券为特征，并要确定某种货币，**投资者购买债券和借款人偿付债券项下的债务，都以这种货币进行**。（表示原因、方式）

(6) But he did not talk at length about the matter, **which was not considered by the White House to be a particularly important question**.

译文：但他并没有详细地谈到这件事，因为白宫没有把这件事看作是一个特别重要的问题。（表示原因）

(7) She wishes to write an article **that will attract public attention to the matter**.

译文：她想写篇文章，以便引起公众对这件事的注意。（表示目的）

(8) A graph of business turnover should be matched by the graph of the advertising budget, and if a business has the opposite point of view—it wants to advertise in October in a way **that would increase turnover in October**—it might mean changing the advertising budget flow away from the pattern of turnover.

译文：营业额图表应与广告速算图表相称。如果商家持相反的观点——想在10月份做广告**以增加10月份的营业额**——那么这将意味着使广告速算的支出与营业额脱节。（表示方式）

(9) Many people become desperate for work, any work, **which will help them to keep alive their families**.

译文：人们极其迫切地要求工作，不管什么工作，只要能维持一家人的生活就行。（表示条件）

(10) While it is not quite the days of the dot-com boom, **when companies lured graduates with promises of six-figure salaries and ping-pong tables in the workplace**, corporate recruiters are once again combing campuses for the best of the Class of 2005.

译文：在网络经济繁荣之时，很多公司曾许以毕业生六位数的薪水、办公区域有乒乓球桌的承诺，来招聘新员工。虽然现在远不能与那时相比，但是各个公司的招聘人员又一次蜂拥至大学校园，搜寻2005届的优秀毕业生。（表示时间）

同位语从句的翻译
(Translating Appositive Clauses)

同位语从句虽然在意思上跟定语从句有区别，但在翻译成汉语时可以采取与定语从句翻译一样的方法，即译成汉语的偏正结构，转译成其他词类或译成独立的分句。

(1) Commerce's other masterstroke was to stick with the bank branch concept in the dotcom boom **when every other bank was trying to coax customers on to the web**.

译文：商业银行的另一个高招是：**在其他所有银行力图诱劝客户上网办理业务的银行网站热中，它仍坚持银行分行的理念。**

(2) The advent of the hybrid mall is a sure sign **that retailers realize that some shoppers have grown tried of the sameness and artificiality of indoor malls.**

译文：混合购物中心的出现是一个确实的信号，**它表明，零售商已经意识到一些购物者对室内购物中心的人造氛围和千篇一律越来越厌倦。**

(3) But we spent six to eight months looking at appliance markets around the world and came to the conclusion that **the consumers and the technology weren't all that different.**

译文：但我们花了6到8个月的时间考察全球各地的家电市场，并得出结论：**世界各地的消费者和技术并没有太大的不同。**

(4) To snatch opportunity, you must spot the signals **that it is time to conquer the new markets, add products or perhaps franchise your hot ideas.**

译文：你想抓住机遇，就得发现各种信号，**如开发新市场的时刻到了，增添新产品或者是抢先推销你的新点子的时刻到了。**

课堂翻译训练

将下列句子译成汉语。

1. The joint venture's marketing is being done by staff from Wu Liang Ye who aim to make good use of the white spirit maker and wine importer's distribution network which goes into 8,000 hotels and restaurants.

2. We Britain rely more than any other major economy on the goods and services that we export, the investment that we attract and we make abroad.

3. With a history of decades, credit cards are at present widely used in many countries as a popular banking instrument which is greatly contributory to the booming development of tourism and commercial and economic communications.

4. The committee prepared this paper because its members recognized that the government has failed to establish an energy policy capable of providing a comprehensive energy source mix that can meet our requirements for the last portion of this century and the greater portion of the next.

5. Spying is rife in consumer product industries where the timing of a $100 million marketing campaign and a product launch can be crucial to success of failure.
6. The company is also switching the balance of its products, from the primarily craft and gift image which still occupies the majority of its catalogue, to more utilitarian products and foodstuffs.
7. The change met the technical requirement of the new age and prevented the decline in efficiency that so commonly spoiled the fortunes of family firms in the second and third generation after the energetic founders.
8. As imports are financed by exports, which help to gain foreign currency to import the badly needed raw materials, technology and equipment, the capacity of a nation to import obviously depends on its export performance.
9. In America, which seems overwhelmed by advertisements and commercials, people are fed up with the propaganda, but nobody can do or wants to do anything about it.
10. Entrepreneurs (企业家移民) must have the intention and ability to establish, purchase or make a substantial investment in a business in Canada that will contribute significantly to the economy and create jobs.

将下列短文译成英语，注意运用本单元所学的翻译技巧。

1.

GM CEO Rick Wagoner is acutely aware of his company's decaying state. He may have the toughest job in corporate America—preventing the world's largest automaker from going under. Wagoner outlined his plan last week, announcing a restructuring that will result in GM's producing 1 million fewer vehicles a year and, he hopes, saving $7 billion annually (GM's sales last year: $193.5 billion). Wagoner has been vigorously trying to crush rumors that GM will seek a bailout in bankruptcy court, following the path of troubled airlines and steel companies. "I'd like to just set the record straight here and now," he wrote in a letter to GM employees. "There is absolutely no plan, strategy or intention for GM to file for bankruptcy."

It's a testament to how bad GM's problems are that Wagoner had to write such a letter. GM is a shell of the company that a half-century ago controlled nearly half the US car market and was such a powerhouse that company executives told Congress they didn't want to cut the price of a Chevy because it might drive the competition out of business. With some 324,000 employees worldwide, GM remains a giant, influencing everything from the price of plastics and steel to the market for mortgages, through its GMAC finance division (part of which may soon be sold). Yet GM can't seem to make money in its core business, manufacturing automobiles at home. In the first nine months of this year, GM's North American operations lost $4.8 billion. Its market share has sunk from 40% in 1984 to a low of 26.1% this year.

GM's decline, which goes back to the energy crisis of the 1970s, has been accelerating lately, compounded by competition from Japanese and Korean brands, another burst of high gasoline prices, the bankruptcy of its largest parts supplier, Delphi, in Troy, Mich., and perhaps most critically, a glut of SUVs and sedans. For all those reasons, Wall Street is discounting GM's chances of survival. Bearish analysts say there's a 40% chance the company will go bust in a couple of years. "The forces working on the auto industry—not just on GM—are gigantic," says Gerald Meyers, a former chairman of American Motors Corp. "GM's future is undoubtedly going to be one of shrinking."

How does GM get out of this mess without a trip through bankruptcy court, which could conceivably lead to a breakup of its storied brands? The company's problems run so deep that only a major overhaul could do the job—and then only if a smooth road lies ahead. Wagoner is getting plenty of advice about how to fix things, from cutting GM's $1.1 billion stock dividend to demanding deeper wage-and-benefit cuts from hourly workers. A confrontation over labor issues is looming, in fact, since GM's contract with the United Auto Workers (U.A.W.) expires in September 2007. Until then, Wagoner seems to be gambling that the company can stay afloat via a series of tune-ups, ranging from having workers bear more health-care costs (annual savings: $3 billion) to eliminating weak models and launching redesigned SUVs and pickups next year—and praying that high gasoline prices don't bog down the plan. Plenty of skeptics believe Wagoner's plan is too limited. "If you have an earthquake and a building falls on someone's leg and he's stuck, you amputate his leg" says Jim Matheson, a management professor at Stanford University. "That's what GM has done." Analysts say GM needs to downsize far more dramatically. Here's what auto experts believe GM will have to do to fix itself.

2.

"What on earth is mechanism design?" was the typical reaction to this year's Nobel prize in economics, announced on October 15th. In this era of "Freakonomics", in which everyone is discovering their inner economist, economics has become unexpectedly sexy. So what possessed the Nobel committee to honor a subject that sounds so thoroughly dismal? Why didn't they follow the lead of the peace-prize judges who know not to let technicalities about being true to the meaning of the award get in the way of good headlines?

In fact, despite its dreary name, mechanism design is a hugely important area of economics, and underpins much of what dismal scientists do today. It goes to the heart of one of the biggest challenges in economics: how to arrange our economic interactions so that, when everyone behaves in a self-interested manner, the result is something we all like. The word "mechanism" refers to the institutions and the rules of the game that govern our economic activities, which can range from a Ministry of Planning in a command economy to the internal organization of a company to trading in a market.

Leonid Hurwicz, Eric Maskin and Roger Myerson won their third-shares of the $1.5m prize for shaping a branch of economics that has had a broad impact, both in academia, in subjects such as incentive theory, game theory and the political science of institutions, and in the real world. It affects everything from utility regulation and auctions to structuring the pay of company executives and the design of elections.

Mechanism-design theory aims to give the invisible hand a helping hand, in particular by focusing on how to minimize the economic cost of "asymmetric information"—the problem of dealing with someone who knows more than you do. Trading efficiently under asymmetric information is hard, for how do you decide what price to offer someone for something—a product, say, or their labor—if you do not know at what price they would sell it? On the one hand, you may not offer enough to get them to deliver the product or work, or at least do so adequately; on the other, you may overpay, wasting resources that might have been better used elsewhere.

佳译赏析

Nine Roads to Riches
生财九道

From *Asiaweek*, November 23, 2001

By Cesar Bacani

The secret to long-term wealth is stocks, stocks and stocks.[1] Diversifying into bonds, hedge funds and works of art is also a sensible ploy.
长期致富的秘诀何在？股票，除了股票还是股票。此外，投资各种债券、对冲基金及艺术品也不失为明智的赚钱手段。

1. Buy bargain blue chips
　　买进低价的蓝筹股

If you look at Morgan Stanley International's Far East index[2], you'll find that it has returned 2,100% in capital gains since its inception[3] in December 1969 — an average of nearly 70% a year. Even Japan, whose economy has been stagnant for a decade, has seen its Morgan Stanley stock index rise 2,166% in the same period. Hong Kong? Up 2,872% over three decades despite its descent into recession this year.[4]
如果看一下摩根斯坦利国际（远东）指数，你就会发现，该指数自1969年12月的基准日到现在，已经获得了2100%的资本收益——平均一年将近70%。即使在10年来经济一直停滞不前的日本，其摩根斯坦利股票指数同期涨幅也达到了2166%。香港？虽然今年的经济出现了滑坡，在过去30年里，该指数同样创造了高达2872%的收益。

In the US, the Dow Jones Industrial Average[5] has soared from around 40 points, when the index was established in 1896, to about 9,700 points last week. Many crises have hit the New York Stock Exchange — the Great Depression of 1929[6], the bombing of Pearl Harbor in 1941[7], the Black October crash in 1987[8], and now, the terrorist attacks on New York and the Pentagon on Sept. 11[9]. Each time the Dow dropped like a stone — only to bounce back to greater heights.[10]

在美国，道琼斯工业平均指数已从 1896 年编制时起的 40 点左右攀升至上周（2001 年 11 月中旬左右）的 9 700 点附近。纽约证券交易所曾遭受过各种危机的打击——1929 年的经济大萧条，1941 年的偷袭珍珠港事件，1987 年的"黑色十月"股市崩盘，以及现在，今年 9 月 11 日，纽约和五角大楼遭到恐怖分子的袭击。每一次危机发生的时候，道琼斯指数都出现了"跳水"——但最终又出现反弹并创出新高。

The lesson: Anchor your portfolio in top stocks — known as "blue chips" in many markets - and hang on to them. Accumulate more shares when there's blood in the streets.[11] "Good quality companies are always the first to turn around when the market rebounds[12]," says Peter Reichenbach, managing director of Swiss-based Gottardo Asset Management[13]. "I'd suggest global blue chips. With internationally strong companies[14], you don't have to worry that they won't be around next year." In addition to direct holdings in blue chips, consider exchange-traded funds[15]. These are listed vehicles that invest in index constituents.[16]

忠告：把你的有价证券投资组合集中在一流股票上（许多市场称其为"蓝筹股"）并紧握不放。市场出现"割肉"时收集更多这样的股票。总部设在瑞士的高特多资产管理公司的总经理彼得·雷千巴克说："市场一旦出现反弹，绩优公司的股价总是率先反转。我主张选购全球性的蓝筹股。持有国际一流公司的股票，你就不愁来年他们不会有突出的表现。"除了直接持有蓝筹股，还可以考虑购买交易所交易基金。这种基金在交易所挂牌交易，并专门投资指数样板股上市公司。

2. Get steady income from cash payers[17]
从派现中获得稳定的收入

There's no better proof of a company's strong fundamentals than the evidence of the dividends it pays out year after year.[18] Small-cap companies often grant the highest and most consistent payouts. At HK$3.20 per share, Hung Hing Printing boasts a dividend yield of nearly 9%[19], while Kingmaker Footwear, at HK$1.40, yields 6.7%. Because they have been sold down, some blue chips now have substantial dividend yields, too.[20] Hang Seng Bank in Hong Kong, Indonesian cigarette maker Gudang Garam and Philippine liquor manufacturer La TondeNa each have a cash return of 6%.

一家公司是否实力雄厚，关键看它每年分给股东多少红利。一些流通盘比较小的公司经常能带来最多和最稳定的回报。宏兴印业的每股市价为 3.20 港元,值得一提的是该公司的派息率接近 9%;而每股股价 1.40 港元的信星集团也有 6.7% 的派息率;一些蓝筹股因价格很低而导致现在的派息率也很可观。香港的恒生银行、印尼烟草制造商盐仓集团及菲律宾烈酒制造商馨泉的派息率都达到了 6%。

3. Lower your risk with bread-and-butter companies
   投资生活必需品公司可降低投资风险

In good times and bad, people have to eat, use water and electricity, take medicine and travel to work and school. [21] Companies that provide these basic services may be boring, but they are dependable investments. [22] That's assuming they do not stray from their core business. A power utility that has sunk money in Internet ventures, for example, has taken on risk that the investor has to take into account.

不论世道好坏,人们总得吃饭、用水用电、吃药和乘车上班上学。提供这类基本服务的公司可能很平常,但其股票却是可靠的投资品种。当然,前提条件是这类公司不偏离它们的主业。例如,一家公用电力事业公司把钱投在因特网企业上,那显然是在冒险,投资者就不得不慎重考虑了。

Power generators and distributors are the havens of choice in uncertain times. [23] Investors have been bidding up their stock price even before Sept. 11 on fears of a global economic recession. "They've outperformed in the last 18 months," notes Markus Rosgen of ING Barings[24] in Hong Kong. "By the second half of next year, when the global economy is expected to recover, they won't be able to increase very much."

当经济形势不稳时,发电站与送配电公司是首选的避风港。即使在 9·11 之前,由于担心全球经济出现衰退,投资者仍在不断炒高这类公司的股价。"这些公司在过去 18 个月里出尽了风头。"香港霸菱集团的马尔库斯·罗斯根指出,"来年的下半年——到那时,全球经济可望复苏——这些股票就不会再有多大的涨幅了。"

Rosgen also likes oil-dependent firms like Hong Kong airline Cathay Pacific. "These companies are cyclical, so as soon as demand comes back up, they'll rebound quickly." People may have fear of flying now, but air travel is still essential.

像香港国泰航空公司这种石油依赖型公司也在罗斯根所喜爱的公司之列。"这类公司的周期性十分明显,因此一旦重新出现需求,它们将很快反弹。"人们现在可能对乘坐飞机感到害怕,但航空旅行是不可缺少的。

Companies in food, medicine and household products are also good bets. "Pharmaceuticals are

always a stable choice," says Norman Chan, head of research at financial adviser Allen Perkins in Hong Kong.
生产食品、药品和家用制品的公司也值得一搏。香港理财公司艾伦·珀金斯市场调研经理诺尔曼·陈说："医药类股票总是一种稳定的选择。"

Mark Monson, head of fund management for Gottardo Asset Management, favors Japan's Takeda Chemicals, which makes medicines, and Kao, the country's biggest maker of detergents. "It's the Japanese Procter & Gamble," he says. Monson praises the two companies for their excellent management, strong brands and dominant market share.[25]
高特多资产管理公司基金管理部经理马克·默恩森偏爱日本的武田药业（生产药品）和花王公司（日本最大的洗涤剂生产商），他说："花王是日本的宝洁公司。"默恩森对这两家公司的优良的管理手段、强大的名牌效应和优势的市场份额极为赞赏。

4. Security-oriented firms can be good short-term bets
国防类股票是很好的短期投资品种

But don't hold them too long. "Security and defense-oriented companies are definitely a good buy[26]," says Gottardo managing director Reichenbach. "They will benefit from increased spending. But they're probably one-off investments.[27]" Warns Rosgen: "People always over exaggerate the potential of safety and security companies when something terrible happens. A few months later, everything is forgotten." Adds Chan: "If the global economy does turn around next year, these stocks could suffer.[28]"
但持有的时间不宜太长。"安全和防务类公司价格低廉，绝对值得投资，"高特多资产管理公司总经理雷千巴克这样说："这些公司将从不断增长的国防开支中受益，但这种股票可能不宜长期持有。"罗斯根警告说："每当有灾难性事件发生，人们总是过度夸大安全和防务类公司的潜力。几个月过后，一切都不再被人提起。"陈补充道："如果明年全球经济真的出现转机，这类股票的价格很可能会走弱。"

5. Ride enterprises at the forefront of China's still booming economy
投资于发展势头不减的中国经济最前沿的上市公司

Almost everyone is bullish on the mainland, which was finally admitted into the World Trade Organization (WTO) last week. "China is the only growing major area in the world," says Chan. "It shouldn't be affected too much by a global recession, as long as the US doesn't completely collapse."
中国最终于上周被接纳为世界贸易组织（WTO）的成员，几乎所有人都对中国内地的经济充满信心。陈说:"中国是世界上唯一经济增长的重要区域。只要美国不完全瘫痪,中国应该不会过多地遭受到全球经济衰退的影响。"

The key is to focus on consumer-oriented companies because exporters are even now getting hit by the global recession. That means retailers, car makers, telecom providers — and even power utilities, because electricity usage in factories and homes will continue surging in an economy that is expanding at 7% or higher every year. But choose carefully. While WTO membership will bring a wave of foreign capital, it will also open the doors to foreign competition.[29]

由于外贸公司现在仍然受到全球经济衰退的打击,所以关键是要把目光集中在那些消费导向型的公司身上。比如零售企业、汽车制造商、电信服务运营商——甚至电力公司,因为在每年以7%甚或更高的增长速度扩张的经济环境下,工厂和家庭的用电量必将持续上涨。但选择时请三思而后行。虽然加入WTO后外资将大量涌入,但中国同时也要开放国门面对国外同行的竞争。

6. Diversify into selected bonds
把资金分散投资于各种精选的债券

No portfolio should be 100% in stocks, and bonds with reasonable yields are better alternatives to bank deposits — and are nearly as safe. Consider the long-term debt of blue chips like Hong Kong's Hutchison Whampoa. Many long-dated corporate bonds have fallen in price as international investors sold them in favor of US Treasuries. At one point last month, Hutchison's bonds maturing in 2011 traded at 230 points over US Treasuries.

不能把你的资金全部投放在股票上,况且一些能够带来一定收益的债券相对于银行存款来说还是一种比较好的选择——而且几乎跟银行存款一样安全。这方面可以关注一下像香港和记黄埔这样的蓝筹股公司的长期债券。由于国际投资者卖掉公司债券转而购买美国国债,所以许多公司的长期债券价格都已下跌。上个月的某个时候,和记公司2011年到期的长期债券交易价比美国国债高出230点。

7. Hedge funds provide safety nets in bad times
市场不好时对冲基金提供安全的净利

Previously available only to millionaires, hedge funds are now within the reach of ordinary investors for as low as $30,000. That's the minimum subscription for AHL Diversified Futures[30] in Hong Kong, which uses sophisticated computer programs to hunt for differences in the prices of futures instruments in different markets.[31] It's up 23% so far this year. "Hedge funds are not hugely exciting, but that's what's good about them," says David Chapman, senior manager of regional financial adviser Towry Law's asset management division. In good times and bad, he says, "they generate steady returns of 10% to 12% a year, and in some cases, 15%." Hedge funds typically take long positions on some securities, shorting others. They won't win big, but they won't lose hugely either.

以前仅仅百万富翁们才能购买的对冲基金，如今普通投资者只要能拿出3万美元便可以拥有。如香港的AHL多元化管理期货（另类）基金，3万美元是最低的认购额。该基金运用复杂的计算机程序在各种市场上寻找不同的期货产品进行投资并博取差价。今年到目前为止，它已上升了23%。"对冲基金不会令人倍感刺激，但那正是它们的好处"，地区财务咨询公司罗德利理财资产管理部的高级经理戴维·查普曼如是说："它们一年能给你带来10%到12%的稳定收入，有时能达到15%。"对冲基金典型的操作手法是做多一些证券，做空另一些。它们不会赚得太多，但同样也不会巨额亏损。

8. Bargain art pieces bring pleasure and capital gains
便宜的艺术品不仅赏心悦目而且收益丰厚

At an art auction in Hong Kong earlier this month, one mainland Chinese woman elicited titters with her unorthodox bidding. She never put down her paddle as others in the room tried to top offers for Nine Buffalos, an ink drawing by Chinese artist Li Keran. The woman won the bidding for the artwork — for $485,000.

本月早些时候，在香港的一次艺术品拍卖会上，一位来自中国内地的妇女那不同寻常的竞价方式引起了场内吃吃的笑声。当拍卖会上其他人试图对中国艺术家李可染的那幅水墨画《九牛图》报出更高的价格时，这位妇女却一直举着她的竞买牌未动。最终她以48.5万美元的价格买走了这件艺术品。

The rise of the cash-rich mainland art collector may be one of the side effects of China's economic boom.[32] "Now is a good time to buy before the mainland Chinese market opens up," says Rose Wong, director for jadeite jewelry at auction house Christie's[33]. She expects jade prices to soar in the next three to five years as Chinese grow wealthier. Because of the prospect of a global recession, many art pieces are priced at bargain levels compared with what owners were asking for 10 years ago. A Ming Dynasty vase that sold for $225,000 in 1998, for example, had a floor price of just $90,000 to $115,000 at a recent auction.

富裕的内地艺术品收藏家的增多也许从一个侧面反映了中国经济的繁荣程度。佳士得拍卖行玉石珠宝部经理罗斯·王说："在中国内地艺术品市场放开之前，现在正是买进的好时机。"她期望在未来3到5年内，随着中国变得更加富裕，玉石的价格会大幅飙升。由于全球经济衰退的预期，与10年前的要价相比，许多艺术品的价格十分低廉。例如，一只1998年卖价22.5万美元的明代花瓶，在最近的一次拍卖会上仅卖出了9万美元至11.5万美元的地板价。

You may want to acquire Chinese pieces now in anticipation of higher prices when mainland collectors hit their stride. [34] Or you may opt for Western works and other antiques to ride renewed interest in art[35] when the global economy gets back on track. Whatever your choice, make sure you buy top-notch works of art that you really like. That Ming vase can sit in your study for five years or more before you see its value appreciate substantially.

随着内地收藏家致富步伐的加快，出于对升值的期盼，你现在可能要买一些中国的艺术品。或者，你也可以选择一些西方的艺术品及其他的古董，以便能在全球经济重新回升，艺术品市场再度转暖时待价而沽。无论你做何种选择，一定要选购那些你真正喜欢的第一流艺术品。在你看到那只明代花瓶大幅增值之前，它可能会在你的书房里呆上5年或者更长时间。

9. Time to buy a dream home — to live in
购置理想住所的时机到了——赶快入住吧

You'd have to look long and hard to find a bullish property analyst these days, especially in Hong Kong. "People here have not yet woken up to the fact that property is no longer an asset class," says Rountree of Prudential Bache. "Property in Hong Kong has seen its better times and we're not going to see the same upside over the next few years." But what's bad for investors can be good news to first-time homeowners. [36] If you're still renting, now may be the time to buy your dream castle.

在这些日子，特别是香港，要想找到一位对房地产前景看好的分析家那简直是难上加难。倍基证券的罗齐说："这里的人们仍未从这样一个事实中醒悟过来，那就是，房地产已不再被归入资产的行列。香港房产的黄金时代已经过去，在未来几年内，我们不会再看到同样的事情发生了。"尽管这对投资者来说是个坏消息，但对首次购买房产的人却是好消息。如果你仍在租房住，现在大概是购买房产实现安居梦的时候了。

Buying property for your own use is a good idea across most of Asia. In some countries, though, it can be a good medium-term investment, too. "I'd buy property in Korea or China," says Rosgen of ING Barings. A middle-class based property boom is starting in Beijing, Shanghai and other cities[37], while domestic consumption in Seoul and Taipei are showing signs of recovery. And if you wait long enough[38], even property values in hard-hit Hong Kong and Singapore could appreciate.

在亚洲的大多数地方，买房自己住是一个好主意。然而，在其他一些国家，它也可以作为一项不错的中期投资。霸菱公司的罗斯根说："我会在韩国或中国购买房产。"北京、上海和其他一些城市正在掀起一股中高收入阶层购买房产的热潮，同时，汉城和台北的内需也正显现出复苏的迹象。而且，如果你耐心等待，即使受到沉重打击的香港和新加坡的房产也会升值。

Words and Expressions

riches	n.	abundant wealth 丰富的财产
		the impassable gulf that lies between riches and poverty 存在于富有与贫困之间的不可逾越的鸿沟
stock	n.	the number of shares that each stockholder possesses 股份（股票持有者拥有的股票份额）
diversify	v.	to spread out activities or investments, especially in business; to vary in order to spread risk or to expand 使多样化（从事多种活动或投资，尤指在商业中）
sensible	a.	acting with or exhibiting good sense 明智的
		a sensible person 通情达理的人
		a sensible choice 明智的抉择
bargain	n.	something offered or acquired at a price advantageous to the buyer 廉价货
blue chip		a stock that sells at a high price because of public confidence in its long record of steady earnings 绩优股，热门股（由于公众对其长期稳定收入的信心而售价很高的股票）
index	n.	in economics and finance an index (for example a price index, a stock market index) is a benchmark of activity, performance or any evolution in general 指数
return	v.	to produce or yield (profit or interest) as a payment for labor, investment, or expenditure 获利，生息
capital gain	n.	the amount by which proceeds from the sale of a capital asset exceed the original cost 资本收益
inception	n.	the beginning of something, such as an undertaking; a commencement 起头，开端
stagnant	a.	showing little or no sign of activity or advancement; not developing or progressing; inactive 不景气的，不发展或前进的
		a stagnant economy 停滞的经济
descent	n.	the act or an instance of descending 下降，降落，下降的动作或实例
recession	n.	an extended decline in general business activity, typically three consecutive quarters of falling real gross national product 衰退（经济活动普遍而持续地衰败，尤指三个连续季度的社会总产品净值的下降）
bounce (back)	v.	to recover quickly, as from a setback 〈经〉（股市价格的）回弹，反弹
hang on (to)	v.	to continue persistently; persevere 坚持，坚持不懈
accumulate	v.	to gather or pile up; amass 收集，堆集
turn round	v.	get better; pick up; cause to get better （使）好转，回转，转向
		The new strategy turned around sales. 新的策略使销售额增加。
rebound	v.	to recover, as from depression or disappointment 重新操作，从诸如衰败或失望中恢复过来

around	a.	in or toward the opposite direction or position 处于相反方向位置的或朝相反方向运行的，反转
exchange-traded funds		Exchange-traded funds（ETFs）are open-ended collective investments traded as shares on most global stock exchanges. 交易所交易基金
listed	a.	将（证券）列入上市名单的，上市交易的
constituent	n.	a constituent part；a component 成分，（股票指数的）样板股
dividend	n.	a share of profits received by a stockholder or by a policyholder in a mutual insurance society 红利，股利，股息
small-cap	a.	of stocks of companies with a market capitalization of less than one billion dollars （高收益的）小资本股票，小盘股 同义词：small-capitalization，small-capitalization
payout	n.	a percentage of corporate earnings that is paid as dividends to shareholders 分红，股息率，付出比率
bread-and-butter	a.	reliable, especially for producing income; basic 赖以为生的（可依靠的，尤指作为收入来源的），基本的 Household appliances are the company's bread-and-butter goods. 家庭用具是这家公司的主要商品。
sink	v.	to invest 投资 sink money into a new housing project 把资金投在一项新的建房计划 to invest without any prospect of return. 丧失（投入资金而没有回报，丧失资金）
haven	n.	a shelter serving as a place of safety or sanctuary 避难所，安全的地方
bid up	v.	to increase the amount bid 哄抬，抬高出价数 bid up the price of wheat 哄抬小麦价格
outperform	v.	to surpass（another）in performance 优过，胜于，在性能上超过（其他的）
bet	n.	one on which a stake is or can be placed 被下赌注的对象 Our product is a sure bet to sell well. 我们的产品肯定能走俏。
pharmaceutical	n.	a pharmaceutical product or preparation 药剂，药品
one-off	a.	happening, done, or made only once 一次性的
bullish	a.	optimistic or confident 乐观的，自信的 bullish on the prospects of reaching a negotiated settlement 对于达到协议妥协持乐观态度
economy	n.	the system or range of economic activity in a country, region, or community 经济体 Effects of inflation were felt at every level of the economy. 通货膨胀影响到每一个经济阶层。

mature	v.	having reached the limit of its time; due 到期的，应支付的
net	n.	remaining after all deductions have been made, as for expenses 纯的，扣除所有开支后剩下的
subscription	n.	agreement to buy new issue of securities 购买新发行证券的合约
futures	n.	(pl) 期货，期货合同 Cotton futures are selling at high prices. 棉花期货以高价出售。
position	n.	the amount of securities or commodities held by a person, firm, or institution 个人资产，公司资产
short	v.	to sell (a stock that one does not own) in anticipation of making a profit when its price falls; make a short sale 卖空
auction	n.	a public sale in which property or items of merchandise are sold to the highest bidder 拍卖
elicit	v.	to bring or draw out (something latent); educe 诱出，引出
titter	n.	a nervous giggle 窃笑
top	v.	to exceed or surpass 多于，超过
side effect		a peripheral or secondary effect, especially an undesirable secondary effect of a drug or therapy 副作用
jadeite	n.	a rare, usually emerald to light green but sometimes white, auburn, buff, or violet mineral, used as a gem and for ornamental carvings 翡翠石（通常指珍贵稀有的祖母绿宝石，有时也指白色、红褐色、暗黄色或蓝紫色的矿石，用作宝石或装饰性的雕刻作品）
hit (one's) stride		to attain a maximum level of competence; to achieve a steady, effective pace 达到最高的水平，达到稳定有效的速度
floor	n.	a lower limit or base 地面，底面
opt	v.	to make a choice or decision 选择或决定
top-notch	n.	first-rate; excellent 第一流的，最高的，顶好的，拔尖的
appreciate	v.	to increase in value or price, especially over time 涨价，增值（尤指经过一段时期后价值或价格上涨）
upside	n.	an upward tendency, as in business profitability or in the prices of a stock 上升（尤指商业利润或股票价格的上涨趋势）
hard-hit	a.	badly or adversely affected 严重影响的
aspire	v.	to have a great ambition or ultimate goal; desire strongly 渴望，追求，有志于

1. The secret to long-term wealth is stocks, stocks and stocks. 长期致富的秘诀何在？股票，除了股票还是股票。
把英语的一句话拆开翻译，前面译成一个问句，后面译成"股票，除了股票还是股票"非常恰当。通过自问自答，既把强调的意味译出来了，又非常符合汉语的表达习惯。

2. Morgan Stanley International's Far East index 摩根斯坦利国际（远东）指数
摩根斯坦利资本国际公司（MSCI）被公认为全球最权威的指数编纂机构，MSCI 系列指数是全球投资经理应用范围最广的基准指数。

3. 英语"inception"是"开始"的意思，但用于"指数的起始"时，行话往往称之为"基准日"。

4. Up 2,872% over three decades despite its descent into recession this year. 虽然今年的经济出现了滑坡，在过去 30 年里，该指数同样创造了高达 2872% 的收益。
整个英语句子中没有动词，关键的副词和介词都转译成了汉语的动词，省掉的词"经济"、"该指数"、"同样"和"收益"也补全了。

5. the Dow Jones Industrial Average 道琼斯工业平均指数
道-琼斯工业平均指数（DJIA）是美国纽约证券交易所指数，于 1896 年 5 月 26 日问世，一直由道－琼斯公司编制，并由该公司出版的《华尔街日报》发表。

6. the Great Depression of 1929 1929 年的经济大萧条
1929 年的经济大萧条是指 1929 年至 1939 年之间全球性的经济大衰退。

7. the bombing of Pearl Harbor in 1941 1941 年的偷袭珍珠港事件
1941 年 12 月 7 日，日本联合舰队袭击美国太平洋舰队基地珍珠港。

8. the Black October crash in 1987 1987 年的"黑色十月"股市崩盘
1987 年 10 月中旬，华尔街的股市带头掀起了一场遍及全球的股灾，使毫无思想准备的人们措手不及。

9. the terrorist attacks on New York and the Pentagon on Sept. 11 9 月 11 日，纽约和五角大楼遭到恐怖分子的袭击

10. Each time the Dow dropped like a stone — only to bounce back to greater heights. 每一次危机发生的时候，道琼斯指数都出现了"跳水"——但最终又出现反弹并创出新高。
将英语"dropped like a stone"译成"跳水"译得非常地道，因为股市上把大幅下跌叫做"股价跳水"。另外，英语"only to"表示该动作出乎人们的意料，应该把这层意思

译出来。此外，"bounce back to greater heights"不宜直译成"回弹至更高的点位"，因为股市下跌后的上涨有的是"反弹"，一般只涨到下跌前的高点又重新下跌，而另一种则是反转，即反弹到下跌前的高点后不再下跌，而是继续上涨并超过前期的高点。所以，这里拆译成"出现反弹并创出新高"。

11 Accumulate more shares when there's blood in the streets.   市场出现"割肉"时收集更多这样的股票。
"there's blood in the streets"是指投资者购买的股票的价格不断下跌，投资者只好低于自己的购买价抛出股票以减少损失，股市上称之"割肉"，译得形象地道。

12 Good quality companies are always the first to turn around when the market rebounds...   市场一旦出现反弹，绩优公司的股价总是率先反转……
"good quality companies"应该译成"绩优公司的股价"，这样意思才准确完整。英语"turn around"表示"转向"，即从下跌趋势转变成上涨趋势，俗称"反转"。

13 Gottardo Asset Management   高特多资产管理公司

14 "With internationally strong companies"译成"持有国际一流公司的股票"比译成"跟国际一流公司在一起"具体准确。

15 exchange traded fund   交易型开放式指数基金（ETF）
它是以被动的方式管理、同时又可在交易所挂牌交易的开放式基金。

16 These are listed vehicles that invest in index constituents.   这种基金在交易所挂牌交易，并专门投资指数样板股上市公司。
这句话中有三个词比较专业。"listed"是"上市交易的"的意思，指发行后的股票和基金等在市场上自由买卖；"vehicle"在这里译成"工具"和"手段"都不理想，实际上是指某种"投资品种"；"index constituents"是指交易所编制股价指数时所采用的"上市公司的股票价格"，通常称为"某某指数样板股"。

17 "cash payers"不能直译成"现金支付人"。这里是指"现金分红丰厚的上市公司"。通常把现金分红称为"派现"，既准确又地道。

18 There's no better proof of a company's strong fundamentals than the evidence of the dividends it pays out year after year.   一家公司是否实力雄厚，关键看它每年分给股东多少红利。
如果将这句话按英语句式译成"衡量一家公司是否具有很强的实力，最好的证据莫过于它每年分给股东的红利"，就显得生硬。其实可以将几个名词转译成其他词类，译出的汉语句子就通顺多了。

19 At HK$ 3.20 per share, Hung Hing Printing boasts a dividend yield of nearly 9%...   宏兴印业的每股市价为3.20港元，值得一提的是该公司的派息率接近9%……
这句话中的"boasts"本来是Hung Hing Pringting发出的动作，但如果直译成"宏兴印业自夸它的派息率接近9%"，读者就会难以理解，所以这里将"boasts"译成"值得一提的是"就非常自然。

20 Because they have been sold down, some blue chips now have substantial dividend yields, too.　一些蓝筹股因价格很低而导致现在的派息率也很可观。

英语状语从句中的主语与主句中的主语为同一个时，从句中用人称代词。但译成汉语时应该注意将主句中的主语先译出来，并把英语的人称代词省略，而不要照英语句式直译成"因为他们……，一些蓝筹股现在……"。

21 In good times and bad, people have to eat, use water and electricity, take medicine and travel to work and school.　不论世道好坏，人们总得吃饭、用水用电、吃药和乘车上班上学。

英语"in good times and bad"不宜译成"不论情况好坏"，因为英语"times"指"the present with respect to prevailing conditions and trends"（时势：反映流行状况和趋势的现今状况）。

22 Companies that provide these basic services may be boring, but they are dependable investments.　提供这类基本服务的公司可能很平常，但其股票却是可靠的投资品种。

英语"boring"如果译成"不大令人喜欢"或者"令人生厌"，读者就很难理解。为什么这类公司会不讨人喜欢呢？没有任何理由。所以，这里不能照译。这里的"boring"意为"what is commonplace, trivial, or unexcitingly routine"，也就是"没有什么特别的"、"平常的"、"不大起眼"的意思。

23 Power generators and distributors are the havens of choice in uncertain times.　当经济形势不稳时，发电站与送配电公司是首选的避风港。

这里的"in uncertain times"究竟是指什么？股市趋势不明，经济形势不稳，还是社会动荡不安？从上下文看，这里似乎不是指"股市动荡时期"，而应该是指"经济形势的发展不确定时"。因为后面提到，投资者担心出现全球经济衰退，大量购入这类股票，而一旦经济复苏，这些股票就难以上涨了。这样翻译同样要回答一个问题：为什么当经济形势不稳时，发电站与送配电公司是首选的避风港呢？因为不管什么情况发生，人们总要用水用电。因此，这里不宜译成"在股市捉摸不定的时期"。

24 ING Barings　霸菱投资

霸菱投资为荷兰国际集团（ING Group）下属资产管理业务中专责产业基金投资管理的专业部门。

25 Monson praises the two companies for their excellent management, strong brands and dominant market share.　默恩森对这两家公司的优良的管理手段、强大的名牌效应和优势的市场份额极为赞赏。

这句话中的三个名词"management"、"brands"和"market share"处理得非常好，因为最后一个名词词组是"市场份额"，所以在"管理"和"品牌"后分别增译了"手段"和"效应"，从而使整个句子连贯通顺。

26 Security and defense-oriented companies are definitely a good buy...　安全和防务类公司

价格低廉，绝对值得投资……

英语"buy"是"something that is underpriced; a bargain"的意思，例如"The couch and stereo are good buys."，所以不要将其译成"抢手货"，而应该拆译成"安全和防务类公司价格低廉，绝对值得投资"。

27 But they're probably one-off investments.   但这种股票可能不宜长期持有。

不错，英语"one-off"是"一次性"的意思，但这里如果直译成"但这种股票可能只能做一次性投资"，不了解股票的读者就很难明白什么叫"一次性投资"。是指只买一次，下次不再买，还是指把资金一次全部押在这类股票上？从上下文看，这里的意思实际上是指：这类股票只能短炒一下，不能长期持有。也可将这句话译成："但这种股票或许只能短炒。"

28 If the global economy does turn around next year, these stocks could suffer.   如果明年全球经济真的出现转机，这类股票的价格很可能会转弱。

主句中的主语是"stocks"，谓语动词是"could suffer"，如果直译成"这类股票很可能会遭受损失"，汉语似乎讲不通。到底是指持有这类股票的投资者将遭受损失，还是指这类上市公司的股价会下跌呢？查查字典就会发现，"suffer"有"to appear at a disadvantage; get worse"的意思，因此应该把"股价可能下跌，被人抛售，转弱，走弱"的意思表达清楚，以免读者误解。

29 While WTO membership will bring a wave of foreign capital, it will also open the doors to foreign competition.   虽然加入WTO后外资将大量涌入，但同时中国也要开放国门面对国外同行的竞争。

这是个典型的英语句子，主语是"WTO membership"，谓语动词是"bring"，宾语是"a wave of foreign capital"。如果按英语句式译成"中国的世界贸易成员地位将带来外国资本的热潮"，就非常拗口，不符合汉语的表达习惯，因此将原主语转译成了汉语的状语，译成"中国加入WTO后"，将原宾语"外资"转译成主语，然后将名词"wave"转译成动词"大量涌入"。后一句的主语"it"显然是指"中国"，而不是指"WTO membership"，所以前句说外资来了，后一句说中国要开放国门，正好形成对照。另外，"foreign competition"不能直译成"国外竞争"，而应该增译成"国外同行的竞争"。

30 AHL Diversified Futures   AHL多元化管理期货

由MAN INVESTMENTS PRODUCTS LIMITED所提供的AHL DIVERSIFIED FUTURES LTD另类基金。该基金乃一开放型基金并投资于约100个包括股票市场指数、债券、货币、短期利率及商品（能源、金属及农产品）期货市场。因此，投资者可在牛市或熊市中获利。MAN INVESTMENTS PRODUCTS的母公司THE MAN GROUP乃伦敦上市之一大金融服务公司。

31 That's the minimum subscription for AHL Diversified Futures in Hong Kong, which uses

sophisticated computer programs to hunt for differences in the prices of futures instruments in different markets. 如香港的 AHL 多元化管理期货（另类）基金，3 万美元是最低的认购额。该基金运用复杂的计算机程序在各种市场上寻找不同的期货产品进行投资并博取差价。

句中的非限制性定语从句不能凭想像译成"该基金运用复杂的计算机程序在不同的金融市场上寻找各种期货证券的差价"，而必须仔细查寻这只基金的详细资料。经查，这只基金乃一开放型基金并投资于约 100 个包括股票市场指数、债券、货币、短期利率及商品（能源、金属及农产品）期货市场。因此，如果将这只基金定义为"在不同的金融市场上寻找各种期货证券的差价"就大错特错了。这就是为什么是"different markets"而不是"stock market"的原因。

32. The rise of the cash-rich mainland art collector may be one of the side effects of China's economic boom. 富裕的内地艺术品收藏家的增多也许从一个侧面反映了中国经济的繁荣程度。

英语"side effects"千万不能译成"副作用"，在这里是"an unexpected or unplanned result of a situation or event"的意思，如"These policy changes could have beneficial side effects for the whole economy."。因此，译成动词"从侧面反映"也行，或者译成"是中国经济繁荣的另一表现"。

33. auction house Christie's 克里斯蒂拍卖行

Christie's is a world-famous auction house located in London. It was founded on December 5, 1766 by James Christie.

34. You may want to acquire Chinese pieces now in anticipation of higher prices when mainland collectors hit their stride. 你现在也许应该买一些中国的艺术品，等着将来内地收藏家出更高的价格来购买。

这个句子中的英语"hit their stride"很令人费解。到底是什么意思呢？能否将后面"when"引导的状语从句提前译成"随着内地收藏家致富步伐的加快，出于对升值的期盼，你现在可能要买一些中国的艺术品"？从上下文看，这个状语从句并不是修饰"You may want to acquire ..."，而是修饰"higher prices"，所以还是按英语句式顺着翻译比较好。"hit their stride"不是"（随着）致富步伐加快"，而应该是"（等到）有足够的资金购买时"。

35. "to ride renewed interest in art"中的"ride"很难直译成汉语。其原意是：或许可以买一些西方的艺术品及其他的古董，等经济重新回升，你就可以利用人们重新燃起的艺术热情而大赚一笔了。

36. But what's bad for investors can be good news to first-time homeowners. 尽管这对投资者来说是个坏消息，但对首次购买房产的人却是好消息。

这个句子如果直译成"那些对投资者来说是坏消息的事情在首次购买房产的人看来却

是好消息"就显得不够简洁，不如接着上文往下译。
37 A middle-class based property boom is starting in Beijing, Shanghai and other cities ...
北京、上海和其他一些城市正在掀起一股中高收入阶层购买房产的热潮……
句中是"a middle-class based property boom"，而不是"a middle-class based on property boom"，所以不能误译成"建立在房产繁荣之上的一批中产阶级正在北京、上海和其他一些城市形成"，而应该是：北京、上海和其他一些城市正在形成或掀起一股中高收入阶层购买房产的热潮。也就是说，是热潮形成，不是中产阶级形成。
38 "And if you wait long enough"不能直接译成"如果你等待的时间足够长"，而应该译成"如果你耐心等待"。

原文1：

Is the sole aim of most Americans to make money and possess luxuries which could be called excessive? The majority of Americans would certainly deny this, though most feel proud to amass wealth and possessions through hard work.

原译：

赚钱和拥有可以称得上过多的奢侈品，是不是大多数美国人唯一的目标？多数美国人肯定会予以否认，虽然他们对通过辛勤劳动而积攒钱财引以为荣。

点评：

① "possess luxuries"不宜译成"拥有奢侈品"。Longman Dictionary of Contemporary English 对"luxury"一词的解释是："very great comfort and pleasure, such as you get from expensive food, beautiful houses, cars, etc."。Random House Webster's Dictionary of American English 对这个词的解释是："a material object, service, etc., that brings physical comfort or rich living, but is not necessity of life"。由此可见，"possess luxuries"在这里就是指过上奢华的生活。

② 限制性定语从句"which could be called excessive"本来是对"luxuries"一词的补充说明，如果直译成"可以称得上过多的"就显得译文生硬，因为这个定语从句的本意是表明：有些人会认为这种奢华的生活太过分，没有必要。而"luxuries"一词本身就有"inessential"的含义，所以翻译时可以将这个定语从句简单地译成"过分的"。

③ 让步状语从句如果就地处理，在汉语中用"不过"比用"虽然"更符合汉语的表达习惯。另外，"amass wealth and possessions"就是"致富"的意思，不必直译成"积攒钱财"。

改译：

美国人是否大都将赚钱和享受过分奢华的生活作为自己唯一的目标？大多数美国人肯定会否认这一点，不过他们仍对勤劳致富甚感自豪。

原文 2：

In practice, a loan is negotiated for an agreed period, at a rate of interest prevailing at the time. Of course, the business should net the bank a profit in the negotiated rate. In order to maintain the trade-off among the above-mentioned three objects in their day-to-day operation, the fundamental principle international commercial banks adopt in their lending is that there should be a match between the type of loan and the type of deposit.

原译：

实际上，当规定期限及现价利率达成一致意见时就可得到贷款。当然，企业应当在协议利率的基础上使银行获得利润。为了在它们每日的操作中保持上述三个目标之间的平衡，国际商业银行在它们的贷款业务中所采取的基本原则就是，应当在贷款类型与存款类型之间有一种对称。

点评：

① "in practice"的意思是"in practical applications"，与"in theory"相对，例如"In theory, the license fee is only ＄5 but, because other costs get added on, in practice it is more like ＄20."。因此，根据上下文这里不宜译成"实际上"，而应该译成"在实际业务中"、"在实际操作中"。

② 将"a loan is negotiated for an agreed period, at a rate of interest prevailing at the time"译成"当规定期限及现价利率达成一致意见时就可得到贷款"让读者一头雾水。什么叫"规定期限及现价利率达成一致意见"？这两个东西又不是人，怎么能达成一致意见呢？其实这个句子是个被动态，变成主动态意思就非常清楚了："The business can negotiate a loan with the bank for an agreed period and at an interest rate prevailing at the time."。

③ "in the negotiated rate"译成"在协议利率的基础上"显得非常生硬，而且不容易理解。"在……的基础上使……获得利润"不如"按……比率让……有利可图"显得自然易懂。

④ 将"to maintain the trade-off among the above-mentioned three objects"译成"保持上述三个目标之间的平衡"非常抽象，读者较难理解，所以应该译得更加具体一点，

以便于读者更好地理解。所谓"trade-off"(平衡)就是指"协调发展,共同实现"。另外,"the above-mentioned three objects"也应该重复一下,以加深读者的印象。

⑤ 最后一句中的"a match"与"the trade-off"属于同一类问题,如果直接译成名词"……之间的一种对称",意思就比较抽象难懂,不如转译成动词"匹配,相称"更加具体一些。

改译:

在实际操作中,贷款方与银行协商确定一笔贷款的期限,贷款利率可采用当时的现行利率。当然,贷款企业应该按双方商定的比率使银行有利可图。为了使每天的业务协调发展,实现流动性、安全性和盈利性三个目标,国际商业银行放贷的基本原则是,贷款类型必须与存款类型相匹配。

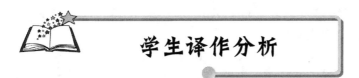

学生译作分析

原文:

Purchase Agreement

This Agreement is entered into this _____ the day, _____ (month) of 2009 by and between Fuji Xerox Industry Development (Shanghai) Co., Ltd., a company organized and existing under the laws of China with its registered address at _____ _____ (the "Purchaser"), and AMC Corporation (the "Vendor") for the procurement by Purchaser from Vendor of certain products and services as specified hereunder. Purchaser and Vendor agree that all transactions with respect to the subject matter between them shall be governed by the terms and conditions of this Agreement, which shall automatically form an integral part of the Purchase Order, which Purchaser may issue to the Vendor from time to time, unless otherwise expressly agreed to in writing.

学生原译文:

采购协议

本协议签订于2009年____月____日。本合同为富士复印工业发展(上海)有限公司,该公司在中国的法律条款下成立,注册地址为_____(采购方)与AMC公司(卖方)基于某产品与服务的招标条款共同签订。采购方与合同商约定在此协议下的双方之间的所有有关交易均受此协议约束,所有的交易均应当自动生成采购合同，该合同由采购方向合同商提出，双方进行磋商直到双方达成书面一致。

分析：

(1) 第一句话是一个被动语态，如果完全按英语的句式翻译，后面的句子就会非常长。为了将这个句子的意思表达清楚，可以采取将句子拆开的方法，即：将一个英语句子拆译成三个汉语句子。

(2) "协议"和"合同"应该只使用一个，避免混用。同样，"买方"和"采购方"，"卖方"和"供货方"选用一个。另外，"Xerox"不能漏掉，必须查字典或上网查实再翻译。

(3) "本合同为……与……共同签订"不大通顺，可以采取变被动为主动的方法来翻译，即译成"协议签订双方为……"，这样可以避免句子过长。

(4) "organized and existing under the laws of China"不宜译成"在中国的法律条款下成立"，可以考虑将动词"organized"和"existing"转译成名词，并将介词"under"转译成动词"符合"。

(5) 介词短语"for the procurement by Purchaser from Vendor of certain products and services as specified hereunder"译成"基于某产品与服务的招标条款"显然意思有误，可以单独译成一个句子。

(6) 第二句话也很长，而且其中有两个非限制性定语从句。首先，谓语动词"agree"不能译成"约定"，因为这个词太含糊，一般不能用于正式的合同或协议中，应该译成"一致同意"。

(7) "all transactions with respect to the subject matter between them"是指买卖双方与本协议主题有关的一切交易或业务，而不是"双方之间的所有有关交易"。翻译合同一类较正式的文件，切忌在意思上含糊不清，例如"所有有关交易"就非常含糊。

(8) "shall be governed by"译成主动态语气更强，效果更好。此外，"terms and conditions"必须翻译出来，不能漏掉。

(9) 第一个定语从句比较好处理，但"form an integral part of the Purchase Order"是"成为订购单的不可缺少的部分"，而不是"生成采购合同"。

(10) 第二个定语从句中的谓语动词"may issue"应该译成"必须提交给……"；后面的"unless otherwise expressly agreed to in writing"表示条件：除非双方另外专门为此达成书面协议。千万不可凭想像译成"双方进行磋商直到双方达成书面一致"。

参考译文：

采购协议

本协议于 2009 年____月____日签订。协议签订双方为富士施乐复印机工业发展（上海）有限公司（以下称买方），公司的成立和运作符合中国的法律，公司的注册地址为_____和 AMC 公司（以下称卖方）。买方为了从卖方获得下述某些产品与服务特与卖方签订本协议。买方和卖方一致同意，本协议中的条款和条件对双方与本协议主题有关的一切业务均有约束力，并自动成为订购单不可缺少的一部分。买方必须经常将该订购单提交给卖方，双方为此另有书面协议除外。

翻译技巧介绍

被动语态的翻译
(Translating Passive Voice)

被动语态在商务英语中经常使用，通常凡是在不必、不愿说出或不知道主动者的情况下均可使用被动语态。因此，掌握商务英语中被动语态的翻译方法非常重要，因为如果被动语态处理不好，就会给读者带来理解上的困难，或让他们阅读译文时感到别扭。汉语中使用完全被动态时往往通过"把"、"被"、"由"等词来表示，但其使用范围远远小于英语中被动语态的使用范围，因此可以采取下列方法来处理英语中的被动语态。

（1）如果英语句子的被动语态强调的是被动动作，翻译时还是应该将句子译成汉语的完全被动态，即带被动标志的被动句，如"被"、"给"、"遭"、"挨"、"作为……而"、"为……所"、"使"、"由……"、"得到"、"受到"等。

① Finally it (invoice) **must be signed** by an authorized employee of the seller, and it may even quote import or export license numbers.

译文：最后发票必须**由**卖方授权的雇员**签字**，甚至还可能要加上进出口许可证的号码。

② For years, personal experience and expert advice **have been widely used** in managing risk and have proved to be very useful and practicable.

译文：多年来，在风险管理中，个人的经验和专家的建议已**得到广泛运用**并证明是十分有效可行的。

③ France and Holland complained that the network, run by Britain's GCHQ and America's National Security Agency, **was being routinely used** to spy on corporate e-mails, causing their national firms to lose deals.

译文：法国和荷兰抱怨说，由英国政府通信总局和美国国家安全局经营的网络**经常被用**于窃取公司电子邮件的秘密，使他们国家公司的生意蒙受损失。

④ What this means is that businesses that once were peripheral to the mall, such as full-service restaurants, major bookstores, cinemas, home-furnishings stores, and services **are grouped together**.

译文：这意味着原来属于购物中心外围的商号，如服务齐全的餐馆、大书店、电影院、家具店和各类服务企业，**都被集中起来**。

⑤ A market **is commonly thought of** as a place where commodities are bought and sold.

译文：市场**通常被认为**是买卖货物的地方。

⑥ The concept "to be bound in case of acceptance" means that once the trade terms raised by the offeror **are accepted** by the offeree, the sales contract is formed, and the offeror has no other choice but to perform the contract even without his consent or confirmation.

译文："接受时承受约束"是指一旦发盘人提出的交易条件**被受盘人接受**，合同即成立，即使发盘人没有同意和确认，他除了履行合同别无选择。

⑦ It recently moved its labor-intensive Master Lock operations to Mexico while opening two cabinet-making factories in North Carolina and Alabama, where each order **is processed** to spec.

译文：集团最近把它的劳动密集型"锁王"生产厂移到了墨西哥，同时在北卡罗莱纳州和亚拉巴马州开设了两家家具制造厂，这里的每一份订单都能**得到**对号入座式的**处理**。

⑧ Frederick Wong, 26, an NTU mechanical and production engineering graduate, **was flatly turned down** when he approached two venture capitalists last year for funds to develop a system to collect car parking fees.

译文：26岁的弗雷德里克·王是新加坡南洋理工大学机械和制造工程专业的毕业生，去年为了开发一个停车场收费装置，他找了两位风险投资商筹措资金却**遭到断然拒绝**。

（2）如果英语句子中的被动语态不强调被动动作，翻译时可译成汉语的简化被动句，即"自然被动句"。这种句子的特点是被动句不带被动标志，常以主动形式表示被动意义。其基本形式是"受动者＋动词"。这种句式结构精练，叙述客观，商务英语中的很多被动语态常用这种句式翻译。

① But he warns that if it is proved that the Air Force unfairly favored Boeing, the contract **should be reopened** for new bidders.

译文：但他警告说，如果有证据表明空军在这项交易中不公正地偏向了波音公司，该合同就**应该对新的竞标者重新开放**。

② You're the child of a successful entrepreneur and the family business **has been entrusted** to you, which is a lot of pressure.

译文：你是成功企业家的子女，而继承家业的重任**又托付于你**，这可是劳神费力的事。

③ Sometimes there are extra charges not quoted in the contract, such as freight and insurance; these **will be shown** in a separate debit note.

译文：有时还有合同中未写上的额外费用，如运费和保险费；**这些费用应在另外的**

收款单上注明。

④ While the banking sector **is scheduled** to liberalize in the coming years, securities will remain tightly restricted, with foreigners limited to minority stakes.

译文：虽然银行业**预计**未来几年内将放开，但证券业仍将受到严格限制，外国人只允许持有小额股份。

⑤ One of the documents presented by an exporter summarizes contract terms, and declares that shipments **have been made** in accordance with them.

译文：出口商向其买主提供的单证之一是商业发票，它包括合同条款，并表明**货物根据合同条款已经装运**。

⑥ And that the credit **can't be cancelled** before the expiry date?

译文：而且信用证在期满前**不得撤销**，对吗？

⑦ Now, rulings **are automatically adopted** unless there is a consensus to reject a ruling—any country wanting to block a ruling has to persuade all other WTO members to share its view.

译文：然而，现在裁决**将自动执行**，除非对一项裁决全体成员方反对——任何想要阻止执行某一裁决的国家必须说服所有其他世贸组织成员方接受它的观点。

⑧ Even if the BOT（Build, Operate, Transfer）project **is completed and transferred** to operation, risks may emerge any time in the course of operation and management.

译文：即使BOT投资（建设、经营、转让）工程**完成并移交使用**，在经营管理中，风险也会随时产生。

⑨ Generally, manufacturer-sponsored discounts are not negotiable, and discounted financing rates **may be limited** by a consumer's credit history.

译文：一般而言，不能对厂家打的折扣讨价还价，而且贷款利率的折扣可能因顾客过去的信用记录而**有所限制**。

⑩ Each equipment and product choice **should be accompanied** by the dealership's suggested retail price; feel free to negotiate those prices.

译文：供选择的每项配件和产品都**应附有**特许经销商的建议零售价；尽可以讨价还价。

⑪ It is because Thailand has poured nearly 30 per cent of its total loans into real estate market since 1992 and most of the loans have failed **to be taken** by now.

译文：这场危机是由于泰国自1992年起就投入到房地产市场中，而到不前为止大部分贷款仍无法**收回**。

（3）商务英语中的大多数被动态常可以译成汉语的主动态，也就是根据上下文将英语被动句中省去（或未省去）的动作发出者译成汉语的主语，并同时将英语的被动式改成汉语的主动式，因为这更符合汉语的表达习惯。

① It means that customers can avoid the trouble of parking the car and queuing in the shop because basic clothes **can be bought** at their computer keyboard.

译文：这意味着**顾客购买普通衣物**只需点击电脑键盘即可，从而免去停车和在商店排队的麻烦。

② Other technologies **are also being used** to make online shopping more interactive.

译文：为了使网上购物双方更好地相互交流，**商家还采用了其他技术**。

③ This request **is made to you** on behalf of my company.

译文：**我代表我公司向你提出这一要求**。

④ Many computer and consumer electronics products offered by Amazon.com **can be viewed** from several different angles by clicking on a series of thumbnail images.

译文：只要点击一连串拇指盖大小的图片，**你便可以从各种不同角度观看亚马逊网上购物（Amazon.com）提供的许多电脑和民用电子产品**。

⑤ The importance of design **is not always recognized** in persuading consumers to make their mind to buy a product.

译文：产品的包装设计能促使消费者做出购买决定，但**人们并不总会意识到它的重要性**。

⑥ The customer **will be provided** with a plastic card carrying a line of credit that, ranging from several hundred to several thousand dollars, varies according to the creditability of the customer.

译文：**银行在向客户签发**塑料信用卡时，将按照客户的资信情况规定一个几百美元至几千美元不等的信用额度。

⑦ So far, personal-computer sales **have been dominated** by Apple, Tandy's Radio Shack and Commodore.

译文：到目前为止，在个人电脑的销售方面，苹果公司、坦迪公司的无线电之家和**康摩多三家公司占着压倒优势**。

⑧ Consequently, **business can be done and cheques can be written** without any legal tender visibly changing hands.

译文：其结果，**大家可以做生意，开支票**，但看不到任何法定货币转手。

（4）在商务英语中，有些被动句是用来描述事物的存在、发生、消失，有时也用来表示人们的看法、态度、告诫、要求、号召等，这时可以将这些被动句译成汉语的无主句，即将被动式改成主动式，省掉动作的发出者，将受动者作为动词的宾语。

① But shares in the bank—the biggest in the euro zone by market capitalization were down as profits were only in line with forecasts once one-time capital gains **were stripped out**.

译文：然而**剥离**一次性资本收益之后，这家银行利润和原来的预计不相上下，所以这家欧元区市值最大的银行股价反而下跌了。

② This is particularly important when spare parts **have to be supplied** promptly to customers, as in the case of consumer goods such as refrigerators.

译文：如果销售电冰箱这类消费品，**一定要能迅速向客户提供零件**，这一点特别重要。

③ If half of the turnover is in December, then half of the advertising budget of ＄9,000 **should be spent** then i. e. ＄4,500.

译文：如果营业额的一半在12月份完成，那么这个月**就应该花**9 000美元广告预算费的一半，即4 500美元。

④ We are sorry to inform you that an accident happened last night, but no great harm **was done** to your goods.

译文：我们很抱歉地告知，昨晚发生了一场事故，但没给你方所订货物**造成**多大损失。

⑤ While two percentage points may not sound like much, it's bad news given how much progress **might have been made** amid explosive growth.

译文：两个百分点听起来可能不算什么，但想想在美国经济飞速发展时期**本可以为人们提供**多得多的升迁机会，下降两个百分点就是坏消息了。

（5）有的英语被动句从意思上表示某种状态，类似形容词，所以可以用汉语中的"是……的"句式来译。

① Today, the vast majority of new vehicle purchases are made with some form of credit, and **most are arranged** through the selling dealer.

译文：如今，绝大多数新车购置采用某种信贷形式，且大多**是**通过经销商**安排的**。

② The internet **was not designed** as platform for commercial transactions.

译文：因特网本来并非**作为**商业交易平台**而设计开发的**。

③ They (term drafts) mean that payment has to be made so many days after the draft is presented and accepted, whereas a sight draft is payable on demand, immediately it's presented, though I think a few days grace **are allowed**.

译文：远期汇票意思是在提出和承兑汇票后的多少天内付款，而即期汇票是要求见票即付，提出后立即付款，不过我想几天的宽限**是允许的**。

④ Because gold has been universally regarded as a very valuable metal, national currencies **were** for many years **judged** as in terms of the so-called "gold standard".

译文：由于黄金已被普遍地看作一种非常贵重的金属，美国的货币多年来就**是**以所谓的"金本位"**来衡量的**。

⑤ They must verify, to prevent dumping and the illegal transfer of funds outside the country, that the goods **are being sold** at the current market rate ruling in the country of origin.

译文：为避免倾销及把资金非法转移到国外，他们必须证实货物**是**按原产地国家的现行市价**出售的**。

⑥ Originally, a valuable metal (gold, silver or copper) served as a constant store of value, and even today the American dollar **is technically backed** by the store of gold which the US government maintains.

译文：起初人们用某种贵重金属（金、银或铜）作为有恒性的价值储存体，甚至今天的美元从技术上说还**是**以美国政府所拥有的黄金储存量**为**"后盾"**的**。

（6）英语中有些句子虽然是被动形式，但译成汉语时可以找到汉语中表示被动动作的词或词组，这时可以采取保留原主语，被动改为主动的翻译方法，即主语照译，作为译文的主语，把原文的被动态译成主动态。这种译法与上面提到的"自然被动式"类似，但不同的是，"自然被动句"的谓语动词前如果加入一个"被"字，句子仍然通顺，而按这种译法翻译的句子中的谓语本身已包含了被动的含义，前面如果再加一个"被"字，句子就不通顺了。

① Today, upward mobility **is determined** increasingly by a college degree that's attainable mostly by those whose parents already have money or education.

译文：如今能否晋升越来越**取决于**大学学历，而取得大学学历的大多数人的父母已具备经济实力或受过文化教育。

② The export trade is subject to many risks. Ships may sink or consignments **be damaged** in transit, exchange rates may alter, buyers default or governments suddenly impose an embargo.

译文：出口贸易常常遇到许多风险，例如船舶可能沉没，货物可能在运输中**受损**，外汇兑换率可能变动，买主可能违约或政府部门突然宣布禁运。

③ No one **is allowed** to obtain a copy of your credit report without your written permission, except where otherwise permitted by law.

译文：除非法律另有明文规定，任何人如无你的书面认可都**不准**获得你的信用记录副本。

④ One is "Public Issue of Bond", that means the issuance **should be made** at public capital market through some financial companies which underwrite the bonds and then resell them to bond buyers.

译文：一种叫"公募债券"，即债券的发行在资本市场上公开**进行**，债券将由一些专业金融公司包销，由它们再转卖给购买者。

⑤ Commerce **has been built** on the belief that selling bank accounts and loans is little different from offloading fresh fruit and breakfast cereal.

译文：商业银行的经营就是**基于**这样的信念：银行吸引存贷也同超市搞新鲜水果、早餐谷物类食品促销非常相像。

（7）商务英语中的被动句有时按上述几种方法翻译读起来都不大顺口，这时不妨采取将被动态转译成其他词类的方法。

① **The contract is made by and between the buyers and the sellers**, whereby the buyers agree to buy and the sellers agree to sell the under-mentioned goods subject to the terms and conditions as stipulated hereinafter.

译文：**经买卖双方同意**，按照以下条款由买方购进，卖方售出以下商品。（转译成动词）

② Consumers will be exposed to constant new products **that will be introduced** from overseas.

译文：消费者将会不断接触到**来自**世界各地的新产品。（将及物动词 introduce 转译成不及物动词）

③ Developed to meet the needs of very high output networks, this new socket is **characterized** first of all **by** its exceptional performance.

译文：这种新型的插座是为了满足高度信息输出网络的需要而开发的产品，它首要的**特点**是性能卓越。（将动词 characterized 转译成名词）

④ Greater emphasis **is also being placed on product innovations** such as single-use packs, microwave packs and zip-up products.

译文：一些**产品革新**，如一次性包装、微波包装盒及拉链包装产品等也**备受重视**。（将介词短语 on product innovation 转成主语）

⑤ They carefully checked the goods which **were being loaded onto s.s. Changfeng** and found Order No. 1234 short-weight by 1,000 kilos.

译文：他们对**长风号轮正在装运**的货物进行了仔细的检查，发现 1234 号订单项下货物短重 1 000 公斤。（将状语 onto s.s. Changfeng 转成主语）

⑥ Because they **have been sold down**, some blue chips now have substantial dividend yields, too.

译文：一些蓝筹股因**价格很低**而导致现在的派息率也很可观。（转译成形容词）

⑦ The fear of SARS and unspecified terrorist threats has kept non-European visitors away, while British tourists **are discouraged** by the strength of Euro.

译文：对非典的恐惧和来路不明的恐怖威胁使非欧洲游客**止步不前**，而英国游客也因为欧元走强**感到囊中羞涩**。（转译成四字词）

课堂翻译训练

将下列句子译成汉语。

1. China has voiced strong opposition to US sanctions over the alleged sale of advanced missile technology to an unnamed country. The purchasing country was not named by the US, but the company, China North Industries Incorporated (Norinco), has been penalized by the US in the past for such sales to Iran.

2. The percentage of discount can be clearly written down in a contract if the seller and the buyer

have reached an agreement. The amount of discount is usually deducted from the buyers' payment.
3. These things had been manufactured in villages which were growing into towns now, away from London.
4. Marketing is seen as the task of finding and stimulating buyers for the firm's output.
5. It is only more recently that it has become increasingly understood that the production of goods is a waste of resources unless those goods can be sold at a fair price within a reasonable time span.
6. And the ability to get people to think passionately and do things as if it were their own business can only be achieved when they are truly part of the business.
7. As most countries are vigorously promoting exports and also because of the tremendous growth of multinational corporations, the international market, in most instances, is characterized by intense competition on an extensive scale.
8. Four major stages in the product life cycle have been identified: introduction, growth, maturity and decline.
9. It is generally agreed that China's current economic readjustment is very much an effort to undertake what was within the country's means.
10. When a bond is sold principally in a country other than the country of the currency in which the issue is denominated, it is called "Euro Bond", and when the bond is sold primarily in the country of the issuance currency, it is called "Foreign Bond".
11. All original and copy of documents called for under this credit must be manually signed and submitted either in English or Arabic.
12. In other words, the advertising budget should be matched and spent in a retail business in proportion to the business being achieved, and at the time it is being generated.

课后练习

一、将下列短句译成英语，注意运用本单元所学的翻译技巧。

1. Customs authorities work closely with the central bank to ensure that goods are only imported or exported in accordance with current regulations.
2. Customs entries are required for both imports and exports. Some articles or commodities may

be actually shipped before an entry is submitted, in this case the shipping note sent to the wharfinger will be marked "Pre-entry not required".
3. One copy of the Consular Invoices is sent to the importing customs, another accompanies documents presented through a bank. Sometimes, however, all what is needed is a certificate of value endorsed by a chamber of commerce, and combined with a certificate of origin.
4. There is additionally a wider sense of the word 'money', covering anything that is used as a means of exchange, whatever form it may take.
5. But the demand for money is related not only to the quantity of business but also to the rapidity with which the business is done.
6. Many small sums of money which might not otherwise be used as capital are rendered useful simply because the bank acts as a reservoir.
7. These airline companies are cyclical, so as soon as demand comes back up, they'll rebound quickly. We like airlines because they've been so badly battered.
8. This type of problem could be avoided if these small firms found out more about their customers at the time of taking them on
9. Although it is said that the operation of a commercial bank aims to maximize its profits, yet, its profitability can not be achieved at the expense of the other two objectives.
10. The company does not condone discrimination of any kind and female employees are fairly promoted and paid.

二、将下列短文译成英语，注意运用本单元所学的翻译技巧。

All values in the economic system are measured in terms of money. Our goods and services are sold for money, and that money is in turn exchanged for other goods and services. Coins are adequate for small transactions, while paper notes are used for general business. Originally, a valuable metal (gold, silver or copper) served as a constant store of value, and even today the American dollar is technically "backed" by the store of gold which the US government maintains. Because gold has been universally regarded as a very valuable metal, national currencies were for many years judged in terms of the so-called "old standard". Nowadays however national currencies are considered to be as strong as the national economies which support them.

Valuable metal has generally been replaced by paper notes. These notes are issued by governments and authorized banks, and are known as "legal tender". Other arrangements such as checks and money orders are not legal tender. They perform the function of substitute money and are known as "instruments of credit". Credit is offered only when creditors believe that they have a good chance of obtaining legal tender when they present such instruments at a bank or other authorized institution. If a man's assets are known to be considerable, then his credit will be good. If his assets are in doubt, then it may be difficult for him to obtain large sums of credit or even to pay for goods with a check.

The value of money is basically its value as a medium of exchange, or, as economists put it, its "purchasing power". This purchasing power is dependent on supply and demand. The demand for money is reckonable as the quantity needed to effect business transactions. An increase in business requires an increase in the amount of money coming into general circulation. But the demand for money is related not only to the quantity of business but also to the rapidity with which the business is done. The supply of money, on the other hand, is the actual amount in notes and coins available for business purposes. If too much money is available, its value decreases, and it does not buy as much as it did, say, five years earlier. This condition is known as "inflation".

Banks are closely concerned with the flow of money into and out of the economy. They often co-operate with governments in efforts to stabilize economies and to prevent inflation. They are specialists in the business of providing capital, and in allocating funds on credit. Banks originated as places to which people took their valuables for safe-keeping, but today the great banks of the world have many functions in addition to acting as guardians of valuable private possessions.

佳译赏析

5 Rules for Finding the Next Dell[1]
如何寻找下一个戴尔？

By Larry Selden and Geoffrey Colvin
July 12, 2004

Sure, companies say they put customers first. But only a few do. They're the ones whose stock you want to own.
不错，每家公司都声称把顾客放在第一位，但能做到的不多。而这些公司的股票正是你想要的。

Dell, Best Buy[2], and Royal Bank of Canada[3] are stocks you wish you'd bought years ago.[4] They've all been knockout performers for shareholders for the same reason: Each has truly put customers at the center of its business.[5] And we mean truly—not in the golly-aren't-customers-great way that most companies have hyped for years but rather in a way that transforms the entire business.[6] If you'd like to spot more such stocks, consider this vignette about electronics retailer Best Buy, related by UBS[7] retail analyst Gary Balter.
你觉得，要是多年前你就买进了美国戴尔公司、百思买家电连锁巨头和加拿大皇家银行的股票，那该有多好。这些企业都为股东带来了丰厚的回报，而它们的秘诀如出一辙：每个企业都真正做到了在经营中将顾客放在首位。我们所说的真正做到，是指这些企业不像大多数公司多年来那样只是高喊顾客就是上帝，而是指真正以顾客为中心，从而改变了整个企业的面貌。如果你想发现更多的此类股票，那就听听瑞银证券公司零售业分析师加里·巴尔特讲述的关于电子产品零售商百思买的小故事吧。

Balter walked into one of the company's stores in Pasadena in May and met an employee named

Matt. What was most remarkable about Matt wasn't his helpful demeanor or plentiful pleases and thank-yous but rather what he knew about his customers—including one key group of them. [8] Best Buy even has a pet name for them. After carefully studying the area around its Pasadena store, the company concluded that one highly promising bunch were upper-income soccer moms, which the company singularized as "Jill". [9] And it wasn't just the store manager who knew about Jill and her shopping ways, but sales people right down the line. Matt, for instance, took the time to explain to the visiting analyst that small appliances hadn't been selling well, even though they'd been chosen with Jill in mind. [10] So, based on interactions with customers, hourly workers moved the items from high shelves above major appliances to low racks along the main walkway. Small appliances are an impulse buy for Jill, and this way, if she needed a kitchen mixer, she wouldn't have to go over to the stoves but could find it along an aisle she frequents. Small-appliance sales soon rocketed.

5月份的一天，巴尔特走进百思买位于帕萨迪那的一家商店，见到了一位名叫马特的员工。马特与众不同之处在于他对自己的顾客——其中包括一群重要的顾客——了如指掌，而不仅仅是待客彬彬有礼，热情周到。百思买对这群重要的顾客甚至有自己的昵称。公司在认真研究了帕萨迪那商店周边的情况后，得出了这样的结论：高收入的足球妈妈是极具潜力的消费群体，为了称呼方便并区别于其他消费群体，公司特将这一群体称为"吉尔"。不仅商店经理了解吉尔和她的购物习惯，而且他手下的销售人员也全都知道。比如，马特借此机会向来访的分析师解释说，以前小家电的销售情况一直不理想，尽管当初公司在选择这些电器时就是将吉尔作为销售对象。因此，在与顾客沟通之后，钟点工把摆放在大型电器上面高层货架上的小家电产品挪到超市主要通道两侧的低层货架上。吉尔购买小家电产品往往出于一时冲动，这样摆置的话，如果她需要一台厨房搅拌器，她就用不着跑到摆放炉灶的地方，而是能够在她经常光顾的走道两侧找到。不久，小家电的销量大幅上升。

But that's not the best part of the story. More surprising was that employees understood how reconfiguring the sales floor would improve the Jill segment's sales and return on invested capital, a measure that drives Best Buy's stock price. In this case they knew that selling more small appliances would not only raise profits but also do so without increasing invested capital, since the store just turns the appliance inventory faster. [11] At most companies, employees haven't a clue what their firm's return on invested capital is, let alone the returns on specific customer segments—and even if they knew, they'd be powerless to do anything about it. But at that Best Buy store in Pasadena—one of 32 pilot stores testing an initiative called "customer-centricity" [12]—they did. Customers loved the results. [13] While Best Buy's same-store sales grew 9% overall in the company's fiscal fourth quarter, sales at its seven customer-centric stores in the Los Angeles area, including Matt's Pasadena outlet, grew 30%. Balter believes the company is now "in a league with Wal-Mart[14] at its zenith and Home Depot[15] under Bernie and Arthur (co-founders Bernard Marcus and Arthur Blank)." In retailing, praise doesn't get higher than that.[16]

但这还不是故事最精彩的部分。更加出人意料的是,员工知道调整店面布局将如何提高针对吉尔的销售量和投资资本的回报,后一指标推动着百思买股价的上涨。在这个事例中,员工们知道出售更多的小家电意味着不仅增加了利润,同时又无须增加投资,因为商店正好将库存的电器产品更快地出售。大多数公司的员工对自己公司的资本投资回报情况一无所知,更别说特定客户群的收益率了——即使他们对此有所了解,也起不了什么作用。但是,在帕萨迪那的那个百思买商店(百思买32家开展名为"以顾客为中心"活动的试点商店之一),员工就能够有所作为。顾客对开展这一活动的效果十分满意。虽然百思买的同店销售总额在第四财政季度增长了9%,但其洛杉矶地区的七家以顾客为中心的商店的销售额则增长了30%,这其中就包括马特所在的帕萨迪那店。巴尔特认为,百思买现在已经和"鼎盛时期的沃尔玛及伯尔尼和亚瑟掌管下的家得宝公司(伯尔尼和亚瑟分别指伯纳德·马库斯和亚瑟·布莱克,他们同为家得宝公司的创始人)同属一个级别"。在零售行业,最高的荣耀也不过如此。

"Customer-centricity" means shareholders as well as customers win, because the customer-centric approach can juice a company's stock with a powerful double boost: rising earnings, plus a higher P/E multiple applied to those earnings.[17] That phenomenon, which we call re-rating the P/E, is critical to making stocks rise in this torpid investment environment. The effect is magical: If a stock is trading at a P/E of 20, which is about the market average, and earnings rise 20%, then the stock will also rise 20% as long as the P/E remains unchanged.[18] But if Wall Street decides that the company can sustain that profit growth for years into the future and thus deserves a new P/E of 40, then that 20% gain in earnings sparks a one-time jump of 140% in the stock, after which earnings increases get multiplied by 40.[19] Re-rating the P/E has been key to Dell's performance as the best stock of the past decade and to Best Buy's doubling over the past year. We believe putting customers in the hands of educated employees like Matt may be the best way for a company to get its P/E re-rated.

"以顾客为中心"意味着股东和顾客能够双赢,因为这种做法能够从两个方面大大增强公司股票的活力,即增加公司的盈利,从而提高公司股票的市盈率。我们把这种现象称之为市盈率调整,在当前疲软的投资环境下它是股价上涨的关键。市盈率调整能够产生神奇的效果:假设某上市公司股票的市盈率现为20倍,接近市场平均水平。如果公司的利润增长20%,股价也将上升20%,而市盈率仍保持不变。但是,如果华尔街的投资人认定该公司能够在今后数年保持这一利润增长速度,那么该股的市盈率应当重新定位在40倍。这样一来,公司利润增长20%将使股价一下子上涨140%,也就是股价=公司盈利×40。过去十年间戴尔公司之所以成为股市中的大黑马靠的就是不断调整股票的市盈率,而去年百思买股价能够翻番的根本原因也在于此。我们认为，让马特那样训练有素的员工为顾客服务，可能是公司实现其市盈率调整目标的最佳办法。

Let's be clear up-front that we're blowing our own horn. A book we've written (Angel Customers & Demon Customers: Discover Which Is Which and Turbocharge Your Stock) is all about how companies can become genuinely customer-centric. One of us, Larry Selden, is an emeritus professor at Columbia University's business school and has a consulting firm that's teaching many companies (including Best Buy and Royal Bank of Canada) in retail, financial services, telecom, technology, and other industries how to apply those concepts. Companies that embrace this core philosophy, we believe, are benefiting, as are their shareholders and customers. Which leads to the obvious question: How can investors spot the next customer-focused winners—and do it before the stocks take off?

我们有言在先，下面我们可要吹嘘一下自己了。我们写的一本书《天使顾客和魔鬼顾客：如何区分他们并让你的股票猛涨》讲的就是关于公司怎样才能真正做到以顾客为中心。我们当中的拉里·塞尔登是哥伦比亚大学商学院的名誉教授，他还开办了一家咨询公司，向零售、金融服务、电信、科技和其他行业的很多公司（包括百思买和加拿大皇家银行）传授如何应用这些理念。我们相信，采纳并贯彻这一核心理念的公司将获益，它们的股东和客户也将获益。这显然就产生了一个问题：投资者怎样（而且要在其股价上涨之前）发现下一个以客户为中心的大牛股呢？

Happily, it's easier than you may think. You don't need access to top management or internal company documents. Your own experience as a customer, in fact, can help you sort the true performers from the pretenders. Here are five questions to ask the best consumer expert around: yourself.

幸运的是，这也许比你想像的要容易。你无须接触公司的高管层，也用不着看公司的内部文件。事实上，你自己作为顾客的体验就可以让你识别那些口头上声称以顾客为中心的公司和那些真正这样做的公司。下面是向最好的消费专家，也就是你自己，提出的五个问题。

1. Is the company looking for ways to take care of you?
   这家公司是否设法满足你的需要？

Only a few companies identify customer needs first, and then create complete experiences to meet them.[20] The vast majority just try to make you buy the products and services they already offer. Those companies are product-centric, no matter what they claim.[21]

只有少数公司首先了解顾客的需要，然后为满足顾客的这些需要而不遗余力。绝大多数公司只是设法让你购买它们所提供的产品和服务。无论这些公司自己怎样说，其实都是以销售产品为中心的。

Here's an example of the difference. Royal Bank of Canada identified an important segment of its customers: snowbirds, Canadians who spend winters in Florida or Arizona. It is obviously a valuable segment, since its members tend to be quite affluent. They want the preferential treatment they get from RBC at home. They want to borrow in the US for condos or houses. They want a US credit rating that reflects their Canadian track record. Through it all, they want to be served by employees who know Canada as well as the US and who can speak French if necessary.

现举一例说明二者之间的区别。加拿大皇家银行确定了一个重要的客户群：那些来美国佛罗里达或亚利桑那过冬的加拿大人。这一群体显然非常有价值，因为这些人通常相当富有。他们希望加拿大皇家银行能给予他们在加拿大本土同样的优惠待遇。他们希望在美国贷款买公寓或房子。他们希望自己在美国的信用等级能够证明他们在加拿大的信用记录。最重要的是，他们希望为其提供服务的银行职员既了解加拿大又了解美国，并能在必要时讲法语。

To meet all those needs, RBC opened a branch in Hollywood, Fla., through its US subsidiary, RBC Centura.[22] The results have been exceptional: Customers are signing up in droves, and the new branch will have moved to profitability in months rather than the typical years. Opening new branches aimed at specific customer segments (rather than spending lots to buy branches) represents a tremendous growth opportunity for RBC's shareowners. They've already seen RBC stock grow 18% a year on average over the past 42 years, thanks in large part to the bank's pioneering customer-centricity efforts.

为了满足客户的所有上述需求，加拿大皇家银行在佛罗里达州的好莱坞市开设了一家支行，由其在美国的分行 RBC Centura 负责管理。这样做的效果相当不错，客户纷至沓来，新支行几个月后就可实现赢利，而一般情况则需要几年时间。开设针对特定客户群体的分支机构（而不是花很多钱去购买分支机构），这使得加拿大皇家银行的股东有机会获得巨额的资本增长。在过去的42年中，加拿大皇家银行的股价平均每年增长18%，这在很大程度上与该银行率先实施以顾客为中心的做法是分不开的。

2. **Does the company know its customers well enough to differentiate between them?**
这家公司是否对自己的顾客了如指掌并能对他们予以区别对待？

Differentiating between customers seems like common sense, and most companies claim to do it. But it's not as simple as, say, offering volume discounts or other special deals to big customers. Real differentiation means knowing who your various customer segments are, what each group wants most, where the groups are shopping, and how to serve the customers individually. Take Best Buy, which configures some stores to serve Jill, as we said, but also knows how to court

"Barry" (an aptly named segment of affluent entertainment lovers) with stores that have such amenities as a home-theater demo room. Still other stores are configured for budget-conscious family men ("Ray") or for young, early adopters of new technologies ("Buzz"), for small business customers, or for combinations of those segments.[23]

区别对待顾客似乎是常识，而且大多数公司也表明要这样做。但这并不像为大客户提供大额折扣或特殊优惠那么简单。真正的区别对待意味着，你应该了解你的各类客户群体是些什么人，每一群体最需要什么，这些群体在哪里购物，以及怎样为不同的顾客提供不同的服务。例如，我们上面说过，百思买为了向吉尔提供服务，改装了部分店面，但它同时也懂得如何讨好"巴里"（富有的、爱好娱乐的消费群体，这一名称颇为恰当），具体做法就是在一些商店配备了家庭影院展厅等娱乐设施。另外，为了迎合比较关注价格的居家男人"雷"，满足追逐新技术的年轻人"巴兹"，吸引小型企业客户，或者同时招揽这几类客户群体，一些商店也对自己的铺面进行了相应的改造。

3. Is someone accountable for you as a customer?
这家公司有人是否对作为顾客的你负责？

At most companies various departments own pieces, but no one owns any specific customer segment. Not so at Dell or RBC. Nor at Best Buy, which has an individual fully accountable for Jills across multiple stores using the same financial measures and operational metrics as Matt in the Pasadena store.

在大多数公司，各部门分工明确，但却没有专门负责某具体客户的部门。戴尔公司和加拿大皇家银行就不是这样。百思买也不是这样。百思买在各连锁店都有完全负责吉尔的人员，使用的财务指标和经营规范与马特在帕萨迪那商店使用的一样。

To see if a company operates this way, ask someone at the company: "Is someone here fully accountable for my relationship with you?" The answer—and the way it's answered—can tell you a lot. (If the rep on the other end of the phone has no idea what you're talking about, that's a clue.) Another way is to check with a part of the business you haven't used before. If you have only a checking account with a bank, call the mortgage people and see if they've ever heard of you.

看一家公司是否按照上述方式经营，只要问问该公司的某位工作人员："你们这里有人专门负责我们客户吗？"这位工作人员的回答及他回答这个问题的方式就可以让你了解很多情况。（如果接听电话的公司代表根本不知道你在说什么，这就说明问题了。）另一个了解情况的方法是，向你以前从未打过交道的业务部门查询。如果你在某家银行只有一个活期存款账户，那就打电话给按揭业务部门，看看他们是否听说过你。

4. **Is the company managed for shareholder value?**
   这家公司的经营是为股东创造价值吗？

If it is, then everyone there knows that the game is about earning a return on invested capital that exceeds the cost of capital, plus investing increasing amounts of capital at that positive spread and maintaining that spread for as long as possible. At the end of the day, those are the only factors that drive the share price. Customer-centric companies apply those criteria to customer segments. They know how much capital they've invested in a segment and how much return they earn on it. They maintain the positive spread by creating and reinventing enduring customer relationships. Thus, when an RBC segment manager created a program to attract first-time mortgage borrowers, she knew those customers were more interested in guidance through the scary home-buying experience than in getting rock-bottom rates (good return on capital for the bank) and were likely to become long-term customers (longer duration of positive spread).[24] Such companies can and do link their success with customers directly to the price of their stock.

如果是的话，那么公司里的每个人就会知道他们的工作是为了使投资资本回报高于资本成本，并加大资本投入以获得更大的差额收入，尽可能延长获得这种收益的时间。归根结底，这就是推动股价的唯一因素。以顾客为中心的上市公司对各个客户群都采用上述标准。它们清楚对某个客户群体投入了多少，能获得多少回报。它们与客户建立并进一步保持长期的关系，以获得长期稳定的投资收益。因此，当加拿大皇家银行某部门的经理制定计划吸引首次办理抵押贷款的顾客时，她很清楚这些客户只希望银行在风险极大的房屋买卖中为他们提供建议，而对获得低息贷款（对这家银行来说，这是很好的投资回报）并不怎么感兴趣，这些客户有可能成为银行的长期客户（银行将因此而长期受益）。此类上市公司之所以能够成功，就是他们能够并真正做到通过客户服务来推动其股价的升值。

Customer-centricity means that all employees understand how their actions affect the share price. Talk to employees. If they speak the language of shareholder value, you may have a winner.[25]
以顾客为中心就是指上市公司的所有员工都明白他们的一举一动将影响公司股价的走势。去找这些员工聊聊吧！如果他们理解股东价值的含义，这家公司的股票可能就是未来的大黑马。

5. **Is the company testing new customer offers and learning from the results?**
   这家公司是否不断研究新的客户服务项目，并从研究结果中得到启发？

Seven-Eleven Japan—consistently one of Japan's most profitable companies—does just that. (Like America's 7-Eleven, it's a subsidiary of Ito-Yokado.) Every week employees from all over Japan meet to discuss specific hypotheses tested and verified in the stores. It can be as obvious as changing the noodle order for the next day's lunch based on the weather forecast. (A cold day? Serve warm noodles!) Relentless learning about what customers want and a formal process for sharing it are critical to customer-centricity.

7-11便利店一直是日本一家最赚钱的公司,它就是这样做的。和美国的7-11便利店一样,该公司是日本伊藤洋华堂(Ito-Yokado)的附属公司。每个星期,7-11在日本各地的员工都会聚集到一起,讨论他们在各个商店中试行的一些具体做法。其中包括根据天气预报更改次日午餐的面条品种(天冷?改上热面条!)等并不复杂的便民措施。不断地了解顾客的需求,并通过正式的会议等方式让每个员工都了解,这是以顾客为中心的关键所在。

You'd think all companies would adhere to all five rules, but few do. Customer-centricity is hard. For investors, that's an attraction: Companies that achieve it hold an advantage that can lead to a jump in share price. They are companies investors should focus on now. Our test can help you tell the real deals from the rapidly proliferating fakes.[26]

你希望所有的公司都能按以上5条原则来经营,然而,几乎没有公司能真正这样做,因为切实做到顾客至上太难了。而对投资者来说,这正是吸引他们的地方:能够按顾客至上原则经营的公司优势明显,其股价也会因此而上涨。投资者从现在起就应当关注这类公司。我们推出的选股方法能助你去伪存真,在茫茫股海中发现真正有投资价值的上市公司。

Words and Expressions

knockout	a.	capable of knocking out 足以击倒的,猛烈的
shareholder	n.	one that owns or holds a share or shares of stock; a stockholder 持股者,持股人(也作 shareowner)
golly	n.	used to express mild surprise or wonder 啊,天哪(用来表达轻微的惊讶或惊奇),神
hype	v.	exaggerated or extravagant claims made especially in advertising or promotional material 广告,夸大的诉求(夸张或过分的宣称,尤其用在做广告或促销物品中)
spot	v.	to detect or discern, especially visually; spy 辨认,认出(特别指用眼睛看出),详查
vignette	n.	a short, usually descriptive literary sketch 小品文(简洁的描述性文学短文)
Pasadena		a city of southern California northeast of Los Angeles 帕萨迪那
pet name		a name of endearment (especially one using a diminutive suffix) 昵称,爱称
bunch	n.	a group of people usually having a common interest or association 一帮,一伙(有共同兴趣或合作关系的一群人)

soccer mom		an American mother living in the suburbs whose time is often spent transporting her children from one athletic activity or event to another 中产阶级妇女（住在郊区且有小孩的职业妇女），在美国选举中被视为强有力的利益团体（interest group），非常重视小孩休闲活动并亲自开车接送小孩参加运动、活动的母亲
right down the line		［口］完全地，彻底地
impulse	a.	characterized by impulsiveness or acting on impulse 冲动的（以冲动或即兴行动为特征的）
		an impulse shopper 即兴的购物者
		impulse buying 即兴购物
frequent	v.	to pay frequent visits to; be in or at often 时常出入，经常在那儿或常常出现
configure	v.	to design, arrange, set up, or shape with a view to specific applications or uses 使成形（为特定设备或用途而进行的设计、安排、设置或塑造）
		an internal security vehicle that was configured for rough terrain 专为崎岖道路而设计的内部安全车辆
turn	v.	to be stocked and sold 进货并销售
		This merchandise will turn easily. 这种商品很容易脱手。
inventory	n.	the quantity of goods and materials on hand; stock 存货总值（手头上货物和材料的数量），库存
returns	n.	收入，投资回报，收益，盈利，利润率
		returns on total assets 总资产收益
initiative	n.	a beginning or introductory step; an opening move 率先，开端，公开的行动
zenith	n.	the point of culmination; the peak 最高点，巅峰
in a league with		in the same league (as someone/something) having qualities or achievements similar to someone or something else 成绩或品格与某人或某物相同
P/E ratio		current stock price divided by trailing annual earnings per share or expected annual earnings per share 市盈率
torpid	a.	deprived of the power of motion or feeling; benumbed 迟钝的，呆滞的（没有行动或感觉的能力的），麻木的
spark	v.	to set in motion; activate 发动，触发
one-time	a.	only once 一次的，只有一次的
demon	n.	an evil supernatural being; a devil 恶魔，魔鬼
turbocharge	v.	(*informal*) to improve dramatically the performance or quality of 大幅度提高成绩或质量
emeritus	a.	retired but retaining an honorary title corresponding to that held immediately before retirement 荣誉退休的
embrace	v.	to avail oneself of 利用
snowbird	n.	one who moves from a cold to a warm place in the winter 打短工的流动工人

preferential	*a.*	of, relating to, or giving advantage or preference 优先的，优势或优先权的、与优势或优先权有关的，给予优势或优先权的 preferential treatment 优先的待遇
condo (condominium)	*n.*	分户出售公寓大厦
credit rating	*n.*	an estimate of the amount of credit that can be extended to a company or person without undue risk 信用等级
track record		a record of actual performance or accomplishment 成绩记录（真正成就或业绩的记录）
subsidiary	*n.*	a subsidiary company 子公司
Hollywood	*n.*	a city of southeast Florida on the Atlantic Ocean north of Miami Beach, which is a resort and retirement community with varied light industries 好莱坞（美国佛罗里达州东南部一城市，临近大西洋，位于迈阿密海滩北部，是旅游胜地和老年退休人员的社区，有各种轻工业）
sign up	*v.*	to agree to be a participant or recipient by signing one's name; enlist 经报名获得（通过签名同意成为……的成员或接受者），应募
in droves		成群结队，陆陆续续
differentiate	*v.*	to constitute the distinction between 区分
volume discount		总额折扣
court	*v.*	to attempt to gain the favor of by attention or flattery 企图获得，通过注意或奉承而试图引起……的好感 a salesperson courting a potential customer 一位正在说服有可能与之成交的顾客的推销员
aptly	*ad.*	适当地，适宜地
amenities	*n.*	a feature that increases attractiveness or value, especially of a piece of real estate or a geographic location 生活福利设施，便利设施，令人愉快之事物
financial measures		(or financial ratios) often used as very simple mechanisms to describe the performance of a business or investment 财务指标
metric	*n.*	a standard of measurement 度量
rep	*n.*	representative 商务代表
checking account		a bank account in which checks may be written against amounts on deposit 活期存款账户
mortgage	*n.*	a temporary, conditional pledge of property to a creditor as security for performance of an obligation or repayment of a debt 抵押
spread	*n.*	a difference, as between two figures or totals 差距，差异，差额，差价
positive spread		正向差幅，正差幅

rock-bottom	a.	the lowest possible level or absolute bottom; well below normal (especially in price) 最低的（价格）
		Prices have hit (reached) rock bottom. 价格降到了最低点。
hypothese	n.	proposal intended to explain certain facts or observations 臆测，假定
relentless	a.	steady and persistent; unremitting 不断的，稳定的，持续的，不松懈的
proliferate	v.	to increase or spread at a rapid rate 激增（高速增长或扩散）
fake	n.	one that is not authentic or genuine; a sham 冒牌货，赝品

Notes

1 Dell 戴尔
戴尔公司于1984年成立于美国，总部设在得克萨斯州奥斯汀（Austin），是全球领先的IT产品及服务提供商。

2 Best Buy 百思买
百思买是全球最大的家用电器和电子产品的零售和分销及服务集团。

3 Royal Bank of Canada 加拿大皇家银行
加拿大皇家银行（Royal Bank Canada）是加拿大最大的银行，同时也是全球性的金融服务机构。

4 Dell, Best Buy, and Royal Bank of Canada are stocks you wish you'd bought years ago.
你觉得，要是多年前你就买进了美国戴尔公司、百思买家电连锁巨头和加拿大皇家银行的股票，那该有多好啊。
这个英语句子看上去并不难译，直接按英语原有的句式译成"戴尔、百思买和加拿大皇家银行是你希望在多年前就已买进的股票"就行。但这样译有两个问题：① 戴尔和百思买也许很多读者并不知道指的是什么，是电脑还是别的什么呢？② 将定语"you wish you'd bought"这个表示愿望的虚拟从句译成"你希望……就已买进的……"，似乎愿望不够强烈。

5 They've all been knockout performers for shareholders for the same reason: Each has truly put customers at the center of its business. 这些年来，这些企业都为股东带来了巨大的回报，而它们的秘诀如出一辙：每家公司都真正做到了在经营中将顾客放在首位。
此句前半句完全采取意译的方法，巧妙地将"knockout performers for shareholders"转译成"为股东带来了丰厚的回报"，并将"reason"意译成"秘诀"，句子通顺自然，词义表达准确。后半句如果译成"每家公司都真正做到了把顾客置于业务的核心位置",感觉就稍微生硬了一点,汉语习惯说"以顾客为中心"、"顾客至上"或者"将顾客放在首位"。

6. And we mean truly-not in the golly-aren't-customers-great way that most companies have hyped for years but rather in a way that transforms the entire business. 我们所说的真正做到,是指这些企业不像大多数公司多年来那样只是高喊顾客就是上帝,而是指真正以顾客为中心,从而改变了整个企业的面貌。

   后半句中的"but rather in a way that transforms the entire business"如果译成"而是以此改变了公司的全部业务","以此"指代不明确,"改变公司的全部业务"也很含糊。"transforms the entire business"应该是指"转变了公司的经营模式或运作方式",所以不妨意译为"改变了公司的面貌或运作方式"。

7. UBS 瑞士银行集团(Union Bank of Switzerland)

8. What was most remarkable about Matt wasn't his helpful demeanor or plentiful pleases and thank-yous but rather what he knew about his customers—including one key group of them. 马特与众不同之处在于他对自己的顾客——其中包括一群重要的顾客——了如指掌,而不仅仅是待客彬彬有礼,热情周到。

   "helpful demeanor"和"plentiful pleases and thank-yous"直译都不大容易,所以采取意译的方法。另外,"what he knew about his customers"根据上下文是指"对顾客了解的程度",而不是"了解的内容",因此转译成"了如指掌"或"非常熟悉"。

9. ... which the company singularized as "Jill". ……为了称呼方便并区别于其他消费群体,公司特将这一群体称为"吉尔"。

   这个句子中的"singularized"一词很费解。查查词典,发现这个词作动词时除了有"成单数"的意思外,还有"to make conspicuous; distinguish"(使奇特,使突出,使惹人注目)的意思。因此,如果将句子直接译成"公司将这一群体冠以单人称的'吉尔'",读者就不容易理解,为什么要冠以单人称呢?所以,不如根据上下文意译成"为了称呼方便并区别于其他消费群体,公司特将这一群体称为'吉尔'"。

10. ... small appliances hadn't been selling well, even though they'd been chosen with Jill in mind. ……以前小家电的销售情况一直不理想,尽管当初公司在选择这些电器时就是将吉尔作为销售对象。

    这个句子的时态是过去完成时,表示过去的过去,尽管没有具体的时间状语,但翻译时应该增加"以前",表示这个动作发生在"小家电的销量不久就猛增"之前。另外,"with Jill in mind"可意译成"将吉尔作为销售对象"。

11. ... since the store just turns the appliance inventory faster. …… 因为商店正好将库存的电器产品更快地出售。

    这句话不宜直译成"因为商店只是使电器库存周转得更快了",英语"turn"在这里不是周转的意思,而是"把存货卖完"之意,再如"A pushcart vendor of applies may turn his stock every day."(推车卖苹果的小贩每天可以把货卖光。)。另外,"just"是"正好"的意思。

12 ... one of 32 pilot stores testing an initiative called "customer-centricity" ... ……百思买 32 家开展名为"以顾客为中心"活动的试点商店之一……
这个句子中的"initiative"是指"公开的行动";"called"不要译成"所谓的",而应该译成"名为"。

13 Customers loved the results. 顾客对开展这一活动的效果十分满意。
紧接上句,这里应该将省略的内容翻译出来。"results"显然是指开展"以顾客为中心"的活动的效果。"loved"可按汉语的表达习惯译成"对……感到满意"。

14 Wal-Mart 沃尔玛
沃尔玛百货有限公司由美国零售业的传奇人物山姆·沃尔顿先生于 1962 年在阿肯色州成立。经过四十余年的发展,沃尔玛百货有限公司已经成为美国最大的私人雇主和世界上最大的连锁零售商。

15 Home Depot 美国家得宝公司
家得宝公司成立于 1978 年,是全球最大的家具建材零售商、美国第二大的零售商。

16 In retailing, praise doesn't get higher than that. 在零售行业,最高的荣耀也不过如此。
这句话中的"praise"不是"赞扬"的意思,而应该是表示一种"荣耀"。

17 "Customer-centricity" means shareholders as well as customers win, because the customer-centric approach can juice a company's stock with a powerful double boost: rising earnings, plus a higher P/E multiple applied to those earnings. "以顾客为中心"意味着股东和顾客能够双赢,因为这种做法能够从两个方面大大增强公司股票的活力,即:增加公司的盈利,从而提高公司股票的市盈率。
首先,这个句子中的英语"juice"一词较难翻译,查查词典,发现作动词用时有"to give energy, spirit, or interest to"(给予活力、精神、兴趣)的意思,因此译成"增加活力"比较恰当。其次,句尾的"rising earnings, plus a higher P/E multiple applied to those earnings"非常专业,不懂股票投资的读者可能不大容易理解,所以翻译时应该格外小心。虽然英语原句中用的是两个名词"rising earnings(增长的利润)和 a higher P/E multiple(更高的市盈率倍数)",但在这里可以转译成动词,以便于后面句子的安排。一般说来,公司盈利的增长必然会降低股票的市盈率,而股票的市盈率越低,该股票就越具有投资价值。但由于投资者预测公司的利润将不断增长,他们就会不断买入该股票,随着股票价格的上升,该股票的市盈率自然就会高于其他股票,将来公司一旦实现预测的盈利,市盈率自然会随之降低。因此,这句话如果译成"因为这种做法能够给公司的股票以强大的双重推动:利润增加,以及按照这些利润计算的市盈率提高",读者就很难理解。

18 The effect is magical: If a stock is trading at a P/E of 20, which is about the market average, and earnings rise 20%, then the stock will also rise 20% as long as the P/E

remains unchanged. 市盈率调整能够产生神奇的效果：假设某上市公司股票的市盈率现为 20 倍，接近市场平均水平。如果公司的利润增长 20%，股价也将上升 20%，而市盈率仍保持不变。

英语"magical"不要译成"有魔力的"，而应该译成"神奇的，不可思议的"；英语"as long as the P/E remains unchanged"不能译成"只要市盈率不变"，这里"as long as"是"since"（既然）的意思。如果把这句话译成"它能够产生魔术般的效果：如果一只股票的市盈率是 20 倍，这大约也是市场的平均水平，这时利润增长 20%，那么，只要市盈率不变，该股的价格也将上升 20%"，"只要市盈率不变"就成了股价上涨的条件。事实上，股价（Price）上涨，市盈率（P/E ratio）必然上升，而只有公司盈利（Earnings）上升，才能使 P/E ratio 保持不变。因此，必须将"价格上升 20%"放在前面，"而市盈率仍保持不变"放在后面。

19 But if Wall Street decides that the company can sustain that profit growth for years into the future and thus deserves a new P/E of 40, then that 20% gain in earnings sparks a one-time jump of 140% in the stock, after which earnings increases get multiplied by 40. 但是，如果华尔街的投资人认定该公司能够在今后数年保持这一利润增长速度，那么该股的市盈率应当重新定位在 40 倍，这样一来，公司利润增长 20% 将使股价一下子上涨 140%，也就是股价 = 公司利润 × 40。

这个句子的原译文是："但是，如果华尔街认为该公司能够在今后数年保持这一利润增长速度，该股的市盈率应当调整为新的 40 倍，那么，利润增长 20% 将导致股价一次性飞涨 140%，此后的利润增长将是 40 倍。"①英语"Wall Street"不宜直译成"华尔街"，因为"华尔街"是指"股票市场"、"股票监管机构"、"券商"，还是指"股票投资人"，读者无从知道，这里还是应该翻译成具体的"华尔街的股票投资人"。②将"deserves a new P/E of 40"仅仅译成"该股的市盈率应当调整为新的 40 倍"，"deserves"的意思没有完全译出来，"new"也宜转译成副词"重新"。③不能将"after which earnings increases get multiplied by 40"译成"此后的利润增长将是 40 倍"。怎么能有如此巨大的增长呢？这里的 40 倍是指公司现有盈利与股价的倍数，而不是指利润增长 40 倍。

20 ..., and then create complete experiences to meet them. ……然后为满足顾客的这些需要而不遗余力。

本句中的"create complete experiences"原本是"创造完美体验"的意思，考虑到后面的不定式短语，将其意译成"不遗余力"也未尝不可。

21 Those companies are product-centric, no matter what they claim. 无论这些公司自己怎样说，其实都是以销售产品为中心的。

句子虽短，并不好翻译。问题出在"no matter what they claim"上。如果一定要把"what"译成"什么"，译文就很难理解：无论它们宣称自己是什么，这些公司都是以产品为中心的。因此，不如将"what"按"how"来处理，将"claim"译成"说"，句子就好处理了。

22 To meet all those needs, RBC opened a branch in Hollywood, Fla., through its US subsidiary, RBC Centura. 为了满足客户的所有上述需求，加拿大皇家银行在佛罗里达州的好莱坞市开设了一家支行，由其在美国的分行 RBC Centura 负责管理。

英语"Hollywood"不是指美国加利福尼亚州洛杉矶的一个区，于1910年并入洛杉矶，长期以来是电影和娱乐中心，而是指美国佛罗里达州东南部一城市。为了避免读者误解，翻译时应该在"好莱坞"后加上"市"。另外，"through its US subsidiary, RBC Centura"不宜直接译成"通过其在美国的附属公司 RBC Centura"，而应译成"由其在美国的附属公司 RBC Centura 负责管理"。

23 Still other stores are configured for budget-conscious family men ("Ray") or for young, early adopters of new technologies ("Buzz"), for small business customers, or for combinations of those segments. 另外，为了迎合比较关注价格的居家男人"雷"，满足追逐新技术的年轻人"巴兹"，吸引小型企业客户，或者同时招揽这几类客户群体，一些商店也对自己的铺面进行了相应的改造。

这是个典型的英语句子，主句"other stores are configured"后一连跟了4个介词短语。翻译时如果直译成"一些商店针对……进行了店面改造"，中间的部分就显得格外长，不太符合汉语的表达习惯。因此，可将4个"for"引导的介词短语译成汉语的目的状语，将主句放到最后，这样读起来似乎更加自然。

24 Thus, when an RBC segment manager created a program to attract first-time mortgage borrowers, she knew those customers were more interested in guidance through the scary home-buying experience than in getting rock-bottom rates (good return on capital for the bank) and were likely to become long-term customers (longer duration of positive spread). 因此，当加拿大皇家银行某部门的经理制定计划吸引首次办理抵押贷款的顾客时，她很清楚这些客户只希望银行在风险极大的房屋买卖中为他们提供建议，而对获得低息贷款（对这家银行来说，这是很好的投资回报）并不怎么感兴趣，这些客户有可能成为银行的长期客户（银行将因此而长期受益）。

这个句子并不复杂，问题是其中包含许多专业方面的词汇，因此在翻译时应该特别注意。①英语"segment manager"指的是部门经理。这个"segment"跟上文提到的"customer segments"不同。②"created a program to attract first-time mortgage borrowers"可以直接译成"制定计划吸引……顾客"。③如果将"were more interested in"原地直译成"对……更感兴趣"，那么介词"in"后面的句子就会拖得很长，不如意译成"只希望……"，将"were more interested in"放到"than in"后译成否定的"不怎么感兴趣"。④"the scary home-buying experience"不宜译成"在可怕的买房过程中"。⑤试与原译文作比较。[原译文：因此，当加拿大皇家银行的部门经理为了吸引首次办理按揭贷款的顾客而制定一项方案时，她知道这些客户更感兴趣的是在可怕的买房过程中得到指导,而不是获得低水平的贷款利率(对这家银行来说,这是很好的投资回报),他们有可能成为长期客户(银行收益持续的时间将变长)。]

25 If they speak the language of shareholder value, you may have a winner. 如果他们理解股东价值的含义,这家公司的股票可能就是未来的大黑马。

整个句子宜意译,因为"speak the language of shareholder value"不好直译;"you may have a winner"译成"这家公司可能就是赢家"也不大合适。

26 Our test can help you tell the real deals from the rapidly proliferating fakes. 我们推出的选股方法能助你去伪存真,在茫茫股海中发现真正有投资价值的上市公司。

此句根据意思意译比较合适,如果译成"我们的测试,能帮助你在当前貌似出众的投资对象日益激增的情况下,发现真正有价值的投资",就显得生硬牵强。

原文 1:

In other words, the advertising budget should be matched and spent in a retail business in proportion to the business being achieved, and at the time it is being generated.

原译:

换句话说,零售商的广告预算费应该与正在实现的营业额成比例,应该在正在产生营业额的时候支付出去。

点评:

① 英语"budget"指"the total sum of money allocated for a particular purpose or period of time",即"专款:为某一特定用途或某段时间拨发的钱财总数",如"a project with an annual budget of five million dollars"(一个年拨款为五百美元的项目)。此句中可以译成"广告费用",并且在后面增译动词"核算和支付",这样就符合汉语的表达习惯了。

② "in proportion to"是"依照比例"或"与……成比例"的意思,而不是"与……成正比"。

③ 将"at the time it is being generated"译成自然被动句,虽然不带被动标志"被",但被动的味道仍十分明显,不如改成其他句型更加自然。

改译:

换句话说,零售企业的广告费用应该根据现有的经营规模按比例进行核算和支付,具体数额以当月的营业额为准。

原文 2：

Conversely, firms in the rest of the world could not hope to compete with American firms technologically. They had to look for niches where the most advances technology was not central to success.

原译：

相反，世界其他地方的公司不会希望在技术上与美国公司竞争，他们不得不寻找最恰当的位置，在那些地方，最先进的技术并不是成功的关键因素。

点评：

① "could" 这里表示"能够"，应该译出来。
② 将 "niches" 译成"最恰当的位置"。不妥，这里是表示"在其他方面，想别的法子"的意思，与前文中的"在技术上"相对应。
③ 将限制性定语从句拆译不妥，应连起来译成汉语的偏正结构。

改译：

相反，世界其他地方的公司不可能希望在技术上与美国公司竞争，他们必须寻找其他不靠顶尖技术取胜的途径。

原文 3：

Customers spent by skimping on savings, borrowing heavily or cashing in stock profits.

原译：

消费者通过提取储蓄存款，大肆举债，或把股票赢利兑换成现金来进行消费。

点评：

① 英语 "skimp" 是 "to be stingy or very thrifty"（吝啬或非常节俭）之意，不宜译成"提取储蓄存款"。
② 英语 "cash in" 在这里不宜直接译成"把股票赢利兑换成现金"，因为 "cash in stock profits" 其实就是"卖掉已经赢利的股票"。

改译：

消费者减少存款，大肆举债并卖掉已经赢利的股票进行消费。

学生译作分析

原文：

Today, more than ever, managers must learn to use their time effectively. Whether you work in a large corporation or in a small business, how you use your time will determine what impact you have on your company. As a manager, you have many responsibilities, and most days seem to have too few hours for you to do all you must do. If you're to have an impact, you must learn to control your time and not let it control you. And you must recognize that if you try to do everything yourself, the days will never have enough hours. That's guaranteed!

学生原译文：

今天比以往任何时候都需要管理者学会有效地利用时间。无论你是在多大规模的公司工作，如何利用时间将决定你公司产生什么样的影响。作为一名管理者，你承担重担，很多时候你没有足够的时间去完成所有必须要做的工作，如果你希望自己有影响力的话，你就得学习掌握时间而不让时间来控制你；而且还得认识到如果你事事亲为，我保证，时间永远不会够。

分析：

(1) "today"在句中是状语，句子的主体是"managers must learn …"。译文将"today"译成主语并将"must"译成"需要"，这在一定程度上削弱了句子的力度。因此，还是按英语原句式翻译比较妥当。

(2) 第二句话中的"how you use your time"虽然是主语，但在前面加上"你"更好，因为这里利用时间的显然是作为管理者的"你"。另外，"将决定你公司产生什么样的影响"有点让人费解，究竟是公司对别的什么产生影响，还是你的行为对公司产生影响呢？译文好像交代得不很清楚。其实原文"will determine what impact you have on your company"就是指你的行为对公司的影响，可以译成"对企业的生产经营产生影响"，这样读者就更加容易理解。

(3) 将"and most days seem to have too few hours for you to do all you must do"译成"很多时候你没有足够的时间去完成所有必须要做的工作"不够准确，因为"most days"不表示"很多时候"，而且"seem"一词的含义也未表达出来。另外，"too few"应该表示"完全没有时间"的意思。

(4) 文中的"If you're to have an impact"不是很好理解，究竟是"如果你希望自己

（对公司）有影响力"，还是"如果你打算（通过自己合理安排时间给公司的经营带来积极影响）提高工作效率/工作卓有成效"呢？

（5）英语两个"control"在翻译时分别译成汉语的两个词，这很好。但选词时应该多斟酌，尽量做到符合汉语的表达习惯。

（6）"That's guaranteed!"最好按英语原句的句式单独成句，以便加强语气。

（7）最后，可以在独立的句子之间增译一些关联词语，使句子读起来比较连贯。

参考译文：

今天，管理者比以往任何时候都更应当学会有效地利用时间。不管你在大公司任职还是管理一家小型企业，你安排时间的方式都将最终影响这个企业的生产经营。作为公司经理，你的责任重大，好像整天手头有干不完的工作。因此，如果你打算工作卓有成效，你就必须学会合理安排时间而不让时间来支配你。另外，你还必须认识到，要是你事必躬亲，那你的时间将永远不够用。情况就是如此！

翻译技巧介绍

长句和复杂句子的翻译
(Translating Long and Complex Sentences)

长句和复杂句的翻译可以算得上一项"系统工程"。商务英语中长句较多，特别是商务合同一类的文件中，长而复杂的句子更加突出。由于英汉两种语言之间的差别，英语句子中并列复合句、主从复合句及包含各种短语的简单句用得比较多，而汉语表达一般提倡用短句和简单句。因此，翻译英语长句和复杂句的关键，就是先必须仔细分析英语句子中的各组成部分，理解它们所表示的各种关系。也就是说，如果句子没有分析清楚，就很难准确理解原文的意思，翻译也就无从下手了。

一、仔细分析，读懂原文

（1）分析句子的结构：确定句子是并列结构、主从结构还是以短语为主的结构。

（2）分析句子的成分：找出句子中的主语、谓语、宾语和其他成分。

（3）分析句中的非谓语形式：理清各种短语、插入语、固定搭配和独立结构与主句之间的关系。

例句 1：

Marketing is being done by staff who have joined the joint venture from Wu Liang Ye and who aim to make good use of the white spirit maker and wine importer's distribution network which goes into 8,000 hotels and restaurants.

这是一个主从复句，全句由一个被动形式的主句（简单句）和三个限制性定语从句组成，其中前两个由关系代词"who"引导的定语从句为并列结构，共同修饰先行词"staff"。后面由"which"引导的定语从句修饰"distribution network"。

例句 2：

The availability of venture capital financing to young, high technology companies has been a primary contributor to the dramatic revenue growth enjoyed by, and the increased competitiveness of, America's high technology industry and to the economic expansion and increased employment levels experienced in California's Silicon Valley and other areas of high technology company concentration.

这个句子虽然很长，但仔细分析，全句的结构为系表结构。句子的主语是"the availability"，表语是"has been a primary contributor"。句子之所以显得非常复杂，主要是句中对主要成分的修饰过多："the availability"后面的"of venture capital financing to young, high technology companies"、"primary contributor"后的"to…to…"、第一个介词短语中的过去分词短语"enjoyed by"和"the increased competitiveness of"、第二个介词短语中的"experienced in"。

例句 3：

(We open one new store a day. We hire 500 new people a month.) And the driving force of the company has always been trying to achieve this very fragile balance between recognizing the company's responsibility for long-term value and profitability for the shareholders, and the most important, constituency and responsibility for me, which is making sure that the people who do the work get rewarded.

这个句子初看并不复杂，但仔细分析一下，就会发现有些地方值得推敲。这个句子属于主从复合句，即：一个主句＋一个定语从句＋一个定语从句。主句是简单句，句子的主语是"the driving force of the company"，谓语是"has always been trying to achieve"，宾语是"this very fragile balance"。正是修饰这个宾语的介词"between"后面连着的几个并列结构、插入语及后面的定语从句使整个句子变得复杂。关键的问题是首先要确定这个"balance"是"between"哪两个部分，也就是说，三个"and"中哪一个是与"between"连用的。然后还要确定"which"引导的定语从句究竟是修饰什么，是修饰有着较长定语的"balance"，还是修饰"constituency and responsibility for me"或者仅仅是"responsibility for me"。

例句 4：

In practice, we have to take a close look at the wording used by the offeror in order to make a correct judgment, to examine whether the offer satisfies the two requirements which will be further explained in the following paragraphs, and whether it contains such qualifying conditions as "subject to our confirmation", which generally is not regarded as an offer, but an "invitation for offer".

这是一个主从复合句，句子中含有两个定语从句。主句中的主语、谓语和宾语非常明显，但"in order"后面的目的状语中却出现了两个不定式"to make a correct judgment"和"to examine"。紧接着又出现了由连接词"whether"引导的两个并列的名词性从句做"to examine"的宾语。在这两个名词性从句的后面分别出现了两个定语从句，第一个是限制性的，修饰名词从句中的宾语"two requirements"，第二个是非限制性的，修饰"such qualifying conditions as 'subject to our confirmation'"

例句 5：

I think, in an American context the trust is much more represented by the nature of the companies that you represent, rather than the individual trust between the people who are negotiating the particular contract that's in place.

这个句子的难度不在句子的结构，而在被动态和相关的词汇，如 in an American context、the nature of the companies、that's in place。

二、反复实践，合理安排

仔细分析了原文的句子结构，理解了原文的意思之后，是否就可以轻易地将原文所表达的意思准确、通顺并按汉语的表达习惯翻译出来呢？回答是否定的。有经验的译者都有这种体会，要想将一个表达比较复杂的概念英语长句和复杂句译成地道的汉语，除了必须熟练地运用前面各单元中所讲到的翻译技巧之外，还必须具有较高的汉语表达能力，也就是将英语原文所传达的意思用地道的汉语表达出来的能力。

人们从大量的翻译实践中发现，英语在表达习惯上倾向于在句子之间用连词或关联词语清楚地表明句子之间的相互关系，而汉语则不同，汉语句子之间只要意义和词序上能表明句子之间的关系，就无需使用关联词语。正因为两种语言的这一不同的特点，英语往往长句较多，汉语提倡使用短句，做层次分明的叙述。了解了这一特点之后，在翻译时就可以根据英语不同的句式从以下几个方面着手。

（1）按英语的语序顺着译：当英语叙述层次与汉语基本一致时，或翻译某些措辞严谨的商务文件时可以按照英语原文的顺序翻译。

（2）与英语的语序反着译：由于英汉两种语言之间在表达同一意思时的时间顺序和逻辑

顺序有时不完全相同，所以翻译时可以按汉语的习惯将语序完全颠倒或部分颠倒来进行翻译。

（3）将英语句子拆开翻译：有时英语长句中主语或主句与修饰词的关系并不十分密切，翻译时可以按照汉语多用短句的习惯，把长句的从句或短语化成句子，分开来叙述，以便使语意连贯。

（4）根据需要融合翻译：一些英语长句单纯采用上述任何一种方法翻译都很难处理，这时可以按照汉语表达习惯的需要，根据时间的先后，或按照逻辑顺序，顺逆结合，主次分明地对全句进行统筹安排。

（5）可以先将英语句子中每个单独的意思译成汉语的分句，然后再根据汉语的时间顺序或逻辑顺序排列。

（6）有时句子虽然不复杂，但由于用词不同或涉及一定的专业知识，所以翻译起来总感觉很难把原文句子中的意思讲清楚，这时应该大胆地根据原文的意思，采取词类转换、增词和拆分原句等方法并按照汉语句子的结构和表意方式重新安排句子。

例句 1：

Marketing is being done by staff who have joined the joint venture from Wu Liang Ye and who aim to make good use of the white spirit maker and wine importer's distribution network which goes into 8,000 hotels and restaurants.

尽管弄清了这个句子的结构，但在翻译时却遇到很大困难。首先，这个句子的主句是被动形式。如果按英语的顺序译成"销售业务正在由……的员工承办"，就会出现以下3个问题：

① 句子一开始就是一个汉语的完全被动态，读起来令人感到别扭，如何处理？

② 修饰动作的发出者"staff"的两个定语从句如果译成"……的员工"的偏正结构，句子就会非常长，从何处断句？

③ "Wu Liang Ye"和后面的"the white spirit maker and wine importer"属于同一个企业，怎样表达？其次，如果不按英语的句式直译，整个句子应该如何安排，谁前谁后呢？

试比较以下3种译文。

译文一：销售业务正在由来自五粮液的员工承办，他们打算好好利用这家分销网络已遍及中国8 000家酒店和餐厅的白酒酿造企业和葡萄酒进口商的销售渠道。

译文二：五粮液是一家白酒酿造企业和葡萄酒进口商，其分销网络遍及中国8 000家酒店和餐厅；合资企业的销售业务目前正是由来自五粮液的员工承办的，他们打算好好利用这一销售渠道。

译文三：五粮液是一家白酒酿造企业和葡萄酒进口商，其分销网络遍及中国8 000家酒店和餐厅，而目前承办合资企业销售业务的正是来自五粮液的员工，他们打算好好利用这一销售渠道。

译文一虽然将句中的第一个定语从句前置于"staff"之前，将第二个定语从句译成单独的并列分句，但前句为汉语的完全被动态，这样读起来很不自然，而后句"the white spirit maker and wine importer"前面的定语也过长，读起来也很费劲。此外，两句中的"五粮液"和"白酒酿造企业和葡萄酒进口商"看不出为同一企业。

译文二采取的是逆序的方法，将整个句子分成两个部分，中间用分号隔开。为了明确表明"五粮液"和"白酒酿造企业和葡萄酒进口商"二者之间的关系，译者首先将后面的句子提到前面来翻译，并将修饰这个企业的非限制性定语从句译成并列分句，这样读起来非常自然，符合汉语的表达习惯。分号之后的句子也是两个并列分句，但将英语的被动态译成汉语"……的"的句型，而下面分句的动作发出者却是"他们"，这样两句间的连贯性较差。此外，"……的"句型的力度也略显不够。

译文三仅仅将译文二中"……的"句型改成了"承办……正是来自五粮液的员工"，这样一来，句子所强调的就是"员工"，与后面句子中的"他们"正好对接。值得注意的是：虽然英语并没有用"It…"的强调句，但强调的意味实际上是非常明显的，因为既然五粮液有着如此庞大的分销网络，那么由来自这家企业的员工负责合资企业的销售业务当然是再好不过了。

例句 2：

The availability of venture capital financing to young, high technology companies has been a primary contributor to the dramatic revenue growth enjoyed by, and the increased competitiveness of, America's high technology industry and to the economic expansion and increased employment levels experienced in California's Silicon Valley and other areas of high technology company concentration.

翻译这个句子可以采取顺序法，因为整个句子的结构并不复杂，翻译时只需将英语的某些词类转译成汉语的另一些词类即可。

译文一：新开业的高技术公司可以获得风险资本融资，这对美国高技术产业收入的大幅度增长和竞争力的提高，以及对加州硅谷和其他高技术公司集中地所取得的经济发展和就业水平的增长，都起了重要作用。

译文二：新兴的高技术公司可以获得风险资本融资，这使得美国高技术产业的收入大幅增长，竞争力不断提高，同时还促使加州硅谷和其他高技术公司集中地的经济蓬勃发展，就业人数大大增加。

译文一"对……都起了重要作用"之间的部分略显过长。

译文二几乎将所有的英语名词全部转译成动词，并将英语的长句译成汉语的并列短句，读起来更加符合汉语的表达习惯。

例句 3：

(We open one new store a day. We hire 500 new people a month.) And the driving force of the company has always been trying to achieve this very fragile balance between recognizing the company's responsibility for long-term value and profitability for the shareholders, and the most important, constituency and responsibility for me, which is making sure that the people who do the work get rewarded.

翻译这个句子时可以先将每层意思译出，然后再按汉语的表达习惯进行排列。

① 公司前进的动力来自公司始终努力在两个方面取得非常微妙的平衡。
② 一方面承认公司有责任使公司长期增值，从而为股东带来收益。
③ 另一方面，而且是最重要的一方面，公司还必须照顾那些给予我支持的员工及我应该履行的义务。
④ 这种照顾和我必须履行的义务就是：保证所有为公司工作的人都能够劳有所获。

译文一：（我们每天开一家新店，每天录用500名新员工。）公司前进的驱动力一直是尽力在两者之间达到这种非常微妙的平衡：一方面是，确认公司实现长期价值的责任和公司为股东创造价值的盈利性；另一最重要的方面是，支持我的员工和我担负的责任，即确保为公司工作的人都得到回报。

译文二：（我们每天开一家新店，每天录用500名新员工。）公司之所以能够持续发展，就是因为公司一直努力在平衡这样一对非常微妙的关系，即：公司不仅有义务使公司长期增值，让股东们受益，更重要的是，公司还必须顾及那些给予我支持的员工的利益，必须让我尽到我应尽的义务，那就是确保所有为公司工作的人都劳有所得。

译文一完全按以上4层意思的顺序排列，但是读起来仍让人感觉生硬和别扭，翻译的痕迹十分明显。为什么会这样呢？首先，译者完全依照英语的词类和句式翻译，而不是将英语的意思用地道的汉语表达出来。例如，将"driving force of the company"直译成"公司前进的驱动力"，但后面的谓语动词又是"尽力在两者之间达到……平衡"，整个句子读起来就是"驱动力是达到平衡"。这样的句子读起来让人难受，而且意思也令人费解。另外"两者之间"和"这种非常微妙的平衡"都存在着汉语表达上的问题，既然"两者"出现在下文，汉语的习惯就必须在"两者"之前增加限定词"以下"；既然"非常微妙的平衡"也是在下文才解释，所以"this"就不能译成"这种"，而应该译成"一种"或"某种"。其次，译者将英语的抽象名词译成对应的汉语，这就造成读者理解上的困难，如将"responsibility for long-term value and profitability"译成"实现长期价值的责任和公司为股东创造价值的盈利性"等。

例句4：

In practice, we have to take a close look at the wording used by the offeror in order to make a correct judgment, to examine whether the offer satisfies the two requirements which will be further explained in the following paragraphs, and whether it contains such qualifying conditions as "subject to our confirmation", which generally is not regarded as an offer, but an "invitation for offer".

译文一：在实际应用中，我们必须看清楚发盘人的措辞，以便做出正确的判断。检查此发盘是否满足下文将要解释的两项要求，以及它是否包含这样的适应条款，如"须经我方认可"，这种措辞通常不被看作发盘，而是一项"要约邀请"。

译文二：在实际业务中，为了准确判断，我们必须仔细阅读发盘人在发盘中的措辞，以便核对该发盘是否符合下节中所规定的两项要求，以及它是否包含"须经我方认可"之类的条件性条款，因为具有这类条款的报盘通常不能认作发盘，而只能看成是"要约邀请"。

① 这句话之前的句子是："The Convention gives no express provisions on how to judge whether the offeror has the 'intention' to be bound by the offer."，因此"in practice"译成"在实际业务中"和"在实际操作中"更加恰当。
② 可以将第一个不定式前置，译成汉语的目的状语，读起来更加通顺。
③ 最后的非限制性定语从句可以译成汉语表因果的状语从句。
④ "satisfies"宜译成"符合"；"qualifying"译成"条件性"更加准确。

例句 5：

I think, in an American context the trust is much more represented by the nature of the companies that you represent, rather than the individual trust between the people who are negotiating the particular contract that's in place.

译文一：我认为，在美国，信赖更多地是由你所代表的公司的本质来表现，而不是由正在就某个特定合同进行谈判的人们之间的个人信赖所表现。

译文二：我认为，如果谈判是在美国进行，那么双方是否能相互信任完全是由各自公司的性质决定的，具体谈判人之间是否信赖不是很重要。

译文三：我认为，美国人谈判，公司之间的信任更重要，具体谈判人之间的信任次之。

译文四：我认为，如果谈判是在两家美国公司之间进行，谈判双方看重的是双方公司之间的相互信任，而不是具体谈判人个人的相互信赖。

① "in an American context"如果译成"在美国"，那为什么原文不直接说"in America"呢？
② 将两个句子都按英语的句式译成汉语的完全被动态，读起来很别扭。"that's in place"是修饰"contract"还是"the individual trust"？
③ 译文三有所突破，已经能够突破原句的句法和词法上的局限，用通俗的汉语将原文的意思表达出来，只不过稍微简单了一点。

课堂翻译训练

将下列句子译成汉语。

1. The World Trade Organization has kicked off five days of ministerial meetings in Cancun, Mexico aimed at breaking the deadlock in trade negotiations as rich and poor nations face off over agricultural subsidies.

2. In the United States, most airlines have produced Customer Service Plans, which, if you cut through the verbiage behind which many are concealed, state precisely what they will do for customers whose flights are delayed or cancelled.

3. A World Bank report released at the time of the conference, which ended on 10 November, insists that Vietnam's overall growth will depend more on its own policies than on the volume of external financing.

4. In order to keep Party A well informed of the prevailing market conditions, Party B should undertake to supply Party A, at least once a quarter or at any time when necessary, with market reports concerning changes of the local regulations in connection with the import and sales of the commodity covered by this agreement, local market tendency and the buyer's comments on quality, packing, price, etc. of the goods supplied by Party A under this agreement.

5. For the emerging company, the association with a corporate partner may not only enhance the emerging company's balance sheet, but may enhance its credibility with customers, suppliers, investors and others, as well as create opportunities for the emerging company to leverage off of the corporate partner's marketing and distribution net work or administrative services.

6. Companies have learned that diversity training, attitudinal training, and other efforts to change how people look at other people can have significant payoffs in changing the way their service employees interact with each other and with the many types of guests who come through the entrance.

将下列短文译成英语,注意运用本单元所学的翻译技巧。

1.

Once people have been a particular organization's guests, their own past experiences with that organization provide the primary basis for their expectations regarding future experiences.

Most hospitality organizations try to provide their guests with accurate information ahead of them so these customers come to the experience with expectations that the organization can meet or exceed. If the hospitality organization does not provide that information, then guests will obtain or infer it, accurately or inaccurately, from other sources, perhaps the organization's general reputation or experiences that friends have had with the organization or that they themselves have had with similar organizations. People going to Wendy's have well-defined expectations about the entire experience and notice quickly when the food is not up to par, the rest rooms are dirty, or something else is different from what they expected.

2.

On Aug. 9, 2007, and the days immediately following, financial markets in much of the world seized up. Virtually overnight the seemingly insatiable desire for financial risk came to an abrupt halt as the price of risk unexpectedly surged. Interest rates on a wide range of asset classes, especially interbank lending, asset-backed commercial paper and junk bonds, rose sharply relative to riskless US Treasury securities. Over the past five years, risk had become increasingly underpriced as market euphoria, fostered by an unprecedented global growth rate, gained cumulative traction.

The crisis was thus an accident waiting to happen. If it had not been triggered by the mispricing of securitized subprime mortgages, it would have been produced by eruptions in some other market. As I have noted elsewhere, history has not dealt kindly with protracted periods of low risk premiums.

The root of the current crisis, as I see it, lies back in the aftermath of the Cold War, when the economic ruin of the Soviet Bloc was exposed with the fall of the Berlin Wall. Following these world-shaking events, market capitalism quietly, but rapidly, displaced much of the discredited central planning that was so prevalent in the Third World.

A large segment of the erstwhile Third World, especially China, replicated the successful economic export-oriented model of the so-called Asian Tigers: Fairly well educated, low-cost workforces were joined with developed-world technology and protected by an increasing rule of law, to unleash explosive economic growth. Since 2000, the real GDP growth of the developing world has been more than double that of the developed world.

The surge in competitive, low-priced exports from developing countries, especially those to Europe and the US, flattened labor compensation in developed countries, and reduced the rate of inflation expectations throughout the world, including those inflation expectations embedded in global long-term interest rates.

In addition, there has been a pronounced fall in global real interest rates since the early 1990s, which, of necessity, indicated that global saving intentions chronically had exceeded intentions to invest. In the developing world, consumption evidently could not keep up with the surge of income and, as a consequence, the savings rate of the developing world soared from 24% of nominal GDP in 1999 to 33% in 2006, far outstripping its investment rate.

  佳译赏析

The Growth of Direct Marketing and Electronic Business
直接营销和电子商务的发展

From Marketing Management
By Philip Kotler[1]

The Direct Marketing Association (DMA)[2] defines direct marketing as follows:
Direct marketing is an interactive marketing system that uses one or more advertising media to effect a measurable response and/or transaction at any location.[3]
直销协会（DMA）给"直接营销"所下的定义如下：
直接营销是一种为了在任何地方可度量的反应或达成交易而使用的一种或多种广告媒体的交互作用的市场营销体系。

This definition emphasizes a measurable response, typically a customer order. Thus direct marketing is sometimes called direct-order marketing.
根据这一定义，直接营销的重点便在于获得一个可度量的反应，亦即从顾客处获得订单。因此，它有时可被称为直接订货营销。

Today, many direct marketers see direct marketing as playing a broader role, that of building a long-term relationship with the customer (direct relationship marketing).[4] Direct marketers occasionally send birthday cards, information materials, or small premiums to select members in their customer base. Airlines, hotels, and other businesses build strong customer relationships through frequency award programs and club programs.[5]
今天，许多直接营销者发现他们扮演的角色越来越广泛，他们可以与顾客建立长期的关系

（直接关系营销）。直接营销者给从他们顾客库中经选择的顾客经常性地寄出生日贺卡、信息资料或小赠品。航空、旅馆及其他一些行业通过各种有奖活动（如老乘客的免费公里数）和其他方案以建立强有力的顾客关系。

THE GROWTH OF DIRECT MARKETING AND ELECTRONIC BUSINESS
直接营销和电子购买的发展

Sales produced through traditional direct-marketing channels (catalogs, direct mail, and telemarketing) have been growing rapidly. The extraordinary growth of direct marketing is the result of many factors. Market "demassification" has resulted in an ever-increasing number of market niches with distinct preferences.[6] Higher costs of driving, traffic congestion, parking headaches, lack of time, a shortage of retail sales help, and queues at checkout counters all encourage at-home shopping. Consumers appreciate direct marketers' toll-free phone numbers available 24 hours a day, 7 days a week, and their commitment to customer service. The growth of next-day delivery via Federal Express, Airborne, and UPS has made ordering fast and easy. In addition, many chain stores have dropped slower-moving specialty items, creating an opportunity for direct marketers to promote these items directly to interested buyers. The growth of affordable computer power and customer databases has enabled direct marketers to single out the best prospects for any product they wish to sell.

通过传统的直接营销渠道（目录单、直接邮寄和电话营销），业务量迅速发展。直接营销之所以能够迅速发展，原因是多方面的。市场"分众化"使得各种偏好的利基市场数量猛增。高昂的驾车开支、交通堵塞、停车的麻烦、时间不足、零售店帮助的缺少及结账时排队都刺激了在家购物。消费者对直接营销者提供的每周7天、每天24小时免费购物电话和客户服务特别青睐。而联邦快递、泰龙及UPS的隔日（24小时）送货制度也使得直接订购快捷而方便。此外，许多连锁店已不再经营销售缓慢的特殊商品，直接营销正好借机向有兴趣的客户推销这些产品。最后，计算机的普及使直接营销者得以建立客户信息库，并从中选出所要推销的最佳对象。

THE BENEFITS OF DIRECT MARKETING
直接营销的益处

Direct marketing benefits customers in many ways. Home shopping is fun, convenient, and hassle-free[7]. It saves time and introduces consumers to a larger selection of merchandise. They can do comparative shopping by browsing through mail catalogs and on-line shopping services. They can order goods for themselves or others. Business customers also benefit by learning about available products and services without tying up time in meeting salespeople.[8]

直接营销给顾客带来许多好处，消费者认为在家中购物有趣、方便并能避免嘈杂之累。这一方式节约了时间并能为顾客提供品种更加多样的商品。顾客通过浏览邮寄目录单和网上购物服务，比较商品，为自己和别人订购商品。工业品采购者也能从中获得好处，尤其是不必花费很多时间与销售人员会面，便可了解各种产品和服务情况。

Sellers also benefit. Direct marketers can buy a mailing list containing the names of almost any group: left-handed people, overweight people, and millionaires. They will personalize and customize their messages. [9]

直接营销给销售人员也带来了好处。直接营销者几乎可以买到一份邮件发送清单，其中包括各类人员：左撇子、超重者、百万富翁，等等。然后，这类信息可以个性化和定制。

Direct marketing can be timed to reach prospects at the right moment, and direct-marketing material receives higher readership because it is sent to more interested prospects. Direct marketing permits the testing of alternative media and messages in search of the most cost-effective approach. Direct marketing also makes the direct marketer's offer and strategy less visible to competitors. Finally, direct marketers can measure responses to their campaigns to decide which have been the most profitable.

直接营销人员可以选择适当的时机与预期的顾客取得联系，并将相关资料直接发送给对其产品有兴趣的消费者，因此营销产品的资料拥有更广泛的读者。此外，直接营销人员还得以尝试使用不同方式来发送相关的产品信息，从而寻找到最划算的销售途径。直接营销人员直接向消费者寄送资料并采取竞争对手难以发现的营销策略进行销售。最后，直接营销人员可以测量到顾客的反应，从而得以准确判断出最佳赢利方案。

FACE-TO-FACE SELLING
面对面推销

The original and oldest form of direct marketing is the field sales call. Today most industrial companies rely heavily on a professional sales force to locate prospects, develop them into customers, and grow the business. Or they hire manufacturers' representatives and agents to carry out the direct-selling task. In addition, many consumer companies use a direct-selling force: insurance agents, stockbrokers, and distributors working for direct-sales organizations such as Avon, Amway, Mary Kay, and Tupperware[10].

直接营销最基础和最原始的形式是销售访问。今天，大多数公司较多地依靠专业销售队伍访问预期客户，将他们发展成顾客，并不断增加业务。或者，它们聘用制造商代表和代理执行直接推销的任务。另外，许多消费者公司，如雅芳、安利、玫琳凯和特百惠，也采用直销队伍：保险公司代理、股票经纪人及为直销机构工作的批发商。

DIRECT MAIL
直接邮寄营销

Direct-mail marketing involves sending an offer, announcement, reminder, or other item to a person at a particular address. Using highly selective mailing lists, direct marketers send out millions of mail pieces each year—letters, flyers, foldouts, mail audiotapes, videotapes, CDs, and computer diskettes to prospects and customers.

直接邮寄营销包括向一个有具体地址的人寄发报价单、通知、纪念品或其他项目。应用高度选择的邮寄清单，直接营销者每年要发出几百万的邮件——信件、传单、折叠广告、音带、录像带，甚至计算机盘片——给预期顾客和客户。

Direct mail is a popular medium because it permits target market selectivity, can be personalized, is flexible, and allows early testing and response measurement. Although the cost per thousand people reached is higher than with mass media, the people reached are much better prospects.

直接邮寄之所以日益流行，是因为它能更有效地选择目标市场，可实现个性化，比较灵活，以及较易检测各种结果。尽管该方法每千人接触成本较之采用大众化广告媒体要高，但所接触的人成为顾客的可能性较大。

Objectives
目标

Most direct marketers aim to receive an order from prospects. A campaign's success is judged by the response rate. An order-response rate of 2 percent is normally considered good, although this number varies with product category and price.

大多数直接营销者的目标是收到预期顾客的订单。推销活动是否成功的标准是预期顾客的回应率。如果有2%的顾客订购就已经不错了，但由于产品类型和价格不同，这一比率也会有所变化。

Direct mail has other objectives as well, such as producing prospect leads, strengthening customer relationships, and informing and educating customers for later offers[11].

直接邮寄也有其他目标，其中之一是为销售队伍寻找预期的顾客线索。另一个是强化顾客关系。有些直接营销者开展这项活动是向顾客通报某些信息，为以后的购买做准备。

Target Markets and Prospects
目标市场和预期的顾客

Direct marketers need to identify the characteristics of prospects and customers who are most able, willing, and ready to buy. Bob Stone[12] recommends applying the R-F-M formula (recency, frequency, monetary amount) for rating and selecting customers: The best customer targets are those who bought most recently, who buy frequently, and who spend the most. Points are established for varying R-F-M levels, and each customer is scored. The higher the score, the more attractive the customer.

直接营销者应该辨别那些最可能购买、最愿意购买及随时准备购买的顾客和潜在消费者的各种特性。鲍勃·斯通建议应用 R-F-M 公式,即近期购买(recency)、购买次数(frequency)、购买金额(monetary amount),将顾客进行排队,并从中进行选择。最佳的目标顾客应该是那些最近购买过的、最经常购买的及花钱最多的顾客。按不同的 R-F-M 水平给每位顾客打分,然后得到每一位顾客的总分:分数越高,该顾客就越有吸引力。

Prospects can also be identified on the basis of such variables as age, sex, income, education, and previous mail-order purchases. Occasions provide a good departure point for segmentation. New parents will be in the market for baby clothes and baby toys; college freshmen will buy computers and small television sets; newlyweds will be looking for housing, furniture, appliances, and bank loans. Another useful segmentation variable is consumer lifestyle groups, such as computer buffs, cooking buffs and outdoor buffs.

理想的预期顾客可以根据诸如年龄、性别、收入、受教育程度、购买邮购商品的历史等变量来加以识别。有时,其他一些因素也可以作为很好的细分标准,如年轻妈妈是婴儿服装和婴儿玩具的主要顾客;刚入学的大学生将购买打字机、计算机、电视机和服装等;新婚夫妇将考虑买房子、家具、家用电器和向银行贷款。另一个有用的细分标准就是消费者生活方式,例如计算机迷、烹调迷、户外活动迷或其他迷等。

Once the target market is defined, the direct marketer needs to obtain specific names. Here is where mailing-list acquisition and mailing-list-database building come into play. Additional names can be obtained by advertising some free offer. The direct marketer can also buy lists of names from list brokers. But these lists often have problems, including name duplication, incomplete data, and obsolete addresses. The better lists include overlays of demographic and psychographic information. Direct marketers typically buy and test a sample before buying further names from the same list.

一旦确定目标市场,直接营销者就需要获得目标市场上可能的顾客名单。这里便要动用邮寄名单以获得和建立邮寄单数据库。通过广告反馈也能增加名单数量。直接营销者也可以从名单经纪人那儿购买其他的名单。但这些名单有各种问题,例如名字的重复、资料不全、地址已废弃不用等。较理想的名单还应包括有关人文统计和心理特征的信息,直接营销者通常在为同样内容购买追加的名单之前,应对其名单样本做一次测试。

Offer Elements
报价要素

Nash[13] sees the offer strategy as consisting of five elements—the product, the offer, the medium, the distribution method, and the creative strategy. Fortunately, all of these elements can be tested.
纳什认为产品战略由 5 个要素构成——产品、报价、媒体、分销方式和创新策略。所幸的是，这些要素都能加以测试。

In addition to these elements, the direct-mail marketer has to decide on five components of the mailing itself: the outside envelop, sales letter, circular, reply form, and reply envelope. Here are some findings[14].
除这些因素外，直接邮寄营销者还必须决定邮件自身的 5 个内容：信封封面、推销信、广告传单、回复表格和回复信封。寄信时可注意以下几点。

- The outside envelope will be more effective if it contains an illustration, preferably in color[15], or a catchy reason to open the envelope, such as the announcement of a contest, premium, or benefit. Envelopes are more effective when they contain a colorful commemorative stamp, when the address is hand-typed or handwritten, and when the envelope differs in size or shape from standard envelopes.
  这样的信封会更有吸引力：封面印有插图，颜色很漂亮，或有一些小花样能诱人打开信封，比如告诉收信人一场比赛、内含一份奖品或某种好处。当然，要是信封上贴有一张色彩鲜艳的纪念邮票，或者地址是手写或用打字机打的，或者信封的大小形状与普通信封不同，信封的效果则更佳。

- The sales letter should use a personal salutation[16] and start with a headline in bold type. The letter should be printed on good-quality paper and be brief. A computer-typed letter usually outperforms a printed letter, and the presence of a pithy P.S. increases the response rate, as does the signature of someone whose title is important.
  推销信应使用称谓，黑体字标题。信纸应使用优质纸，信的内容应该简单明了。用计算机打印的信通常比统一印制的信效果更好。另外，在信尾加上简练的"附笔"可提高回复率。同样，在所签姓名边加上头衔也是很重要的。

- In most case, a colorful circular accompanying the letter will increase the response rate by more than its cost.
  在很多情况下，随函附寄彩色的广告传单也会提高回复率，并可弥补它的成本。

- Better results are obtained when the reply form features a toll-free number and contains a perforated receipt stub and guarantee of satisfaction.
在回复表格上印上以下内容效果更好：免费电话号码，可撕下的收据存根，以及使对方满意的承诺。

- The inclusion of a postage-free reply envelope will dramatically increase the response rate.
附上一个邮资已付的回复信封则会大大增加回复率。

Testing Elements
测试直接营销的各要素

One of the great advantages of direct marketing is the ability to test, under real marketplace conditions, the efficacy of different elements of an offer strategy, such as product features, copy, prices, media, or mailing lists. [17]
直接营销的巨大优势之一便是它能够在一个真实的市场条件下对组成提供战略的各个要素的效能进行测试。直接营销可以测试产品特色、价格、媒体、邮寄名单等。

Direct marketers must remember that response rates typically understate a campaign's long-term impact. [18] Suppose only 2 percent of the recipients who receive a direct-mail piece advertising Samsonite luggage place an order. A much larger percentage became aware of the product (direct mail has high readership), and some percentage may have formed an intention to buy at a later date (either by mail or at a retail outlet). [19] Furthermore, some of them may mention Samsonite luggage to others as a result of the direct-mail piece. To derive a more comprehensive estimate of the promotion's impact, some companies are measuring direct marketing's impact on awareness, intention to buy, and word of mouth.
直接营销者必须记住，直接营销广告的响应率通常低估了该广告的长期影响。假设只有2%的人看了直接营销新秀丽（Samsonite）箱包的直接邮寄广告后提出订购，但是，有相当一部分人知道这一品牌的箱包（如果有直接邮件有较高的可读性），有一部分人可能准备过些时候就去买（他们可能到一个零售店去买）。也有这种可能，譬如一些看过有关直接营销邮件的人会向其他人提及新秀丽箱包。现在，有些公司在检测直接营销效果时还包括对品牌的知晓度、打算购买的意向和口碑等，这样得到的促销效果就超过了单纯以回复率测算的结果。

Measuring Campaign Success: Lifetime Value
衡量直销活动的成功性: 生命周期价值

By adding up the planned campaign costs, the direct marketer can figure out in advance the needed break-even response rate. This rate must be net of returned merchandise and bad debts. Returned merchandise can kill an otherwise effective campaign. The direct marketer needs to analyze the main causes of returned merchandise (late shipment, defective merchandise, damage in transit, not as advertised, incorrect order fulfillment).
将计划中的直销活动成本加起来,直接营销者便可以事先计算出达到保本所需要的响应率。这个响应率必须将退货和不能收回的货款(债务)排除在外。退货能使一次本来十分成功的直接营销活动前功尽弃。直接营销者应该分析退货的原因(送货不及时、次品、在运输途中受损、与广告宣传不符或者交付订单有误,等等)。

By carefully analyzing past campaigns, direct marketers can steadily improve their performance. Even when a specific campaign fails to break even, it can still be profitable.[20] Consider the following situation.
通过对以往的直销活动进行仔细分析,直接营销者可以不断地改善他们的业绩。甚至当某一场直销活动亏了本,它依然可能是有利的。研讨下述例子。

Suppose a membership organization spends $10,000 on a new-member campaign and attracts 100 new members, each paying annual dues of $70. It appears that the campaign has lost $3,000 ($10,000 - $7,000). But if 80 percent of the new members renew their membership in the second year, the organization gets another $5,600 without any effort. It has now received $12,600 ($7,000 + $5,600) for its investment of $10,000. To figure out the long-term break-even rate, one needs to know the percentage who renew each year and for how many years they renew.
假设一个会员制组织花 1 万美元搞了一次吸引新会员的活动,结果吸纳了 100 个新会员,每位新会员每年支付了 70 美元的会费,那么,看似这场活动亏了 3 000 美元(10 000 美元 - 7 000美元)。但是,如果其中 80% 的新会员第二年延长会员资格,那么,这一组织无需额外推销活动又可获得 5 600 美元。结果,该组织当初投资 10 000 美元却收到了 12 600 美元(7 000美元 + 5 600美元)的回报。因此,要计算长期的保本率,不能只考虑第一年的响应情况,还应该考虑今后若干年内每一年的续订率。

This example illustrates the concept of customer lifetime value. A customer's ultimate value is not revealed by a purchase response to a particular mailing. Rather, the customer's lifetime value is the expected profit made on all future purchases net of customer acquisition and maintenance costs. [21] For an average customer, one would calculate the average customer longevity, average customer annual expenditure, and average gross margin, minus the average cost of customer acquisition and maintenance (properly discounted for the opportunity cost of money). [22] Data Consul claims it is able to estimate the expected lifetime value of a customer from as few as three or four transactions. This information enables marketers to adjust the nature and frequency of communications.

上面例子说明了有关顾客生命周期价值（lifetime value）这一概念。顾客的最终价值并非在某一次邮寄时便显露出来。顾客的最终生命周期价值乃是他或她在一段时间内总的采购额减去他获得商品和保留商品所耗费的成本。在计算一个平均客户时，要计算平均持续时间、每年的客户开支和平均毛利（对机会成本的适当折扣），减去获得平均客户的成本。数据咨询公司声称，只需计算3次或4次交易便能估算出顾客生命周期价值。营销者可根据这些信息决定如何与不同的客户进行联系及联系的频率。

Words and Expressions

direct marketing		marketing via a promotion delivered directly to the individual prospective customer 直接营销
electronic business		(or "e-business") may be defined broadly as any business process that relies on an automated information system 电子商务
interactive	a.	acting or capable of acting on each other 互相作用的或能互相作用的
measurable	a.	of distinguished importance; significant; valuable 重要的，重大的，值得注意的，有价值的
premium	n.	something offered free or at a reduced price as an inducement to buy something else 赠品（为刺激购买其他物品而免费赠送或减价销售的东西）
frequency	n.	the property or condition of occurring at frequent intervals 频繁性（有规律间歇出现的特性或情况）
telemarketing	n.	use of the telephone in marketing goods or services 电话销售（使用电话销售货物或销售服务）
demassification	n.	breaking up of a large company: the restructuring of a company into smaller independent operating entities 分众化
niche	n.	a special area of demand for a product or service 产品或服务所需的特殊领域 One niche that is approaching mass-market proportions is held by regional magazines. (Brad Edmondson) 正在接近群众（大的、集中的）市场比例的领域被地方性杂志占据着。（布拉德·埃德蒙森）

		A niche market is a focused, targetable portion of a market sector. 利基市场是指那些高度专门化的需求市场。 market niche 也可以翻译成"推销缝隙产品"。 niche market 可以翻译成"利基（小的、分散的）市场"或"缝隙市场"。
prospect	n.	a potential customer, client, or purchaser　可能的顾客
hassle	n.	trouble; bother　麻烦，打扰
browse	v.	to read something superficially by selecting passages at random　浏览文章
tie up		to keep occupied; engage　占用
customize	v.	to make or alter to individual or personal specifications　定做
readership	n.	the readers of a publication considered as a group　读者人数，读者群
cost-effective	a.	economical in terms of the goods or services received for the money spent　划算的
stockbroker	n.	one that acts as an agent in the buying and selling of stocks or other securities; a broker　证券经纪人（股票或其他证券买卖的代理人），经纪人
reminder	n.	a letter sent to remind somebody: a letter or message sent to remind somebody about something　催函，催单，催款函 If they don't settle the bill next week, send them a reminder. 如果下周他们仍不付账，就给他们发一封催款函。
flyer (flier)	n.	a pamphlet or circular for mass distribution　广告传单
foldout	n.	a folded insert or section, as of a cover, whose full size exceeds that of the regular page　折页
selectivity	n.	the state or quality of being selective　选择，选择性
recency	n.	the quality or state of being recent　崭新状态
mail-order	a.	an order for goods that is received and filled by mail　邮购的
segmentation	n.	division into segments　分割
variable	n.	something that varies or is prone to variation　易变的东西
buff	n.	one that is enthusiastic and knowledgeable about a subject　狂热爱好者，……迷（对一个主题感兴趣并且了解很多的人）
obsolete	a.	outmoded in design, style, or construction　过时的
overlay	n.	a transparent sheet containing graphic matter, such as labels or colored areas, placed on illustrative matter to be incorporated into it　透明塑料膜
demographic	a.	of or relating to demography　人口统计的，与人口统计有关的
psychograph	n.	a graphic representation or chart of the personality traits of an individual or a group　心理记录表（一种个人或群体的性格特征的图示或图表）
sales letters		推销函
circular	n.	a printed advertisement, directive, or notice intended for mass distribution　印制的广告，传单

catchy	a.	attractive or appealing 动人的或迷人的 easily remembered 易记的
commemorative	a.	honoring or preserving the memory of another 纪念性的
outperform	v.	to surpass (another) in performance 优过，胜于
pithy	a.	precisely meaningful; forceful and brief 简练有力的，言简意赅的
perforated	a.	having a hole or holes, especially a row of small holes 有孔的或多孔的（尤指有一排小孔的）
stub	n.	the part of a ticket returned as a voucher of payment 票根
marketplace	n.	an open area or square in a town where a public market or sale is set up 市场 the world of business and commerce 商贸界
efficacy	n.	power or capacity to produce a desired effect; effectiveness 效验（产生预期效果的力量或能力），效力
understate	v.	to express with restraint or lack of emphasis, especially ironically or for rhetorical effect 轻描淡写地陈述（带限制地或缺乏重点地表达，尤指讽刺性地或为修辞作用）
word of mouth		gossip spread by spoken communication 口碑
break-even	a.	marked by or indicating a balance of investment and return; having or showing neither profit nor loss 得失相当的，不盈不亏的，显示或标明不盈不亏的
dues	n.	a charge or fee for membership, as in a club or organization 会费（对成员资格征取的费用，如俱乐部或某一组织的会费）

Notes

1. 菲利普·科特勒（Philip Kotler）是国际上公认的市场营销学权威。
2. The Direct Marketing Association is Europe's largest trade association in the marketing and communications sector. The DMA was formed in 1992, following the merger of various like-minded trade bodies, forming a single voice to protect the direct marketing industry from legislative threats and promote its development.
3. Direct marketing is an interactive marketing system that uses one or more advertising media to effect a measurable response and/or transaction at any location.　直接营销是一种为了在任何地方可度量的反应或达成交易而使用的一种或多种广告媒体的交互作用的市场营销体系。这个句子的翻译太长，读起来有些拗口。其主要的问题是将"that"所引导的定语从句直

接放在"市场营销体系"前修饰该词组,从而出现了"而使用的"、"多种广告媒体的"和"交互作用的"三个偏正结构,使得句子过长。可以采取拆译的办法解决这个问题:"直接营销是一种交互式的营销体系,即:通过一种或多种广告手段随处获得顾客可度量的反应和(或)与顾客达成交易。"

4. Today, many direct marketers see direct marketing as playing a broader role, that of building a long-term relationship with the customer (direct relationship marketing). 今天,许多直接营销者发现他们扮演的角色越来越广泛,他们可以与顾客建立长期的关系(直接关系营销)。

这个句子有些特别,"that of building a long-term relationship with the customer"应该是"role"的同位语。翻译时可以采取两种办法:一是将"direct marketing"转译成"营销者",省去"see",将句子译成"许多直接营销者发现他们扮演的角色越来越广泛,他们可以……",这样所有的动作都由"direct marketers"发出;二是采取直接译法,将"that of"译成同位语,即"今天,许多直接营销者认为,直接营销的作用更加广泛,即:与顾客建立长期的业务关系"。

5. Direct marketers occasionally send birthday cards, information materials, or small premiums to select members in their customer base. Airlines, hotels, and other businesses build strong customer relationships through frequency award programs and club programs. 直接营销者给从他们顾客库中经选择的顾客经常性地寄出生日贺卡、信息资料或小赠品。航空、旅馆及其他一些行业通过各种有奖活动(如老乘客的免费公里数)和其他方案以建立强有力的顾客关系。

这句译文虽然意思无误,但有些用词和句子可以更加准确和精炼一点。试比较:"直接营销者时常从自己的顾客数据库中选出一些顾客,给他们寄送生日贺卡、信息资料或小赠品。航空公司、旅馆及其他一些商业企业也经常通过开展各种有奖活动和会员活动来加强与顾客的联系。"

6. "demassification"、"niches"这两个词都是比较专业的词语,翻译时可以采取直译和意译两种方法。"分众化"和"利基市场"是直接译法,即使读者不懂,可以查阅相关的辞典。①demassification 即非大规模生产。de-是英语中常用的前缀,表示"分离,反,非",如 deemphasize 意为"不再强调,不再重视"。这个词通常被译成"分众化"、"去大量化"、"去大众化"、"反集体"、"非大众化"等。该词的来源是:阿尔温·托夫勒(Alvin Toffler)在他1970年出版的《未来的冲击》(Future Shock)一书中,首创了"分众"(demassification)这个新词,并且预测美国社会在未来的10年之内,将面临社会结构的问题。②niches 即"利基",是指针对企业的优势细分出来的市场,这个市场不大。产品推进这个市场,有盈利的基础,特指针对性、专业性很强的产品。除了"利基"外,还有人将其译成"缝隙市场"、"细化市场"、"隙间市场"、"小众市场"等。如果为让读者能够直观地读懂这些专业术语,也可以考虑采取意译的方法来翻译,如将其分别译成"高度多样化"和"区别偏好的市场"。

7 Direct marketing benefits customers in many ways. Home shopping is fun, convenient, and hassle-free.　直接营销给顾客带来许多好处，消费者认为在家中购物有趣、方便并能避免嘈杂之累。

此句中的"hassle-free"译成"避免嘈杂之累"似乎不太准确，因为英语"hassle"虽然有"trouble, bother"（麻烦，打扰）之意，但这里难道是购物时的嘈杂嘛？显然不是，这里应该是指"an argument or a fight"（争论或争斗），即"讨价还价之累"。例如：Customers are hassling with merchants over high prices. 顾客和商人因为过高的价格争吵起来。

8 Business customers also benefit by learning about available products and services without tying up time in meeting salespeople.　工业品采购者也能从中获得好处，尤其是不必花费很多时间与销售人员会面，便可了解各种产品和服务情况。

英语"business customers"译成"工业品采购者"不如译成"企业客户"。"available"还是翻译出来比较好，可译成"可供产品"。另外，汉语句中的"尤其"好像英语原文中并没有，不如译成因果句。因此，这句可以译成："企业客户也能从中获得好处，因为它们无须花费很多时间与销售人员会面，便可了解各种可供产品和服务的情况。"

9 They will personalize and customize their messages.　然后，这类信息可以个性化和定制。

将这个句子译成被动有些不妥，因为前面的句子是说：销售人员可以轻而易举地得到各类客户的邮购地址清单，接下来还是应该顺着说他们得到这份清单后会怎样做。所以，将这句话译成主动更妥帖，即："然后，他们将根据客户不同的要求向其发送相关的商品信息。"

10 Avon, Amway, Mary Kay, and Tupperware

Avon（雅芳）：雅芳公司是全美最大的500家企业之一，1886年创立于美国纽约。

Amway（安利）：美国安利公司创立于1959年，是世界知名的家庭日用品生产商和销售商，美国安利公司总部位于美国密执安洲亚达城，占地28万平方米。

Mary Kay（玫琳凯）：玫琳凯化妆品公司是美国最大的皮肤保养品公司及第二大化妆品公司，玫琳凯品牌也是美国面部保养品销量第一的品牌。

11 "and informing and educating customers for later offers"中的"educating"不可译成"教育"。"educate"一词有"to provide with information; inform"（教导，提供信息，通知）的意思，所以这里可以将其译成"向顾客通报某些信息"。

12 Bob Stone 鲍勃·斯通

美国前直接营销协会主席、著名学者，著有被专家誉为直接营销"圣经"的《成功的直接营销方法》一书。他认为直接营销具有这样几个方面的关键性质：①互动性；②利用"一种或多种广告媒体"；③"可测量的反应"；④"不受地域限制的交易"。

13 Nash 纳什

约翰·纳什，普林斯顿大学数学系教授，1994年诺贝尔经济学奖得主，美国科学院院士，国际公认的天才数学家、博弈论的创始人。

14 "finding"一词在这里不太好翻译。该词的英文解释为"the information that someone has

learnt as a result of their studies". 如果直接翻译成"研究结果",读者自然不容易明白。其实下面所说的的确是作者的"研究成果",所以译文将其转译为"留意以下几点",请读者"注意"或"留意"的当然是作者总结出来的经验。

15. 翻译"it contains an illustration, preferably in color"这句话中的"illustration"和"preferably"两词时应该注意,"illustration"不宜译成"插图","preferably in color"不应译成"颜色很漂亮"。"illustration"在这里的意思是"a visual representation (a picture or diagram) that is used make some subject more pleasing or easier to understand",但汉语"插图"往往指书籍中的"图解"和"图示",这个词用在信封的封面显然不妥,所以可以考虑译成"图片"。而"preferably in color"可译成"最好是彩色照片"。

16. "salutation"一词不宜译成"称谓",因为汉语"称谓"的意思是"人们由于亲属和其他方面的相互关系,以及身份、职业等而得来的名称,如父亲、师傅、厂长等"(《现代汉语词典》)。而英语"salutation"的意思是:"a word or phrase used at the beginning of a letter or speech, such as 'Dear Mr. Smith'"(Longman Dictionary of Contemporary English)。因此,"personal salutation"在这里是指不要简单地称收信人"顾客"、"客户"、"先生"、"女士"等,而应该热情地称呼对方,如"Dear Mr. Li Ning"或"Dear Mrs. Rachel, our dear friend"。

17. ①"efficacy"不是"效能",而是"效果,功效"。二者的区别是:"效能"指"事物所蕴藏的有利的作用(如充分发挥水利和肥料的效能)";"效果"指"由某种力量、做法或因素产生的结果"。②"offer strategy"不能翻译成"提供战略",而应该翻译成"报价策略"。③"copy"不能省略,这里是指"[uncountable] technical something written in order to be printed in a newspaper, magazine, advertisement; the words to be printed or spoken in an advertisement"(文字说明:广告中的印刷文字说明或解说词)。④"media"不是"媒体",而是"广告媒介"的意思。⑤另外,将"One of the great advantages of direct marketing is the ability to test, under real marketplace conditions, the efficacy of different elements of an offer strategy, such as product features, copy, prices, media, or mailing lists."全句分别译成"直接营销的巨大优势之一便是它能够在一个真实的市场条件下对组成提供战略的各个要素的效能进行测试。直接营销可以测试产品特色、价格、媒体、邮寄名单等"显得前面的句子太长,后面的句子又太突然,因此不如改成:"直接营销的优势非常明显,其中之一就是能够在真实的市场条件下从各方面检测某一报价策略的效果,如产品的特色、相关文字说明、价格、广告媒介、邮寄名单等。"

18. Direct marketers must remember that response rates typically understate a campaign's long-term impact.
这句话中的"understate"一词较为难处理。译成"通常低估了该广告的长期影响"显然让读者摸不着头脑。其实上下文所表达的意思非常明确,即:回复率并不能完全表明这一营销方式的长期功效,所以应该译成:"直接营销者必须记住,直销邮件的回复数量往往无法表明该种推销方式的长期效果。"

19. Suppose only 2 percent of the recipients who receive a direct-mail piece advertising Samsonite luggage place an order. A much larger percentage became aware of the product (direct mail has high readership), and some percentage may have formed an intention to buy at a later date (either by mail or at a retail outlet).
Samsonite：新秀丽。Samsonite（新秀丽）是一个享誉世界的箱包品牌。
这个句子中的 suppose 一词不能翻译成"假如"，因为后面没有主句，后面如果接"但是"，句子就不通顺。可以考虑译成："尽管/虽然收到直接邮寄广告的人中只有2%的读者愿意订购新秀丽箱包，但更多的人却因此而了解了这一品牌的箱包（阅读直销邮件的大有人在）。还有一部分人可能打算过些时候去买（也可能到一个专卖店购买）。"

20. By carefully analyzing past campaigns, direct marketers can steadily improve their performance. Even when a specific campaign fails to break even, it can still be profitable.
翻译此句时应该注意省略和增词："通过对以往的直销活动进行仔细分析，直接营销者可以不断改善（他们的）业绩。这样，即使某一次直销活动亏了本，（它）依然可能赢利。"

21. Rather, the customer's lifetime value is the expected profit made on all future purchases net of customer acquisition and maintenance costs. 顾客的最终生命周期价值乃是他或她在一段时间内总的采购额减去他获得商品和保留商品所耗费的成本。
这句译文的意思有误。① 英语句子 "the customer's lifetime value is the expected profit" 的意思应该是"顾客的最终生命周期价值是销售产品公司预期的赢利"，不可能是"在一段时间内总的采购额"。② 后面的介词短语 "on all future purchases net of customer acquisition and maintenance costs" 修饰 "profit"，意思是"未来销售总额减去公司获得和留住顾客的全部成本后的 profit"。翻译时首先应该将"价值＝赢利"这层意思译出来，因为顾客的价值是相对推销售公司而言的，顾客购买越多，对销售公司的价值就越大。因此，可考虑改译成："顾客的最终生命周期价值为：公司销售总额（即顾客从公司购买产品的总额）减去公司获得并留住客户的全部费用（即公司通过各种手段推销并留住客户所需的成本）之后的预期利润率。"

22. For an average customer, one would calculate the average customer longevity, average customer annual expenditure, and average gross margin, minus the average cost of customer acquisition and maintenance (properly discounted for the opportunity cost of money).
在计算一个平均客户时，要计算平均持续时间、每年的客户开支和平均毛利（对机会成本的适当折扣），减去获得平均客户的成本。
① 这里不能译成"平均客户"，应该考虑增词，即："在计算每位客户的平均生命周期价值时"。② 剩下的句子可以译成一个公式。因此，可改译为："在计算每个客户的平均生命周期价值时，可按这个公式进行：先计算出该客户与销售公司的平均业务年限、该客户每年购买本公司产品的平均支出及公司的平均毛利，再减去公司获得并留住该

客户的平均成本（适当降低了机会成本）。"

他山之石

原文 1：

Advertising is any paid form of nonpersonal presentation and promotion of ideas, goods, or services by an identified sponsor. Advertisers include not only business firms but also charitable, nonprofit, and government agencies that advertise to various publics.

原译：

广告是由明确的主办人发起，通过付费的任何非人员介绍和促销其构思、商品或服务的行为。广告主不仅有商业性的公司，也包括慈善组织、非营利机构与政府机构，它们也对各种公众做广告宣传。

点评：

① 将"nonpersonal presentation and promotion"译成"任何非人员介绍和促销"让读者较难理解，意思其实就是"不是通过人，而是通过公共媒体来传播"。

② 公众就是公众，不宜译成"各种公众"。

公众：社会上大多数的人，大众（《现代汉语词典》）。"public"一词的英文解释为：
- people in general considered as a whole—"He is a hero in the eyes of the public."
- a body of people sharing some common interest—"the reading public"
- a place accessible or visible to the public

改译：

广告是指由特定的广告主以付费的方式通过媒体向社会公众介绍和宣传其观念、商品或服务。广告主不仅可以是商业企业，也可以是慈善组织、非营利机构和政府机构。

原文 2：

The practice of her company specializes in advising companies on how to build and maintain that more metaphysical aspect of what brands are about: the brand's reliability as what she calls a "repository of knowledge about the things that people are going to buy or use".

原译：

她所在的公司的业务主要是向企业提供咨询，协助它们树立并维持品牌概念中那更加抽象、玄妙的一面，即品牌的可信度——用她的话说，品牌的可信度就是"一部关于各种商品的百科全书"。

点评：

① 将"advising in"拆译成"提供咨询，协助……"可能让读者产生这样的误解："这家公司既提供咨询服务，又协助企业……"。

② 将"to build and maintain that more metaphysical aspect of what brands are about"翻译成"树立并维持品牌概念中那更加抽象、玄妙的一面"让读者感到费解，因为人们很难理解和想像出什么是"品牌概念中那更加抽象、玄妙的一面"，虽然后面解释说是"可信度"，但仍然有点儿玄乎。另外，"建立""可信度"似乎更加符合汉语的表达习惯。

③ 将"repository of knowledge about the things that people are going to buy or use"翻译成"一部关于各种商品的百科全书"显然过于草率，因为英语中"that"所引导的是定语从句，修饰"the things"，即：人们打算购买和使用的东西。另外，将"repository of knowledge"意译成"百科全书"也不恰当，因为"百科全书"一般指"比较全面系统地介绍文化科学知识，收录各种名词和术语"的词典。

改译：

她所在的公司专门从事为企业提供这样的咨询服务业务，那就是建议企业该如何建立并维护品牌的可信度，这可是品牌内涵中最让人琢磨不透的东西，用她的话说，"是人们打算购买或使用的商品的全部知识"。

学生译作分析

原文：

Today the Whirlpool brand is the No. 1 major-appliance brand in the world. But when we went to Europe, people had never heard of it. It was our view that there was a great advantage to global branding and that you could build it with the right advertising. You could build a loyal relationship with consumers in which they felt the brand was theirs, even though in many places they couldn't pronounce Whirlpool. But if you spend enough on advertising, they learn to.

学生原译文：

今天，惠普是世界第一的主要器械品牌。但我们去欧洲就没有听说过这个牌子。我们认为，打造全球品牌和通过适当的广告来建立这个品牌大有好处。你可以与消费者建立起忠诚的关系，让他们感觉这是他们自己的品牌。尽管在许多地方人们甚至连"Whirlpool"这个字都不会念，但只要你大量做广告，他们就能学着念。

分析：

（1）将"Whirlpool"（惠而浦）译成"惠普"（Hewlett-Packard）说明翻译时没有认真查找相关资料。实际上全球领先的家用电器品牌——惠而浦创立于1911年，总部位于美国密歇根州的奔腾港，是目前世界上最大的家用电器制造商之一，亦是美国《财富》杂志全球500强企业。而惠普公司（Hewlett-Packard）则是世界最大的计算机公司之一。该公司制造的产品正用于工业、商业、工程、科学和教育等领域。HP总部设在加利福尼亚州的Palo Alto，该公司有雇员8万多人。

（2）将"major-appliance"译成"主要器械品牌"说明没有认真查阅词典。根据Wikipedia的解释："A major appliance is usually defined as a large machine which accomplishes some routine housekeeping task, which includes purposes such as cooking, food preservation, or cleaning, whether in a household, institutional, commercial or industrial setting.", 也就是说，这里的"major-appliance"是指家电产品。

（3）"when we went to Europe, people had never heard of it"显然是过去和已经完成的动作，必须译清楚。

（4）"you could build it"中的"it"一词不是指"惠而浦"这个品牌，而应该是泛指"global branding"。

（5）"loyal"一词不宜译成"忠诚、忠实"等，因为这些词太含糊，究竟是厂商对客户忠诚还是客户忠诚厂商呢？

（6）整段文章翻译得太口语化，可以再严谨一点，多用一些书面语，这样文章读起来更加上口。

参考译文：

今天，惠而浦是世界第一的家电品牌。但从前我们进入欧洲时，那儿的人根本没听说过我们。我们认为，品牌全球化大有裨益，可以通过适当的广告（宣传）来建设（打造）品牌。你可以与消费者建立起稳固的关系，让他们感觉这个品牌属于他们自己。虽说在许多地方，许多人甚至连"Whirlpool"的音都不会发，但只要你在广告宣传上大量投入，他们会学会的。

翻译技巧介绍

商务词语和专业术语的翻译
（Translating Business Terms）

商务的快速发展使人们在日常生活中接触的商务方面的词汇越来越多，这些词汇涉及商务的各个领域，如金融、外贸、国际工程、保险等。由于各个领域都有大量的专业术语，从事商务方面的翻译除了需要掌握必要的专业知识外，还必须熟悉并了解相关的词汇和术语，否则翻译出来的句子就会让读者难以理解，甚至误解原文的意思。

一、注意词语在商务英语中的特殊用法

英语中的很多词汇在商务英语中有特殊的意义，在一般的辞典中不一定都能查找到，所以必须利用专业辞典，辨清词义，然后再进行翻译。例如：

（1）Few managers seriously question the benefits of **delegation**, but many are still reluctant to **delegate**.

译文：公司经理大都对**授权**的好处深信不疑，但其中大多数仍不愿意**授权**他人。

这句话中的"delegation"和"delegate"是"to commit or entrust to another"（委托他人）的意思，译成"代表"就不对了。

（2）As its most basic, the **hospitality industry** is made up of organizations that offer guests courteous, professional food, drink, and lodging services, alone or in combination.

译文：**旅游饭店业**的根本就是众多的企业和机构为顾客提供周到和高水平的饮食和住宿服务，这种服务可以是其中某一项，也可以是全方位的。

句中的"hospitality industry"就是指"a catchall phrase covering a variety of Service Industries. It is often applied to Hotels and Resorts.", 也就是"restaurant and food service"。如果不查相关的辞典，直译成"好客行业"，就会让人难以理解。

（3）Amendments to this Contract may be made only by a written **instrument** signed by a duly authorized representative of each of the parties.

译文：对本合同的修改，只能通过各方正式授权的代表签署**协议**进行。

此处"instrument"是指"a legal document"（文书，契约，合同），而不是指"仪器"。

（4）Credit is offered only when creditors believe that they have a good chance of obtaining legal tender when they present such **instruments** at a bank or other authorized institution.

译文：只有当债权人相信，一旦他们向银行或其他授权机构递交此类信用**票据**就有把握获得法定货币时，他们才会提供信贷。

这里的"instruments"是指"票据"，如 a credit instrument（信用票据）、an inchoate instrument（空白票据）、a negotiable instrument（可转让票据）。

（5）Our bank doesn't **negotiate** foreign cheques.

译文：我们银行不**恰兑**国外支票。

"negotiate"在这里不是"洽谈"的意思，而是指"to transfer title to or ownership of (a promissory note, for example) to another party by delivery or by delivery and endorsement in return for value received"[让渡：为取得价值，通过交货或交货并担保把权力或所有权（比如一张期票）转交给另一方]，即"议付，押汇，恰兑"之意。

（6）The IOC also expects a surge of brands trying to **hijack** the games with "ambush marketing" and has already taken measures to outlaw activity from non-sponsors as part of its commitment to limit the commercialization of the games.

译文：国际奥委会也预料很多商家会借助黑市手段从奥运会身上**揩油**，并已对那些非赞助商的不法活动采取了措施，以此作为限制奥运商业化承诺的组成部分。

"hijack"是"to take control of something and use it for your own purposes"（即"揩油"）的意思。

二、符合汉语惯用法

商务英语中的一些词语在汉语中有习惯的表达方式，翻译时应该加以考虑，否则即使意思正确，读起来却缺乏韵味。例如：

(1) After the deal was signed in December 1998, it took a relatively short 16 months from design to completion of the plant buildings, which used local Chinese **materials and labour.**

译文：合资协议于1998年12月签署后，整个厂子的建设从设计到完工只用了短短16个月，使用的是中国本地的**人力和物力**。

这个"人力和物力"不仅意思准确，而且符合现在的习惯用法，读起来很上口。

(2) Marketing people the world over will be rubbing their hands and thinking of ways **to take advantage** of the tremendous tide of opportunity in China.

译文：全世界的营销商都将摩拳擦掌，想方设法在中国的这一波商机大潮中**抢占先机**。

"take advantage"若译成"利用一下"自然不如"抢占先机"适用。

(3) In my personal portfolio, the only industry **I won't invest in** is tobacco.

译文：在我个人的投资组合中，我唯一**不碰**的是烟草行业。

"I won't invest in"谁都认识，但能将其译成"不碰"的却只有真正了解股市行话的人。

(4) The impulse to invest ethically is praiseworthy, but I'm skeptical of "**one size fits all**" approaches to it.

译文：促进合乎道义的投资是值得赞赏的，但我怀疑这种"**一刀切**"的做法能否行得通。

好一个"一刀切"，多么准确而传神。

(5) When you are **managing other people's money**, your job is maximize performance.

译文：当你为别人**理财**时，你的任务就是要取得最好的业绩。

将"manage one's money"翻译成"理财"真是恰到好处。

(6) Private banks that offer capital protection using new financial instruments and strategies

have come into favor.

译文：使用新型金融工具和策略提供资本保护的私人银行**受到人们的青睐**。

"喜爱"和"青睐"相比，后者更贴切。

三、专业术语要专业

商务英语的一大特点就是专业术语非常多，这些术语涉及国际贸易、金融、保险、旅游、运输、海外工程和投资等领域，因此在翻译这方面的资料时，一定要先理解相关的专业术语，其至向行内人士请教，以免译文不够专业。例如：

(1) The Chinese Government has supported cattle production by encouraging the use of stalks from harvested crops for feed, and **stock numbers** have risen.

译文：中国政府提倡饲养家畜，鼓励人们使用庄稼收获后留下的秸秆来喂养牲口，因而牲口**存栏数量**有所上升。

这里的"stock numbers"是很专业的术语，叫"存栏"，即牲畜在饲养中（统计术语）。如果译成"储存数量"，味道就差远了。

(2) What was different was that these were mass-produced at a time when most people either made their own clothes or had them made by tailors, making Max Mara one of the first **ready-to-wear** companies in the world, facing the challenge of convincing **fabric shops** to stock its garments.

译文：所不同的是，在大多数人要么自己亲手做衣服要么请裁缝做衣服的那样一个时代，这些衣服是批量生产的，从而使马克斯·玛拉服装公司成为世界上最早的**成衣**公司，面临的难题是说服纤维**面料**商店出售它生产的服装。

制成后出售的衣服叫"成衣"，做衣服鞋帽等的面儿用的料子叫"面料"，二者均为服装行业专业术语。

(3) A credit card thief may be sitting on a potential gold mine, particularly if there is a delay in **reporting the loss of the card**.

译文：信用卡窃贼可能会大发横财——尤其是在失主未能及时**挂失**的情况下。

"report the loss of"在银行业中叫"挂失"或"报失"。

(4) Despite its troubles, Coke has seen its stock jump 19% since Jan. 31, after **languishing** near a six-year low for most of 2001.

译文：尽管麻烦不少，但可口可乐公司的股票价格今年1月31日至今已飙升了19%，而2001年几乎一年的时间股价都在6年来的最低点附近**盘整**，无人问津。

"languish"除了"to remain unattended or be neglected"（备受冷落）的意思之外，同时还描述了股价波动不大的走势，将其译成"盘整"恰如其分。

(5) Employees and Manufacturers Association (Northern) chief executive Alasdair Thompson questions if **public companies** have a right to diver share holders' money

into areas such as social activities.

译文：雇主与制造商协会（北方区）会长阿拉斯戴尔·汤普森质疑**上市公司**是否有权利将股东的钱花在社会活动等其他领域。

如果将"public companies"译成"公共公司"，读者可就难以明白了。

(6) Finally, excellent hotel managers must know how to make profits **when times are good** and occupancies and revenues are high and also **when times are bad** and costs must be controlled closely.

译文：最后，优秀的饭店经理还必须懂得如何赢利，**经济景气**和客房出租收入高的时候如此，**经济萧条**和开支必须紧缩的时候亦如此。

(7) Despite the changes, however, Wall Street remains a treacherous place for the **small investors**.

译文：然而，尽管出现了种种变化，对于**散户投资者**来讲，华尔街依然布满了陷阱。

四、习语的译法

除了大量的专业术语外，由于中西文化上的差异，商务英语中时常出现的一些习语往往很难找到对应的汉语来翻译，这就需要译者认真分析这些习语，并弄懂其在文章中的准确含义，然后酌情将意思意译出来。例如：

(1) Some people were convinced that IBM would be unveiling a new **Holy Grail**.

译文：有些人相信国际商用机器公司会展出一个新的**圣杯**。

(2) China, with an estimated capital pool of ＄621 bn, is **the holy grail**.

译文：中国的资本容量估计为6 210亿美元，是最大的**淘金地**。

(3) Western businesses who have already exhausted opportunities in mature markets such as America and Europe, cracking China in a major way is something of **a holy grail.**

译文：对于在美洲、欧洲这样的成熟市场中难觅商机的西方商家来说，开启中国市场的大门正是他们**梦寐以求的**。

以上三个句子中都使用了"holy grail"一词。一查词典，发现其意思有二：① "a cup or plate that, according to medieval legend, was used by Jesus at the Last Supper and that later became the object of many chivalrous quests（also called Holy Grail）"; ② " the object of a prolonged endeavor; something you try very hard to get or achieve but never can"。这个词跟宗教有关，如果将其直接翻译成"圣杯"，读者自然会感到费解。

① 将第一个句子中的"a new Holy Grail"译成"一个新的圣杯"不如译成"有些人认为国际商用机器公司一定会很快推出一款人们期盼已久的新机型"。

② 第二个句子中的"the holy grail"被译成了"淘金地"，这显然没有将"the object of a prolonged endeavor"的含义翻译出来，因此不如译成："中国的资本容量估计为6 210亿美元，是梦想家心中的宝地。"

③ 第三个句子中的 "a holy grail" 通过采取转换手法译成形容词 "梦寐以求的"，意思准确，将原文的意思完全表达出来了。

（4）Customers, he says, are starting to **vote with their feet** and go to other businesses when they find a particular company rude, or uncaring, or basically unaware of the customer's needs.

译文：他称，如果顾客发现某公司对待顾客粗鲁、冷漠，或是对顾客的需要根本一无所知，他们就会**一走了之，去选择**其他的商家。

"to vote with one's feet" 的意思是 "to indicate a preference or an opinion by leaving or entering a particular locale"。如果直接将此习语译成 "用脚投票"（尽管现在有人这样翻译，表示投反对票），则原来 "有权选择" 的意思便没有翻译出来。因此，上述译文既将 "feet" 用汉语表达出来，又没有失去原有的 "选择" 之意。

（5）If you own stock in a company, but don't know what it actually does to make a profit, you deserve to **take a bath** if the share price plunges.

译文：如果你拥有一家公司的股票，却不知道该公司实际是靠什么来盈利的，一旦股价暴跌，你的钱财**打了水漂**也是活该。

这个句子中的习语 "take a (financial) bath" 并不难译，查查 A Dictionary of Informal Words and Expressions 就知道，这个俚语的意思是 "to lose money on an investment; to lose a large amount of money (in a business deal)"。但如果直接将其翻译成 "遭受重大损失"，意思虽然没错，但语言的魅力已荡然无存。因此，不如译成汉语的 "打了水漂" 或者 "血本无归"，这样可以使译文在意思和语言特色两个方面尽量忠实于原文。

（6）Workers have charged that they were locked inside stores at night and that managers secretly "**shaved**" their time sheets to meet budgets.

译文：员工们指控说，他们夜里被硬留在店里，经理们还为不超过预算暗地里在工时卡上"**做手脚**"。

将 "shaved" 译成汉语的习语 "做手脚" 比译成 "克扣" 等词自然得多。

课堂翻译训练

将下列句子译成汉语。

1. It is easy to be brave and keep buying during a bull market.

2. He said inflation could still trend lower from its already low pace. Underlying inflation is close to one per cent.
3. But the importance of trade in our economy has exploded in the past three years.
4. The hammer came down quickly on Wall Street after the stock-market bubble burst.
5. Foreign banks, not to be outdone, lure new customers with pricey freebies (in Hong Kong, it's Palm organizers and DVD players), and old-fashioned nudging (in Israel, banks could call potential customers at home).
6. Once you have a core investment portfolio in something solid such as blue-chip stocks, look around for satellite investments that may spice up your portfolio.
7. But for banks, personal, unsecured loans represent one of the most profitable niches.
8. With an organization of this size and status, anyone who says something is not going to go dump in the night is not being realistic.
9. All of which proves that the best defense may be a twist on the old warning: caveat investor.
10. Many businesses today realize that the bottom line—the profit figure—should include not only monetary gain, but gains for society and the environment.
11. Stroll and Chou intend to change that by turning Michael Kors into a $1 billion brand within a decade and taking the company public along the way, which is an ambitious plan to say the least.
12. The revelation that the *Sun*—Britain's biggest newspaper—believes it is losing daily circulation sales to its website has caused quite a stir in the online publishing industry.

课后练习

将下列短文译成汉语，注意运用本单元所学的翻译技巧。

1.

After reaping benefits from globalization for decades, the developed world is having second thoughts about its value.

Pollsters in advanced economies report declining public support for open markets and free trade; politicians increasingly gain more political mileage by being identified as a globalization skeptic than globalization booster; and essays fretting over the sustainability of international economic integration fill the opinion pages of the world's leading financial newspapers and international-affairs journals.

Yet at the same time, globalization itself continues apace, as trade and investment flows surge around the globe, tying national economies ever closer together and delivering perhaps the strongest period of growth for the world economy since the Second World War.

Can this dichotomy persist, or will the rich world's rising globalization angst be sufficient to send the integration process into reverse?

Certainly, there are clear signs that the international policy environment is becoming less globalization-friendly, a development marking a pronounced reversal in the general trend since the 1980s. After the failed meeting in Potsdam, the Doha round of international trade negotiations looks to be on its way from intensive care to the crematorium. Meanwhile, protectionist sentiment is on the rise in the US and Western Europe, manifesting itself in public and political disquiet over offshore outsourcing, foreign investment in sensitive areas, migration and, in particular, trade with China.

Nevertheless, the foundations for globalization are no longer as solid as they once were.

Instead, many of the loudest attacks on the consequences of globalization now come from those countries that were the architects and builders of the new global economy.

2.

The National Council for US-China Trade has its members and associates companies raging from the very largest, such as General Motors, down to the very small company, companies with as few as 10 employees.

In the United States, much new technology and many new products, components and services now reside in, and are owned by, small companies. These small, even tiny companies, are frequently formed when professors and research scientists, engineers and technicians, who have been studying and doing research in certain fields, leave large institutions and form small entrepreneurial type companies to exploit and produce their new findings. Examples would include professors leaving the Universities of Wisconsin, Iowa State and Purdue and forming companies in the new bio-genetics areas, performing gene splitting, and producing new products in animal and plant life, and pharmaceuticals as well. Other examples would include professors leaving the Massachusetts Institute of Technology, the University of California at Berkeley and Stanford University to form new small companies in the computer science and electronic areas. Former scientists at the University of Utah now own and operate several companies producing artificial human organs such as mechanical heart and the artificial ear.

Employees of large companies (such as IBM, General Electric and Hewlett Packard), also frequently break away and form their own small companies to develop, produce and market new advanced products, services and technologies, such as the gallium arsenide high-speed semiconductor as a replacement for silicon.

CITIC may want to deal with some of these very small, advanced technology firms. These emerging small companies would like to do business with countries such as China; however, they have concerns about such a relationship. My presentation reflects the thinking of these new small high technology companies.

Small high technology companies have several good business reasons why foreign opportunities might be considered in spite of the difficulties inherent in capitalizing on them.

The first is to gain a supply of needed resources.

The second is to lower production cost—either to be more competitive in one's home market or to serve a new area.

The third is to penetrate the market where the investment is to be made.

These reasons, of course, could apply to anything from establishing a new office in the next town to building a whole new manufacturing plant half way around the world; but when a foreign location is involved, some of the questions that must be asked to evaluate the options properly, become much more difficult to answer.

综合测试 1

班级_____   姓名_____   时间：90 分钟

I. Translate the following sentences into Chinese. (55)

1. According to the Motion Picture Association of America (MPAA), the losses are around $2.5 billion in the music business, which has grappled with piracy for far longer. (7)
2. There has been much talk recently of the Wal-Martization of America, a reference to the giant retailer's fervent attempts to keep its cost—and therefore its prices—at rock-bottom levels. (7)
3. The fairy-dust of creativity, when built on a very wise, experienced base of research and fact, can make the difference between walking and flying. (7)
4. Gretchen Adams has more than a few bones to pick with Wal-Mart, but she figures its treatment of women is a good place to start. (6)
5. If you foul things up, the family business not only goes south but Mom or Dad's legacy sinks, too. (6)
6. Despite an illustrious heritage of influencing politics and making and breaking celebrities, the once brash young tabloid might be starting to show its age. (7)
7. Risk aversion is a key component of how economists analyze individual behavior and accurate measurements of individual risk aversion is particularly useful to the insurance and pensions industries and to explain saving and investment behavior. (8)
8. To prevent the stores from cherry picking, they made the unusual stipulation that in order to carry any part of the collection, retailers would have to buy from each category. (7)

II. Translate the five sentences underlined into Chinese. (25)

You must have heard about General Motors. But do you know that in 1973, the annual sales of GM were actually greater than the combined GNP of Switzerland, Pakistan and South Africa? Yes, corporations such as GM, IBM, and ITT are extremely powerful. In fact the combined physical assets of all global corporations were estimated at more than $200 billion. And that was more than twenty years ago. Today their power has greatly increased, and is still growing. <u>1. So much so, that some observers believe that by the end of this century, the 300 largest corporations will account for more than half of the world's industrial production.</u>

The most commonly used term for this type of transnational organization is "multinational corporation". It does not mean that they are all transnational in personnel. The top level of management usually comes predominantly from one country. In most cases, the country is clearly identifiable as the home country. GM for example, is based in the United States. So are the others mentioned above. What makes them multinational is the scope of their operations. 2. They manufacture and sell their products where it is most profitable, by passing the formal boundaries of states as much as they can and dealing with the governments of states as little as they can. Being "multinational", they have little loyalty toward any one country. When their interests conflict with the political interests of a country, they will always put their business interest first. To them, political boundaries are irrelevant to the business of selling automobiles or coca Cola. 3. The chair of Dow Chemical Company (陶氏化学公司) once expressed the wish that he could buy an island owned by no nation, on which to establish his World Headquarters so that the corporation could be truly on neutral ground.

4. Today there is widespread agreement that multinational corporations will have an important effect on international relations and world economy. But there is little agreement on exactly what that effect will be. There are those who see them as benevolent and those who see hem as evil.

Among those who see multinational corporations as benevolent, many emphasize their importance in helping reduce the gap between rich countries and poor ones. 5. These business giants are referred to as "engines of development", because it is claimed that they do more to improve the economic life in less developed countries than all governmental foreign aid programs have ever done. By setting up factories abroad, they provide jobs; by equipping these factories with the latest machines and equipment, they make available the most modern technology. Because goods are now produced within the less developed countries, there is less need for them to import from abroad, and their balance of payments will improve.

III. Translate the following letter into Chinese. (20)

Dear Cliff,

Sixteen "Swatch" miniature pocket watches with a tennis motif case were sent today by UPS to replace the watches you received in error. You should have them by now.

You know, one would think it would be impossible to make an error like this one, Cliff. You clearly specified in your letter that these watches were to be awarded to winners of the Annual Lakeside Tennis Club Tournament on October 20. The stock number you supplied was correct. There was no reason for a slip-up at this end, and I can't even guess now it happened.

I am much relieved, however, that you will have the right watches in time for the awards dinner. I really don't know what a tennis player's reaction would be to having a classic golf swing in bas-relief on his prize.

  When you get around to it, would you please ship the golf watches to me by DHL collect? I apologize for the anxiety we've caused you, and I truly hope that everything turns out just the way it's posed to.

Yours very sincerely,

Chinese-English
汉译英

Part

Unit 10

佳译赏析

全球性失衡和高油价双重威胁[1]下的世界经济与中国
World Economy and China Threatened by Global Economic Disequilibrium and Surging Oil Prices

在经历了 2004 年的高速增长之后，2005 年世界经济增长速度回落。根据 IMF[2] 在 9 月份的预测，2005 年全球经济增长速度将从 2004 年的 5.1% 降至 4.3%。虽然 IMF 在 12 月份表示将调高对全球经济增长的预测，但估计很难超过 4.6%。在全球经济失衡和高油价的双重冲击下，世界经济取得这样的增长速度，并且全球经济没有出现大的动荡和危机，已经超出了很多学者和官员的预期。根据 IMF 等国际经济组织的研究，世界经济能够在全球性失衡和高油价的环境中平稳地走过 2005 年，主要得益于各国审慎且合适的货币和财政政策、宽松的国际金融环境和企业资产负债表的改善。[4]

The growth of the global economy slowed in 2005 after sizzling expansion the previous year. According to the forecast of the International Monetary Fund (IMF) in September 2005, the growth rate of the global economy in 2005 would drop to 4.3 percent from 5.1 percent in 2004. Although the IMF said in December it would raise its prediction, sources estimated that the adjusted rate would hardly surpass 4.6 percent. Despite the impact of global economic disequilibrium and surging oil prices, the world economy has performed well beyond the expectations of many economists and officials by running at speed, yet avoiding turbulence and crisis. According to the analysis of many international research organizations, including the IMF, the steady development of world economy in 2005 mainly benefited from prudent and appropriate monetary and fiscal policies, as well as an easy international financial environment and improved corporate balance sheets.

在世界经济整体保持较高增长的同时，不同国家的经济增长存在显著差异[5]。美国在高油价和高赤字的条件下[6]，通过美联储[7]审慎的加息措施抑制通货膨胀、吸引外部资金持续流入，美元在2005年以前的贬值效应逐步发挥出来，推动了美国出口的增长；"卡特里娜"飓风[8]以后，美国财政支出增加。这些因素结合在一起，使得美国在财政和贸易双赤字条件下保持了物价稳定和经济平稳增长。[9]欧元区国家依然受制于内部结构性问题和财政政策冲突，经济增长乏力；虽然过去几年中欧元对美元的升值有助于欧元区国家出口的增加和实现既定的通货膨胀目标[10]，但是2005年油价持续上涨及欧元对美元的贬值，给欧元区经济带来了极大的风险，不仅影响消费和投资的信心，也带来了极大的通胀压力。这使得欧元区的货币政策更加难以抉择。日本通过极度宽松的货币政策刺激经济逐步摆脱通货紧缩的困境，日元币值走低也进一步刺激了日本的出口。这有助于日本在物价水平继续下跌的情况下，保持整体经济较好的增长势头。中国通过紧缩的货币政策和财政政策的调整，成功地抑制了经济过热问题[11]，内需和出口的增长推动了中国经济的高速增长。

While the overall global economy kept a relatively high growth, various countries featured strikingly different development. In the United States, where oil prices and deficits ran high, inflation was dampened and foreign capital maintained its momentum thanks to prudent interest rate rises adopted by the Federal Reserve. Meanwhile, exports increased partly due to a depreciating dollar and US fiscal expenditures expanded after Hurricane Katrina devastated the south. All these factors combined to help the United States stabilize its prices and maintain a steady economic growth. Baffled by internal structural problems and fiscal policy conflicts, the economic growth of euro zone countries was lackluster. Although the euro zone countries had seen their exports expand and had well controlled the inflation with the appreciation of euro to the dollars, the surging oil price and a weakening euro to the dollar in 2005 brought enormous risks to the economic operation of the euro zone, which not only dampened consumption and investors' confidence, but also inflicted more risk of inflation. All this has made it even more difficult for euro zone countries to decide on their monetary policies. In Asia, Japan gradually extricated itself from deflation through its extremely loose monetary policy, and the depreciating yen also promoted its exports. Thus, its overall economy maintained the momentum of growth though prices continued sliding. China successfully cooled its overheating economy through tight monetary and fiscal policies, and the growing domestic demand and exports propelled its rapid economic development.

整体性失衡问题严重
Losing equilibrium

过去几年中，美国的贸易逆差及全球性经济失衡现象始终是人们关注的焦点。2005年中，人们所关注的全球经济失衡的潜在威胁没有转变成现实，没有出现大的金融动荡甚至是全球经济崩溃。然而，在历经了美元持续贬值[12]、人民币汇率调整[13]及各国经济政策调整以后，美国的贸易逆差和全球性经济失衡依然未能走上人们所期待的调整之路。[14]

  During the past few years, the US trade deficits and the uneven development of the global economy remained the focus of worldwide attention. In 2005, neither the potential threat of global economic disequilibrium nor big financial turbulence, even global economic collapse, came true. But the US trade deficits and the global economic disequilibrium didn't improve though the world witnessed a weakening US dollar, an adjusted Chinese yuan and economic policy amendments of various countries.

  美元及相关国家货币汇率的调整，已经对美国的出口产生积极影响。2003 年以来，美国的出口持续增长，2004 年和 2005 年美国的出口增长率分别为 8.4% 和 8.2%。与此同时，美国进口的增长速度显著降低，从 2004 年的 10.7% 降至 2005 年的 6.6%。在这种情况下，如何调整各国的储蓄行为和财政收支政策，成为调整全球性失衡的关键。

  But the dollar and the adjusted exchange rates of relative countries have exerted positive influences on US exports. Since 2003, US exports have increased steadily. In 2004 and 2005, the growth rate of US exports stood at 8.4 percent and 8.2 percent, respectively. Meanwhile, US import growth declined by a large margin, reaching 6.6 percent in 2005 against 10.7 percent in 2004. Under these circumstances, how to adjust the savings and fiscal revenue and expenditure policies of various countries has become the key to address the global economic disequilibrium.

  进入 2005 年，虽然面对美国贸易逆差和全球性经济失衡的潜在风险，但美元却一改过去几年的下跌势头，对日元和欧元等主要货币开始升值。这是因为亚洲中央银行大量购进美元，导致亚洲国家的外汇储备大量流入美国。同时，由于美国经济形势良好，美国资产对私人投资者仍然有相当的吸引力，私人资本回流美国[15]。这种情况将进一步加剧世界经济失衡及调整的风险。官方储备和私人资本的大量流入会阻碍美元的调整；同时大量外部资金的流入，也不利于美国国内储蓄行为和财政收支政策的调整。

  In 2005, though facing potential risks of the US trade deficits and global economic disequilibrium, the dollar reversed its sliding momentum and began to appreciate against such main currencies as the yen and euro. This is because the Asian central banks purchased a great deal of dollars, leading to a large amount of foreign reserves of Asian countries flowing to America. Meanwhile, thanks to a sound domestic economic situation, American assets remained attractive to private investors, resulting in the inflow of a huge amount of private capital. But this would aggravate the risk of global economic disequilibrium and adjustment. The inflow of official reserves and private capital would also interfere with the dollar's adjustment. Meanwhile, the inflow of a large amount of external capital would be unfavorable for America's internal savings and revenue and expenditure policy.

油价的影响
Oil impact

  2005 年，世界石油价格持续攀升，给各国经济和世界经济整体的运行带来了巨大的风险。从世界石油的整体供求来看，由于近年来石油需求的急剧增加，产能和需求之间的差额逐步减小。2004 年以后，每日供求差额不足 200 万桶。世界经济的持续增长，特别是那些依赖于石油进口的新兴市场经济体的快速增长，进一步强化了石油需求增长的预期。在另一个方面，石油供给的弹性不足[16]成为推动石油价格在 2005 年近一年上涨的主要原因。"卡特里娜"飓风和"丽塔"飓风对世界石油供求产生短期冲击，进一步推动了石油价格的上升。2005 年 6 月，世界市场的石油价格突破 60 美元每桶，8 月份更是突破了 70 美元的大关。

  In 2005, international oil prices continued to soar, bringing enormous risks to the operation of the economies of various countries and the global economy as a whole. As oil demand worldwide has surged over recent years, the gap between production and demand has gradually been narrowed. After 2004, the daily gap was reduced to less than 2 million barrels. The continuous growth of the world economy, especially the rapid expansion of emerging markets, heavily dependent on oil imports, further intensified the expectation of an oil demand increase. Oil supply insufficiency was mainly to blame for the oil price rise in 2005, and the short-term impact of Hurricanes Katrina and Rita on global oil demand further drove up the oil price. In June 2005, the oil price on the international market surpassed $60 per barrel and in August it rose further to top $70.

  到目前为止，世界石油价格的上升并没有对各国经济和世界经济产生过大的负面冲击，或者，至少可以说，石油价格高涨的负面影响在目前并没有全部显示出来。世界经济之所以能够在 2005 年成功应对石油价格的冲击，得益于如下几个方面的政策反应。首先是增加能源产业的投资，提高石油开采能力，推动节约石油和替代性能源的投资，增加石油的储备；其次是通过审慎的货币政策稳定通货膨胀预期，避免石油价格变化引发严重的通货膨胀。这些因素结合在一起，使得世界经济在 2005 年避免石油价格上升的负面影响[17]。但是，如果高油价持续维持下去，生产者和消费者都将调整自己的供求行为，导致工资和物价上升，进而引发严重的通货膨胀，对经济增长产生严重的负面影响。特别是那些依赖于石油进口的发展中国家和地区，持续的油价将导致其国际收支恶化，甚至是整体性金融危机和经济危机。

  So far, the international oil price hike has not produced huge negative impacts on the economies of various countries and the global economy as a whole. Or at least it's safe to say that the negative impact of the surging oil price has not shown entirely. The policies—increasing investment in the energy industry, improving oil exploitation capacity, promoting investment in oil conservation and alternative energy resources, increasing oil reserves, and introducing prudent monetary policies to pin down the expectation of inflation sparked by soaring oil prices have made it possible for the global economy to shun the negative impact of a rocketing oil price. However, if the oil price continues to hover high, both producers and consumers would adjust their supply and demand, thus leading to salary and price rises and further to serious inflation. In this case, economic growth might be eroded. For those developing countries and regions that rely on oil imports, particularly, ongoing oil price rises would deteriorate their balance of payments, possibly giving rise to an overall financial and economic crisis.

中国经济面临诸多风险
Challenges for China

2005 年中国经济保持了较好的增长势头，同时由于宏观经济调控措施的逐步生效，通胀压力得到控制。据预测，全年 GDP 增长速度达到 9.4% 左右，全年的通货膨胀率在 3% 以下。这就使得人们在年初最担忧的中国经济下滑和通货膨胀上升问题，并没有变成现实。[18] 中国经济在面对全球性经济失衡、房产价格泡沫、石油价格冲击、人民币汇率制度调整压力等众多不利因素的情况下，实现了经济的持续、平稳增长。

In 2005, the economic growth in China maintained a good momentum. As macro-economic adjustment measures gradually took effect, the pressure of inflation was eased. The country's gross domestic product (GDP) for the year is expected to rise by 9.4 percent, and the inflation rate to stand below 3 percent. The most worrying problems at the beginning of 2005—an economic slide and inflation escalation—didn't occur. Despite many disadvantages, such as global economic disequilibrium, a property bubble, surging oil prices and foreign exchange rate adjustment, China achieved continuous and steady economic growth.

在中国良好的增长态势的背后，也蕴藏着众多矛盾和风险。年初为了应对投资过热所引发的通货膨胀问题，中国开始实施全面的宏观调控，包括紧缩货币政策、压缩投资、调整财政支出行为。这些政策调整已经发挥实际的作用。但是截至 11 月底，全社会固定资产投资增长率仍然高达 27.8%，与 2004 年相比只回落了 1.1 个百分点。投资增长率的居高不下使得中国经济在短期内无法摆脱通货膨胀的威胁，鉴于 2006 年金融业将全面开放，通货膨胀压力一旦变成现实，中国经济的稳定和增长都将遇到严重挑战。

But many contradictions and risks also hide behind China's economic growth. At the beginning of 2005, China initiated overall macro-economic adjustment measures, such as tightening the monetary policy, checking on investment and adjusting fiscal expenses, to deal with the inflation sparked by overheated investment. By November, however, fixed asset investment still had grown by 27.8 percent, only 1.1 percentage points down from the same period of 2004. The hovering investment growth rate made it hard for China to get rid of the threat of inflation in the short term. In 2006, China is expected to completely open its financial sector. If inflation does show up in 2006, it would pose great challenges to China's economic stability and growth.

2005年7月份人民币汇率制度进行了调整,转向参考一篮子货币、更多反应市场供求力量的汇率形成机制。[19] 汇率制度的调整,一方面减缓了外部对人民币汇率施加的压力;另一方面也没有对国内金融体系产生过大的冲击。但是由于2005年世界经济整体性失衡现象依然严重,加之中国的贸易顺差继续扩大,国际上对人民币汇率制度施加的调整压力很快将重新加剧,要求增加人民币汇率弹性的呼声也将变得更大[20]。由此而引发的外汇和资本账户管理体制调整,将考验中国的决策部门和金融部门。而在全球失衡加剧的背景下中国的贸易顺差继续扩大,也将引发更严重的贸易摩擦和冲突,并引发国际社会对中国经济增长战略和增长模式的非议。

In July 2005, China revalued the yuan against the US dollar and introduced a currency basket to determine the exchange rate against the previous dollar peg. While such an adjustment has helped to relieve the pressure on the yuan, it did not exert a noticeable impact on the domestic financial system. However, as the global economic disequilibrium remained serious and China's trade surplus continued to widen in 2005, the international pressure on the yuan adjustment and the demand for a more flexible yuan will make a comeback soon. The adjustment in foreign exchange and the capital account management system arising from it will test China's policy makers and financial departments. Meanwhile, China's widening trade surplus will also result in more trade frictions and conflicts, sparking arguments from the international community on the strategy and mode of China's economic growth.

随着2006年中国金融业的全面开放,追逐高收益的投机性资金必然随着中国金融开放步伐的加快而找到更多的进入中国市场的途径。这将对中国未来的金融稳定性和货币稳定性施加更大的压力,并可能压缩货币当局在未来的政策调整空间。

As China's financial sector will be fully opened in 2006, speculative capital will definitely find more access to the Chinese market, placing more pressure on the country's financial and monetary stability and leaving less room for policy regulation.

Words and Expressions

失衡	disequilibrium; lose equilibrium; uneven development; loss or lack of stability or equilibrium 不平衡，失调
高速增长	sizzling expansion The summer sidewalks were sizzling. 夏日的人行道非常热。
调高	raise
得益于	benefit from
审慎的	prudent
宽松的	easy
财政政策	fiscal policies
企业资产负债表	corporate balance sheets
赤字	deficits the amount by which a sum of money falls short of the required or expected amount; a shortage large budget deficits 大量的财政赤字
美联储	the Federal Reserve
抑制	dampen
持续流入	momentum impetus of a nonphysical process, such as an idea or a course of events
贬值	depreciate; weaken
财政支出	fiscal expenditures
欧元区国家	euro zone countries
受制于	baffled by
乏力	lackluster; lacking brightness, luster, or vitality; dull
带来	inflict
摆脱	extricate oneself from
通货紧缩	deflation
抑制	cool
经济过热	overheating economy
内需	domestic demand
推动	propel to cause to move forward or onward; push
贸易逆差	trade deficits
潜在威胁	potential threat
显著降低	decline by a large margin
调整	address to deal with
一改……势头	reverse ... momentum
升值	appreciate

外汇储备	foreign reserves
回流	inflow
加剧	aggravate to make worse or more troublesome
攀升	soar; surge; hike; rise; rocket; hover high
新兴市场	emerging markets
强化	intensify
弹性不足	insufficiency
突破……大关	top; exceed or surpass
稳定	pin down
避免	shun to avoid deliberately; keep away from; escape
引发	give rise to occasion or opportunity
宏观经济调控	macro-economic adjustment
房产价格泡沫	a property bubble
不利因素	disadvantages
压缩投资	check on investment
金融业	financial sector
变成现实	show up to put in an appearance; arrive
人民币汇率制度	the yuan against the US dollar
汇率形成机制	peg a fixed price at a certain level or within a certain range
贸易顺差	trade surplus
增加人民币汇率弹性	a more flexible yuan
呼声	demand for
重新加剧	comeback
资本账户管理体制	capital account management system
贸易摩擦	trade frictions
国际社会	the international community
非议	arguments
投机性资金	speculative capital

Notes

1　"全球性失衡"指的是"全球经济失衡",这里因为是标题,所以汉语将"经济"省略了,翻译时应该将"经济"译出,以免意思含糊不清;"双重威胁"译成英语时无需译为"threatened by both ..."或者"double threat";另外,"高油价"译为"surging oil prices"表示油价仍然在继续上涨,而这种持续的上涨才是威胁所在。因为造成石油价格上涨的因素很多,所以价格的波动也很大,故此处不宜译成"high prices"。

2 IMF(International Monetary Fund)   国际货币基金组织
国际货币基金组织是政府间的国际金融组织。

3 "增长速度"在这一段中出现了三次,但是译文却不同。第一个"增长速度"将"速度"省译,因为主语就是"the growth",只用动词"slow"就将意思表示得非常清楚了。第二个"增长速度"后面因为出现了具体的百分比,如果还采用前一种译法,句子就会变成"the growth ... would drop to ...",因此将其译成了"the growth rate",这样句子就非常自然通顺了。第三个句子中的"取得……增长速度"是汉语的表达方式,如果硬译,难免出现不地道或者重复的问题,所以将其译成"has performed well",既简单又准确。

4 "根据 IMF 等国际经济组织的研究"中的"研究"实际上指的是"analysis"或者是"the result of the research";"世界经济能够在全球性失衡和高油价的环境中平稳地走过 2005 年",看到"平稳地走过",容易想到"pass ... smoothly"的句型,这里转译成名词"the steady development of world economy in 2005"正好做"主要得益于"的主语,更加符合英语的表达习惯;"企业资产负债表的改善"指的是"通过包括注入资本、缩减负债、盘活资产等方法改善企业的资产负债比例",这里也可以译成"better corporate balance sheets"。

5 在"……经济增长存在显著差异"中,汉语的主语是"经济增长"。如果按汉语句式直译,"存在"一词就不好处理。如果硬译,就很容易出现类似"there is a great difference ... in the development"这样的汉语句式,因此这里将汉语句子中的定语"不同国家的"译成主语,将主语"经济增长"译成英语句子中的宾语,即"various countries featured strikingly different development",这样译出的句子非常地道,但英语谓语动词的选择至关重要。"feature"一词的意思是"to have or include as a prominent part or characteristic"(包含……作为主要部分或特点)。英语中常出现这样的句子: "The automobile exhibition features a variety of new models.",如果对"feature"这个词不熟悉,就很难译出这样地道的句子。

6 "美国在高油价和高赤字的条件下"
受原油价格上涨等因素影响,美国商务部 2006 年 3 月 14 日公布的 2005 年经常项目赤字(包括商品及服务贸易、投资收益及经常性转移)再创历史新高,达到 8 049 亿美元。

7 美联储   the Federal Reserve
美国联邦储备局(简称"美联储")扮演着美国"中央银行"的角色。

8 "卡特里娜"飓风   Hurricane Katrina
2005 年 8 月 29 日,来自大西洋的"卡特里娜"飓风重创美国墨西哥湾沿岸地区,造成至少 1 800 多人死亡,数百万人无家可归,新奥尔良市 80% 被洪水淹没,造成的损失超过千亿美元，成为美国历史上最为严重的自然灾害之一。由于政府事后应急措施迟缓，造成数万灾民被困在新奥尔良，悲惨场景受到全世界普遍关注，布什政府因此受到国内外舆论的共同指责。

9 美国在高油价和高赤字的条件下……保持了物价稳定和经济平稳增长。

这个句子非常长，但主要是想表明：在高油价和高赤字的条件下，美国的经济运行平稳，所以这个句子可以采取两种译法。第一种是完全按英语的习惯译成："The United States stabilizes its prices and maintains a steady economic growth at home, where oil prices and deficits ran high, inflation was dampened, foreign capital maintained its momentum thanks to prudent interest rate rises adopted by the Federal Reserve, and exports increased partly due to a depreciating dollar and US fiscal expenditures expanded after Hurricane Katrina devastated the south."。如果这样翻译，原文中"这些因素结合在一起，使得……"的意思就没有完全表达出来。第二种方法即课文采取的拆译法，最后将这句话完全按汉语的句式译成"All these factors combined to help the United States stabilize its prices and maintain a steady economic growth"似乎更加准确，而且也与后面几句的句式保持一致。另外，原文中有"在财政和贸易双赤字条件下"，因为前面已经有"where oil prices and deficits ran high"，所以这里省译，以免重复。

10 "……实现既定的通货膨胀目标"指通胀没有超出预计，所以不能硬译成"meet the fixed inflation target"。也可以译成"succeeded in keeping the inflation under control/within their expectation"。

11 "……抑制了经济过热问题"，这个汉语句子有语病，可以抑制经济过热，也可以解决经济过热问题，但不能说"抑制……问题"，所以翻译时要灵活，千万不能死译、硬译。

12 美元持续贬值

2002年上半年，美元对西方主要货币的比价开始走下坡路，此后一蹶不振，美元对欧元汇率曾创下1欧元兑1.3667美元的低位，对日元也曾跌破105点关口，三年多时间贬值超过65%。

13 人民币汇率调整

2005年7月，我国汇率制度实行了历史性的改革。随后，又出台了一系列配套政策，使改革不断得以深化和更加符合市场实际。整体上看，新的外汇汇率机制运行良好，汇改达到了预期目的。

14 "……依然未能走上人们所期待的调整之路"的主语"贸易逆差和全球性经济失衡"，走上调整之路就是指得到改善，译文译得很巧，一个"improve"就把整个句子的意思表达出来了。

15 这是因为亚洲中央银行大量购进美元，导致亚洲国家的外汇储备大量流入美国。同时，由于美国经济形势良好，美国资产对私人投资者仍然有相当的吸引力，私人资本回流美国。这个句子中的"私人资本回流美国"前也可以使用一个"以致"或"导致"，译文用一个"leading to"和一个"result in"把两个句子自然地连接起来。

16. "弹性不足"不能随便翻译,先必须弄清楚它的确切含义,然后再动手翻译,直译或硬译都可能造成读者难以理解原文。

17. "世界经济之所以能够在2005年成功应对石油价格的冲击……使得世界经济在2005年避免石油价格上升的负面影响"中的第一句和最后一句意思重复,翻译成英语时应该避免重复,否则句子显得臃肿。

18. "这就使得人们在年初最担忧的中国经济下滑和通货膨胀上升问题,并没有变成现实。"这个汉语句子用的是使动句式,如果直译成"使得……并没有变成现实",英语句子就不通顺,因此译文没有采用汉语的句式,而是将其译成:"The most worrying problems at the beginning of 2005—an economic slide and inflation escalation—didn't occur."。

19. "人民币汇率制度"不能简单地翻译成"the RMB exchange rate system",而应该译成"the yuan against the US dollar"。另外,"转向参考一篮子货币、更多反应市场供求力量的汇率形成机制"意思是指"人民币汇率不再盯住单一美元,而是按照我国对外经济发展的实际情况,选择美元、欧元、日元等若干种主要货币,赋予相应的权重,组成一个货币篮子。同时,根据国内外经济金融形势,以市场供求为基础,参考一篮子货币计算人民币多边汇率指数的变化,对人民币汇率进行管理和调节,维护人民币汇率在合理均衡水平上的基本稳定。参考一篮子表明外币之间的汇率变化会影响人民币汇率,但参考一篮子不等于盯住一篮子货币,它还需要将市场供求关系作为另一重要依据,据此形成有管理的浮动汇率。"因此,在翻译这种政策性很强的术语时,一定要查找相关的资料,准确理解原文的意思后再动手翻译。

20. "但是由于2005年……要求增加人民币汇率弹性的呼声也将变得更大"中的"弹性"是指汇率根据市场供求关系浮动调整,译成"flexible"很准确。另外,"呼声"应该译成"demand";"也将变得更大"应该是又会卷土重来的意思,所以这里没有将其译成英语的比较级,而是和前面的"调整压力(很快将重新加剧)"并列,共用一个"make a comeback soon",句子准确自然。

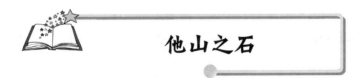

原文:

面向未来,中化公司将继续秉承"创造价值、追求卓越"的理念,牢固树立科学发展观,坚持走质量效益型发展道路,全面加快战略转型,以能源、农业投入品和化工产业为核心,以营销服务能力为基础,继续向相关产业的上下游和国内外延伸,逐步形成资源控制、技术研发、市场营销和金融服务相互支撑的产业价值链和相关产业群,建成具有较强市场竞争力和影响力的综合性国际企业集团,为国家能源安全、农业安全和化工产业发展持续做出贡献。

原译文:

Looking into the future, Sinochem will continue carrying on the vision of "creating value and pursuing excellence", practice the scientific concept of development, give top priority to quality and profitability, accelerate strategic transformation, take the energy, agricultural inputs and chemicals industries as the core and the marketing and servicing capability as the foundation to continue to expand related businesses towards upstream and downstream sectors both internationally and domestically. It will gradually build and strengthen an integrated industrial chain incorporating resources control, R&D, marketing and financial services to develop into an international with strong competitiveness and influence and make sustainable contributions to China's energy security, agricultural security and chemical industry.

点评:

① "继续秉承'创造价值、追求卓越'的理念,牢固树立科学发展观"是下文"坚持走质量效益型发展道路"等动作的前提条件,所以不一定按汉语的句式译成句子的谓语,可以译成其他成分。另外,"秉承……理念,树立……发展观"可以用"following the (management) philosophy of"来表示,不必分开翻译。

② "以能源、农业投入品和化工产业为核心,以营销服务能力为基础"是"全面加快战略转型"的具体体现,所以与其译成并列谓语,不如译成方式状语,修饰谓语"giving top priority to ..."。

③ "以能源、农业投入品和化工产业为核心,以营销服务能力为基础"指的是加快传统外贸企业向现代营销服务型企业转型,因此可以理解为:营销和服务是企业核心经营能力的基础。

④ 原译中的断句有点问题,"逐步形成资源控制、技术研发、市场营销和金融服务相互支撑的产业价值链和相关产业群"很显然是上句"继续向相关产业的上下游和国内外延伸"的结果和目的,所以还是连起来比较合理。

⑤ 企业所做的这一切努力都是为了将企业"建成具有较强市场竞争力和影响力的综合性国际企业集团,为国家能源安全、农业安全和化工产业发展持续做出贡献",所以可以将后面的句子并到一起,使整个句子完整自然。

改译:

Looking into the future, Sinochem, by following its management philosophy of "creating value and pursuing excellence", will continue giving top priority to quality and profitability in its steady scientific development, and accelerate the strategic transformation by basing the energy, agricultural inputs and chemicals industries on its marketing and servicing capability to further expand related businesses towards upstream and downstream sectors both home and abroad so as to gradually build and strengthen an integrated industrial chain incorporating resources control, R&D, marketing and financial services, thus developing into a powerful and competitive international conglomerate to make sustainable contributions to China's energy and agricultural security and chemical industry.

学生译作分析

原文：

我们从1998年开始出版梅塞尔（Messer）中国杂志，至今已经是第14期了。这份杂志的宗旨始终是改善我们的内部交流，我们希望我们的同事们能清楚了解公司的远景计划、近期目标及我们努力实现目标的进展情况。同时，我们也希望提供一个论坛，让大家都有机会就公司政策和存在的问题畅所欲言。公司总部正在整个梅塞尔中国范围内，从技术、安全、人力资源、财务等各个领域努力推行标准化管理模式，希望标准化活动有助于改善公司的效率和效力。

学生原译文：

It has been the 14th volume since we started to publish Messer-China Magazine in 1998. The objective of this magazine is always to improve our internal exchange. We hope our colleagues have a clear idea about the long-term plan and the target in the near future of our firm, as well as the situation of the target we are striving for. We also hope to provide a forum where everyone can have an opportunity to comment the policy of our firm and the existing problems freely. The headquarters of our corporation is trying hard to promote a standard management style from several fields such as technology, security, human resource and finance within the area of Messer, China. It is hoped that the standard management will be benefit for the improvement of the efficiency and the effectiveness of our firm.

分析：

（1）原文中的"出版"应该理解成"print"，因为这只是一份企业内部的刊物，发行的范围有限。

（2）"内部交流"这里是指员工之间的沟通。

（3）"同事们"不宜直译成"colleagues"，而应该译成"fellow workers"或者"staff"。

（4）"清楚了解"译成"have a clear idea about"不够准确，应该译成"better

understand"更加贴切,因为仅仅知道是不够的,还应该理解。

(5) "畅所欲言"译成"comment ... freely"太生硬,不如用"say one's say"或者"air one's views"。

(6) 最后一句"公司总部正在……,希望……"是一句话,不能拆译,将后面的句子译成表目的的分句比较妥切。

参考译文:

In 1998 we first printed this journal, Messer China Quarterly and this is the 14th issue. Since then we have been following our original aim of the publication: to make an easier communication between the workers within the organization, to have the long, short-term targets and our efforts better understood by our fellow workers, and to provide a forum where everyone can have an opportunity to air his views on the policy and the existing problems of our organization at any time. Now the headquarter of the Messer Group is working hard to standardize its management style within Messer China team in the fields such as technology, security, human resource and finance in the hope of improving the efficiency and the effectiveness of the whole corporate.

翻译技巧介绍

连动式的处理

汉译英中最常碰到的问题就是如何处理好汉语连动式的问题。汉语中"用连动词组充当谓语的句子叫'连动式'"。连动式谓语通常只有一个主语,谓语中间不能加上关联词语,但在意义上与同一主语形成主谓关系。虽然从句子的形式看,这些连动式很像英语中的并列句,但英语中的并列句是互相对等的,成平行排列。因此,在翻译较长的汉语联合复句时,首先应该判断这个句子是属于汉语的连动式(一个主语 + 多个谓语分句,不能用关联词语)、连贯复句(不同的主语 + 多个分句,可以用关联词语)还是并列复句(一个主语 + 多个谓语分句,可用或不用关联词语)。另外,汉语的联合复句除了表示动作和动作的先后次序(连贯复句)和并列动作(并列复句)外,充当谓语的多个连动词组还可表示原因、目的、结果和伴随状况,所以弄清楚各动词(动词词组)之间的逻辑关系是翻译汉语连动句式的关键。

例句 1:

政府只要将财政更多地**投入**到公共领域,**完善**各种保障机制,并通过各项政策**调整**居民与居民、居民与政府间的收入分配格局,就有可能真正**调动**居民的消费热情,**提升**居民的消费潜力,从而**促成**居民消费更快地增长,从而也就可以**改变**中国目前主要依靠投资拉动的经济增长模式。

译文1:

If the government increases investment in the public sector, improves various security systems and adjusts the income distribution structure, it can possibly arouse the people's enthusiasm to spend, tap residents' consumption potential, speed up the nation's consumption capability and transform the current investment-oriented economic growth pattern.

译文2:

With the government's effort to **increase investment in** the public sector, to **improve** various security systems and to **adjust** the income distribution structure, the people's enthusiasm to spend will be **aroused**. This will help **tap** residents' consumption potential, **speed up** the nation's consumption capability and **transform** the current investment-oriented economic growth pattern.

例句1的汉语句子中一共出现了7个动词,读起来似乎都与主语"政府"形成主谓关系。然而,如果仔细分析,就会发现整个汉语句子其实是个表连贯关系的联合复句,并不是"连动式"。除了关联词语"就"以外,其中"调动"、"提升"、"促成"和"改变"只是政府"投入"、"完善"和"调整"行为的结果,所以译文2将"调动"译成了英语的被动语态,另外在其他三个动词前增加了另一个主语"this",这样就使得英语句子中动词之间的相互关系非常明确,比译文1更加准确清楚。

例句2:

我们要**以**加入世贸组织**为契机**,进一步**扩大**对外开放,**争取**主动,**推动**国民经济持续健康快速发展。我们要认真**分析研究**加入世贸组织对我国的各种影响,及时**提出**有针对性的措施,既要**敢于开放**市场,又要**善于保护**自己。

译文1:

We should take our WTO entry as an opportunity, further our opening to the outside world, get initiatives into our own hands, and boost the sustained, healthy and rapid development of the national economy. We should make conscientious analysis and study of the various influences brought on China by WTO entry and promptly put forward purposeful measures. We should dare to open the market and be good at protecting ourselves.

译文2:

We should **take** our WTO accession as an opportunity **to further open** to the outside world and **strive** for initiatives **in winning** the sustained, healthy and rapid development of the national economy. A thorough analysis and study should be made **to find out** the various influences on us from the WTO membership **so that** we **can cope with** them in time with effective measures, **which enables us to open** the market boldly **while protecting** ourselves against any risks therefrom.

例句 2 汉语句子中一共出现了 11 个动词。整个句子只有一个主语"我们",也就是说所有动作都是"我们"发出的。整个句子虽然是汉语的连动结构,但是各个动作从先后次序和重要性方面来看与主语的关系却不一样,如果将所有动词一律译成句子的谓语(译文1),那么各动词与主语逻辑上的关系就非常含糊。因此,译文 2 在仔细分析汉语原文之后,做了如下处理:① 将第一句中的"以……为契机"和"争取"译成了英语句子的谓语,将"进一步扩大……"译成英语的不定式短语修饰"opportunity"(作定语),并将"推动"译成英语的介词短语修饰"initiatives"。这样一来,句子的意思就非常明了,即"我们要抓住时机做某事,争取主动做某事",而不是"将……作为机会,进一步……,争取主动和推动……",其中"take ... as an opportunity"和"strive for initiatives"好像是没有任何目的的行为;② 将第二句中的"分析研究"译成谓语(被动式和词类转换),将其他动词以状语从句和定语从句的方式译成谓语动作的结果,动作的先后次序和逻辑关系一目了然;③ 将"又要善于保护自己"译成分词短语表伴随状况。

例句 3:

我们将**借鉴**世界知名展会的先进经验,**坚持**以人为本、全面、协调、可持续的科学发展观,积极**开拓创新**,通过优质服务**推动**贸易发展,**促进**经济和社会进步。

译文:

We will **insist on** the scientific strategy of human-oriented, all-around, harmonious and sustainable development while learning advanced experience drawn by world's renowned fairs. We shall **spare no efforts** in fair innovating and providing quality services in order to promote trade, economic and social development.

例句 3 的汉语句子中动词多达 6 个,究竟哪个或哪些应该译成英语的谓语,哪些译成其他句子成分呢?译者经过认真分析原文,找出"坚持"和"积极"两个词充当句子的谓语,并以其他形式(分词、介词短语和不定式)将其他动词或词组译成别的成分,符合英语的表达习惯,意思准确明了。

例句 4:

面向未来,中土畜总公司**坚持**"永远不变的追求,奉献自然与健康"的经营理念,**以振兴**中国土畜事业**为己任**,**努力**把中土畜总公司**打造**成为具有核心竞争力的中国土产、畜产、茶叶行业的龙头企业。

译文:

Facing the future, China Tushu, **by adhering** to its unswerving business philosophy of satisfying customers with natural and healthy products and **bearing** the vitalization of the whole china's business of native produce, animal by-products in mind, will **spare no effort to reach its goal of becoming** a pilot enterprise with core competitive edge in the line of native produce, animal by-products and teas.

例句4的汉语句子中的动词虽然不多，但整个句子也是连动式。翻译时将"面向"译成分词短语，将"坚持"和"以……为己任"译成英语的方式状语，表示这样做的目的是"努力把……打造成……龙头企业"。如果将"坚持"和"以……为己任"也译成英语句子中的谓语，其动作与后面动词逻辑上的关系就无法表达了。

例句5：

以上海浦东开发开放**为龙头**，进一步**开放**长江沿岸城市，**尽快把**上海**建成**国际经济、金融、贸易中心之一，**带动**长江三角洲和整个长江流域地区经济的新飞跃。

译文：

We should **open** more cities along the Yangtze River, **while concentrating on** the development and opening of the Pudong Area of Shanghai so **as to make** Shanghai one of the international economic, financial and trade centers as soon as possible and **to bring about** a new leap in economic development in the Yangtze River Delta and the whole Yangtze River basin.

从例句5的汉语句子中可以看出，"以上海浦东开发开放为龙头，进一步开放长江沿岸城市"与"尽快把上海建成国际经济、金融、贸易中心之一，带动长江三角洲和整个长江流域地区经济的新飞跃"之间存在逻辑上的联系，虽然汉语中没有用关联词语，但意思非常明确，即：以上海浦东开发开放为龙头，进一步开放长江沿岸城市的目的就是为了尽快把上海建成国际经济、金融、贸易中心之一，带动长江三角洲和整个长江流域地区经济的新飞跃，所以翻译时将后面的句子译成了目的状语。

总之，汉语的长句比较复杂，有时一段话全用逗号连接，这些句子有些是连动式，有的只是一些连贯复句。因此，每当读到较长的汉语句子时，就应当仔细揣摩句子的含义，分析句子之间的内在联系，合理选择一个或几个动词作为句子的谓语，切忌胡子眉毛一把抓，造成译文意思含糊不清，逻辑混乱。具体方法如下。

（1）如果汉语中的联合复句表示并列意义，翻译时可考虑将其中大多数动词或动词词组译成谓语，形式除了动词之外，还可采用现在分词和过去分词表示伴随状况。

例句6：

公司紧紧围绕总体工作目标，**坚持**"保安全、保市场、保稳定、增效益"的工作方针，以市场为基础，以效益为中心，**发挥**整体优势，适时**调整**经营策略，**强化**内部管理，**优化**生产运行，**取得**了较好的经营业绩。

译文：

Focusing on the overall business targets, the Company **stuck** to the business guidelines of "Ensuring Safety, Market, Stability and Increasing Profitability", and driven by the market and profitability, the Company fully **leveraged** its overall advantages, timely **adjusted** operation strategies, **strengthened** internal management and **optimized** production and **has thus**

accomplished remarkable operating results.

（2）如果汉语中的联合复句表示连贯意义，翻译时可将各动词或动词词组按次序来排列。如果汉语句子中间出现关联词语，可以将句子拆开分段翻译。

例句 7：

与外资银行相比，在高端客户业务的竞争中，中资银行**缺乏**优势，"而争夺高端客户是外资银行在中国的主要竞争策略之一，他们青睐、争夺的**也正是**这块'肥肉'"。

译文：

Compared with foreign-funded banks, Chinese-funded banks **lagged behind** in the competition to win more high-end clients. "To contend for high-end clients is one of the competition strategies of foreign-funded banks in China because that **is** exactly what they favor and come here for."

（3）如果确定句子属于汉语的连动式，翻译时可考虑将表示方式、目的、结果、伴随状况的动作以英语不定式、介词短语、现在分词和过去分词等形式译成英语的状语；还可以合并动词，运用系表结构，采用定语从句，甚至将句子拆开翻译。

例句 8：

公司总部**设**在北京，在境内外**拥有**全资、控股和参股企业几十家，**形成了**横跨土、畜、茶三大类商品的全球性营销网络，并**通过**自己的远洋运输船队与国内外客商**建立了**广泛密切的业务联系。

译文：

China Tuhsu, **with** its headquarter in Beijing, solely **owns** and **holds** majority interests or joint shares of scores of businesses and subsidiaries at home and abroad, and also **has** its own marine fleets **linking up** itself closely with its clients worldwide, thus **forming** global ramifications of trade in the line of native produce, animal by-products, and teas.

例句 9：

日本只**进口**原产于韩国的紫菜，而不**进口**中国产的同类紫菜，明显**违反**了世贸组织有关协定的规定，**构成了**对中国产紫菜出口日本的贸易壁垒。

译文：

Japan only **imports** laver produced in South Korea but not products from in China, which has obviously **violated** related regulations of the World Trade Organization (WTO) **to have formed** a trade barrier for Chinese laver exports to Japan.

例句 10：

广东省**地处**沿海，**毗邻**香港和澳门，经济繁荣，人口密集，交通发达，**成为**各路商家争夺中国市场的一个滩头阵地，**是**中国音像产业 3 大基地之一，每年从这里发出的正版音像制品占全国市场销量的 70% 以上，同时也**是**盗版者格外活跃的地带。

译文：

Guangdong is a coastal province **bordering** Hong Kong and Macao. **With** a prosperous economy, dense population and convenient transportation, the province **is** a battleground for companies wanting a larger slice of the lucrative Chinese market. As one of the three major bases for China's audio-video industry, it **is responsible for** more than 70 percent of original audio-video products sold across the country every year. However, it **is** also an ideal place for copyright piracy.

课堂翻译训练

将下列句子译成英语。

1. 我们要以加入世贸组织为新的起点，努力提高开放水平。要充分利用加入世贸组织的有利条件，实施多元化战略，千方百计扩大出口。

2. 中国经济的更加繁荣和开放，不仅会大大增进中国十几亿人民的福祉，而且还会给包括广大华商在内的世界各国企业家提供广阔的市场和无限的商机，也必将对世界经济的繁荣和发展做出更大贡献。

3. 每次盛会，展览商品琳琅满目，吸引国际诸多大商贾前来参观并洽谈商务，效果显著，为中国商品出口和中外工商贸易，创造出辉煌成果。

4. 专家还指出，中国农产品流通体系发育仍十分落后，不能适应当前的国际化竞争形势。他们说，多数农民在市场风险面前仍处在"单兵对阵"状态，加上有关农作物种植面积的预测与动态发布信息十分稀缺，农民安排种植品种和面积，仍然是"今天下雨，明天打伞"。

5. 中国商务部部长薄熙来强调，中国各项鼓励外商投资的政策、措施和法律法规不变，特别是所得税政策不变，外资准入政策不变，并将进一步扩大开放，改善投资环境。

6. 中国会继续依靠获利的出口市场来赚取外汇以发展和增长自己的经济。同时，中国可用进口的机械和技术来加速它继续发展的速度。对于美国来说，在不断涌现的市场上，新的贸易机会将以最快的速度增长。这将意味着为美国工人创造就业机会，使美国人民提高生活水平。

7. 反对者说，迪斯尼乐园对中国人来说还是属于高档消费，属于"奢侈品"，在中国还存在大量贫困地区和贫困人口的今天，政府应该把更多精力和财力放到解决民生大计上。另外，在已经有香港迪斯尼乐园的情况下，如果国内再建第二个乐园就属于重复建设，盲目投资。
8. 商务部长薄熙来说，这次谈判是复杂的，也是困难的，正因为如此才谈到七轮，有几次已经走到了悬崖的边缘。
9. （纺织）企业赴海外建厂可以向这些发展中国家转移，这样做的好处是可以缓解贸易摩擦、分散企业经营风险，同时也可以享受到欧美发达国家与一些发展中国家建立的优惠贸易政策，以及东道国提供的优惠政策等。
10. 21世纪商业竞争中重要的一部分就是高级人才的比拼，在中国越来越多的企业愿意依托专业公司帮助它们寻找人才，跨国猎头公司的中国客户也越来越多
11. 尽管大多数专家认为去年的贸易逆差有特定的原因，今年情况将有所好转，但其中不少人也还是不甚乐观地指出，由于中国农业自身存在的问题及诸多外部因素的作用，中国未来几年的农产品贸易可能依然面临较大压力。
12. 中国将继续稳步开放市场，创新引进外资的形式，完善有关鼓励和保护外商投资的法律法规，改革涉外经济管理体制，加强知识产权保护，努力为中国的对外经贸合作和外国来华投资提供一切便利，创造更好的环境。

课后练习

将下列短文译成英语，注意连动式的处理。

1.
我公司是一家具有52年历史的外贸企业。半个世纪以来，公司始终如一地运用其丰富的商务经验、完善的海内外渠道及雄厚的融资能力来为客户提供最大化价值的服务。在社会各界的支持与海内外客户的关爱下，公司在我国对外贸易史上创造出了诸多"第一"，书写了动人的篇章。

伴随着科技革命和新经济的发展，我公司正在以"新思路、新姿态、新视角"来实现公司的可持续发展，我们的目标凝聚成一句："将企业做强做大"。依托50余年来造就的良好商誉、人才优势和国内外经营网络及业务渠道，通过自我发展与整合社会资源等多种有效方式，公司在专业化经营的领域内不断提升项目开发、集成与管理能力，实现由传统的进出口贸易代理向国际工程承包、咨询和项目管理方向的转型，为客户提供更加专业化及附加值更高的产品和服务。

2.
当年为了实现乌拉圭回合，各个成员费了很大劲儿，但事后的结果并不乐观，世界经济

更不平衡,两极分化越加严重。面对这一现象,发展中国家不能容忍,发达国家也感到了危机。正因为如此,大家才把多哈回合定为发展回合。这是 WTO 历史上巨大的进步,也是各个成员富有远见的选择。果能如此,不论富国还是穷国,都会因为生活在一个更加和谐的世界而获得持久发展的环境。反之,如果发展的主题仅仅是口号,没有实际内容,谈判将失去意义,失去动力,也会令世人对世贸组织感到失望。

乌拉圭回合已经过去十年,现在是发达国家下决心的时候了。发达国家的农民在全球不到 4%,而发达国家财力雄厚,完全有能力在取消补贴、降低关税之后,把自家的农民照顾好。我们坚定地支持取消发达成员的各种形式的出口补贴,并定出 2010 年的时间表以体现诚意;坚定地支持实质性大幅度削减发达成员扭曲贸易的国内支持。

3.

近两年来,关于人民币汇率改革的问题一直是国内外广泛关注的焦点。从 1994 年至今,我国对外汇管理体制进行了重大改革,在实现了经常项目下的完全可兑换后,人民币汇率实行了名义上的有管理的浮动汇率制度,多年来始终保持在 8.27 水平左右。由于近几年来我国经济持续高速发展,外贸顺差不断扩大,外汇储备急剧增加,人们越来越认识到,有必要实行更加灵活的调控机制。

7 月 21 日,央行宣布开始实行以市场供求为基础、参考一篮子货币进行调节、有管理的浮动汇率制度。央行宣布的人民币汇率改革主要有三方面的内容:一是汇率由 1 美元兑 8.28 元调整到 8.11 元,升幅为 2%;二是人民币与美元脱钩,汇率参照一篮子货币制定;三是在前一交易日收盘价基础上,人民币汇率每天波幅在 0.3% 以内。

8 月 9 日,央行宣布改革银行间外汇市场,为非银行金融机构和非金融企业进入该市场开了"绿灯",同时首次引入询价这种更为市场化的交易方式,首次允许在该市场内开展远期外汇交易和掉期交易。这意味着,央行正致力于逐步推进人民币汇率的市场化。

  佳译赏析

外资信用卡不赚钱?
Is There Profit in China's Foreign Credit Card Market?

近日银行业研究顾问公司 Lafferty Group[1] 的一份研究在中国引起了广泛讨论[2]。该报告称,争相进入中国信用卡市场的西方银行有可能发现,2010 年前它们可能无法赢利。

Recently, a survey by Lafferty Group, a provider of business information on global retail banking, has attracted much attention in China. The survey claims that Western banks that are rushing into the Chinese credit card market may find that it's impossible for them to make profits in China before 2010.

该集团推算,中国各银行去年在信用卡业务上的税前亏损达 8 400 万美元,并预测说,如果当前这一趋势继续下去,2010 年的亏损可能猛增[3]至逾 10 亿美元。Lafferty 旗下 World Cards Intelligence 的资深分析师詹姆斯·巴克利表示,中国与墨西哥等其他增长迅速的市场之间对比十分鲜明,World Cards Intelligence[4] 估计,墨西哥各银行的信用卡业务去年利润达约 15 亿美元。

Lafferty found that in 2005, Chinese banks suffered a pretax loss of $84 million on their credit card business. If the present trend continues, the loss is expected to jump to more than $1 billion by 2010. According to James Buckley, an analyst at World Cards Intelligence, Lafferty Group's online source for critical market and competitor intelligence on credit cards and consumer lending, China is a sharp contrast to other fast-growing credit card markets, such as Mexico, which produced a profit of about $1.5 billion in 2005.

"我们发现,令人吃惊的是,西方银行已在中国银行业投资了约 250 亿美元,目的基本上是想创造消费金融[5]业务,而无论是现在还是近期,我们看不到银行在中国赢利的前景[6]。"他说。

"It's a surprise that although Western banks have invested $25 billion into China's banking sector, aiming to build up the business of consumer finance, there is no sign that these banks are able to make profits now or in the near future," said Buckley.

与之相反的是,对国际信用卡公司而言,拥有13亿以上的人口,2005年GDP超过18万亿元并经济稳步增长的中国,仍是个充满希望的市场。面对2006年12月1日信用卡业务对外资的开放期限,国际信用卡公司早早就在中国做好了准备。[7] 早在2002年12月,浦发银行[8]就与花旗国际有限公司[9]签署《信用卡业务协议》。双方将共同成立一家新的信用卡公司,各占50%的股权,但信用卡公司中的高管人员多数由花旗派出。[10]

To the Western credit card companies, China remains a promising market, which has a population of 1.3 billion and whose GDP in 2005 exceeded 18 trillion yuan based on a steadily growing economy. International credit card companies have already made sufficient preparation for the day when the restriction on foreign banks' engagement in the credit card business is nullified, on December 1, 2006. As early as December 2002, Shanghai Pudong Development Bank (SPDB) and Citibank signed a credit card business agreement, under which the two will jointly set up a new credit card company, with each possessing 50 percent of the shares. The company's high-level managerial personnel will be provided by Citibank.

通过这次合作,花旗绕过政策限制[11],提前开展信用卡业务。而浦发银行则能引进先进的技术、经验,提高自身管理水平并弥补其个人金融业务薄弱的不足。浦发银行2005年报显示,报告期内,浦发银行联手花旗推出的信用卡,年内发卡20万多张。而这种中外合作模式后来也成为许多国际信用卡公司进入中国的普遍模式。

On the one hand, by cooperating with SPDB, Citibank is able to begin the credit card business in China ahead of others by avoiding restrictions on foreign banks. On the other hand, SPDB is able to seize this opportunity to import advanced techniques and experience to enhance its own managerial level and make up for its weak individual finance business. A 2005 report by SPDB shows that by the time this report was finished, 200,000 credit cards that are jointly produced by SPDB and Citibank had been issued in 2005. The Sino-foreign cooperation model set by SPDB and Citibank had now been widely followed by other companies.

除了国际信用卡公司之外,全球最大的零售商美国沃尔玛(Wal-Mart)也计划在中国推出自己的信用卡。信用卡将由该公司与美国GE Money[12]和中国深圳发展银行[13]联合推出。而沃尔玛信用卡将会成为第一种由外资零售商在中国发行的此类信用卡。

Apart from foreign credit card companies, Wal-Mart, the largest retailer in the world, is planning to issue its own credit card in China. This card will be a joint product of Wal-Mart, GE

Capital of the United States and Shenzhen Development Bank. The Wal-Mart credit card will be the first credit card issued by a foreign retailer in China.

一方面是不容乐观的前景,一方面是不断涌入中国市场的国际信用卡公司,究竟外资信用卡能否如它们期望的在中国这个广阔的信用卡市场上淘到黄金?[14]

Against the bleak prospect of profit, are credit card companies naively rushing into the Chinese market? Is it possible for them to succeed in their "gold rush" in China?

信用卡靠什么赚钱
How to make money?

麦肯锡[15] 2006年初的数据统计显示,目前中国的信用卡人数已经从2003年年初的300多万人猛增至现在的1 200多万人,发放的标准信用卡[16]将近2 000万张。可是如此蓬勃的市场增长速度,并没有从国际信用卡公司在中国投资的账本上显示出来。[17] Lafferty认为,在华投资的外国银行需要一代人的时间,才能使其信用卡业务产生大量利润,而那些进入拉美和其他成长性市场的银行比起进入中国的银行,其回报将更强劲,获得回报的时间也将早得多。[18]

According to statistics from McKinsey & Co., at the beginning of 2006, credit card users in China soared to 12 million from just slightly over 3 million at the beginning of 2003. Nearly 20 million credit cards have been issued. However, foreign credit card companies seem to have benefited little from such a booming market. Lafferty believes that a generation's time is needed for foreign banks engaged in China's credit card business to win big profits. The Chinese banking market is different from that in Latin America or other growing markets that are able to produce large amounts of profits within a shorter period of time.

这个悲观的预测是基于中国市场"完全不同的经济状况",中国市场有很高比例的无利客户,他们每月还清全部账单,同时商户支付的费用也很低,且还在下降。

This pessimistic prediction is based on "the totally different economic condition" of the Chinese market, which has a high proportion of clients who bring no profits, as they pay off all their debts every month. Even commercial clients pay small fees, which themselves are falling.

万事达卡[19]国际组织资深副总裁兼大中华区总经理冯炜权介绍,目前国内信用卡有三部分直接的利润来源:一是年收费,二是手续费,三是透支利息收入,即循环信贷。

According to Feng Weiquan, Senior Vice President and General Manager of Greater China branch of MasterCard International, credit cards in China currently have three direct profit sources: Annual fees, handling fees and overdraft fees from "frequent revolvers".

所谓"循环信贷"即客户无需在收到信用卡账单时一次性还清所有款项，而只需每月交付一个最低金额还款数目，这样做的好处在于很大程度上缓解了客户的还款压力，同时也直接刺激了国内市场的消费。

Clients who are frequent revolvers do not need to pay off all the debt on the credit card at one time; they only need to pay off a monthly minimum. This has greatly relieved clients of the pressure of heavy debts, and has also stimulated domestic consumption.

这也同时意味着银行将向每一位"循环信贷"的客户收取一定比例的贷款利息，虽然这个利息并不是很高，但一旦银行的发卡量达到一定规模，那么信用卡的利息收益累计起来也将会是一个大数目。根据麦肯锡的统计，在国外成熟市场，例如美国，利息收入可占信用卡业务全部收入的三分之二。

Of course, while providing this service, clients are required to pay a certain proportion of loan interest to banks, which can become quite large amounts. In line with statistics from McKinsey, in mature card markets—the US market for instance—interest income accounts for two thirds of all profits related to the credit card business.

而中国目前的状况是，年费收入是中国信用卡市场的最主要收入来源，平均比例高达55%；其次是利息透支收入，平均比例为22%；第三为刷卡手续费，平均比例达到16%；最后是平均7%的其他收入。

In China, however, annual fees are the major income source for credit card issuers, which compose 55 percent of the total income on average. Second is overdraft interest income, accounting for 22 percent. Third is the handling fee, making up 16 percent. Other income accounts for 7 percent.

银行业人士普遍认为，导致中国信用卡市场透支利息收入比例低的原因主要表现为以下两个方面：一是中国信用卡市场发展的程度较低，社会上还没有普遍形成透支消费的观念[20]；二是由于信用体系建设的落后导致发卡机构信用卡的营销策略大多表现为稳健型的经营风格，重视稳定且风险低的年费收入，而对具有信用风险的透支消费的营销力度不够。"中国内地居民的消费习惯直到目前还是'赚多少，花多少'[21]，缺乏循环信贷可以说是制约内地信用卡发展的一个瓶颈，也是内地银行发卡的一个盈利盲点。"冯炜权说。

Those familiar with China's banking sector believe that there are two reasons that have led to low overdraft interest income in China's credit card market: One is that China's credit card market is not fully developed, and few people are in the habit of spending tomorrow's money. Second, due to the outdated credit system, card issuers tend to adopt a stable method in carrying out their business. The stable and low-risk incomes from annual fees are thus quite popular with Chinese banks, while the overdraft business—which may incur big losses—is quite limited. "The Chinese are used to 'just making ends meet', and the lack of frequent revolvers has become a bottleneck that has restricted credit card issuing in China," said Feng.

据麦肯锡公布的《2005年中国信用卡市场调研报告》称,目前中国一半以上的信用卡客户不能给发卡行带来盈利,只有2%的客户经常使用循环信贷,即信用卡上几乎总有欠款的消费者。长此以往,中国信用卡市场有可能全线走向亏损,而Lafferty对最坏情形的预测是2010年将出现10.3亿美元的亏损。

According to a report on China's credit card market in 2005 issued by McKinsey, more than half of the card users in China will not bring profits to card issuers. Only 2 percent of the clients are frequent revolvers who delay debt payment. If this trend continues, all the credit card issuers will suffer from losses, and Lafferty predicts that banks will suffer from a big loss of $1.03 billion in 2010.

但多位接受《北京周报》采访的银行界人士表示,国内信用卡市场的盈利前景未必如麦肯锡报告中所说的如此黯淡,中国信用卡市场在经过长时间的磨炼之后,出现突破性的增长也是完全有可能的。

Nevertheless, a number of personnel from the banking industry told Beijing Review that the Chinese credit card market is not doomed to meet such a dark fate. After a certain period of effort, it's quite possible that there will be a breakthrough in credit card incomes for the issuers.

上海交通大学国际金融研究中心主任潘英丽在接受采访时表示,当一个国家的人口老龄化问题严重时,信用卡市场也必然进入衰退期。目前中国25岁至45岁这一年龄层占总人口比重较大,而中国的人口基数又很大,因此现在信用卡市场的发展空间是很大的。一位不愿意透露姓名的外资银行管理人员透露:"信用卡本来就是一项中长期投资,一般国外要3到5年能盈利,印度的大银行用了8年时间才持平。而且从长远来看,前期客户基础打得越好,后期收益就越可观,因此尽管现在账面亏损,但所有的银行都不愿在争夺客户上落后半步。[22]"

Pan Yingli, Director of the International Finance Research Center of Shanghai Jiao Tong University, said during an interview that if a nation has a large aging population, the credit card market would surely wane. China, however, has a high proportion of the population aged 25 to 45 while the whole population is more than 1.3 billion, so there is great room for credit card business to achieve further development, according to Pan. A manager with a foreign bank, who refused to reveal his name, pointed out that the "credit card is a long and medium-term investment. It took three to five years for card issuers to make profits in many other countries. Take the credit card business in India for example. It cost the banks eight years to reach a balance. In the long run, the more clients that are attracted in the early period, the more profits will be produced in the late period. Despite the book loss at present, all the banks are still competing for more clients."

未来的市场有多大
What is the market potential?

虽然麦肯锡和 Lafferty 都为中国的信用卡市场做了最坏的打算,但是它们同时也认为最有可能的结果是收支大致平衡。据 Lafferty 计算,如果中国市场的卡费和商户费用能维持在去年的水平,账单和有息结余能有大幅增加,损失率和利差能达到全球平均水平,则该行业到 2010 年能实现 20 亿美元的税前利润。与之类似的预测是麦肯锡 2005 年底发布的一份调研报告,其中预计中国的信用卡市场将呈指数增长,2013 年将成为仅次于房贷的第二大零售信贷产品,并且信用卡业务占整个银行业的利润将由现在的 4% 增长到 14% 左右,金额约合人民币 130 亿元。

Although McKinsey and Lafferty have painted the darkest prospect for Chinese banks, they still believe the enterprises can break even. According to Lafferty's calculation, the credit card sector could earn $2 billion in pretax profits by 2010 if the following occurs: The card fees and fees paid by commercial clients are no less than those of last year, there is a sharp increase in customer accounts and interest-bearing debts, and the loss rate and interest margin reach average international levels. A similar prediction is made by McKinsey in one of its survey reports issued at the end of 2005, which indicates that China's credit card business will greatly grow and become a large retailing credit product second only to the real estate industry in 2013. By that time, the credit card business, which currently accounts for 4 percent of the overall profits of the banking sector, will rise to 14 percent, amounting to 13 billion yuan.

市场也在近期给了众多处于迷茫中的信用卡公司一个好的答案。2006 年较早进入信用卡市场的广东发展银行,在历经 10 年磨炼之后,于 2005 年率先实现盈亏平衡;后来居上的招商银行信用卡业务在 2005 年底实现盈亏平衡,并且在 2006 年第一季度盈利 6 000 万元。招商银行信用卡中心总经理助理彭千对这样的结果表现得十分兴奋,他认为 2006 年将成为中国信用卡快速发展年,起步较早的本土股份制银行在信用卡市场的盈利也给进入中国市场的国际信用卡公司带来一个好的讯息。

Recently the market shows some hope for credit card companies at sea. After 10 years of a hard struggle, Guangdong Development Bank, which entered the credit card market a bit ahead of other banks, reached breakeven in 2005. China Merchants Bank also achieved a profit and loss balance in its credit card business at the end of 2005 and a profit of 60 million yuan in the first quarter of 2006. Peng Qian, Assistant Manager of the Credit Card Center of China Merchants Bank, feels quite excited about this result. In his opinion, in 2006, China's credit card business will begin to boom. The initial success of those Chinese joint-stock banks that have been involved in the credit card business for a long time, is also good news for foreign credit card companies in the Chinese market.

彭千认为：" 国际信用卡公司对我们而言是重量级的竞争对手。" 他解释首先目前中国信用卡市场还没有领导者而利润前景又非常可观；其次，信用卡业务并不像存款业务一样需要很多分行网点，而且主要集中在大城市。更为重要的是，由于国内银行卡已实现联网，这意味着不管是哪家发的卡都可以在全国任意一台 ATM 上使用，这使得本土银行和外资银行站在了同一起跑线上，而凭借丰富的经验和国际影响力，国际信用卡可能导致 "后来者居上"。[23]

Peng believes: "Foreign credit card companies will prove to be tough rivals for Chinese banks." First of all, he explained, the promising Chinese credit card market is now short of leading issuers. Second, unlike the deposit business, the credit card business does not need a lot of branches around the country. The branches are in big cities. More importantly, because a computer network has linked Chinese banks, cards issued by any bank can be used at any ATM. As a result, Chinese banks and foreign banks begin at the same starting line, and the latter, with their rich experience and international influence, can easily leave the former behind.

麦肯锡关于中国信用卡客户的调查报告也显示：35% 的大众富裕消费者和富裕消费者（富裕消费者是指家庭年收入超过 6 500 美元的消费者，大众富裕消费阶层是指家庭年收入在 4 000 至 6 500 美元间的消费者），都居住在中国的四大主要城市：上海、北京、广州和深圳。更让外国发卡机构鼓舞的是，中国的持卡人偏爱获得新卡，然后将大部分支出转到这些新卡上。

McKinsey's survey of Chinese credit card users shows that 35 percent of "mass rich" consumers and rich consumers (the former refers to families with an annual income of \$4,000 – \$6,500 and the latter families with an annual income of more than \$6,500) live in the four major cities: Shanghai, Beijing, Guangzhou and Shenzhen. Foreign card issuers find that Chinese card users like new cards and they always transfer most of their expenses onto these new cards.

民生银行信用卡中心总裁杨科称 2006 年底，外资金融机构被允许在中国独立发行信用卡必定对中国本土的信用卡形成有力竞争。他说很多外资机构的信用卡处理系统设在香港，只要政策放开，外资派出高管，兼之成熟的经验和雄厚的资金实力，很快就会打垮中国本土银行的信用卡。[24]

Yang Ke is President of the Credit Card Center of China Minsheng Banking Corp., Ltd. In his opinion, when foreign financial institutions are allowed to issue credit cards independently in

China at the end of 2006, they will become competitive rivals to Chinese credit card companies. He also reveals that quite a lot of foreign banks have their credit card processing systems set up in Hong Kong. As long as the policy restriction is removed, they will send experienced high-level managerial staff to China's mainland, accompanied by large amounts of capital, and Chinese credit cards will be easily defeated.

而在麦肯锡公司看来，即使中国银行业向外资全面开放以后，外资银行单独在华开展信用卡业务也不是一项能够轻松盈利的选择，因为中国高达50%的持卡人是在自己的工作单位被发展为信用卡用户的，而那些发卡银行正是借助自己广泛的客户网络才敲开了这些企事业单位的大门。

However, McKinsey believes that even if China's banking industry is open to foreign banks on the whole, it's not an easy job for foreign banks to manage the credit card business independently. The fact is that in China, 50 percent of card users come to have them by way of their companies or work units. By forging extensive relationships with company clients, card issuers are able to win business opportunity in these areas.

除此之外，麦肯锡认为，就信用卡而言，外国品牌在中国人眼里不值一分钱。国际信用卡公司更有可能获得成功的途径是先与中国本土银行合作做开放前的热身准备。[25]目前一些全球知名的发卡组织陆续在中国境内发行联名卡，如汇丰银行[26]和上海银行联合推出的VISA[27]美元信用卡、花旗银行与浦发银行联合推出的VISA双币种信用卡、美国运通[28]与中国工商银行[29]发行的牡丹运通卡、日本JCB与中国银行发行的长城JCB白金卡等。通过这样的合作，一方面国际信用卡可以通过网点和客户较多的本土银行进入中国市场，另一方面国内的商业银行也可以借助它们的国际化网络走出国门[30]。

In addition, McKinsey points out that when it comes to credit cards, foreign brands are nothing at all. It's better for them to first cooperate with Chinese banks before they are allowed to compete in the Chinese credit market. At present, some well-known card issuers have already come to cooperate with their Chinese counterparts: HSBC and Bank of Shanghai have jointly produced the VISA USD credit cards. Citibank and SPDB produced the VISA dual-currency card. American Express and China Industrial and Commercial Bank jointly issued ICBC American Express cards. In this way, on the one hand, foreign credit card issuers are able to enter the Chinese market through big Chinese banks. On the other hand, Chinese banks are able to operate abroad by making use of the international network of these foreign banks.

2006年底信用卡业务对外资的全面开放，目前不得不选择合作发卡方式的国际信用卡银行具备了单独发卡的权利，中外银行在信用卡业务上将由目前的合作走向面对面的竞争。

招行信用卡中心总经理仲跻伟预测，明年的中外信用卡竞争集中在大型城市的中高收入阶层上。对于中高端客户，中外竞争的焦点还是在产品功能与服务水平上。由于信用卡目标客户锁定为收入和资产状况良好、有贷款偿还能力的高消费客户群体，因此信用卡产品设计与服务只有尽量满足客户群体的市场需求才有竞争优势。[31] 交通银行私人金融业务部负责人刘立志表示，以客户为中心无疑是中外银行都遵循的服务理念，然而在理念的把握和实施上，经验丰富的外资银行显然具有更多的优势，也很有可能成为信用卡市场的赢家。[32]

At present, foreign credit card banks can only issue cards by cooperating with Chinese banks, but when the restriction over them is removed at the end of 2006, they will have the independent right to issue cards, which will make the present cooperative partners rival in the credit card business. Zhong Jiwei, General Manager of the Credit Card Center of China Merchants Bank, predicts that the middle and high-income classes will be the major targets for both Chinese and foreign credit card issuers. Competition will focus on product function and service level, Zhong said. Because the targeted clients are relatively rich, or are rich consumers capable of paying off loans, only when the card design and service can meet and exceed clients' needs can they succeed in competition. Liu Lizhi is in charge of individual financial business at the Bank of Communications. He indicates that the concept of client-centered service is undoubtedly followed by both Chinese and foreign banks. But clearly, he said, experienced foreign banks can beat their Chinese counterparts in putting this concept into practice, and so are more likely to be winners.

Words and Expressions

税前亏损	a pretax loss
消费金融	consumer finance
高管人员	high-level managerial personnel
绕过政策限制	avoid restrictions on
弥补	make up for
报告期内	by the time this report was finished
不容乐观的前景	bleak prospect
蓬勃的市场	a booming market
年收费	annual fees
手续费	handling fees
透支利息收入	overdraft fees
循环信贷	frequent revolvers
成熟信卡市场	mature card markets
银行业人士	those familiar with China's banking sector

透支消费	spending tomorrow's money
信用体系	credit system
落后	outdated
赚多少，花多少	just making ends meet
瓶颈	bottleneck
长此以往	if this trend continues
银行界人士	personnel from the banking industry
人口老龄化	aging population
衰退期	wane
持平	reach a balance
账面亏损	the book loss
做了最坏的打算	have painted the darkest prospect for
收支平衡	break even
商户费用	fees paid by commercial clients
账单	customer accounts
有息结余	interest-bearing debts
损失率	loss rate
利差	interest margin
税前利润	pretax profits
房贷	real estate industry
零售信贷产品	retailing credit product
处于迷茫中	at sea
磨炼	hard struggle
盈亏平衡	breakeven
盈亏平衡	a profit and loss balance
股份制银行	joint-stock banks
重量级的竞争对手	tough rivals
领导者	leading issuers
存款业务	deposit business
站在了同一起跑线上	begin at the same starting line
后来者居上	leave the former behind
外资金融机构	foreign financial institutions
政策放开	policy restriction is removed
工作单位	work units
走出国门	operate abroad
产品功能	product function

服务水平	service level
尽量满足	meet and exceed clients' needs
私人金融业务部	individual financial business
理念的把握和实施上	put the concept into practice

Notes

1 Lafferty Group   银行业研究顾问公司
2 "在中国引起了广泛讨论"不宜直译成"bring forth broad discussions in China",因为这里实际上是引起了广泛的注意。
3 "China is a sharp contrast to"和后面的"This card will be a joint product of …"均采用了转译方法,将汉语的动词转换成英语的名词,既可避免动词的重复使用,又表达得更加地道。
4 World Cards Intelligence   银行业研究顾问公司属下的公司
5 消费金融   consumer finance
   Consumer finance in the most basic sense of the word refers to any kind of lending to consumers. However, in the United States financial services industry, the term "consumer finance" often refers to a particular type of business, sub prime branch lending (that is lending to people with less than perfect credit).
6 "而无论是现在还是近期,我们看不到银行在中国赢利的前景"这个句子容易译成"We can't see the prospect of … now and in the near future"。这样翻译不如"there is no sign that these banks are able to make profits now or in the near future"自然和地道。
7 面对2006年12月1日信用卡业务对外资的开放期限,国际信用卡公司早早就在中国做好了准备。 International credit card companies have already made sufficient preparation for the day when the restriction on foreign banks' engagement in the credit card business is nullified, on December 1, 2006.
   这句话中涉及国家的政策,翻译时应该将内容译出,否则难以理解。
8 浦发银行   (即上海浦东发展银行)Shanghai Pudong Development Bank (SPDB)
9 花旗国际有限公司   Citicorp International Limited
   花旗银行(Citibank)是花旗集团(Citigroup)属下的一家零售银行,其主要前身是1812年6月16日成立的纽约城市银行(City Bank of New York)。

10 双方将共同成立一家新的信用卡公司,各占50%的股权,但信用卡公司中的高管人员多数由花旗派出。... under which the two will jointly set up a new credit card company, with each possessing 50 percent of the shares. The company's high-level managerial personnel will be provided by Citibank.
这句话为双方签订的协议的内容,所以译成非限制性定语从句,符合英语表达习惯。

11 "花旗绕过政策限制"中的"绕过"翻译起来很麻烦,怎样绕呢?译文译得很巧妙。

12 GE Money GE 消费者金融集团
GE 消费者金融集团(GE Money)是通用电气公司中有关消费者金融的一个业务部分,是全球领先的银行和金融服务提供者,为全球51个国家的消费者、零售业及商业合作伙伴提供服务。

13 深圳发展银行 Shenzhen Development Bank
深圳发展银行是第一家在深圳证券交易所上市(深圳股票交易所代码:000001)的股份制商业银行,总部位于因经济迅速发展而驰名的深圳。

14 一方面是不容乐观的前景,一方面是不断涌入中国市场的国际信用卡公司,究竟外资信用卡能否如它们期望的在中国这个广阔的信用卡市场上淘到黄金? Against the bleak prospect of profit, are credit card companies naively rushing into the Chinese market? Is it possible for them to succeed in their 'gold rush' in China?
汉语"一方面……一方面"容易让人想到英语的句型"on the one hand ... on the other hand",但这里的两个方面实际上是并列的关系。因此,前句采用介词短语,后面增译了副词"naively"并采用问句的形式,既解决了句式上的问题,又将后句中"如它们期望的"的意思表达出来了。最后的"淘到黄金"也译得非常巧妙和传神。

15 麦肯锡 McKinsey & Co.
麦肯锡咨询公司是美国1926年成立的专门为企业高层管理人员服务的、世界级领先的全球管理咨询公司。

16 注意,这里的"标准信用卡"不宜译成"standard credit cards",因为所谓"标准信用卡"是针对其他银行卡(如储蓄卡)而言的。

17 "可是如此蓬勃的市场增长速度,并没有从国际信用卡公司在中国投资的账本上显示出来。"这句话似乎有点不大容易理解,"蓬勃的市场增长速度……没有从……的账本上显示出来"究竟想表达什么意思呢?如果直译,"账本显示速度"也不好处理。从下文中可以看出,这句话的意思是:市场发展这么快,可是……并没有赚到钱,所以译成"However, foreign credit card companies seem to have benefited little from such a booming market."。

18 而那些进入拉美和其他成长性市场的银行比起进入中国的银行,其回报将更强劲,获得回报的时间也将早得多。 The Chinese banking market is different from that in Latin America or other growing markets that are able to produce large amounts of profits within a

shorter period of time.

将主语转译成"the Chinese banking market",后面跟一个限制性定语从句,仍然用同一个主语,解决了汉语中主语不明的问题。

19　万事达卡　MasterCard

万事达卡国际组织(MasterCard INTERNATIONAL)是全球第二大信用卡国际组织。

20　一是中国信用卡市场发展的程度较低,社会上还没有普遍形成透支消费的观念。One is that China's credit card market is not fully developed, and few people are in the habit of spending tomorrow's money.

注意汉语中的概念词"程度"、"社会上"和"观念"的译法。英译汉时应该适当增译概念词,汉译英时应该省译或者转译。下文中的"风格、力度、瓶颈、盲点、人口基数、老龄化问题和衰退期"等等都属于这种情况。

21　将"赚多少,花多少"译成"just making ends meet",非常准确。类似的用法还有"within one's means",如"China's current economic readjustment was very much an effort to undertake what was within the country's means."。

22　而且从长远来看,前期客户基础打得越好,后期收益就越可观,因此尽管现在账面亏损,但所有的银行都不愿在争夺客户上落后半步。 In the long run, the more clients that are attracted in the early period, the more profits will be produced in the late period. Despite the book loss at present, all the banks are still competing for more clients.

这句话中有几句地道的汉语不太好处理,即:①"基础打得越好";②"收益就越可观";③"不愿……落后半步"。译文没有直译,而是采取了意译的方法,将①译成"the more clients that are attracted",将②译成"the more profits",将③译成"still competing for more clients"。还有下面的那个标题:"未来的市场有多大",将译文"What is the market potential?"与"How big the future market will be?"对比一下,优劣自明。

23　……这使得本土银行和外资银行站在了同一起跑线上,而凭借丰富的经验和国际影响力,国际信用卡可能导致"后来者居上"。 As a result, Chinese banks and foreign banks begin at the same starting line, and the latter, with their rich experience and international influence, can easily leave the former behind.

这句汉语中的"可能导致'后来者居上'"如果按英文句式直译,会碰到麻烦,因为"导致'后来者居上'"实际上是"导致后来者居上的情况发生"的省略。因此,这里干脆将其译成"the latter, ... can easily leave the former behind.",准确而自然。下面段落中的"……必定对中国本土的信用卡形成有力竞争"也是指"必定与中国本土的信用卡公司形成有力竞争",所以也译成"they will become competitive rivals to Chinese credit card companies",否则"外国卡与中国本地卡形成竞争"就表达得不很清楚了。

24　……只要政策放开,外资派出高管,兼之成熟的经验和雄厚的资金实力,很快就会打垮中国本土银行的信用卡。 As long as the policy restriction is removed, they will send experienced high-level managerial staff to China's mainland, accompanied by their rich experience and large amounts of capital, and Chinese credit cards will be easily defeated.

① 这个连动式乍看像是个条件句,"只要政策放开,外资派出高管,……"。但仔细一读,发现"外资派出高管,……"应该是"政策放开"的结果,所以翻译时千万要小心。

② "政策放开"不等于"政策开放",这里是指国家放开对国外银行在中国经营的限制,因此译成"policy restriction is removed"十分贴切。

③ "and Chinese credit cards will be easily defeated" 还是译成 "and Chinese credit card competitors will be easily defeated" 更好。

25 国际信用卡公司更有可能获得成功的途径是先与中国本土银行合作做开放前的热身准备。 It's better for them to first cooperate with Chinese banks before they are allowed to compete in the Chinese credit market.

注意,这里的"热身准备"不宜译成"warming-up"。

26 汇丰银行 HSBC (Hongkong and Shanghai Banking Corporation)
汇丰集团是全球规模最大的银行及金融服务机构之一,总部设在伦敦。

27 VISA 维萨信用卡
VISA 卡是维萨国际组织于 1982 年末开始发行的信用卡。

28 美国运通 American Express
美国运通公司创建于 1850 年,现已成为多元化的全球旅游、财务及网络服务公司,提供签账卡及信用卡、旅行支票、旅游、财务策划、投资产品、保险及国际银行服务等。

29 中国工商银行 Industrial and Commercial Bank of China (ICBC)
中国工商银行成立于 1984 年 1 月 1 日,总部设在北京,是中国内地规模最大的银行。

30 "另一方面国内的商业银行也可以借助他们的国际化网络走出国门"中的"走出国门"和上段中的"……敲开了这些企事业单位的大门"可采取意译的方法,分别译成"operate abroad"和"win business opportunity in these areas"。

31 ……因此信用卡产品设计与服务只有尽量满足客户群体的市场需求才有竞争优势。
... only when the card design and service can meet and exceed clients' needs can they succeed in competition.

这里的"尽量满足"可以翻译成"meet and exceed clients' needs",服务行业常用这个表达方法。

32 以客户为中心无疑是中外银行都遵循的服务理念,然而在理念的把握和实施上,经验丰富的外资银行显然具有更多的优势,也很有可能成为信用卡市场的赢家。 He indicates that the concept of client-centered service is undoubtedly followed by both Chinese and foreign banks. But clearly, ... experienced foreign banks can beat their Chinese counterparts in putting this concept into practice, and so are more likely to be winners.

"在理念的把握和实施上"中的"把握"一词指的是"理解程度",如果直译,就成了

"in understanding and putting this concept into practice",但实际上中外银行在这一点上的理解是相同的,只不过外国银行从事这项业务时间更长,经验更加丰富,所以译文将"把握"一词省去了。

他山之石

原文 1:

尽管欧盟声称在调查中发现了充分的证据,表明中国鞋业存在廉价融资、免税期等严重的政府干预,但在中国人看来,欧盟的上述指控多半是子虚乌有,甚至与事实南辕北辙。

译文:

Although the EU announced that it has found in its investigation that low-cost financing, free tariff period and other government measures should be blamed in the Chinese shoe-making industry, Chinese enterprises said that those were just excuses, and the reality was to the contrary.

点评:

① "充分的证据表明……"还是译成"sufficient evidence shows that..."更准确。

② "多半是子虚乌有"如果按汉语直译成"probably unreal",语气就不够肯定,也就达不到驳斥对方的效果,因此译成"just excuses"或"sheer fiction",就译得非常到位。

原文 2:

我认为,至少在最近的 5 年内,中国内地还没有建设第二个迪斯尼乐园的需要。中国的经济发展稳健而快速,人民群众对文化消费的要求也越来越高,当老百姓口袋里的钱越来越多的时候,除了迪斯尼,我们还需要更多的乐园。在此之前,我们应该冷静下来,避免将迪斯尼乐园当作一种新的"形象工程",一窝蜂地钻进去。

原译文:

I think there is no need for China to build a second Disneyland, at least not in the next five years. With the Chinese economy growing robustly in recent years, the public has higher demands in their cultural consumption. As they earn more and more money, we need Disneyland and much more. So we have to cool down rather than rush into a Disneyland as an "image project".

点评:

① "当老百姓口袋里的钱越来越多的时候"直译成"As they earn more and more money"与后面的句子有些连接不上,不妨采取意译的办法。

② "we need Disneyland and much more" 似乎没有把原文的意思表达出来,因为原文明明是说:我们不仅需要建迪斯尼乐园,还应该建更多的其他乐园。
③ 最后一句的译文好像又与前面的句子脱节,应该将"在此之前"的意思译出来。

改译:

I think there is no need for China to build a second Disneyland, at least not in the next five years. With the Chinese economy growing robustly in recent years, the public has higher demands in their cultural consumption. They do need more Disneylands and even many other theme parks to meet their cultural needs as their income keep increasing. Now, however, we have to cool down rather than rush into building a Disneyland as an "image project".

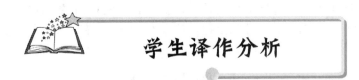
学生译作分析

桂林集琦药业股份有限公司坐落在"山水甲天下"的桂林市国家高新区,它是一家以健康产业为核心的高新制药企业,主要从事中成药、天然药物、化学原料及制剂、医疗器械、抗菌材料、医药网络的研究、生产和销售。公司注册资金2.15亿元人民币,总资产12亿元人民币,净资产6.8亿元人民币,员工3 000人。"集琦"二字,精练地传达了30多年来企业执著追求的使命——汇集英才,致力健康。

学生原译文:

Guilin Jiqi Pharmaceutical Co., Ltd. locates in the National High & New Technology Development Zone in Guilin city, whose hills and water are ranking the first in the world. Taking health industry as its core mission, Jiqi Company mainly engages in the research, production and sales of Chinese patent medicines, natural medicines, chemical raw materials, preparation, medical equipments, anti-bacterial materials as well as medical network. Its registered capital is RMB 215 million, total asset is 1,200 million, and net asset is 604 million. There are 3,000 employees in work now. The word "Jiqi" succinctly/laconically conveys its consistent enterprise mission—collecting talents, dedicating to the health—which is what they pursue perseveringly for more than 30 years.

分析:

(1) 将"……坐落在'山水甲天下'的桂林市国家高新区"译成"...locates in the National High & New Technology Development Zone in Guilin city, whose hills & water are ranking the first in the world"虽然准确,但译得稍生硬,也就是说中文的

用词和句式都基本跟英文一样,这是翻译中的大忌,可否考虑译成:"Surrounded by the best mountains and rivers in the world, Guilin Jiqi Pharmaceutical Co., Ltd. ...",或者用"With the best view..."句型,那样似乎更符合英语的表达习惯。

(2) 将"'集琦'二字,精练地传达30多年来企业执著追求的使命——汇集英才,致力健康。"译成"Thus, the word 'Jiqi' succinctly/laconically conveys its consistent enterprise mission-collecting talents, dedicating to the health- which is what they pursue perseveringly.",完全按汉语的句式直译,显得生硬,而且并没有完全将原文所要表达的内涵译出。翻译时可以灵活一点,尽量用英语来思维,即讲英语的国家的人们会怎样来表达这层意思。

参考译文:

Surrounded by the best mountains and rivers in the world, Guilin Jiqi Pharmaceutical Co., Ltd locates in the National High & New Technology Development Zone in Guilin city, Guanxi Zhuang Autonomous Region. "Jiqi", the company's name in Chinese, well tells its consumers what the enterprise has been pursuing perseveringly for over 30 years—pool able and virtuous personage (persons of outstanding ability) to produce quality medicine for people's health.

翻译技巧介绍

习语及商务术语的翻译
(Translating Idioms and Business Terms)

在商务英语文献翻译中同样经常需要处理大量的习语,如成语、俗语、谚语、汉语的四字结构等。这些习语如果在翻译时处理不当,轻者外国读者很难理解原文的含义,重者将使读者误解原文,从而造成沟通上的障碍,甚至经济上损失。因此,处理好习语的翻译是非常重要的。通常,有以下几种方法可以考虑。

一、能直译则直译

因为中英两种文化存在着巨大的差异,英语中与汉语习语完全对等或相似的习语并不多见。有些习语意象虽然不同,但意义却基本相同。这一类习语可以尽量采取直译的方式来处理。所谓直译,就是指两种语言中习语的意思和形式完全一样或者十分类似。

(1) 竞争已经进入**白热化**,在接下来的五年中,很可能是中国零售业市场格局**重新洗牌**的五年,并购将**称王**中国的零售业市场。

译文:Retail industry competition is **white hot**, with acquisitions **being the ultimate trump cards** in the following five-year **reshuffle** in China's retail market.

(2) 这种恶性的出口竞争最终将导致出口企业**自食其果**。

译文:The vicious low-price export competition eventually will cause the export companies to **eat the bitter fruit of their own making.**

(3) 去年,很多像申银万国这样的大证券公司皆因财务丑闻而**轰然倒下**。

译文:Last year, many big security companies like SYWG (Shenyin & Wangou) **were brought to their knees** by high-profile scandals.

(4) 中国车市经历了连续几年的超高速增长后,目前被**一股始料不及的"寒流"所深深笼罩**。

译文:The accelerated growth that the Chinese automobile market has witnessed over the past several years has **shifted to a lower gear**.

(5) "一朝被蛇咬,十年怕井绳",自从股市被套后,她就再也没有买过新的股票,也没有再投资过证券市场的其他产品。

译文:**Once bitten, twice shy.** After losing lots of money, she has never again dabbled in stocks. Neither has she invested in other products in the securities market.

(6) 要在啤酒市场生存,现在主要的方法就是靠兼并小啤酒厂家。未来在中国啤酒市场上到底**谁主沉浮**,无人能够预料。

译文:One of the ways to survive in this market is to buy smaller companies, but only time will tell **who will sink and who will swim** in China's beer market in the coming years.

(7) 星巴克的定位就是"**第三生活空间**",就是家和办公室之间还应该有一个地方可以提供大家休息、畅谈,包括来洽谈一些商务的环境。

译文:Starbucks' shops are intended to fit into people's lives as "**a third living space**" besides home and office, where people can linger, relax and talk about business.

(8) 7年的时间里,开这么多店,基本上是一个半月开1家店。这种规模让美国星巴克总部看着有点儿**眼馋**。

译文:Against a time span of seven years, opening up so many shops equals a new shop in these two cities every one and a half months, which draws **envy** from Starbucks headquarters in the United States.

二、不能直译则意译

汉英两种语言中很多的习语是可以采取意译的方式翻译的,即采用译入语中意思相同但不一定是习语的词句来表达原文习语的意思。这种处理方式虽然在意象上译文和原文无法等同或相似，但只要意义相同，不影响读者对原文的理解，也是可以接受的。

(1) 近年来，随着国内经济强劲增长，拥有工商管理和会计学双硕士学位的毕业生成了**香饽饽**。

译文：With the strong growth of economy at home these years, students with a combined Masters of Business Administration and accounting degree **become kings among graduates**.

(2) 从本周二开始，商场将对 SK-II 的产品进行清仓**大甩卖**，各种产品的价格将大幅度下调，降幅约 20%。

译文：Starting Tuesday, prices of SK-II will be **slashed** for a clearance sale, a reduction of about 20 percent for each item.

(3) 为了能吸引新人加盟，公司已经提高了福利待遇，比如当员工太忙无暇外出**跑腿**时，公司可以提供侍从服务，专门为员工**跑腿办事**。

译文：To lure new hires, the company has boosted benefits—including a concierge service for employees too busy to **run errands**.

(4) 为了拓展在华的业务，沃尔玛采取了收购兼并的策略，今年头两个月就**吞掉**了 10 个小型超市。

译文：To open up its business in China, Wal-Mart took the strategy of acquisitions and **snapped up** 10 small local supermarkets in the first two months of this year.

(5) 荷兰银行中国区认为中国的个人理财市场是一座有着巨大潜力的金山，而其他外资大行也在加大对中国个人高端理财业务的投入，竞相到中国争**一席之地**。

译文：ABN AMRO China revealed that China's personal wealth management market is a **bonanza** full of opportunities and other foreign-funded banks are clambering to gain a **foothold** by increasing their input in high-end personal wealth management in China.

(6) 前几年零售业进入**门槛太低**，许多人把开超市当作敛财的好方法，使零售超市门店**扎堆经营**。

译文：Several years ago, retail market **access was easy**, resulting in a **surging number** of supermarkets throughout the country, which became a good way to accumulate wealth for many people.

(7) 北京对 2008 年奥运会可能带来的美好前景**寄予厚望**，并想借此机会向世界展示一个"**焕然一新**"的中国，以吸引新的投资者和游客。

译文：Beijing has **pinned hopes of** a successful future on the Beijing 2008 Olympics being a showcase for a "**transformed**" China, attracting new investors and tourists alike.

(8) 2005年1月，国有银行也"**登陆**"了热度极高的人民币理财市场。建行、工行和中行相继发售了各自的人民币理财产品。几大行的理财产品首日面世可谓**风头出尽**。

译文：State-owned banks **entered** the personal wealth management market in January 2005. China Construction Bank（CCB）, ICBC and Bank of China（BOC）did **brisk** business with their wealth management products as soon as they launched them.

三、直译和意译都不行就省译、暗译或者转译

跟英译汉一样，汉语有些习语采用直译或意译的方法都不太好处理，非要译出来甚至会使译文生硬难懂，翻译的痕迹非常明显，这时不如考虑省译或暗译，目的无非就是要将原文的意思表达出来罢了。

(1) 显然，外资银行在中国多年的耕耘已经**尝到一定甜头**，并且希望获得更大的获利空间。面对外资银行对高端客户的争夺，中资银行也**不甘示弱**，纷纷开始加快争夺高端理财市场的脚步。

译文：It is obvious that foreign-funded banks are already **profitable** and are hoping to build on these profits further. Facing competition from them for high-end clients, Chinese-funded banks are also revving up to capture this segment. （不必将"不甘示弱"译成"refuse to admit being inferior"，因为英语"rev up"已经暗含了"争夺"的意思。）

(2) 韩国为即将举行的亚太经合组织领导人峰会新建了一座会议中心，据说这里不仅可以抵挡炸弹、地震，即使遇到海啸也**固若金汤**，而每小时将近1 000万美元的**代价也着实不菲**。

译文：Costing nearly 10 million dollars for each hour APEC leaders will meet there, South Korea's newest convention hall is said to be capable of withstanding bombs, earthquakes and **even a tsunami**. （暗译"固若金汤"和"代价也着实不菲"。）

(3) 星巴克中国总部目前的重点是瞄准了中国的二线城市。很可能不久之后，星巴克将和麦当劳、肯德基一样，会在中国**遍地开花**。

译文：Starbucks' China headquarters has attached more importance to regional centers. It is expected that in the near future Starbucks cafes **will be seen** across the country, like the fast food chains McDonald's and KFC. （暗译"遍地开花"。）

(4) 现实中像她这样从事外贸经营活动的个人有很多，这早就不是什么秘密了。但因为**名不正言不顺**，这份钱赚得很是辛苦。

译文：This under-the-table practice had long been no secret, as there are quite a number of individual foreign trade dealers like her. However **it was extremely difficult**, because their way of doing business **wasn't approved by law**. （意译"名不正言不顺"；暗译"这份钱赚得很是辛苦"。）

（5）中国彩电业把下一个市场目标转向东盟，完全是一种市场行为，但是，我们的终极目标还是要转向欧美等发达地区，这是中国彩电业在品牌国际化道路上**绕不过去的一道"坎"**。

译文：Though it is a natural market behavior in approaching the ASEAN market for Chinese color TV industry, our ultimate goal should not be limited to that. We still aim for markets in developed countries in our brand internationalization. （省译"绕不过去的一道坎"。）

（6）在"**瓷老大**"的心态支配下，"精品意识强、商品意识淡"的景德镇丧失了多次重新崛起的机会。

译文：Accustomed to its **dominant status in the field**, Jingdezhen authorities were reluctant to **shift production to porcelain for everyday use** and lost many chances to promote an economic revival. （暗译"瓷老大"，省译"精品意识强、商品意识淡"。）

（7）近年来中国冰淇淋市场的状况：口味**更新变换多端**；价格**血拼肉搏上阵**；品牌**造势声声逼人**；资本**巨舰破浪向前**。

译文：China's ice cream market is booming because of four reasons: **Changing** tastes, **competing** prices, **new** brand names and **injected** capital. （用四个形容词转译"更新变换多端"、"血拼肉搏上阵"、"造势声声逼人"和"巨舰破浪向前"。）

课堂翻译训练

将下列句子译成英语。

1. 到2004年底，老王手里的股票市值已经缩水到2～3万元，心痛之余也只能是回天乏术。
2. 随着中国入世以来对外资银行的开放，中外银行纷纷推出个人理财服务项目，个人理财产品竞争开始"白热化"。
3. 第二，门票价格设计要合理，价格要有竞争力，对青少年应有优惠价；要让孩子进了迪士尼之后，一票玩到底。千万要摒弃目前国内某些景点大票套小票的做法。
4. 中国的并购市场还是一个缺乏法律和规章、缺乏流程限制的粗放市场，就像一个篱笆稀松的"菜园子",外资不抓紧这个时候收购,更待何时?
5. 深圳市计划要在9月底前实现95%的"零就业家庭"中至少有1人实现就业,力争年底让这些"零就业家庭"全部"归零"。
6. 欧盟内部决策机制的缺陷提高了发生贸易争端的风险概率,正是这些缺陷使得几个南欧、东欧国家小小的纺织和制鞋业就能够"绑架"整个欧盟,强迫整个欧盟的消费者、进口商、零售商和对华出口商为它们"买单"。
7. 人们已开始恢复到原来的正常生活。受非典影响最严重的一蹶不振的消费领域及投资服务业不久将会复苏。
8. 首要的问题是,中国一旦被迫按照全球经济秩序所要求的规则行事,是否能养活13亿人。
9. 然而,对那些具有其他杰出专业证书的人,我们也将给予认真考虑。这些具有挑战性的机遇将为那些称职的申请人提供大量的回报。
10. 滞港卡关的损失主要是由欧盟的进口商、零售商来承担。但是作为负责任的贸易大国,在处理纺织品滞港问题上,中国是合情合理的,并没有袖手旁观,因为中欧经贸合作关系是长远和全面的,不是一锤子买卖。

课后练习

1. 将下列短文译成英语,注意习惯用语的处理。

经过近30年的改革开放,中国越来越多的国有和民营企业具备了走向国际市场的条件。截止到目前,已有10 000多家中国企业在170个国家和地区投资办厂,其中绝大多数在发展中国家,经营状况普遍较好。

中国企业走出去的主要优势表现在三个方面。首先,目前中国的国际地位和国际声誉日益提高,外部环境对中国企业走出去十分有利。其次,大多数准备走出去的企业集中在中国的纺织、化工、能源、建筑等传统强势领域,它们大多国际竞争力较强,推出的技术既先进又适合大部分对象国的国情。其三,由于中国与世界的融合程度不断提高,许多企业已逐渐形成了国际化的管理体制。加之技术较先进,劳动力成本较低,使得企业的综合竞争力处于较高水平。此外,中国的企业家们大多具有吃苦耐劳、勇于开拓的精神和同舟共济、互利共赢的经营理念,易于与他们的外国同行开展真诚有效的合作。

当然,中国企业也还存在一些不利于走出去的弊端,如有些企业的机制陈旧,不适合在国外投资办厂;有些企业对投资对象国的情况不太了解,主观想像,盲目决策;还有些企业实力不够,一时冲动就决定走出去,结果投资失败。近年来,为扶持鼓励中国企业走出去,政府有关部门在工商、财政、保险、税收等方面出台了一系列优惠措施并在各部门的门户网站上公布，接受社会各界的咨询和监督。

2. 将下列短文译成英语。

　　说话间，来到闹市。只见有一隶卒在那里买物，手中拿著货物道："老兄如此高货，却讨恁般贱价，教小弟买去，如何能安心！务求将价加增，方好遵教。若再过谦，那是有意不肯赏光交易了。"唐敖听了，因暗暗说道："九公，凡买物，只有卖者讨价，买者还价。今卖者虽讨过价，那买者并不还价，却要添价。此等言谈，倒也罕闻。据此看来那'好让不争'四字，竟有几分意思了。"只听卖货人答道："既承照顾，敢不仰体！但适才妄讨大价，已觉厚颜；不意老兄反说货高价贱，岂不更教小弟惭愧？况敝货并非'言无二价'，其中颇有虚头。俗云：漫天要价，就地还钱。今老兄不但不减，反要加增，如此克己，只好请到别家交易，小弟实难遵命。"唐敖道："'漫天要价，就地还钱'，原是买物之人向来俗谈；至'并非言无二价，其中颇有虚头'，亦是买者之话。不意今皆出于卖者之口，倒也有趣。"只听隶卒又说道："老兄以高货讨贱价，反说小弟克己，岂不失了'忠恕之道'？凡事总要彼此无欺，方为公允。试问那个腹中无算盘，小弟又安能受人之愚哩。"谈之许久，卖货人执意不增。隶卒赌气，照数付价，拿了一半货物，刚要举步，卖货人那里肯依，只说"价多货少"，拦住不放。路旁走过两个老翁，作好作歹，从公评定，令隶卒照价拿了八折货物，这才交易而去。唐、多二人不觉暗暗点头。

  佳译赏析

一般货物进口合同
PURCHASE CONTRACT

合同号码：_____
Contract No：

签约日期：_____
Date：

买方：_____
The Buyer：

卖方：_____
The Seller：

本合同由买卖双方缔结，用中、英文字写成[1]，两种文本具有同等效力，按照下述条款[2]，卖方同意售出买方同意购进以下商品：
The Contract, made out, in Chinese and English, both version being equally authentic, by and between the Seller and the Buyer whereby the Seller agrees to sell and the Buyer agrees to buy the under mentioned goods subject to terms and conditions set forth hereinafter as follows：

第一部分
SECTION 1

1. 商品名称及规格：_____

1. Name of Commodity and specification

2. 生产国别及制造厂商：_____
2. Country of Origin & Manufacturer

3. 单价（包装费用包括在内）：_____
3. Unit Price（packing charges included）

4. 数量：_____
4. Quantity

5. 总值：_____
5. Total Value

6. 包装：_____（适合海洋运输）
6. Packing（seaworthy）

7. 保险：_____（除非另有协议，保险均由买方负责）
7. Insurance（to be covered by the Buyer unless otherwise agreed upon）

8. 装船时间：_____
8. Time of Shipment

9. 装运口岸：_____
9. Port of Loading

10. 目的口岸：_____
10. Port of Destination

11. 装运唛头：卖方负责在每件货物上用牢固的不褪色的颜料明显地刷印或标明下述唛头，以及目的口岸、件号、毛重和净重、尺码和其他买方要求的标记。如系危险及/或有毒货物，卖方负责保证在每件货物上明显地标明货物的性质说明及习惯上被接受的标记。

11. The Seller shall have the marks shown as below in addition to the port of destination, package number, gross and net weights, measurements and other marks as the Buyer may require stenciled or marked conspicuously with fast and unfailing pigments on each package. In case of dangerous

and/or poisonous cargo(es), the Seller is obliged to take care to ensure that the nature and the generally adopted symbol shall be marked conspicuously on each package.

12. 付款条件：买方于货物装船时间前一个月通过_____银行开出以卖方为抬头的不可撤销信用证，卖方在货物装船启运后凭本合同交货条款第 18 条 A 款所列单据在开证银行议付货款。[3] 上述信用证有效期将在装船后 15 天截止。[4]

12. One month prior to the time of shipment the Buyer shall open with the Bank of _____ _____ an irrevocable Letter of Credit in favor of the Seller payable at the issuing bank against presentation of documents as stipulated under Clause 18.1 of the Terms of Delivery of this Contract after departure of the carrying vessel. The said Letter of Credit shall remain in force till the 15th day after shipment.

13. 其他条件：除非经买方同意和接受[5]，本合同其他一切有关事项均按第二部分交货条款之规定办理[6]，该交货条款为本合同不可分的部分，本合同如有任何附加条款将自动地优先执行附加条款，如附加条款与本合同条款有抵触，则以附加条款为准。

13. Other Terms: Unless otherwise agreed and accepted by the Buyer, all other matters related to this contract shall be governed by Section II, the Terms of Delivery which shall form an integral part of this Contract. Any supplementary terms and conditions that may be attached to this Contract shall automatically prevail over the terms and conditions of this Contract if such supplementary terms and conditions come in conflict with terms and conditions herein and shall be binding upon both parties.

第二部分
SECTION 2

14. FOB/FAS 条件
14. FOB/FAS TERMS

14.1 本合同项下货物的装运舱位由买方或买方的运输代理人_____租订。
14.1 The shipping space for the contracted goods shall be booked by the Buyer or the Buyer's shipping agent _____.

14.2 在 FOB 条件下，卖方应负责将所订货物在本合同第 8 条所规定的装船期内按买方所通知的任何日期装上买方所指定的船只。
14.2 Under FOB terms, the Seller shall undertake to load the contracted goods on board the vessel

nominated by the Buyer on any date notified by the Buyer, within the time of shipment as stipulated in Clause 8 of this Contract.

14.3 在 FAS 条件下，卖方应负责将所订货物在本合同第 8 条所规定的装船期内按买方所通知的任何日期交到买方所指定船只的吊杆下。

14.3 Under FAS terms, the Seller shall undertake to deliver the contracted goods under the tackle of the vessel nominated by the Buyer on any date notified by the Buyer, within the time of shipment as stipulated in Clause 8 of this Contract.

14.4 货物装运日前 10～15 天，买方应以电报或电传通知[7]卖方合同号、船只预计到港日期、装运数量及船运代理人的名称，以便卖方与该船运代理人联系及安排货物的装运。卖方应将联系结果通过电报或电传及时报告买方。如买方因故需要变更船只或者船只比预先通知卖方的日期提前或推迟到达装运港口[8]，买方或其船运代理人应及时通知卖方。卖方亦应与买方的运输代理或买方保持密切联系。

14.4 10 - 15 days prior to the date of shipment, the Buyer shall inform the Seller by cable or telex of the contract number, name of vessel, ETA of vessel, quantity to be loaded and the name of shipping agent, so as to enable the Seller to contact the shipping agent direct and arrange the shipment of the goods. The Seller shall advise by cable or telex in time the Buyer of the result thereof. Should, for certain reasons, it become necessary for the Buyer to replace the named vessel with another one, or should the named vessel arrive at the port of shipment earlier or later than the date of arrival as previously notified to the Seller, the Buyer or its shipping agent shall advise the Seller to this effect in due time. The Seller shall also keep in close contact with the agent or the Buyer.

14.5 如买方所订船只到达装运港后，卖方不能[9]在买方所通知的装船时间内将货物装上船只或将货物交到吊杆之下，卖方应负担买方的一切费用和损失，如空舱费、滞期费及由此而引起的及/或遭受的买方的一切损失。

14.5 Should the Seller fail to load the goods on board or to deliver the goods under the tackle of the vessel booked by the Buyer within the time as notified by the Buyer, after its arrival at the port of shipment the Seller shall be fully liable to the Buyer and responsible for all losses and expenses such as dead freight, demurrage and any consequential losses incurred upon and/or suffered by the Buyer.

14.6 如船只撤换或延期或退关等而未及时通知卖方停止交货，在装港发生的栈租及保险费损失的计算，应以代理通知之装船日期（如货物晚于代理通知之装船日期抵达装港，应以货物抵港日期）为准，在港口免费堆存期满后第十六天起由买方负担，人力不可抗拒的情况除外[10]。上述费用均凭原始单据经买方核实后支付。但卖方仍应在装载货船到达装港后立即将货物装船，并承担费用及风险。

14.6 Should the vessel be withdrawn or replaced or delayed eventually or the cargo be shut out etc., and the Seller be not informed in good time to stop delivery of the cargo, the calculation of the loss in storage expenses and insurance premium thus sustained at the loading port shall be based on the loading date notified by the agent to the Seller (or based on the date of the arrival of the cargo at the loading port in case the cargo should arrive there later than the notified loading date). The abovementioned loss to be calculated from the 16th day after expiry of the free storage time at the port should be borne by the Buyer with the exception of Force Majeure. However, the Seller shall still undertake to load the cargo immediately upon the carrying vessel's arrival at the loading port at its own risk and expenses. The payment of the afore-said expenses shall be effected against presentation of the original vouchers after the Buyer's verification.

15. C&F 条件
15. C&F Terms

15.1 卖方在本合同第8条规定的时间之内应将货物装上由装运港到中国口岸的直达船。未经买方事先许可，不得转船。货物不得由悬挂中国港口当局所不能接受的国家旗帜的船装载。
15.1 The Seller shall ship the goods within the time as stipulated in Clause 8 of this Contract by a direct vessel sailing from the port of loading to China port. Transhipment on route is not allowed without the Buyer's prior consent. The goods shall not be carried by vessels flying flags of countries not acceptable to the Port Authorities of China.

15.2 卖方所租船只应适航和适货。卖方租船时应慎重和认真地选择承运人及船只。买方不接受非保赔协会[11]成员的船只。
15.2 The carrying vessel chartered by the Seller shall be seaworthy and cargoworthy. The Seller shall be obliged to act prudently and conscientiously when selecting the vessel and the carrier when chartering such vessels. The Buyer is justified in not accepting vessels chartered by the Seller that are not members of the PICLUB.

15.3 卖方所租载货船只应在正常合理时间内驶达目的港，不得无故绕行[12]或迟延。
15.3 The carrying vessel chartered by the Seller shall sail and arrive at the port of destination within the normal and reasonable period of time. Any unreasonable aviation or delay is not allowed.

15.4 卖方所租载货船只船龄不得超过 15 年。对超过 15 年船龄的船只其超船龄额外保险费应由卖方负担。买方不接受船龄超过 20 年的船只。

15.4 The age of the carrying vessel chartered by the Seller shall not exceed 15 years. In case her age exceeds 15 years, the extra average insurance premium thus incurred shall be borne by the Seller. Vessel over 20 years of age shall in no event be acceptable to the Buyer.

15.5 一次装运数量超过一千吨的货载或其他少于一千吨但买方指明的货载，卖方应在装船日前至少 10 天用电传或电报通知买方合同号、商品名称、数量、船名、船龄、船籍、船只主要规范、预计装货日、预计到达目的港时间、船公司名称、电传和电报挂号。

15.5 For cargo lots over 1,000 M/T each, or any other lots less than 1,000 metric tons but identified by the Buyer, the Seller shall, at least 10 days prior to the date of shipment, inform the Buyer by telex or cable of the following information: the contract number, the name of commodity, quantity, the name of the carrying vessel, the age, nationality, and particulars of the carrying vessel, the expected date of loading, the expected time of arrival at the port of destination, the name, telex and cable address of the carrier.

15.6 一次装运一千吨以上货载或其他少于一千吨但买方指明的货载，其船长应在该船抵达目的港前 7 天和 24 小时分别用电传或电报通知买方预计抵港时间、合同号、商品名称及数量。

15.6 For cargo lots over 1,000 M/T each, or any other lots less than 1,000 metric tons but identified by the Buyer, the Master of the carrying vessel shall notify the Buyer respectively 7 (seven) days and 24 (twenty-four) hours prior to the arrival of the vessel at the port of destination, by telex or cable about its ETA (expected time of arrival), contract number, the name of commodity, and quantity.

15.7 如果货物由班轮装运，载货船只必须是_____船级社最高船级或船级协会条款规定的相同级别的船级，船只状况应保持至提单有效期终了时止，以装船日为准船龄不得超过 20 年。超过 20 年船龄的船只，卖方应负担超船龄外保险费。买方绝不接受超过 25 年船龄的船只。

15.7 If goods are to be shipped per liner vessel under liner Bill of Lading, the carrying vessel must be classified as the highest _____ or equivalent class as per the Institute Classification Clause and shall be so maintained throughout the duration of the relevant Bill of Lading. Nevertheless, the maximum age of the vessel shall not exceed 20 years at the date of loading. The seller shall bear the average insurance premium for liner vessel older than 20 years. Under no circumstances shall the Buyer accept vessel over 25 years of age.

15.8 对于散件货[13],如果卖方未经买方事前同意而装入集装箱,卖方应负责向买方支付赔偿金,由双方在适当时间商定具体金额。

15.8 For break bulk cargoes, if goods are shipped in containers by the Seller without prior consent of the Buyer, a compensation of a certain amount to be agreed upon by both parties shall be payable to the Buyer by the Seller.

15.9 卖方应和载运货物的船只保持密切联系,并以最快的手段通知买方船只在途中发生的一切事故[14],如因卖方未及时通知买方而造成买方的一切损失卖方应负责赔偿。

15.9 The Seller shall maintain close contact with the carrying vessel and shall notify the Buyer by fastest means of communication about any and all accidents that may occur while the carrying vessel is on route. The Seller shall assume full responsibility and shall compensate the Buyer for all losses incurred for its failure to give timely advice or notification to the Buyer.

16. CIF 条件:在 CIF 条件下,除本合同第 15 条 C&F 条件适用之外,卖方负责货物的保险,但不允许有免赔率[15]。

16. CIF Terms: Under CIF terms, besides Clause 15 C&F Terms of this contract which shall be applied, the Seller shall be responsible for covering the cargo with relevant insurance with irrespective of percentage.

17. 装船通知:货物装船完毕后 48 小时内,卖方应即以电报或电传通知买方合同号、商品名称、所装重量(毛/净)或数量、发票价值、船名、装运口岸、开船日期及预计到达目的港时间。如因卖方未及时用电报或电传给买方以上述装船通知而使买方不能及时保险,卖方负责赔偿买方由此而引起的一切损害及/或损失。

17. Advice of Shipment: Within 48 hours immediately after completion of loading of goods on board the vessel the Seller shall advise the Buyer by cable or telex of the contract number, the name of goods, weight (net/gross) or quantity loaded, invoice value, name of vessel, port of loading, sailing date and expected time of arrival (ETA) at the port of destination. Should the Buyer be unable to arrange insurance in time owing to the Seller's failure to give the above mentioned advice of shipment by cable or telex, the Seller shall be held responsible for any and all damages and/or losses attributable to such failure.

18. 装船单据
18. Shipping Documents

18.1 卖方凭下列单据向付款银行议付货款[16]:

18.1 The Seller shall present the following documents to the paying bank for negotiation of payment:

18.1.1 填写通知目的口岸的_____运输公司的空白抬头、空白背书的全套已装运洋轮的清洁提单[17]（如系 C&F/CIF 条款则注明"运费已付"，如系 FOB/FAS 条款则注明"运费待收"）。
18.1.1 Full set of clean on board, "freight prepaid" for C&F/CIF Terms or "Freight to collect" for FOB/FAS Terms, Ocean Bills of Lading, made out to order and blank endorsed, notifying _____ at the port of destination.

18.1.2 由信用证受益人签名出具的发票5份，注明合同号、信用证号、商品名称、详细规格及装船唛头标记。
18.1.2 Five copies of signed invoice, indicating contract number, L/C number, name of commodity, full specifications, and shipping mark, signed and issued by the Beneficiary of Letter of Credit.

18.1.3 两份由信用证受益人出具的装箱单及/或重量单，注明每件货物的毛重和净重及/或尺码。
18.1.3 Two copies of packing list and/or weight memo with indication of gross and net weight of each package and/or measurements issued by beneficiary of Letter of Credit.

18.1.4 由制造商及/或装运口岸的合格、独立的公证行签发的品质检验证书及数量或重量证书各两份，必须注明货物的全部规格与信用证规定相符。
18.1.4 Two copies each of the certificates of quality and quantity or weight issued by the manufacturer and/or a qualified independent surveyor at the loading port and must indicate full specifications of goods conforming to stipulations in Letter of Credit.

18.1.5 本交货条件第17条规定的装船通知电报或电传副本一份
18.1.5 One duplicate copy of the cable or telex advice of shipment as stipulated in Clause 17 of the Terms of Delivery.

18.1.6 证明上述单据的副本已按合同要求寄出的书信一封。
18.1.6 A letter attesting that extra copies of abovementioned documents have been dispatched according to the Contract.

18.1.7 运货船只的国籍已经买主批准的书信一封。
18.1.7 A letter attesting that the nationality of the carrying vessel has been approved by the Buyer.

18.1.8 如系卖方保险需提供投保不少于发票价值110%的一切险和战争险的保险单。
18.1.8 The relevant insurance policy covering, but not limited to at least 110% of the invoice value against all and war risks if the insurance is covered by the Buyer.

18.2 不接受影印、自动或电脑处理，或复印的任何正本单据，除非这些单据印有清晰的"正本"字样，并经发证单位授权的领导人手签证明。
18.2 Any original document(s) made by rephotographic system, automated or computerized system or carbon copies shall not be acceptable unless they are clearly marked as "ORIGINAL" and certified with signatures in hand writing by authorized officers of the issuing company or corporation.

18.3 联运提单、迟期提单、简式提单不能接受。
18.3 Through Bill of Lading, Stale Bill of Lading, Short Form Bill of Lading, shall not be acceptable.

18.4 受益人指定的第三者为装船者不能接受，除非该第三者提单由装船者背书转受益人，再由受赠人背书后方可接受。
18.4 Third Party appointed by the Beneficiary as shipper shall not be acceptable unless such Third Party Bill of Lading is made out to the order of shipper and endorsed to the Beneficiary and blank endorsed by the Beneficiary.

18.5 信用证开立日期之前出具的单据不能接受。
18.5 Documents issued earlier than the opening date of Letter of Credit shall not be acceptable.

18.6 对于C&F/CIF货载，不接受租船提单，除非受益人提供租船合同、船长或大副收据、装船命令、货物配载图及/或买方在信用证内所要求提供的其他单据副本各一份。
18.6 In the case of C&F/CIF shipments, Charter Party Bill of Lading shall not be acceptable unless Beneficiary provides one copy each of the Charter Party, Master's of Mate's receipt, shipping order and cargo or stowage plan and/or other documents called for in the Letter of Credit by the Buyer.

18.7 卖方须将提单、发票及装箱单各两份副本随船带交[18]目的口岸的买方收货代理人_____。

18.7 The seller shall dispatch, in care of the carrying vessel, two copies each of the duplicates of Bill of Lading. Invoice and Packing List to the Buyer's receiving agent, _____ at the port of destination.

18.8 载运货船启碇后,卖方须立即航空邮寄全套单据副本一份给买方,三份给目的口岸的 _____ 运输公司。
18.8 Immediately after the departure of the carrying vessel, the Seller shall airmail one set of the duplicate documents to the Buyer and three sets of the same to _____ Transportation Corporation at the port of destination.

18.9 卖方应负责赔偿买方因卖方失寄或迟寄上述单据而使买方遭受的一切损失。
18.9 The Seller shall assume full responsibility and be liable to the Buyer and shall compensate the Buyer for all losses arising from going astray of and/or the delay in the dispatch of the above mentioned documents.

18.10 中华人民共和国境外的银行费用由卖方负担。
18.10 Banking charges outside the People's Republic of China shall be for the Seller's account.

19. 合同所订货物如用空运,则本合同有关海运的一切条款均按空运条款执行。
19. If the goods under this Contract are to be dispatched by air, all the terms and conditions of this Contract in connection with ocean transportation shall be governed by relevant air terms.

20. 危险品说明书:凡属危险品及/或有毒物品,卖方必须提供其危险或有毒性能、运输、仓储和装卸注意事项及防治、急救、消防方法的说明书,卖方应将此项说明书各三份随同其他装船单据航空邮寄给买方及目的口岸的_____运输公司。
20. Instruction leaflets on dangerous cargo: For dangerous and/or poisonous cargo, the Seller must provide instruction leaflets stating the hazardous or poisonous properties, transportation, storage and handling remarks, as well as precautionary and first-air measures and measures against fire. The Seller shall airmail, together with other shipping documents, three copies each of the same to the Buyer and _____ Transportation Corporation at the port of destination.

21. 检验和索赔:货物在目的口岸卸毕60天内(如果用集装箱装运则在开箱后60天)经中国进出口商品检验局复验,如发现品质、数量或重量及其他任何方面与本合同规定不符,除属于保险公司或船方负责者外,买方有权凭上述检验局出具的检验证书向卖方提出退货或索赔。因退货或索赔引起的一切费用包括检验费、利息及损失均由卖方负担。在此情况下,凡货物适于抽样及寄送时[19]如卖方要求，买方可将样品寄交卖方。

21. Inspection & claims: In case the quality, quantity or weight of the goods be found not in conformity with those as stipulated in this Contract upon re-inspection by the China Commodity Import and Export Inspection Bureau within 60 days after completion of the discharge of the goods at the port of destination or, if goods are shipped in containers, 60 days after the opening of such containers, the Buyer shall have the right to request the Seller to take back the goods or lodge claims against the Seller for compensation for losses upon the strength of the Inspection Certificate issued by the said Bureau, with the exception of those claims for which the insurers or owners of the carrying vessel are liable, all expenses including but not limited to inspection fees, interest, losses arising from the return of the goods or claims shall be borne by the Seller. In such a case, the Buyer may, if so requested, send a sample of the goods in question to the Seller, provided that sampling and sending of such sample is feasible.

22. 赔偿费：因"人力不可抗拒"而推迟或不能交货者除外，如果卖方不能交货或不能按合同规定的条件交货，卖方应负责向买方赔偿由此而引起的一切损失和遭受的损害，包括买价及/或买价的差价、空舱费、滞期费，以及由此而引起的直接或间接损失。买方有权撤销全部或部分合同，但并不妨碍买方向卖方提出索赔的权利[20]。

22. Damages: With the exception of late delivery or non-delivery due to "Force Majeure" causes, if the Seller fails to make delivery of the goods in accordance with the terms and conditions, jointly or severally, of this Contract, the Seller shall be liable to the Buyer and indemnify the Buyer for all losses, damages, including but not limited to, purchase price and/or purchase price differentials, deadfreight, demurrage, and all consequential direct or indirect losses. The Buyer shall nevertheless have the right to cancel in part or in whole of the contract without prejudice to the Buyer's right to claim compensations.

23. 赔偿例外：由于一般公认的"人力不可抗拒"原因而不能交货或延迟交货，卖方或买方都不负责任。但卖方应在事故发生后立即用电报或电传告知买方并在事故发生后15天内航空邮寄买方灾害发生地点之有关政府机关或商会所出具的证明，证实灾害存在。如果上述"人力不可抗拒"继续存在60天以上，买方有权撤销合同的全部或一部。

23. Force Majeure: Neither the Seller nor the Buyer shall be held responsible for late delivery or non-delivery owing to generally recognized "Force Majeure" causes. However in such a case, the Seller shall immediately advise by cable or telex the Buyer of the accident and airmail to the Buyer within 15 days after the accident, a certificate of the accident issued by the competent government authority or the chamber of commerce which is located at the place where the accident occurs as evidence thereof. If the said "Force Majeure" cause lasts over 60 days, the Buyer shall have the

right to cancel the whole or the undelivered part of the order for the goods as stipulated in Contract.

24. 仲裁：双方同意对一切因执行和解释本合同条款所发生的争议，努力通过友好协商解决。在争议发生之日起一个合理的时间内，最多不超过 90 天，协商不能取得对买卖双方都满意的结果时，如买方决定不向他认为合适的有管辖权的法院提出诉讼，则该争议应提交仲裁。除双方另有协议，仲裁应在_____举行，并按_____所制订的仲裁规则和程序进行仲裁，该仲裁为终局裁决，对双方均有约束力。仲裁费用除非另有决定，由败诉一方负担[21]。

24. Arbitration：Both parties agree to attempt to resolve all disputes between the parties with respect to the application or interpretation of any term hereof of transaction hereunder, through amicable negotiation. If a dispute cannot be resolved in this manner to the satisfaction of the Seller and the Buyer within a reasonable period of time, maximum not exceeding 90 days after the date of the notification of such dispute, the case under dispute shall be submitted to arbitration if the Buyer should decide not to take the case to court at a place of jurisdiction that the Buyer may deem appropriate. Unless otherwise agreed upon by both parties, such arbitration shall be held in _____, and shall be governed by the rules and procedures of arbitration stipulated by _____. The decision by such arbitration shall be accepted as final and binding upon both parties. The arbitration fees shall be borne by the losing party unless otherwise awarded.

卖方：_____   买方：_____
FOR THE SELLER   FOR THE BUYER

Words and Expressions

缔结	make out
在下文（在本文件、声明或书的以下的部分）	in a following part of this document, statement, or book
与……一致，通过……，借以	whereby in accordance with which; by or through which; hereinafter
按照	subject to
规格	specification
生产国别	country of origin
包装	packing
适合海洋运输的	seaworthy
装运唛头	mark
毛重和净重	gross and net weights

刷印	stencil
明显地	conspicuously
牢固的	fast
不褪色	unfailing
颜料	pigments
习惯上被接受的	generally adopted
以……抬头（受益人）的	in favor of
不可撤销信用证	irrevocable Letter of Credit
有效	remain in force
交货条款	terms of delivery
凭	against
不可分的部分	an integral part
附加条款	supplementary terms and conditions
抵触	in conflict with
于此，在这里，此中	herein
装运舱位	shipping space
运输代理人	shipping agent
所订货物	the contracted goods
装船期	time of shipment
FAS	an abbreviation (for "free alongside ship") used in international trade statistics and t sales contracts; a method of valuing traded goods that does not include the cost of shipment from the exporting to the importing country 船边交货价格 ["船边交货（……指定装运港）"是指卖方在指定的装运港将货物交到船边，即完成交货。买方必须承担自那时起货物灭失的责任。FAS 术语要求卖方办理出口清关手续。]
吊杆	tackle
货物装运日	date of shipment
预计到港日期	ETA of vessel
其（有关这、那或它的变更）	thereof: of or concerning this, that, or it
	replace
带有那个（这个）意思	to this effect
及时	in due time, in good time, timely
空舱费	dead freight
滞期费	demurrage
结果的，相因而生的	consequential

退关	the cargo being shut out
栈租费	storage expenses
保险费	insurance premium
免费堆存期	free storage time
人力不可抗拒的情况	Force Majeure
支付……费用	effect payment of ...
凭原始单据	against presentation of the original vouchers
核实	verification
直达船	direct vessel
转船	transhipment on route
租船	charter
适航和适货	seaworthy and cargoworthy
保赔协会	PICLUB
装运数量	cargo lots
船公司	carrier
预计抵港时间	ETA (expected time of arrival)
班轮	liner vessel
散件货	break bulk cargoes
途中	on route
免赔率	insurance with irrespective percentage
付款银行	paying bank
议付	negotiation
提单	Bills of Lading
运费已付	freight prepaid
运费待收	freight to collect
空白抬头	to order
空白背书	blank endorsed
受益人	beneficiary
装箱单	packing list
重量单	weight memo
品质检验证书	certificate of quality
副本	duplicate copy
保险单	insurance policy
一切险和战争险	against all and war risks
联运提单	Through Bill of Lading
迟期提单	Stale Bill of Lading

简式提单	Short Form Bill of Lading
赔偿	compensate
费用由……负担	for ... account
检验	inspection
索赔	claims
中国进出口商品检验局	China Commodity Import and Export inspection Bureau
凭检验证书	upon the strength of the Inspection Certificate
仲裁	arbitration
中国国际贸易促进委员会	Foreign Trade Arbitration Commission of the China Council for the Promotion of International Trade

Notes

1. "用中、英文字写成"即"文本为中、英文",所以应译成"made out in Chinese and English"或者"executed/written in Chinese and English"。

2. "按照下述条款"的译文"subject to terms and conditions set forth hereinafter as follows"中的"hereinafter as follows"重复,也可只用"below"代替。

3. 买方于货物装船时间前一个月通过_____银行开出以卖方为抬头的不可撤销信用证,卖方在货物装船启运后凭本合同交货条款第 18 条 A 款所列单据在开证银行议付贷款。One month prior to the time of shipment the Buyer shall open with the Bank of _____ an irrevocable Letter of Credit in favor of the Seller payable at the issuing bank against presentation of documents as stipulated under Clause 18.1 of the Terms of Delivery of this Contract after departure of the carrying vessel.

   这是一个长句,也是进出口业务中常见的句子,中间有很多专业术语,因此翻译时应该注意英语中词语的用法和搭配。如 open with、in favor of、at the issuing bank、against presentation of、as stipulated under Clause 等。

4. 上述信用证有效期将在装船后 15 天截止。The said Letter of Credit shall remain in force till the 15th day after shipment.

   将"信用证的有效期"转译成动词词组"remain in force"更符合合同和商务文件中的表达习惯。

5. "除非经……同意和接受"为合同中常用语,英文合同中有对应的译法,即"Unless

otherwise agreed and accepted by ...".

6 "本合同其他一切有关事项均按第二部分交货条款之规定办理"中的"办理"一词不好处理,译成"shall be governed by ..."准确地表达了这层意思,因为"govern"一词有"(法律,规律)适用于,作……原则"之意。再如:"本合同的解释和履行应依据中华人民共和国的有关法律。"(This contract shall be governed by the relevant laws of the People's Republic of China as to interpretation and performance.)

7 买方应以电报或电传通知…… the Buyer shall inform the Seller by cable or telex ...
20世纪80年代最快捷的通信方式就是电传和电报,但价格昂贵。后来出现的传真使通信更加快捷,而且成本降低。特别是随着网络的迅猛发展,电子邮件已完全取代了电传和电报,所以现在这两种通信设备已不再使用。

8 "如买方因故需要……"中的"如"是表示可能发生的事。因此,按照合同一般译法,将其译成"should ..."。"should"一词的用法是:"used to express probability or expectation"(用于表示可能性或期望)。下文译法相同。句型可以是"if ... should ...",也可以采取倒装的形式。

9 合同中的"不能",一般不翻译成"cannot"或"not be able",因为这里的"不能"实际上是"未能"的意思,所以应该译成"fail"。

10 如船只撤换或延期或退关等而未及时通知卖方停止交货,在装港发生的栈租及保险费损失的计算,应以代理通知之装船日期(如货物晚于代理通知之装船日期抵达装港,应以货物抵港日期)为准,在港口免费堆存期满后第十六天起由买方负担,人力不可抗拒的情况除外。 Should the vessel be withdrawn or replaced or delayed eventually or the cargo be shut out etc., and the Seller be not informed in good time to stop delivery of the cargo, the calculation of the loss in storage expenses and insurance premium thus sustained at the loading port shall be based on the loading date notified by the agent to the Seller (or based on the date of the arrival of the cargo at the loading port in case the cargo should arrive there later than the notified loading date).
此句很长,全句均采用被动语态翻译,这也是合同用语的特色之一,因为英语中只要无须提及动作的发出者,就可以使用被动语态。另外,合同中大量使用被动语态还可以起到简化句子的作用。

11 保赔协会 PICLUB
保赔协会又称保赔保险协会,它是由船东们自愿成立的一种互相保险的组织,其会员各自交纳保险费,共同分担各个会员所应承担的船东责任的损失赔偿额。所以,保赔协会的会员,既是投保人,又是承保人。

12 不得无故绕行。 Any unreasonable aviation or delay is not allowed.
将"绕行"译成"unreasonable aviation"更准确合理,因为这里的"绕行"并一定是"绕远路"或"绕道而行"的意思,不宜译成"pass round"或"make a detour"。

13. "散件货"的概念是:"loose cargo, such as cartons, stowed directly in a vessel's hold as opposed to containerized or bulk cargo"。
14. "一切事故"不应只译成"all accidents",这里的"一切"指"可能发生的任何……"。为了准确严谨,英语合同中一般译成"any and all"。
15. 免赔率 irrespective of percentage
    免赔额是指在保险合同中规定的损失在一定限度内保险人不负赔偿责任的额度,可分为"绝对免赔额"和"相对免赔额"。免赔额的规定主要是为了减少一些频繁发生的小额赔付支出,提高被保险人的责任心和注意力,避免不应发生的损失发生,同时也可以降低保险公司的经营成本。免赔率的规定是国际和国内保险公司的通行做法。
16. "卖方凭下列单据向付款银行议付货款"即"向……银行提交单据进行议付",因此译成"... present the following documents to the paying bank for negotiation of payment"。
17. "空白抬头、空白背书的全套已装运洋轮的清洁提单"也可以翻译成"full set of clean on board Ocean Bills of Lading, made out to order and endorsed in blank"。
18. "随船带交"即转交,因此译成"in care of"(信封上用语,略作c/o,意为"烦……转交")。
19. "凡货物适于抽样及寄送时"指"假设……,只有当……",所以译成"provided that"。
20. 将"并不妨碍买方向卖方提出索赔的权利"采用介词短语译成"without prejudice to the Buyer's right to claim compensations",译得非常地道。
21. 仲裁费用除非另有决定,由败诉一方负担。The arbitration fees shall be borne by the losing party unless otherwise awarded.
    这里的"决定"不是"decide",而是"仲裁决定",因此应译成"award"。

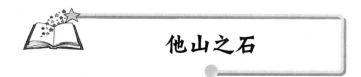

他山之石

原文 1:

如果在颁发中标函后发生双方无法控制的任何情况,使双方中任何一方不可能或是不能依法履行自己在合同中的义务,或根据合同法双方均被解除继续履约时,如果合同已按第97条的规定被终止,则雇主为已实施的工程向承包商支付的金额应与按第97条规定应支付的金额相等。

原译文:

If any circumstance outside the control of both parties arises after the issue of the Letter of Acceptance which renders it impossible or unlawful for either party to fulfil his contractual obligations, or under the law governing the Contract the parties are released from further performance, then the sum payable by the Employer to the Contractor in respect of the work executed shall be the same as that which would have been payable under Clause 97 if the Contract had been terminated under the provisions of Clause 97.

点评：

① 英语"circumstance"一词作"the sum of determining factors beyond willful control"解时常为复数形式，而且一般与介词"beyond"连用。

② 汉语"依法"在此应理解为"按本合同的规定"。此外，"不能依法……"也不等于"it's unlawful to do ..."。

③ 汉语"履约"不宜直译成"performance"，这个词后常跟"obligations"等，用"execution"更准确。

④ 汉语"如果合同已按第 97 条的规定被终止"应与前面的两个条件并列，因为如果没有这一条件，即使有上面两个条件，后面的规定也不能照办。因此，英语"if the Contract had been terminated under the provisions of Clause 97"还是放在主句之前更加妥当。

改译：

In case of any events beyond the parties' control which prevent one party from performing any of its obligations under this Contract in accordance with the provisions hereof after the service of the Letter of Acceptance, or release both parties from further execution of this Contract by the law governing the Contract, and if the Contract had been terminated under the provisions of Clause 97 hereof, the sum payable by the Employer to the Contractor in respect of the work executed shall be the same as the sum which would have been payable under Clause 97.

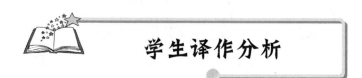

学生译作分析

原文：

本协议的任何一方发生了违约行为，另一方应以书面的形式通知其纠正。如若违约一方在三个月内仍未纠正其违约行为，则另一方有权中止本协议。

学生原译文：

If a noncompliance has taken place to either party of this agreement, another party should inform him to correct by written. If the delinquent party does not correct its noncompliance yet within three months, then another party has the right to discontinue this agreement.

分析：

（1）将汉语"违约行为"译成"noncompliance"欠妥，因为"noncompliance"的意思是"failure or refusal to comply"。因此，应该译成"failure"或者直接将"不能履行其职责"的意思译出。

（2）"发生"不应该译成"has taken place to"，因为这种违约就是其中的一方的行为。

（3）"另一方"应为"one party"，因为前面用的是"either party"。

（4）"应以书面的形式通知其纠正"中的"应"应该译成"shall notify"，而不是"shall inform"，因为英语合同中表示按合同规定有义务做……，助动词往往用"shall"，而"inform"一词过于随意。另外，这句话中的"其"应为另一方或违约方，所以不能译成"him"，而应译成"the defaulting party"或"the delinquent party"。

（5）汉语"纠正"一词不能简单地译成"correct"，因为英语的"correct"一词指"to eliminate faults, errors, or defects"，而"remedy"则指"remove or counteracting something considered a cause of harm or damage"，所以用英语的"remedy"一词更准确。另外，"以书面的形式"应该为"by a written notice"或者"notify in writing"。

（6）汉语"仍未"不宜译成"does not do ... yet"这样的句型。

参考译文：

Either Party shall have the right to terminate this Contract if the other party fails to fulfill or perform any of its obligations hereunder in the event that such failure remains unremedied three months after the service of a written notice by the party to the defaulting party specifying the failure in question and requiring it to be remedied.

翻译技巧介绍

商务合同的翻译
(Translating Business Contracts)

商务合同用词行文准确严谨，属于一种特殊的应用文体，重在记实。

由于商务合同属于法律性公文，因此无论是英译汉还是汉译英，都必须力求准确严谨。尽量使用两种语言中惯用的词句，从而使译文语言地道、逻辑缜密、结构严谨。

一、注意惯用词语的使用

商务合同毕竟是法律文件，所以翻译时要尽可能地使用惯用词语，因为这些词语能够使译文表意准确明了、正式规范。

1. 副词

英语商务合同中常使用惯用副词，这些副词通常不能用普通词语代替。英译汉时有时可以省译这些副词，但汉译英时就应该酌情加上，否则必然影响译文的质量。

英语商务合同中的惯用副词一般由 here、there、where 等副词分别加上 after、by、from、in、of、on、to、under、upon、with 等副词构成。这类副词虽然不多，但却不可缺少。例如：

hereafter 从此以后，今后
hereby 因此，据此
hereinabove/hereinbefore 在上文
hereinafter/hereinbelow 在下文
hereof 于此，关于此点
hereto 对于这个
thereafter 此后，以后
therein 在那里
thereinbefore 在上文中，在上一部分中
thereinafter 在下文中，在下一部分中
thereof 在其中，关于……，将它，它的
thereon/thereupon 在其上
thereunder 在其下
therewith 与此，与那、这或它
whereby 与……一致，通过……，借以
wherein 在何处，在其中
whereto 对于那个

例句：

(1) The terms and conditions contained **herein**, including the Appendices **hereto**, shall constitute the entire agreement between the parties **hereto** and shall supercede any and all previous oral and written notices, memoranda, documents, agreements and contracts between the parties.

译文：**本合同**包含的条款和条件，包括**合同**附件，构成**合同**双方的完整协议，并取代双方以前所有的口头或书面通知、备忘录、文件、协议和合同。

(2) The requirements and specifications are specified in the Equipment Purchase Contract

（EPC）of which the delivery and payment are subject to the provisions **thereof**.

译文：设备合同的交付规定和交付办法，按**设备合同**的规定执行。详见《设备引进合同》。

(3) The undersigned **hereby** agrees that the new products **whereto** this trade name is more appropriate are made in China.

译文：下述签署人同意在中国制造新产品，其品牌**以此**为合适。（省译 hereby）

(4) The covering Letter of Credit must reach the Sellers before _____ and is to remain valid in _____ China until the 15th day after the aforesaid time of shipment, failing which the Sellers reserve the right to cancel this Sales Contract without further notice and to claim from the Buyers for losses resulting **therefrom**.

译文：该信用证必须在_____前开到卖方，信用证的有效期应为上述装船期后第 15 天，在中国_____到期，否则卖方有权取消本售货合约，不另行通知，并保留**因此**而发生的一切损失的索赔权。

(5) In accordance with the Joint Venture Law and other relevant Chinese laws and regulations, both parties of the joint venture agree to set up in China a joint venture limited liability company (**hereinafter** referred to as the joint venture company).

译文：按照中国的合资企业法和其他有关法律和法规，合同双方同意在中国建立合资公司（**以下称合资公司**）。

(6) Licensee agrees that it will not during the term of this agreement, or **thereafter**, attack the title or any rights of Licensor in and to the Name or attack the validity of this license.

译文：被许可方同意在协议有效期内及**其后**，不质疑许可方就该商标享有的所有权和其他权利，不质疑本协议的有效性。

(7) From time to time after Licensee has commenced selling the articles and upon Licensor's written request, Licensee shall furnish without cost to Licensor not more than 10 additional random samples of each article being manufactured and sold by Licensee **hereunder**, together with any cartons, containers and packing and wrapping material used in connection **therewith**.

译文：对被许可方开始出售协议产品后，应许可方的要求，将免费向许可方提供不超过 10 件的随机抽样样品及相关的纸箱、包装箱和包装材料。（省译）

(8) "Patented Technology" means those letters patent, and applications **therefor** presently owned or **hereafter** acquired by Party B and/or which Party B has or may have the right to control or grant license **thereof** during the term **hereof** in any or all countries of the world and which are applicable to or may be used in the manufacture of Contract Products.

译文:"专利技术",系指乙方目前拥有的或**未来**获得的和/或有权或可能有权控制的,或在**本合同**有效期间在世界任何国家许可转让的,适用于或可能适用于制造本合同产品的专利和专利申请。(有的省译,有的不省)

2. 常用词或词组

除了惯用副词外,英语商务合同中所使用的一些词或词组也比较规范,掌握这些词和词组的使用规律,就能提高商务合同英汉互译的质量。不同的商务合同所使用的词和词组不尽相同,以下所举实例基本上在大多数商务合同中都能见到。通过反复对比译文和翻译实践,熟悉、掌握并运用这些词汇是能够办到的。例如:

(1) The Buyers agree to buy and the Sellers agree to sell the following goods **on terms and conditions as set forth below**:

译文:**双方同意按下列条款**由买方售出下列商品:

类似的表达还有:

on terms and conditions mutually agreed upon as follows:

according to the terms and conditions stipulated below and overleaf:

subject to the terms and conditions stated below:

upon the terms and subject to the conditions set forth in this Agreement:

(2) **Unless otherwise agreed and accepted by** ...

译文:除非经……同意和接受

类似的表达还有:

unless otherwise indicated in ...

unless otherwise stated herein ...

unless otherwise instructed ...

unless otherwise noted ...

unless otherwise agreed upon ...

unless waived or otherwise agreed in ...

unless otherwise required by ...

unless otherwise provided by ...

unless otherwise specified in ...

(3) ... the Sellers **reserve the right to cancel this Contract without further notice and to claim from the Buyers** for losses resulting therefrom.

译文:……卖方**有权取消本合约,不另行通知,并保留**……**权**。

类似的表达还有:

reserve the right to withhold ...

reserve the right to refuse, cancel, or suspend ...

reserve the right to cancel, re-name or relocate ...

reserve the right to delete and clear up ...
reserve the right to cancel or reject ...
reserve the right to update and change ...
reserve the right to transfer ...
reserve the right to restrict access to ...
reserve the right to limit the amount of ...

(4) shall be **governed by**

  译文：按……之规定办理

类似的表达还有：

shall be governed, controlled, interpreted and defined by ...
shall be governed by and construed in accordance with ...
shall be governed in all respects by ...
shall be governed solely by ...

(5) both version being **equally authentic**

  译文：两种文本**具有同等效力**

类似的表达还有：

both texts being equally authentic
each version being equally authentic
the two texts being equally authentic
both languages being equally authentic
both language versions being equally authentic
all being equally authentic
the texts in each of these languages being equally authentic

(6) ... shall be fully liable to ... and responsible for ...

  译文：……应**负担**……的一切费用和损失

类似的表达还有：

shall be responsible for ...
shall assume full responsibility for ...
shall be held responsible for ...
shall be held partially responsible for ...
shall be held liable for ...
shall be of the sole responsibility of ...

(7) ... found not **in conformity with** ...

  译文：发现……与本合同规定**不符**

类似的表达还有：

found not conforming to ...

found not to comply with ...

found not identical in ...

found not to be in substantial conformity with ...

found lacking conformity with ...

(8) In case of **discrepancy**, the original version in Chinese shall prevail.

译文：一旦产生歧义，以中文本为准。

类似的表达还有：

if there are discrepancies in ...

in the event of any conflict between the meaning of ...

in case of litigation and misinterpretation ...

where this disclaimer is available in ...

in case of disputes arising from ...

in case of a disagreement between ...

in the event of inconsistencies between ...

3. 注意所用词语与日常意义的差异

商务英语合同中有一些词或词组具有特殊的含义，因此在进行商务英语合同翻译时，一定要勤查字典，仔细辨别这些词语或词组的含义，切不可信手拈来，否则轻者将引起歧义，重者将给合同双方造成经济损失。例如：

(1) **instrument**：a formal, legal document　文书：法律文件

- Amendments to this Contract may be made only by a **written instrument** signed by ...

译文：对本合同的修改只能通过……**签署协议**进行。

(2) **execution**：validation of a legal document by the performance of all necessary formalities; the signing, sealing, and delivering of a contract or agreement making it valid　使……生效：通过执行各种必要的手续（签署、盖章、发布）使法律文件（协议、合同）生效

- This Contract shall take effect from the date of its **execution** by ...

译文：本合同自……**签署**之日起生效。

(3) **service**：the delivery of a writ, summons and complaint, criminal summons, or other notice or order by an authorized server upon another　（法律文件的）送达，寄出

- Either party may terminate this Contract if the other party fails to ... 90 (ninety days) after the **service** of a written notice by ...

译文：如果一方未能在另一方向该方**送达**书面通知后的 90 天内……，另一方可以终止本合同。

(4) **counterpart**：a copy or duplicate of a legal paper　副本：法律文本的复制品或副本

- This Contract is executed in Chinese in 3 (three) **counterparts**, and each party shall hold one copy.

译文：本合同文本为中文，一式三（3）**份**，三方各执一份。

（5）**in question**：under consideration, referring to the subject being discussed
- One party shall send to the defaulting party a written notice specifying the failure **in question** and requiring it to be remedied.

  译文：其中一方可以向违约一方发出书面通知，指出**该方的**违约行为并要求该方予以改正。

（6）**exercise**：to make use of something, such as a right or option　行使权力等
- Failure or delay on the part of any party to **exercise** any right, power or privilege under this Contract shall not operate as ...

  译文：任何一方未能或延迟**行使**本合同规定的任何权利、权力或特权，不得视为……

（7）**acknowledge**：to accept or certify as legally binding【法律】公证，确认：作为法律约束力而接受或确认
- The Seller **acknowledges** and agrees that the Buyer shall have the right ...

  译文：卖方**确认**并同意买方有权……

（8）**award**：a decision, such as one made by a judge or arbitrator　判定，判决：决定，如法官或仲裁者所做出的
- No party may appeal in connection with the matters relating to the arbitration **award**.

  译文：任何一方均不得就仲裁**裁决**所涉及的事项起诉。

二、注意典型的句子结构

商务英语合同的句子不像普通英语句子那么松散，文中一般没有多余的词句，句子结构严谨。无论句子多长，翻译时能够直译就直译，尽量少采用意译。例如：

（1）在合同签字后12年内，买方不得全部或部分地披露按本合同所获得的专有技术、技术资料和其他信息。

译文：Within twelve years after signing the Contract, the Buyer shall not disclose in whole, or in part, the know-how Technical Documentation and other information of the Process obtained under the Contract.

（2）"合同生效日"系指本合同双方管理机构和有关权力机关中最后一方批准合同的日期。

译文："The Date of Coming into Effect of the Contract" means the date of ratification of the Contract by the managing constructure of the parties or by the competent authorities of both parties, whichever comes later.

（3）合同是指合同条款及其附件，包括说明书、图纸、规范、工程量表、投标书、中

标函、合同协议书，以及其他明确列入中标函或合同协议书（如已完成）中的此类进一步的文件。

译文："Contract" means this Contract, the Specification, the Drawings, the Bill of Quantities, the Tender, the Letter of Acceptance, the Contract Agreement (if completed) and such further documents as may be expressly incorporated in the Letter of Acceptance or the Contract Agreement (if completed).

(4) 信用证内容须严格符合本售货合约的规定，否则修改信用证的费用由买方负担，卖方并不负因修改信用证而延误装运的责任，并保留因此而发生的一切损失的索赔权。

译文：The contents of the covering Letter of Credit shall be in strict conformity with the stipulations of the Sales Contract. In case of any variation thereof necessitating amendment of the L/C, the Buyers shall bear the expenses for effecting the amendment. The Sellers shall not be held responsible for possible delay of shipment resulting from awaiting the amendment of the L/C and reserve the right to claim from the Buyers for the losses resulting therefrom.

(5) 附加条款（本合同其他条款如与本附加条款有抵触时，以本附加条款为准。）

译文：Supplementary Condition(s) (Should the articles stipulated in this Contract be in conflict with the following supplementary condition(s), the supplementary condition(s) should be taken as valid and binding.)

(6) 商品检验：以中国_____所签发的品质/数量/重量/包装/卫生检验合格证书作为卖方的交货依据。

译文：Inspection: The Inspection Certificate of Quality/Quantity/Weight/Packing/Sanitation issued by _____ of China shall be regarded as evidence of the Sellers' delivery.

课堂翻译训练

将下列句子译成英语。

1. 仲裁应在北京举行。仲裁委员会的裁决为最后裁决，对双方都有约束力；任何一方均不得向法院或其他当局要求再判。仲裁费由败诉方负担。
2. 异议：品质异议须于货到目的口岸之日起30天内提出，数量异议须于货到目的口岸之日起15天内提出，但均须提供经卖方同意的公证行的检验证明。

3. 本合同其他条款如与本附加条款有抵触时,以本附加条款为准。
4. 在合同条款中,无论何处述及由任何人发出或颁发任何通知、同意、批准、证明或决定,除另有说明者外,均指书面的通知、同意、批准、证明或决定,而通知、证明或决定字样均应据此解释。
5. 乙方如需查核甲方的账目时,应在接到甲方依上述第 3.4 款规定开出的书面通知后 10 天内通知甲方,其具体的查账内容和程序详见本合同附件四。
6. 付款交单:货物发运后,卖方出具以买方为付款人的付款跟单汇票,按即期付款交单(D/P)方式,通过卖方银行及_____银行向买方转交单证,换取货物。
7. 买方凭其委托的检验机构出具的检验证明书向卖方提出索赔(包括换货),由此引起的全部费用应由卖方负担。若卖方收到上述索赔后_____天未予答复,则认为卖方已接受买方索赔。
8. 本合同用中英文两种文字写成,两种文字具有同等效力。本合同共_____份,自双方代表签字(盖章)之日起生效。

课后练习

1. 将下列合同条款译成英语,注意运用本单元所学的翻译技巧。

(1) 迟交货与罚款:除合同第 21 条不可抗力原因外,如卖方不能按合同规定的时间交货,买方应同意在卖方支付罚款的条件下延期交货。罚款可由议付银行在议付货款时扣除,罚款率按每_____天收_____%,不足_____天时以_____天计算。但罚款不得超过迟交货物总价的_____%。如卖方延期交货超过合同规定_____天时,买方有权撤销合同,此时,卖方仍应不迟延地按上述规定向买方支付罚款。
买方有权对因此遭受的其他损失向卖方提出索赔。

(2) 不可抗力:凡在制造或装船运输过程中,因不可抗力致使卖方不能或推迟交货时,卖方不负责任。在发生上述情况时,卖方应立即通知买方,并在_____天内,给买方特快专递一份由当地民间商会签发的事故证明书。在此情况下,卖方仍有责任采取一切必要措施加快交货。如事故延续_____天以上,买方有权撤销合同。

(3) 基于本协议授予的独家代理权,甲方不得直接或间接地通过乙方以外的渠道向美国顾客销售或出口第二条所列商品,乙方不得在美国经销、分销或促销与上述商品相竞争或类似的产品,也不得招揽或接受以到美国以外地区销售为目的的订单,在本协议有效期内,甲方应将其收到的来自美国其他商家的有关代理产品的询价或订单转交给乙方。

2. 改译下列句子。

商业机密：本协议的任何一方均不得在有效期内及期满的一年内向第三者泄漏双方之间的商业秘密，若由此而造成另一方的利益损失，则另一方有追索泄漏商业秘密一方的经济责任的权利。

原译：

Business Secret: In the period of validity and one year after expiry, either party of this agreement shouldn't let out the business secret between both parties to the other person. If lead to the fact therefrom that the interests of another Party suffers, another party has the right of demanding the economic responsibility of the party which lets out business secret.

Unit 13

佳译赏析

猎头公司[1]瞄准中国公司[2]
China's Green Pastures Beckon Headhunters

  21 世纪商业竞争中重要的一部分就是高级人才的比拼，在中国越来越多的企业愿意依托专业公司帮助它们寻找人才，跨国猎头公司的中国客户也越来越多。[3]

  Competition for talent is an important aspect of business competition in the 21 century and more Chinese companies are now turning to local professional headhunters who are winning growing number of Chinese clients.

  "今天你被猎了吗？[4]" 如果听到这样的询问，潘伟会很高兴地说："是的，这是另外一种赞赏。"潘伟是中国一家知名工业企业的项目经理，但是凭借优秀的工作能力已经完成了几个业内交口称赞的项目，猎头公司的电话也就随之而来。[5]

  "Are you sought after by headhunters?" Pan Wei, Project manager of a well-known enterprise, answers happily, "This is another way of praise for my job." He is already much sought after by headhunters thanks to successes in his professional life.

  最近有一家猎头公司又找上了他，为潘伟提供的是一家民营企业的高级职位，并有丰厚的薪金，但潘伟并没有跳槽的打算就一口回绝了。但之后的几个星期，猎头公司并未放弃，甚至请求和他面谈。潘伟说："以前跟我联系的猎头公司多是介绍一些外企的工作，中国的企业还是第一次。"

  Recently, a headhunting company called him with an attractive offer in a private company. But Pan turned it down as he did not want to abandon his current job. But the headhunting company did not give up and even invited him for face to face discussions. Pan says, "Earlier, headhunting companies introduced mostly foreign enterprises to me. This is the first time it is finding me a Chinese enterprise."

猎头公司在外国已有几十年的历史，而中国出现猎头行业不过近几年的事。[6] 早期主要是为外企在中国的机构寻找本土人才。近年来经济的日益开放使中国企业面对的竞争日益加强，尤其是中国加入 WTO 后面临越来越国际化的竞争，因此许多国企，特别是一些上市的股份公司、民营高科技企业也跻身于猎头公司客户的行列。

Headhunting has been popular for a few decades abroad and is becoming a recent phenomenon in China. In the beginning, headhunters focused on finding local talent for foreign enterprises. But now, with China opening up and joining the World Trade Organization, Chinese enterprises are facing more intense foreign competition. This has forced many of them, especially stock and high-tech enterprises, to turn to headhunters.

与其他行业不同，跨国猎头公司在中国并没有遭遇水土不服的阻碍。在 2003 年之后，外资猎头公司在中国市场经营得有声有色。[7] 目前 90% 的在华外资公司都和猎头有过交往。爱立信（中国）有限公司曾多次使用猎头服务，其人力资源部主任刘黛娜说：" 从时间上讲，猎头公司利用其专业技能可以节省我们的时间；从质量上讲，猎头公司从第三者的角度更客观地来考察和判断人才。"这些外资公司为了尽快适应市场需要，往往去委托一些能明白它们企业要求，帮助它们解决困难的"猎头公司"为它们寻找一个熟悉本土文化、工作习惯、竞争规则的关键人才。

Unlike other foreign businesses, foreign headhunters didn't have much difficulty on the new Chinese market, and their business really picked up after 2003. At present, about 90 percent of Chinese foreign-funded companies deal with headhunters. Ericsson China, for example, has gone through headhunting companies many times. Diana Liu, human resources director of Ericsson China, says, "On the one hand, headhunting companies can save time for us by using their professional skills to find the right people; on the other hand, they can also judge more objectively the candidates from the third party's angle." These Chinese foreign-funded companies prefer to obtain senior executives through headhunters who understand the requirements well, can help resolve any problems that may arise and find local people who are familiar with the local culture, work habits and market rules.

中国的本土猎头在数量上发展迅速，仅以北京为例，根据北京市人事局的统计，北京目前有合法的人才中介机构 180 余家[8]，真正专业的猎头公司有 37 家，其中包括新近批准的和已经申请的 6 家外国人才猎头机构。北京赛思卓越企业管理顾问有限公司总经理黄剑介绍，北京没有经过正式审批的猎头公司至少是这个数字的两倍，目前在北京市场开展猎头活动的单位至少在 400 家左右，国外猎头公司在 100 家左右。

The number of local headhunting companies has increased rapidly. In Beijing alone, according to the Beijing Municipal Personnel Bureau, there are about 180 licensed human resources intermediary firms, of which 37 are professional headhunting companies, including six foreign ones that have just been authorized or have been waiting for approvals. According to Huang Jian, general manager of CIASE Management Consultation Company, the number of headhunting companies without official authorization stands at twice over the above-mentioned statistical number. At present, there are at least 400 headhunting companies operating in Beijing, of which about 100 are foreign companies, says Huang Jian.

温军是广西某家高新企业的老板，一年之前和几个朋友一起投资办购物网站，但是缺少网络技术人员，情急之下就花了3万元[9]定金委托某家本土猎头公司，但猎头公司最后推荐的人工作能力并不能让他满意，并且工作不到一年就离开了公司。温军失望之余说："如果早知道是这样，我宁愿多花点钱找外国猎头公司，服务质量也许会高一点儿。"目前国内猎头公司的收费一般为年薪的20%～30%，外资猎头公司是年薪的三分之一。但更多企业认为，专业的外资猎头公司收费高昂不是没有道理的。

Wen Jun heads a high and new technological company in Guangxi. A year ago, he and his friends decided to set up an online shopping site but lacked the technical expertise. Desperated, they forked out 30,000 yuan ($3,623) to a local headhunter for a suitable candidate. However, the appointed person turned out unsuitable and eventually left the company in less than one year. Wen Jun says, disappointed, "If I could have foreseen the result, I would rather have spent more money to ask a foreign headhunting company for help. Perhaps the service quality may be better." At present, a local headhunting company charges 20 – 30 percent of a worker's annual salary while a foreign one always charges one third of a worker's annual salary. But most companies seem okay with the higher service fees of foreign headhunters.

猎头工作极费时间。猎头公司能帮助客户即雇主们就所招职位正确地评估其期望值并寻找到合适的面试人选。猎头顾问及时向面试人选提供客观真实的意见反馈，并及时向雇主提出建议。猎头顾问能替用人公司对面试人选的资格条件进行调查，并得到有关面试人选过去的工作表现及背景情况。这些，都需要调动很多的人力和资源，往往是一些小公司所不能胜任的。

Headhunting demands much time. Headhunter can help their clients evaluate their expectations and find the right candidates. They relieve companies of the job of verifying the qualifications and experience of the candidates and check out their recommendations. Small companies may not have the time and resources for this exercise which requires much work and resources. They also help prospective candidates by providing them with invaluable feedback that can improve their chances in future job openings.

相比之下，历时短暂、资金有限和管理经验匮乏，已经成为悬在中国本土猎头业头上的一把达摩克利斯剑。那么，面对洋猎头的咄咄逼人态势，本土猎头公司是否已无生存空间？[10]

Local headhunters compare poorly with their foreign counterparts when it comes to experience, fund invested and management. Does this mean that local headhunters can hardly survive the aggressive intrusion that endangers the headhunting industry in China?

北京科锐总经理高勇表示前景并没有那么悲观："猎头行业的空间很大。据估计，整个中国猎头行业有 25 亿的市场份额，即使是目前做得最好的猎头公司，它的市场份额也没有占到 1%。对于国内的猎头企业来说，都有机会做大做强。[11]"

Wallace Gao, general manager of the Beijing Chinacareer Company is not that pessimistic. He says "The headhunting industry has a great potential. It is estimated that there is a 2.5 billion yuan ($301.93 million) market. Even the current best headhunting company has not conquered 1 percent of the total headhunting market. All Chinese headhunting companies have the opportunity to become stronger."

网上抢市场
Online Business

4 月 19 日，美国最大的猎头公司 MONSTER 公司斥资 5 000 万美元收购国内三大招聘网站之一中华英才网 40% 的股份。在今后的三年中，MONSTER 将帮助中华英才网完成 IPO 上市[12]。上市后，MONSTER 将购买其 51% 甚至更多的股份。如果在三年时间内，中华英才网未能上市，MONSTER 同样有义务购买其超过 51% 的股份，成为实际控股股东[13]。

On April 19, Monster, the biggest headhunter in USA, spent $50 million to buy 40 percent of ChinaHR.com stocks, which is one of China's three largest human resources websites. In the next three years, Monster will help ChinaHR.com launch its initial public offering (IPO). Monster will then buy 51 percent or more of its stocks. Even if ChinaHR.com does not get listed on the market in three years, Monster will be obliged to buy 51 percent of its stock and become the majority shareholder.

据中华英才网内部人士透露，该公司虽然名列国内 3 大网络招聘公司，但 2004 年总收入仅 6 500 万元左右。资金一直是该公司发展中最头疼的问题之一。"作为一个想上市的企业，最需要的是资金。其次是专业的服务技术和人才。"中华英才网市场总监周茜这样说[14]。

According to ChinaHR.com insiders, although it is among China's three biggest headhunting companies, its total income in 2004 was only about 65 million yuan ($7.85 million). The company has always been plagued by funds shortage. "As a company wanting to go public, fund is the most important thing, followed by professional service technology and personnel," said Zhou Qian, marketing director of ChinaHR. com.

据统计,中国的招聘市场2004年达到41.6亿元人民币,预计2006年将达到51.2亿元人民币,平均年增长率达到10%。网上招聘在2003年为3.1个亿,到2004年为5.5个亿,一年当中以占8.1%的比例跃升到了13.2%,到2006年将增长到16.9亿元人民币,平均增长率为73.9%,2006年网上招聘收入将占整体招聘市场收入的33%。在未来,网上招聘市场将达到整个招聘市场的60%~70%。

It is estimated that the human resources market that was worth 4.16 billion yuan ($502.42 million) in 2004 will grow to 5.12 billion yuan ($618.36 million) in 2006. The annual average increase rate is 10 percent. The online human resources market was worth 310 million yuan ($37.44 million) in 2003, and it grew to 550 million yuan ($66.43 million) the following year. Within just one year, the online market share had grown from 8.1 percent of the human resources market to 13.2 percent. It will reach 1.69 billion yuan ($204.11 million) in 2006. The annual average increase rate stands at 73.9 percent. In 2006, revenue from the online market will account for 33 percent of the market total. This share is expected to grow to 60 – 70 percent.

而早在2001年,MONSTER就把目光投向了中国市场,但由于当时政策的限制,MONSTER延缓了其在中国的收购计划[15]。现在面对中国开放的人才市场,MONSTER再次展开它的"中国之旅"。MONSTER的创始人杰夫·泰勒表示,MONSTER对中华英才网的投入不是简单逐利的风险投资,而是着眼于长远的产业资本,以打造中国第一的网上招聘品牌。

Monster first began eyeing the Chinese market in 2001 but owing to official policy at the time, had to defer its plans. Today, the company has once again launched its China journey. According to Jeff Taylor, founder of Monster, his company invested in ChinaHR. com not for temporary benefits but to create China's No. 1 human resources brand.

面对机遇多多的中国人才市场,不仅仅是MONSTER,海德思哲、斯图亚特、澳大利亚EL集团、光辉国际等全球十大猎头公司早已在北京、上海、深圳等地落户,并展开与本土企业的合作。在2003年底,光辉国际就与"上海人才"合资成立了上海光辉人力资源咨询有限公司。据艾瑞公司[16]预测,2002—2006年是招聘网站的成长期,2007—2010年进入成熟期后,新的招聘网站就不适宜再进入。

China's large human resources market is already attracting the world top 10 headhunters, such as Monster, Heidrick & Sruggles, Spencer. Stuart, Australia's EL Group and Korn Ferry International. All these companies have established businesses in Beijing, Shanghai and Shenzhen, and are even cooperating with local enterprises. By the end of 2003, for instance, Korn Ferry International had set up a joint consultancy with Talent Shanghai Co. Ltd. According to iResearch, 2002 to 2006 is the peak growth period for human resources websites. Post 2007, demand is expected to taper off and by 2010 the market will not see any new entrants.

正如光辉国际董事长兼全球总裁 Paul C. Reilly 所说的：国际上最大的猎头公司都在盯着中国市场，我们也一样。

As Paul C. Reilly, CEO of Korn Ferry International, puts it, "Like other international headhunting companies, we are also paying more attention to the China market."

Words and Expressions

牧地，草原，牧场	pasture
招手，召唤	beckon
猎头	headhunter
跳槽	abandon one's current job
回绝，拒绝	turn ... down
有起色，改善	pick up; improve in condition or activity
中介机构	intermediary firms
专家的意见，专门技术	technical expertise
支付	fork out, expend, spend
咄咄逼人	aggressive
首次公开募股	Initial Public Offering (IPO)
上市	get listed, go public
内部人士	insiders
使苦恼，烦扰	plague
把目光投向	eye
延缓	defer
逐渐减弱，消失	to diminish or lessen gradually

Notes

1 猎头公司   headhunter

A headhunter is a private employment agency specializing in the recruiting of professional and managerial personnel; also called executive search firm. The fees charged by these agencies range up to one-third of the first year's total salary and bonus package for the job to be filled.

2. 猎头公司瞄准中国公司　China's Green Pastures Beckon Headhunters

将"猎头公司瞄准中国公司"译成"China's Green Pastures Beckon Headhunters"（中国的绿色牧场吸引猎头们）很有创意，因为"猎头"的另一个意思是"a savage who cuts off and preserves the heads of enemies as trophies（猎取人头的蛮人）"，这样翻译准确地表达出了外国猎头公司对潜力巨大的中国猎头市场垂涎三尺的含义。

3. 21世纪商业竞争中重要的一部分就是高级人才的比拼，在中国越来越多的企业愿意依托专业公司帮助它们寻找人才，跨国猎头公司的中国客户也越来越多。Competition for talent is an important aspect of business competition in the 21 century and more Chinese companies are now turning to local professional headhunters who are winning growing number of Chinese clients.

"高级人才的比拼"并不是高级人才相互倾轧的意思，所以译成"competition for talent"非常贴切。"愿意依托专业公司帮助它们寻找人才"这句话并没有译成"rely on … for finding talents"，而是按英文的习惯译成"are now turning to local professional headhunters"，这样就将"原来靠自己的人事部门招人才，现在找猎头公司"的意思表达出来了。后面的"……跻身于猎头公司客户的行列"被译成"This has forced many of them, especially stock and high-tech enterprises, to turn to headhunters."也是采用了同样的手法。

4. 今天你被猎了吗？　Are you sought after by headhunters?

这一句话并未译成"Are you headhunted today?"，这是因为"headhunt"这个词一般不作动词用，否则就是"出外猎取人头"的意思。

5. 潘伟是中国一家知名工业企业的项目经理，但是凭借优秀的工作能力已经完成了几个业内交口称赞的项目，猎头公司的电话也就随之而来。Pan Wei, Project manager of a well-known enterprise, answers happily, "This is another way of praise for my job." He is already much sought after by headhunters thanks to successes in his professional life.

译者并未直译"猎头公司的电话也就随之而来"这句话，而是译成"He is already much sought after by headhunters"，这样正好前后呼应，效果很好，既意译了"电话也就随之而来"，又通过回答"Are you sought after by headhunters?"这一问题，将猎头公司紧追不舍的意思译出。

6. 猎头公司在外国已有几十年的历史，而中国出现猎头行业不过近几年的事。Headhunting has been popular for a few decades abroad and is becoming a recent phenomenon in China.

此句中的"不过近几年的事"不太容易处理，英译时用了"phenomenon"一词。这样翻译并非要直译"事"，而是英语常用这个词来表示某种状况和现象，如："There is a growing number of economists who believe today's brutally tough labor market is not a temporary

American phenomenon."（越来越多的经济学家认为，当今劳动力市场的惨状，并不是美国一国出现的暂时现象。）

7 　与其他行业不同，跨国猎头公司在中国并没有遭遇水土不服的阻碍。在 2003 年之后，外资猎头公司在中国市场经营得有声有色。 Unlike other foreign businesses, foreign headhunters didn't have much difficulty on the new Chinese market, and their business really picked up after 2003.

"没有遭遇水土不服的阻碍"中的"水土不服"本来是"unaccustomed to the climate of a new place"的意思，但这里仅仅是个比喻，所以译成"didn't have much difficulty on the new Chinese market"。

这句明显有刚开始经营一般，现在大有好转的意思，所以用了英语"pick up"一词，将"有起色"的意思译出来了。

8 　合法的人才中介机构 180 余家　there are about 180 licensed human resources intermediary firms

此句中的"合法"一词应该译成"licensed"，而不宜译成"legal"，因为这里指的是政府发放了经营许可证的公司。后面"已经申请的"译成"which have been waiting for approvals"也是采用了意译的方法。

9 　商务英语中，有时会遇到用某种货币统计出来的数额，一般的原则是英译汉时，可以酌情将其他货币的数额照译，然后再将人民币的等值译出，并用括号括上；汉译英时，则反之。

10 　相比之下，历时短暂、资金有限和管理经验匮乏，已经成为悬在中国本土猎头业头上的一把达摩克利斯剑。那么，面对洋猎头的咄咄逼人态势，本土猎头公司是否已无生存空间？ Local headhunters compare poorly with their foreign counterparts when it comes to experience, fund invested and management. Does this mean that local headhunters can hardly survive the aggressive intrusion that endangers the headhunting industry in China?

这句话的主语本来是"历时短暂、资金有限和管理经验匮乏"，宾语是"一把达摩克利斯剑"。"达摩克利斯剑"是个比喻，表示时刻存在的危险或到来的杀身之祸。句子的原意是：中国本土的猎头业面对洋猎头的大举入侵，正处于生死存亡的关头。英译采取意译的方法将原文的内涵完全表达出来。

11 　猎头行业的空间很大。据估计，整个中国猎头行业有 25 亿的市场份额，即使是目前做得最好的猎头公司，它的市场份额也没有占到 1%。对于国内的猎头企业来说，都有机会做大做强。 The headhunting industry has a great potential. It is estimated that there is a 2.5 billion yuan ($301.93 million) market. Even the current best headhunting company has not conquered 1 percent of the total headhunting market. All Chinese headhunting companies have the opportunity to become stronger.

此句中的"份额"可以理解为范畴词，汉译英时可以省略，直接译成"there is a ...

market"即可,不一定非要用"market share"。

12 "IPO 上市"即首次公开募股。首次公开募股(Initial Public Offerings, IPO)是指企业通过证券交易所首次公开向投资者增发股票,以期募集用于企业发展资金的过程。

13 在今后的三年中,MONSTER 将帮助中华英才网完成 IPO 上市。上市后,MONSTER 将购买其 51% 甚至更多的股份。如果在三年时间内,中华英才网未能上市,MONSTER 同样有义务购买其超过 51% 的股份,成为实际控股股东。 In the next three years, Monster will help ChinaHR. com launch its initial public offering (IPO). Monster will then buy 51 percent or more of its stocks. Even if ChinaHR. com does not get listed on the market in three years, Monster will be obliged to buy 51 percent of its stock and become the majority shareholder.

句中两次出现"上市"一词,但前后的意思并不完全一样,前者是指首次公开募股(Initial Public Offerings),即在一级市场上向投资者增发股票,以期募集用于企业发展资金的过程,并非通常所指的"上市流通"。而后者(get listed)是指某公司股票在证券交易所(挂牌)上市流通,即投资者将首次发行的股票在二级市场出售变现的过程。再如:"The company is planning to obtain a London Stock Exchange list."(该公司正计划在伦伦敦股票交易所挂牌上市。)

14 "作为一个想上市的企业,最需要的是资金。其次是专业的服务技术和人才。"中华英才网市场总监周茜这样说。"As a company wanting to go public, fund is the most important thing, followed by professional service technology and personnel," said Zhou Qian, marketing director of ChinaHR. com.

此句中的"其次是专业的服务技术和人才",译文采用了英语的过去分词短语,译得非常地道。

15 而早在 2001 年,MONSTER 就把目光投向了中国市场,但由于当时政策的限制,MONSTER 延缓了其在中国的收购计划。 Monster first began eyeing the Chinese market in 2001 but owing to official policy at the time, had to defer its plans.

此句中的"政策的限制"是指限制外国猎头公司进入的政策,这里没有直接译出,但并不妨碍对原文的理解。

16 艾瑞公司 iResearch
艾瑞市场咨询是一家专注于网络媒体、电子商务、网络游戏、无线增值等新经济领域,深入研究和了解消费者行为,并为网络行业及传统行业客户提供市场调查研究和战略咨询服务的专业市场调研机构。

他山之石

原文:

中国将继续稳步开放市场,创新引进外资的形式,完善有关鼓励和保护外商投资的法律法规,改革涉外经济管理体制,加强知识产权保护,努力为中国的对外经贸合作和外国来华投资提供一切便利,创造更好的环境。

译文1:

China will continue to open its market in a steady manner, adopting new approaches to attract foreign investment, improving laws and regulations to encourage and protect foreign investment, reforming foreign-related economic management mechanisms, strengthening the protection of intellectual property, and making efforts to provide facilitation and better environment for foreign trade and economic cooperation and foreign investment in China.

译文2:

China will keep opening up its market step by step. We will try to explore new ways of attracting foreign capital, improve the legal framework for encouraging and protecting foreign investment, streamline the management of businesses with foreign elements, and step up the protection of intellectual property rights. Great efforts will be made to create a more favorable business climate to facilitate economic and trade cooperation outwardly and to make things smooth for the inflow of foreign investment.

点评:

整个段落为汉语的连动式。译文1将汉语中所有的并列分句译成英语的分词短语;译文2虽然将句子拆开翻译,但表达的意思却与译文1基本相同。两种译文基本上都按照汉语的句式进行对译。其实,仔细阅读原文,"努力为中国的对外经贸合作和外国来华投资提供一切便利,创造更好的环境"虽然放在整个段落的最后,但却是这段话的中心,也就是说,前面的"继续稳步开放市场,创新引进外资的形式,完善有关鼓励和保护外商投资的法律法规,改革涉外经济管理体制,加强知识产权保护"只不过是"提供一切便利,创造更好的环境"的具体表现而已。因此,在翻译汉语的连动式时,一定要分析句子的内在含义,分清主次,否则译文虽然通顺,但却违背原文所要表达的意思。

改译:

China will exerts itself to provide a more favorable business climate for Sino-foreign trade and cooperation as well as foreign investment by keeping opening up its market step by step, adopting new approaches to attract foreign investment, improving the legal framework for encouraging, protecting foreign investment, streamlining the management of businesses with foreign elements and strengthening the protection of intellectual property rights.

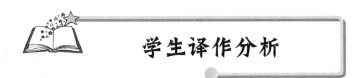

学生译作分析

原文：

显然从拉动中国经济增长的"三驾马车"看，投资和进出口的增长仍然是主要的，与发达国家消费占 GDP 比重 70% 以上的比例相比，消费水平仍然偏低。

学生原译文：

Obviously, among the three carriages that have been driving China's economic growth, investment and export played the leading role, and the consumption level is lower than that of developed countries which accounts for more than 70 percent of the GDP.

分析：

(1) "三驾马车"不宜直接译成"carriages, a troika, three carts"或者"wagons"，因为汉语中"三驾马车"只是个比喻，实质上指推动中国经济持续增长的三种动力或者因素。因此，将其意译成"locomotive"或许更加贴切，如："The US could no longer serve as the locomotive for the world economy. 美国再也无力承担世界经济推动力的重任了。"如果译成"factors"，后面的动词可以使用"driving"或者"powering"。

(2) "投资和进出口"译成"investment and export"似乎过于简单，应该将其完整的意义译出，以免让外国读者产生误解。

(3) "消费水平仍然偏低"不是"is lower than that of..."，而是相比之下，我国的消费水平占 GDP 的比重偏低。

(4) "消费水平"中的"水平"属于范畴词，译成英语时可以考虑省略。

参考译文：

Of the three primary contributors to the Chinese economic growth, fixed-asset investment and foreign trade are dominating. Compared with the situation in developed countries where consumption constitutes more than 70 percent of the total GDP, the Chinese consumption is still low.

翻译技巧介绍

顺序法、逆序法和变序法

一、顺序法

顾名思义,顺序法就是指按时间、逻辑的先后顺序和汉语原来的句式进行翻译。由于这种译法与汉语的表达顺序基本相同,差别不大,译者完全可以做到顺序而下,逐步翻译。这种译法在翻译合同等比较严谨的文体时常用。

例句1:

①卖方在每批货发货前两个月通知买方是否参加该批货检验。②买方收到通知后至少在开箱检验日期前20天将检验日期通知卖方,③并为卖方检验人员提供检验工作的便利条件。

译文:

①The Seller shall notify the Buyer two months prior to each shipment whether his inspectors will join in the inspection of the shipment. ②The Buyer after receiving the notice shall inform the Seller of the date of inspection at least 20 days before the date of open-package inspection ③and shall also render convenience to the Seller's inspectors in their inspection work.

例句2:

①由于小作坊"一统天下",面对激烈的市场竞争,②景德镇的陶瓷产品不仅陷入了恶性的价格战,③而且"景德镇"这个品牌逐渐被滥用。

译文:

① Dominated by private workshops and facing furious competition, ② porcelain manufacturers in Jingdezhen have become entangled in vicious price wars for products. ③The "Jingdezhen" brand has been commandeered as well by many small workshops selling wares branded with "fine porcelain from Jingdezhen," despite the fact that a majority of them are of low quality.

例句3:

①若需要,②在本合同签字后的第18个月,卖方将自行出资派遣技术人员到中国,就买方的最终土木建筑设计进行讨论,③如需要对最终土木建筑设计条件做更改,④双方对其结果应在协议书中签署同意。⑤买方的图纸须盖章注明"双方同意",并签署实际日期。

译文:

①If necessary, ②the Seller shall send in the 18th month after signing the Contract at his own expense technical personnel to China to discuss the Buyer's final civil design ③and if there are revisions regarding the final information of civil engineering, ④both parties shall discuss and reach an agreement on the consequences thus incurred in a protocol. ⑤The drawings of the Buyer will be sealed and marked "Approved by both parties" and stamped with the actual date.

例句4：

①该信用证必须在10月10日前开到卖方，②信用证的有效期应为上述装船期后第15天，在中国杭州到期，③否则卖方有权取消本售货合约，不另行通知，并保留因此而发生的一切损失的索赔权。

译文：

①The covering Letter of Credit must reach the Sellers before October 10 and ②is to remain valid in Hangzhou, China until the 15th day after the aforesaid time of shipment, ③failing which the Sellers reserve the right to cancel this Sales Contract without further notice and to claim from the Buyers for losses resulting therefrom.

二、逆序法

所谓逆序法，就是指由于汉英两种语言在表达方面存在差异，在翻译时应按各自的语言表达习惯重新组合。在组合过程中，原文的一些语句顺序将被打乱，或前置，或后置。也就是说，或顺译，或倒译。这种倒译，即从原文的后面往前译的方法，通常称之为逆序译法。

例句1：

①凡在制造或装船运输过程中，②因不可抗力致使卖方不能或推迟交货时，③卖方不负责任。

译文：

③The Seller shall not be responsible ②for the delay of shipment or non-delivery of the goods due to force Majeure, ①which might occur during the process of manufacturing or in the course of loading or transit.

例句2：

①中国知名大型彩电企业——创维集团在首届"中国－东盟博览会"上与马来西亚、印度尼西亚等5个东盟国家的经销商签订了10万台彩电、总价值2 000万美元的出口合同。②这是继TCL和长虹两大彩电企业今年9月进入泰国市场之后，③又一个彩电企业为抢占东盟市场而采取的实质性举措。

译文：

②Following the lead of color TV makers like TCL Holding Co. and Sichuan Changhong Electric Co., which started selling in Thailand from this September, ③the Skyworth Group, a leading Chinese color TV producer, delved into the Southeast Asian market ①by signing contracts worth $20 million with dealers from five Southeast Asian countries that are members of the Association of South East Asian Nations (ASEAN), including Malaysia and Indonesia, for 100,000 color TV sets.

例句 3：

①当卖方完成了运输货物的责任，②货物的丢失或损坏及承受与货物相关的费用的责任，③便从卖方转移到买方。

译文：

②The risk of loss of or damage to the goods, as well as the obligation to bear the costs relating to the goods, ③passes from the seller to the buyer ①when the seller has fulfilled this obligation to deliver the goods.

例句 4：

①加入 WTO 后，②世界银行业的龙头企业也必然进入中国市场，这是无法回避的现状，也是市场竞争的必然趋势。③面对外资银行挑起的这场来势凶猛的"中国富人争夺战"，④中国银行业唯有创新才能求生存。

译文：

④ The Chinese banking sector, ① with China's WTO membership, ④ has to seek for innovation to survive ③the fierce rivalry for Chinese wealthy people triggered by foreign-funded banks ② facing the inevitable and natural tendency of competition spurred by world's leading banks' access to the Chinese market.

三、变序法

变序法是指在将汉语句子译成英语时，不考虑原文句子的顺序，并完全根据英语的表达的习惯来安排句子。这种情况往往出现在汉语句子特别长的时候，翻译时必须首先抓住文章中的主句，然后按照英语的表达方式来合理安排句子。如果仅仅按汉语的句式来翻译，虽然意思也能表达清楚，但毕竟不是英语的习惯表达方式。

例句 1：

①货物在目的口岸卸毕 60 天内（如果用集装箱装运则在开箱后 60 天）经中国进出口商品检验局复验，②如发现品质、数量或重量及其他任何方面与本合同规定不符，③除属于保险公司或船行负责者外，④买方有权凭上述检验局出具的检验证书向卖方提出退货或索赔。⑤因退货或索赔引起的一切费用包括检验费、利息及损失均由卖方负担。⑥在此情况下，⑦凡货物适于抽样及寄送时如卖方要求，⑧买方可将样品寄交卖方。

译文：

②In case the quality, quantity or weight of the goods be found not in conformity with those as stipulated in this Contract ①upon re-inspection by the China Commodity Import and Export inspection Bureau within 60 days after completion of the discharge of the goods at the port of destination or, if goods are shipped in containers, 60 days after the opening of such containers, ④ the Buyer shall have the right to request the Seller to take back the goods or lodge claims against the Seller for compensation for losses upon the strength of the Inspection Certificate issued by the said Bureau, ③with the exception of those claims for which the insurers or owners of the carrying vessel are liable, ⑤ all expenses including but not limited to inspection fees, interest, losses arising from the return of the goods or claims shall be borne by the Seller. ⑥In such a case, ⑧the Buyer may send a sample of the goods in question to the Seller if so requested, ⑦provided that sampling and sending of such sample is feasible.

例句2：

①虽然贴牌生产已成为国内企业海外扩张中成功概率最高的一种形式，②然而，如何创立自主品牌才是广大企业需要把握的，③因为中国东南沿海贴牌生产企业只能赚取微薄的加工费用，而大部分利润为国外品牌企业所赚取，④而贴牌生产往往因为加工出口量大而容易遭遇国外的贸易壁垒，⑤近来欧盟和美国对中国皮鞋、彩电等接连采取了反倾销措施，大量的贴牌生产也是招来反倾销的重要原因。

译文：

③ Facing the facts that southeast China's OEM (Original Equipment Manufacturer) businesses only make slim processing fees, with most of the profits going to foreign brand owners, ⑤and that large OEM production volumes have been cited as the culprits for recent anti-dumping cases involving Chinese-made leather shoes and color TV sets initiated by the European Union and the United States, ②these OEM-oriented businesses should place their focus on creating more independent brands ④ when more and more trade barriers are erected by foreign countries in retaliation against large export volumes, ①although OEMs have traditionally been the way through which domestic companies successfully made their way into the world market.

课堂翻译训练

1. 商人，只要不是买空卖空者，即便只有百分之五、百分之二，甚至百分之一的利润也会感到心满意足。
2. 秉承"造中国人买得起的好车"的理念，奇瑞汽车一上市便因良好的产品质量和性价比一直受到消费者的青睐。

3. 欧盟劳动力市场过分僵化，为了降低畸高的劳动力成本，需要向海外转移部分丧失竞争力的产业，尤其是劳动密集型产业。
4. 文化产业是21世纪具有战略意义的黄金产业，但由于中国文化产业起步较晚，仍然处于散乱弱小的初级发展阶段，企业的规模与国际巨头相比差距甚大。
5. 在这些市场上，高利润率并不意味着高价格，高利润率也不意味着非要提供高端产品。我们对于中小企业市场及新兴市场都极为关注。
6. 作为一个对外贸易迅速增长的大国，发生贸易争端很正常。对出口企业来说更重要的是，如何学会国际游戏规则，并调整自身的出口行为，而不要把希望一味寄托在政府创造更大的数量增长空间上。
7. 作为世界最大紫菜消费国的日本，一方面向中国出口大量相关机械设备，另一方面又禁止中国紫菜的进口，令人难以理解。
8. 多数农民在市场风险面前仍处在"单兵对阵"状态，加上有关农作物种植面积的预测与动态发布信息十分稀缺，农民安排种植品种和面积，仍然是"今天下雨，明天打伞"。

课后练习

将下列短文译成英语，注意运用本单元所学的翻译技巧。

1.

25年来，中国坚定不移地推进改革开放，社会主义市场经济体制初步建立，开放型经济已经形成，社会生产力和综合国力不断增强，各项社会事业全面发展，人民生活总体上实现了由温饱到小康的历史性跨越。从1978年至2003年的25年间，中国经济年均增长9.4%。25年前，中国年国内生产总值为1 473亿美元，去年已达到14 000多亿美元。25年前，中国年进出口贸易总额为206亿美元，去年已达到8 512亿美元。25年前，中国外汇储备为1.67亿美元，去年已达到4 033亿美元。目前，中国经济总量居世界第六，进出口贸易总额居世界第四。中国之所以能够发生这样巨大的变化，最关键的原因是我们始终坚持走中国特色社会主义道路，始终坚持改革开放，激发了全体人民的积极性、主动性、创造性。

中国虽然取得了很大的发展成就，但中国人口多，底子薄，生产力不发达，发展很不平衡，生态环境、自然资源与经济社会发展的矛盾比较突出。虽然中国人均国内生产总值已经突破1 000美元，但仍排在世界一百位以后。中国要实现现代化，使全体人民都过上富裕生活，还需要进行长期不懈的艰苦奋斗。

我们已经明确了本世纪头20年的奋斗目标，这就是全面建设惠及十几亿人口的更高水平的小康社会，到 2020 年实现国内生产总值比 2000 年翻两番，达到 4 万亿美元，人均国内生产总值达到 3 000 美元，使经济更加发展、民主更加健全、科教更加进步、文化更加繁荣、社会更加和谐、人民生活更加殷实。

2.

尽管大多数专家认为去年的贸易逆差有特定的原因，今年情况将有所好转，但其中不少人也还是不甚乐观地指出，由于中国农业自身存在的问题及诸多外部因素的作用，中国未来几年的农产品贸易可能依然面临较大压力。

根据入世协议的规定，今后几年中国农产品市场将进一步开放，关税水平继续降低。2005 年，中国农产品关税水平将降至 15.35%，而世界农产品关税平均水平为 62%，中国将成为世界上关税最低的国家之一，2008 年还将进一步降至 15%；农产品关税配额数量将逐年增加，2006 年将取消植物油关税配额管理。

2005 年，中国免税进口小麦可达 900 多万吨，占中国小麦产量差不多 10%，亦即城市居民消费量的 1/4 强。近年来国际小麦价格基本和国内的价格差不多，但是进口小麦的质量和纯度都优于国产小麦，国产小麦在国内市场上将遇到的激烈竞争是可以想像的。

国际农产品市场是全球贸易自由化进展相对滞后的一个市场，各国政府给予的保护程度普遍高于其他市场。由于在各种非关税措施中，技术性贸易壁垒有其特殊的作用，所以进入本世纪以来，技术壁垒已经成为一个国家保护国内经济最堂而皇之的手段，并成为中国农产品出口中的一个重要障碍。

除了贸易壁垒，农产品反倾销也是中国出口企业今后可能要经常面对的问题。特保条款、"非市场经济"的反倾销、过渡性审议机制这些措施，"同样对农产品有效"。

很多国家在进口上都卡得很严，层层把关，而我们国家在这方面就弱得多。我们加入 WTO 既有义务也有权利，不能只执行义务而放弃了应有的权利。

Unit 14

佳译赏析

追求公平
A Developing Inequity

　　为期5天的世界经济论坛¹达沃斯年会于1月29日结束了，围绕"创新——势在必行"主题，针对世界经济、政治面临的重大挑战及其应对之道，来自全球89个国家和地区的2 340名嘉宾们举行了240多场讨论。²本次论坛设置了8项议题，包括中国与印度的崛起、经济发展区域的改变、创造更多未来就业、处理国际危机中有效的领导能力等。在笔者看来，可以基本归结在国内公平、国际公平、发展中国家之间的竞争与合作等三个方面。

　　The annual meeting of the World Economic Forum at Davos, Switzerland concluded January 29 after five days of vibrant debate around the theme of "the creative imperative." Some 2,340 guests from 89 countries and regions participated in more than 240 discussion sessions on major challenges facing the world economy and politics as well as the solutions to these problems. "The Emergence of China and India," "The Changing Economic Landscape," "Creating Future Jobs" and "Effective Leadership in Addressing Global Risks" were among the eight sub-themes of the forum this year. In my opinion, these topics can be summed up as national equity, international equity and competition and cooperation between developing countries.

　　近年世界经济增长强劲，2004年全球经济增长5.1%，为30年来最高记录；预计2005年增长率可达4.3%；2006年经济增长也不太可能出现大逆转，国际货币基金组织等国际经济组织已从去年下半年起纷纷提高了对世界经济增长率的预测。然而，各国收入分配格局大面积恶化给这幅繁荣图景投下了阴影。就在此次论坛开幕前的1月23日，英国新经济基金会³发表的研究报告表明，过去10年来，世界最贫困人口的收益趋向锐减。根据这份研究报告，1990—2001年间，全球人均收入每增长100美元，最贫困人口收入仅增长60美分，比上世纪80年代的2.20美元锐减73%。⁴

The world economy has maintained robust growth in recent years. In 2004, it grew by 5.1 percent, hitting a record 30-year high. The growth rate is projected at 4.3 percent in 2005, and is unlikely to experience any dramatic setback in 2006. International economic organizations including the International Monetary Fund (IMF) began to have higher predictions of the world economy growth rate as of the second half of last year. However, the across-the-board deterioration of the income distribution pattern in various countries has cast a dark shadow on this rosy landscape. Shortly before the World Economic Forum opened, the London-based New Economics Foundation published a report January 23, revealing that the share of benefits from global economic growth reaching the world's poorest people drastically shrunk in the past 10 years. According to the report, between 1990 and 2001, for every $100 worth of growth in the world's income per person, only $0.6 found its target and contributed to reducing poverty for those living on less than a dollar a day—73 percent less than in the 1980s, when $2.2 of every $100 worth of growth contributed to reducing poverty for those living on less than a dollar a day.

问题的严重性不仅在于贫困的普遍和程度，更在于扶贫力度削弱，以及贫困人口向上流动机会减少。就国内扶贫而言，即使在号称发展中国家经济成功模范的亚洲，上世纪80至90年代，国民收入增量中用于扶贫的比例也从10.2%锐减到了2.9%。在国际扶贫方面，上世纪90年代以来，发达国家几乎都大幅削减了其国际官方援助，对剩余的官方援助也增加了许多附加条件。[5]

The seriousness of the problem is not only evident in the prevalence and magnitude of poverty but also in the slackened poverty alleviation efforts as well as narrowed opportunities for the poor to move up. In terms of national poverty reduction, even in Asia, the purported testament to developing countries' economic success, the proportion of national income growth devoted to poverty alleviation plummeted from 10.2 percent in the 1980s to 2.9 percent in the 1990s. Regarding international poverty reduction, almost all developed countries have reduced official international aid by a large margin and attached more strings to remaining aid projects since the 1990s.

授人以鱼，不如授人以渔。[6]要减少贫困，最重要的不是直接扶助，而是向贫困人口、贫困阶层、贫困地区提供依靠自我奋斗向上流动的机会。[7]此次论坛的组织者们注意到了这个问题，他们设置的第4项议题是"创造更多未来就业"，其主要内容包括"了解增长和创造就业方面出现的变化性质，全球就业形势，对新技能的要求，劳动力迁徙，以及由此导致的社会和经济结果"。然而，很多强势国家和阶层在取得了较大影响力后，就迫不及待地企图树立对他们片面有利的规则，大幅度提高贫困人口、贫困阶层向上流动的壁垒，固定对他们有利的社会分化格局；而在当前的政治游戏规则下，这种企图又常常能够得逞。遗憾的是，此次论坛对此讨论不足,最终也只能感叹一番"反饥饿斗争路漫漫"了事。[8]

A time-honored Chinese saying goes, "It is better to teach others to fish than to provide them with fish." What is most important to poverty alleviation is not direct assistance but affording the impoverished with opportunities to pull themselves up by their bootstraps. Aware of this fact, organizers of this year's Davos summit singled out "Creating Future Jobs" as the forum's fourth sub-theme, which includes understanding the changing nature of growth and job creation, global employment, new skill requirements, labor mobility and resulting social and economic consequences. However, many advantaged social strata and nations are anxious to establish rules that are skewed in their favor as soon as they gain prominence. They attempt to perpetuate the favorable social division by imposing more barriers to the upward mobility of the poor. Under the current political rules, this attempt usually turns out successful. Regretfully, not well prepared for discussions in this regard, the Davos summit ended up with nothing more than a discouraging announcement that "roads can go a long way in fighting hunger".

此次世界经济论坛高度关注中印这两个最大的发展中国家,头号议题就是"中国与印度的崛起"。论坛首日就专门以"中国的崛起"为题举行了研讨会,中国银行业发展前景、环境保护、农村问题、中国崛起对外部世界的冲击、中印能源需求,等等,无不引发热烈讨论。在闭幕会上,伦敦商学院院长劳拉·泰森演讲的主题仍然是中国和印度。与会人士"言必称中国",堪称本届论坛最大的特色。

China and India, the two largest developing countries, were in the spotlight during the Davos summit and the hottest topic of discussion is "the rise of China and India". A symposium exclusively dedicated to China's emergence was held on the very first day. Topics such as the prospects of China's banking sector, its environmental protection, rural problems, the impact its emergence has on the outside world and the energy demands of China and India all triggered heated discussions. At the closing session, Laura Tyson, Dean of London Business School, delivered a speech on China and India. The participants' obsession with China can easily be called an outstanding feature of this year's forum.

此次世界经济论坛如此高度关注以中印为代表的发展中国家,其背景是近年发展中国家经济增长业绩可观,影响力日增。日前,英国《经济学家》杂志[9]发文声称,2005年新兴市场[10]产出总量占全球比重已经过半;新兴市场出口总量占全球比重从1970年的20%提高到现在的42%;过去5年新兴市场出口增量占全球比重过半;发达经济国家和新兴市场间贸易增速是发达经济国家内部贸易增速的两倍;新兴市场外汇储备占全球2/3;石油消费量占全球47%;过去3年新兴市场平均经济增速超过6%,而发达经济国家仅为2.4%;去年新兴市场GDP总量增加1.6万亿美元,发达经济国家GDP增量仅1.4万亿美元;国际货币基金组织预测,未来 5 年新兴经济体经济增速仍将是发达经济国家的两倍。如果这种相对增长趋势能够维持下去,20 年后新兴经济国家产出将占全球的 2/3。

The highlighting of developing countries, as represented by China and India, during the Davos summit was set against a background of these countries' remarkable economic performance and growing influence in recent years. Not long ago, The Economist magazine stated in an article that in 2005 the combined output of emerging economies rose above half of the global total. Their share of exports has jumped to 42 percent, from 20 percent in 1970. Over the past five years, they have accounted for more than half of the growth in world exports. Developed economies' trade with developing countries is growing twice as fast as their trade with one another. Emerging economies are now sitting on two thirds of the world's foreign exchange reserves and they consume 47 percent of the world's oil. In the past three years, their growth has averaged more than 6 percent, compared with 2.4 percent in rich economies. Last year, their combined GDP grew in current dollar terms by $1.6 trillion, more than the $1.4 trillion increase of developed economies. The IMF forecasts that in the next five years they will roll along twice as fast as developed economies. If this relative pace is sustained, in 20 years' time emerging economies will account for two thirds of global output.

发展中国家经济增长要求有关各国相应做出调整,特别是在全球经济失衡日益加剧的背景下,发达国家与主要发展中国家之间需要改进经济协调。此次世界经济论坛也开宗明义地向与会者提出了这样的思考问题——"全球发展中心转向亚洲,各国面临的挑战与机会"。令人欣慰的是,西方世界的不少有识之士对此趋势给予了积极的评价,劳拉·泰森就认为中国和印度国内消费的增加将带动全球经济的增长。然而,我们也不可忽视与此截然相反的思潮,劳拉·泰森就指出,发达国家人民往往将本地失业问题归咎于全球化,迫使政府采取贸易保护主义政策;她在论坛接触到的美国人,有人视中国发展为威胁,有人对中国满怀恐惧、焦虑和愤怒。部分出于上述原因,中国已经步入国际经贸争端高发期,世贸组织多哈回合谈判[11]也格外艰难。

The economic revival of developing countries requires countries involved to make adjustments accordingly. Especially given escalating imbalances in the global economy, economic coordination between developed countries and major developing countries needs to be improved. At the beginning of the Davos meeting, a thought-provoking topic was presented before all participants: "the shift of gravity to Asia and the challenges and opportunities for the global community". To great comfort, many resourceful persons in the West commented positively on this trend. It is Laura Tyson's belief that increasing domestic consumption in China and India will boost the growth of the world economy. However, opposite views do exist. Tyson pointed out that people in developed countries tend to attribute local unemployment to globalization, urging the government to adopt trade protectionism policies. She noted that some of the Americans she met during the forum viewed China's development as a threat and others were full of fear, concern and anger toward China. Partly for this reason, China has been plunged into an era of frequent international economic and trade disputes. The Doha Round of WTO negotiations will prove to be an uphill battle, too.

其实,经济发展更多的是"双赢"而不是零和博弈[12];发展中国家经济发展给发达国家带来的主要是新的发展空间而不是冲击威胁。在此次论坛上,年会联席主席、哈佛大学校长劳伦斯·萨默斯强调,世界经济不能仅仅依靠美国一台发动机。英国《金融时报》首席评论员马丁·沃尔夫则强调,资本正在流向最富裕的国家,发展中国家是资本净供给者。何况,目前的国际经贸规则对发展中国家极为不公平,在这个经济全球化的时代,这一点无时不在威胁着发展中国家乃至整个世界经济可持续发展的前途,人们不能指望小块繁荣孤岛能够长久安然矗立在浩瀚的贫困海洋之上。坚持多哈回合的"发展导向"并不是给予发展中国家额外的优惠,而是平衡它们分享的全球化收益和承担的调整负担。毕竟,任何"发展"的成果都必须让尽可能广大的社会成员分享,一国之内如此,国际社会也不例外。假如对发展中国家谋求发展的合理需求掉以轻心,全球化进程未必没有可能全面逆转,导致南北两败俱伤[13]。目前,正如加纳贸易与工业部长阿伦·克列梅滕在此次论坛上警告的那样,越来越多的国家怀疑多边贸易体系能否兑现其承诺;印度信心工业公司[14]董事长兼总裁穆克什·阿巴尼更直言,国际社会担心世贸组织进程自身会走向崩溃。

As a matter of fact, economic development is more of a "win-win" situation than a zero-sum game. In the wake of the emergence of developing countries, developed countries have mostly found new room for development rather than being adversely impacted or threatened. Lawrence H. Summers, President of Harvard University and Annual Meeting Co-Chair, emphasized at the forum that the world economy should not depend on the United States as its only engine. Martin Wolf, Chief Economics Commentator for the *Financial Times*, noted that capital is flowing into the richest countries, and the developing countries are actually net capital suppliers. The present international economic and trade rules are extremely unfair to developing countries. In an era of economic globalization, the inequity poses a grave threat to the sustainable economic development of developing countries and the world at large. On the vast ocean of poverty, small, isolated islands will be unable to maintain their prosperity for long. Adherence to the "development orientation" of the Doha Round does not mean granting privileges to developing countries, but striking a balance between their share of benefits from globalization and the burden they have to shoulder. After all, benefits derived from development should be shared by as many people as possible. Both individual countries and the international community should stick to this principle. Insufficient consideration of the reasonable demands of developing countries might lead to a major setback in the globalization process, harming both developing and developed nations. Alan Kyerematen, Minister of Trade, Industry of Ghana, warned in Davos that many countries are increasingly becoming disillusioned about whether the multilateral trading system can deliver on its promises. Mukesh D. Ambani, Chairman and Managing Director of India's Reliance Industries, stated bluntly that the international community is worried about the collapse of the WTO process.

好在主要西方国家代表在此次论坛中表现出了某些积极姿态。欧盟贸易委员曼德尔森和美国贸易代表波特曼一致认为，在此次论坛期间的世贸小型部长级会议上，气氛有所改变，曼德尔森敦促各方抓住机会，尽可能改善气氛，声称他将乐于看到由发展中国家自己实施且有利于发展中国家的农业改革；波特曼则强调，如果多哈回合谈崩，有关各方将满盘皆输，美国支持当前谈判中一切朝向自由化的方面，呼吁各方共同努力。世界贸易组织总干事帕斯卡尔·拉米则敦促有关各方面对现实，欧盟应在开放农产品市场方面做出更大让步，美国应削减其国内农业补贴，瑞士和日本则应同时改革上述两个方面。我们希望多哈回合谈判未来达成的协议能够得到各国的切实遵守。毕竟，世贸组织规则不能得到有效的执行，特别是发达国家不遵守其对世贸组织的承诺，曲解世贸组织规则，或以本国国内法取而代之，在入世以来的贸易争端中，中国对此已经领教得足够多，也足够深重。[15]

However, representatives from leading Western countries showed some positive signs in Davos. Both EU Trade Commissioner Peter Mandelson and US Trade Representative Robert Portman agreed the atmosphere took a turn for the better in a small-scale ministerial meeting during the forum. Mandelson urged all players to capture and use the opportunity to maximize the improved "mood music," claiming that he prefers to see a case made for agricultural reform "on behalf of developing countries by developing countries." Portman cautioned that if the current Doha Round fails, everyone stands to lose. He indicated that the United States supports "all of the liberalizing aspects of the current round" while appealing for the concerted efforts of different players. Pascal Lamy, WTO Director General, called on relevant parties to face up to reality. He urged the EU to move on market access of agricultural produce, the United States to move on domestic subsidies, and Japan and Switzerland to do both. We hope the countries will abide by the agreements reached in future Doha Round negotiations. China has suffered too much and too severely from trade disputes that resulted from failures to follow WTO rules, especially developed countries' breach of their WTO commitments, misinterpretation of WTO rules and replacing WTO rules with domestic laws.

发展中国家经济增长很大程度来自周期性因素或取决于发达国家宏观经济政策；经济增长势头能否保持，存在很大的不确定性。近年推动发展中国家经济增长的周期性因素莫过于大宗初级商品价格屡创新高，但初级产品价格不可能始终上涨，大幅度下跌的阴影日趋浓重。[16] 2000 年下半年以来，发达国家相继大幅度下调利率，低利率一方面激励了资本流向发展中国家，另一方面刺激了发达国家消费，从而拉动了发展中国家的出口。然而，2004 年 6 月以来，美联储发动新一轮加息周期，发达国家利率日益高涨，一方面可能导致国际资本流动方向大规模逆转；另一方面，高利率必然遏制发达国家的负债消费，对发展中国家出口的影响可想而知。

The economic growth of developing countries relies heavily on cyclic factors and the macroeconomic policies of developed countries. It remains uncertain whether their economic growth can be sustained. The prices of bulk primary products soared in recent years, a main cyclic factor powering the economic growth of developing countries. However, the prices will not be able to remain high. In fact, there has been an ever-growing tendency toward price drops. The series of interest rate cuts in developed countries beginning from the second half of 2000 stimulated capital inflow to developing countries while boosting consumption in the developed world, a trend that led to export expansion in developing countries. However, the US Federal Reserve initiated a new round of interest rate hikes in June 2004. The rising interest rates may reverse the direction of global capital flow and rein in credit consumption in developed countries, exerting adverse influence over developing countries' exports.

发展中国家存在竞争与合作双重关系，中印两大发展中国家的这种关系最为显著。[17] 近几年，在国际政治、经济、学术和舆论界，中印比较似乎已经成为一门"显学"[18]，举凡政治、军事、经济、文化各个领域，无不被拿出来评头品足一番。[19] 此次世界经济论坛也对中印两国给予了高度的关注。在西方资本主导的国际传媒中，中印两国几乎已经被渲染成"既生瑜，何生亮"的关系。其影响所至，两国国内舆论也颇受感染[20]，"中国纺织品受限，印度工厂拣便宜日夜加班"，"科尔尼管理咨询公司[21]编制的全球投资者信心排行榜上印度大有赶超中国之势"，诸如此类的新闻总能在我国国内引起关注。我国一些人往往下意识地高估印度的综合国力，进而过度看重中印之间的竞争关系。

The relationship between developing countries is two-pronged, characterized by both competition and cooperation. China-India relations provide a telling example. In recent years, the comparative study of China and India has become a highly charged subject in academia as well as the media, being discussed in political, military, economic, cultural and many other contexts. It is a hot-button topic at the Davos summit as well. In the Western-dominated international media, China and India are usually described as two rival powers. Media in the two countries have proven vulnerable to their influence. Reports that "Indian factories work around the clock to take advantage of the restrictions facing China's textiles" and "India is likely to catch up with China in terms of global investor confidence as shown in a survey made by A. T. Kearney" cause a nationwide stir in China. Some Chinese people unconsciously overvalue India's comprehensive strength, placing too much emphasis on competition between the two countries.

其实，对于海外舆论界的这类比较，我们无须过分认真。首先，由于印度大体沿袭了英国人安排的政治体制，在盎格鲁－萨克逊国家主导国际经济秩序的格局下，在他们进行的中印比较中，中国的任何缺陷都会被成倍放大，而印度的任何成绩也都会被成倍放大，在西方人看来，印度治理良好的企业和杰出企业家数目远远多于中国，他们对印度的金融体系稳定性、股市给予了较高的评价，都说明了这一点。中印两国之间虽然确实在领土、经济等方面存在一些问题，甚至是严重的问题，但中印矛盾在相当程度上是被西方舆论界有意无意放大了。在中印之争中，恰恰是综合国力相对虚弱的印度在殖民地时代培育出了一个"盎格鲁－萨克逊化"的统治精英阶层，他们受到西方舆论界更多的"支持"，实在是理所当然。对此，我们与其过度敏感，不如下工夫从根本上扭转西方对国际舆论的主导权。[22]我们也应当认识到，印度社会各界向我们提出的某些劝诫未尝不符合我国自身的利益（如此次论坛上印度财政部长奇丹巴兰姆要求我国提高消费率）。我们不必过分看重海外媒体渲染的中印竞争，而是需要探询两国良性协作之道。归根结底，同属人口众多的发展中国家，这一共同的基本国情决定了两国可以分享许多国内发展的经验教训，在国际经济、政治事务中也存在众多共同利益，因此存在合作的基础。从能源开发到多边贸易回合谈判，我们也欣慰地看到了两国化竞争为协作的趋势。[23]

We needn't take comparisons made by the international media too seriously. India has largely inherited a political system devised by the British. When China and India are compared in an international economic order dominated by Anglo-Saxon countries, China's defects are usually magnified and so are the successes of India. In the eyes of people from the West, India has many more well-governed enterprises and outstanding entrepreneurs than China does, as evidenced by their high praise for India's financial stability and stock market. It should be admitted that China and India have territorial, economic and other problems, some of which are quite serious, but conflicts between the two countries largely result from intentional or unintentional exaggeration by Western media. As India, whose comprehensive strength is inferior in the China-India rivalry, nurtured a group of Anglo-Saxon bureaucratic elites during its colonial era, it is no wonder that it receives support from the West. Instead of making a fuss about this, China is expected to fundamentally reverse the Western dominance of mainstream international opinion. In fact, some warnings from India are good to China. For example, Indian Finance Minister Palaniappan Chidambaram called on China to increase consumption at the Davos summit. China should remain dispassionate in the face of the much-touted China-India rivalry, and explore ways for the two countries to cooperate amicably. In the final analysis, both being populous developing countries, China and India have much to share with each other in respect to their national economic development and a wide range of common interests in international economic and political affairs.

These common grounds have formed the basis for their cooperation. From energy exploration to trade negotiations, we are glad to see an emerging trend of the two countries turning competition into collaboration.

  经济全球化时代造就了全球化的利益和问题，客观上要求各个国家、社会各界广泛协调，以便解决问题。我们并不奢望世界经济论坛能够直接解决多少问题，但我们有理由期望，通过让来自众多国家或地区的社会各界人士共处一堂讨论问题，世界经济论坛能够有助于推动解决问题。[24]

  Economic globalization has also brought along globalized interests and problems, which call for broad coordination of all countries and all sections of society. We do not expect the World Economic Forum to solve any problems directly, but we have reason to believe that the big gathering of worldwide representatives can make a difference to their solution.

Words and Expressions

年会	annual meeting/conference/session/symposium
势在必行	imperative an obligation; a duty
议题	sub-theme
崛起	emergence
区域	landscape
强劲	robust
预计	project
逆转	setback
收入分配格局	the income distribution pattern
大面积	across-the-board
恶化	deterioration
荣图	rosy landscape
锐减	drastically shrink, plummet
普遍	prevalence
程度	magnitude
扶贫	poverty alleviation/reduction
号称	purport
证明	testament
大幅	by a large margin
附加条件	attach strings to
贫困人群	the impoverished

依靠自我奋斗	pull oneself up by his bootstraps
迁徙	mobility
强势	advantaged
阶层	social strata
曲解	skew
固定	perpetuate
壁垒	barrier
社会分化格局	social division
政治游戏规则	political rules
得逞	turn out successful
研讨会	symposium
高度关注	highlighting
新兴市场	emerging economies or emerging markets
产出总量	combined output
外汇储备	foreign exchange reserve
思考问题	thought-provoking topic
令人欣慰的是	to great comfort
有识之士	resourceful person
贸易保护主义	trade protectionism
艰难的	uphill
多哈回合谈判	the Doha Round of WTO negotiations
双赢	win-win
零和博弈	zero-sum game
发展导向	development orientation
掉以轻心	insufficient consideration of
多边贸易体系	multilateral trading system
兑现	deliver on
直言	state bluntly
总干事	director general
开放农产品市场	market access of agricultural produce
国内农业补贴	domestic subsidies
不遵守	breach
承诺	commitments
周期性因素	cyclic factors
大宗初级商品	bulk primary product
美联储	the US Federal Reserve

遏制	rein
负债消费	credit consumption
分支，支流	prong
学术界	academia
显学	highly charged subject
国际经济秩序	international economic order
精英阶层	elites
敏感	make a fuss
归根结底	in the final analysis
协调	coordination

Notes

1. 世界经济论坛　World Economic Forum（WEF）
   世界经济论坛是一个非官方的国际组织，总部设在瑞士日内瓦。

2. 为期5天的世界经济论坛达沃斯年会于1月29日结束了，围绕"创新——势在必行"主题，针对世界经济、政治面临的重大挑战及其应对之道，来自全球89个国家和地区的2 340名嘉宾们举行了240多场讨论。 The annual meeting of the World Economic Forum at Davos, Switzerland concluded January 29 after five days of vibrant debate around the theme of "the creative imperative." Some 2,340 guests from 89 countries and regions participated in more than 240 discussion sessions on major challenges facing the world economy and politics as well as the solutions to these problems.
   这句话在英译时增译了"vibrant debate"，这就把原文中"围绕'创新——势在必行'主题进行了激烈的辩论"这层意思准确地表达出来了，后面紧接着说：辩论之激烈，来自89个国家和地区的2 340名嘉宾举行了240场讨论会。将汉语拆开翻译，并适当增词，使译文的层次更加分明。

3. 新经济基金会　New Economics Foundation（NEF）
   英国"新经济学基金会"成立于1986年，以研究如何提高人们生活质量为主旨，并为政府提供咨询和建议，迄今在社会福利和地方事务等许多方面的建议得到政府和地方的考虑或采纳。

4. 根据这份研究报告，1990—2001年间，全球人均收入每增长100美元，最贫困人口收入仅增长 60 美分，比上世纪 80 年代的 2.20 美元锐减 73%。According to the report, between 1990 and 2001, for every ＄100 worth of growth in the world's income per person, only ＄0.6 found its target and contributed to reducing poverty for those living on less than a dollar a day—73 percent less than in the 1980s, when ＄2.2 of every ＄100 worth of growth contributed to reducing poverty for those living on less than a dollar a day.

此句中的"100 美元"不是单纯指美元，而是指相当 100 美元的价值或财富，因此翻译时增加了"worth"一词。另外，"最贫困人口"也没有译成"the poorest people"，而是将其译成"those living on less than a dollar a day"。这样，读者就能够更加具体地理解原文所传达的意思。

5. 问题的严重性不仅在于贫困的普遍和程度，更在于扶贫力度削弱，以及贫困人口向上流动机会减少。就国内扶贫而言，即使在号称发展中国家经济成功模范的亚洲，上世纪 80 至 90 年代，国民收入增量中用于扶贫的比例也从 10.2% 锐减到了 2.9%。在国际扶贫方面，上世纪 90 年代以来，发达国家几乎都大幅削减了其国际官方援助，对剩余的官方援助也增加了许多附加条件。

此段原文中连续出现了表示"减少"的词，译文使用了 slackened poverty alleviation efforts、narrowed opportunities、plummeted、reduced 等不同的词汇。用词的多变化可以使译文不至于呆板和生硬。

6. 授人以鱼，不如授人以渔。Teaching how to fish is better than giving fish.

这句古话的出处不明，有的说是老子说的，但没有查到。但翻译这种成语一类的句子，一定要先弄懂句子的内在含义，否则读者无法理解。这个句子的含义非常明确，译法也很多，列在下面，供参考。

① Giving a man fish will keep him starving today, but teaching a man how to fish will keep him from starving for a lifetime.

② Give a man a fish and you will feed him for a day. Teach him how to fish and you will feed him for a lifetime.

③ Give me a fish and I will eat today. Teach me to fish and I will eat for a lifetime。

7. 要减少贫困，最重要的不是直接扶助，而是向贫困人口、贫困阶层、贫困地区提供依靠自我奋斗向上流动的机会。What is most important to poverty alleviation is not direct assistance but affording the impoverished with opportunities to pull themselves up by their bootstraps.

"贫困人口、贫困阶层、贫困地区"实际上指的就是"贫困的人们"，汉语经常采用这种的方法来表示强调，译成英语时可考虑将有些不必要的部分省略。

8. 遗憾的是，此次论坛对此讨论不足，最终也只能感叹一番"反饥饿斗争路漫漫"了事。Regretfully, not well prepared for discussions in this regard, the Davos summit ended up with nothing more than a discouraging announcement that "roads can go a long way in fighting

hunger"。

"讨论不足"并没有译成"not well discussed",而是译成"not well prepared for discussions in this regard"。这样,原文的意思表达得更加清楚,因为如果说"not well discussed",读者可能不太容易理解,而"not well prepared for discussions in this regard"就表明此次论坛的重点并没有放在这些方面,所以讨论自然就不可能充分,也就更不可能解决实际问题了。另外,"感叹一番……了事"并没有直译成"end up . . . with a sigh"。这里的"感叹"其实只是表示遗憾的意思,最好是意译,所以译文为"... ended up with nothing more than a discouraging announcement that . . . ",准确而自然。

9 《经济学家》杂志 The Economist magazine(也称《经济学人》杂志)

10 这里的"新兴市场"实际上就是"新兴经济国家",即"emerging economies",也可以译成"emerging markets"。
关于新兴经济体,目前还没有公认的定义。一些国家与其叫新兴经济体,不如叫复兴经济体,因为它们其实是东山再起。

11 世贸组织多哈回合谈判 the Doha Round of WTO negotiations
2001年11月,在卡塔尔首都多哈举行的世贸组织第四次部长级会议启动了新一轮多边贸易谈判。新启动的多边贸易谈判又称"多哈发展议程",或简称"多哈回合"。

12 零和博弈 a zero-sum game
即"彼之所得必为我之所失,得失相加只能得零"、"竞争者此长彼消,胜者之所得加败者之所失等于零"。所谓零和,是博弈论里的一个概念,意思是双方博弈,一方得益必然意味着另一方吃亏,一方得益多少,另一方就吃亏多少。之所以称为"零和",是因为将胜负双方的"得"与"失"相加,总数为零。在零和博弈中,双方是没有合作机会的。
"零和游戏"就是:游戏者有输有赢,游戏参与各方的得失总和为零。在一般情况下,玩家中总有一个赢,一个输,如果获胜算为1分,而输为-1分,那么这2人得分之和就是:$1 + (-1) = 0$。
零和博弈属于非合作博弈,是指博弈中甲方的收益,必然是乙方的损失,即各博弈方得益之和为零。在零和博弈中各博弈方决策时都以自己的最大利益为目标,结果是既无法实现集体的最大利益,也无法实现个体的最大利益。除非在各博弈方中存在可信性的承诺或可执行的惩罚作保证,否则各博弈方中难以存在合作。

13 "导致南北两败俱伤"中的"南北"就是指发展中国家和发达国家。当今世界上的200多个国家和地区,根据它们的生产力发展水平和贫富程度,被分为发达国家和发展中国家两类。因为发展中国家大多在南半球,所以通常被称为"南方";发达国家大多在北半球,通常被称为"北方"。翻译时可直译成"developing and developed nations"。

14 印度信心工业公司 Reliance Group
The Reliance Group, founded in 1932 – 2002, is India's largest private sector enterprise, with businesses in the energy and materials value chain.

15. 毕竟，世贸组织规则不能得到有效的执行，特别是发达国家不遵守其对世贸组织的承诺，曲解世贸组织规则，或以本国国内法取而代之，在入世以来的贸易争端中，中国对此已经领教得足够多，也足够深重。China has suffered too much and too severely from trade disputes that resulted from failures to follow WTO rules, especially developed countries' breach of their WTO commitments, misinterpretation of WTO rules and replacing WTO rules with domestic laws.

这句汉语中的"在入世以来的贸易争端中"如果直译成英语的状语，则"已经领教得足够多，也足够深重"就很难准确地表达，因为汉语的"领教"在这里是讽刺的意义，即"经历过"的意思，等于英语的"have experienced of; encounter"。因此，将"争端"译成"领教"的宾语，后面再用定语从句说明造成这些"争端"的直接原因，更加符合逻辑，表意更加明确，读者也更容易理解。请看例句："同时，在和平崛起进程中，中国又要以自己为主，来关注和解决自己的问题。"这里的"自己的问题"到底指什么问题呢？所以最好不要直译成："At the same time, in the course of its peaceful rise, China must rely on itself to pay attention to and resolve its own problems.", 而应该译成："At the same time, China must address itself to and deal with problems arising in her peaceful rise."。

16. 近年推动发展中国家经济增长的周期性因素莫过于大宗初级商品价格屡创新高，但初级产品价格不可能始终上涨，大幅度下跌的阴影日趋浓重。The prices of bulk primary products soared in recent years, a main cyclic factor powering the economic growth of developing countries. However, the prices will not be able to remain high. In fact, there has been an ever-growing tendency toward price drops.

"创新高"还可以译成"set (make, establish) a new record, chalk up a record, top the highest record in history"或者"to be an all-time high", 但这里是"屡创新高", 所以将其译成"soar", 表示价格高涨，即"to ascend suddenly above the normal or usual level"（突然上升到超过正常或平常的水平），这样更加形象自然。另外，"阴影日趋浓重"是比喻，所以意译成"there has been an ever-growing tendency toward price drops", 表示价格下跌的趋势非常明显。

17. 发展中国家存在竞争与合作双重关系，中印两大发展中国家的这种关系最为显著。The relationship between developing countries is two-pronged, characterized by both competition and cooperation. China-India relations provide a telling example.

本句中的"双重关系"其实就是表示"发展中国家之间既合作又相互竞争", 可以将"关系"看成是一个范畴词，这与下文中"'既生瑜, 何生亮'的关系"中的"关系"相同，翻译时不一定译出来。如"在西方资本主导的国际传媒中，中印两国几乎已经被渲染成'既生瑜，何生亮'的关系"一句就译成了"In the Western-dominated international media, China and India are usually described as two rival powers."。因此，这句话也可以译成"While competing against each other, developing countries also associate for their own benefit in the development."。

18 "显学"

"显学"通常是指与现实联系密切,引起社会广泛关注,或者在思想学术界占统治地位的学说。在先秦思想史中特指儒家、墨家这两种学说。有时也指在整个中国思想史上占重要地位的儒、道、佛三家。显学一词最早出于《韩非子·显学篇》:"世之显学,儒、墨也。儒之所至,孔丘也。墨之所至,墨翟也。"

这里根据意思将其译成"highly charged subject",意指引起社会广泛关注的话题。

19 举凡政治、军事、经济、文化各个领域,无不被拿出来评头品足一番。

"举凡"就是"凡是"的意思,也可以译成"from...to..."或"all...such as"的句型,这里直接译成"being discussed in political, military, economic, cultural and many other contexts"也同样表达了"在各个领域"这层意思。"评头品足"在这里既不是"评论他人外表"(make frivolous remarks about sb's appearance)的意思,也不是"挑剔"(find fault with; be overcritical)的意思,而是"被广泛讨论"之意,所以译成"being discussed"。

20 "既生瑜,何生亮"表示有我无他的竞争关系,所以不宜直译,而应该将两国成为竞争对手这层意思译出。"两国国内舆论也颇受感染"中的"感染"表示"易诱惑的,易受影响的,易于屈服的(如受到劝说或诱惑)",即"liable to succumb, as to persuasion or temptation"之意,所以译成"vulnerable to their influence"。

21 科尔尼管理咨询公司　A. T. Kearney

科尔尼公司作为一家全球领先、针对企业提供高价值管理咨询服务的公司,以其高质量的服务、可实施的成果及创新精神而闻名。

22 对此,我们与其过度敏感,不如下工夫从根本上扭转西方对国际舆论的主导权。

Instead of making a fuss about this, China is expected to fundamentally reverse the Western dominance of mainstream international opinion.

本句中的"敏感"不要直接译成"oversensitive",因为这里不是"对外界事物反应很快"的意思,而是指"无须大惊小怪"(no need to be in a state of excessive and unwarranted concern over an unimportant matter),所以译成"make a fuss"非常贴切。下文中的"不必过分看重"也是这个意思,所以译成"China should remain dispassionate in the face of the much-touted China-India rivalry"。

23 从能源开发到多边贸易回合谈判,我们也欣慰地看到了两国化竞争为协作的趋势。

From energy exploration to trade negotiations, we are glad to see an emerging trend of two countries turning competition into collaboration.

句中"欣慰地"一词不太容易处理,如果直接译成"We feel relieved/gratified"好像与上文中的"Instead of making a fuss"和"remain dispassionate"有些不协

为汉语"欣慰"表示喜欢和安心，既然无须大惊小怪，也就没有什么心不心安的问题了，所以要么将"喜欢"的意思译出，即"we are glad to see ..."，要么干脆译成"there is an emerging trend ..."。

24 我们并不奢望世界经济论坛能够直接解决多少问题，但我们有理由期望，通过让来自众多国家或地区的社会各界人士共处一堂讨论问题，世界经济论坛能够有助于推动解决问题。

We do not expect the World Economic Forum to solve any problems directly, but we have reason to believe that the big gathering of worldwide representatives can make a difference to their solution.

最后一句语中的"能够有助于推动解决问题"并没有直接译成"help solve those problems"，而是译成"make a difference to their solution"，这样就避免了重复，而且非常地道、自然和准确。

他山之石

原文 1：

中美两国互为重要贸易伙伴，中美经贸关系的顺利发展符合两国人民的根本利益，也有利于中美关系的健康发展。我们希望美方能够从两国关系的大局出发，进一步促进中美经贸关系在良好、健康的环境中发展。

原译文：

...na and the US are important trading partners for each other. The smooth development of ...d trade relations serve the fundamental interests of the two peoples and the healthy ... the bilateral ties. We hope that the US can proceed from the overall interests of the ...her promote the development of economic and trade relations in a sound and

...翻译汉语中的"符合"和"有利"，比分别用两个英语单词翻...为"serve"一词有"contribute or conduce to"的意思，如...to increase the popularity of their products."。

...系的大局出发"译成英语时最好不要译成一个分句，因为..."进一步……"，"从……大局出发"只不过是某种做事的方...果完全按汉语的句式翻译，一来"proceed"的动作意义不够明确，二来"proceed"和"promote"之间用逗号隔开也不符合英语的语法习惯。所以，可以考虑将"从……大局出发"直接译成英语的方式状语，或者用一个有实际意义的词替代"proceed"，然后将后面的句子译成目的状语从句。

改译：

China and the US are important trading partners for each other. The smooth development of economic and trade relations serve the fundamental interests of the two peoples and the healthy development of the bilateral ties. We hope that the US stress itself to further promoting the development of economic and trade relations in a sound and healthy environment by taking the overall interests of the bilateral ties into account.

原文 2：

保护知识产权是中国的国家战略。保护知识产权是中国扩大开放、改善投资环境和提高自主创新能力的需要。中国政府在保护知识产权方面态度是明确的，决心是坚定的，行动是积极的，成效也是有目共睹的。我们今后将继续健全有关法律体系，加大执法力度，严厉打击各种侵权行为，依法保护各国知识产权权利人在华合法权益。

原译文：

It is China's national strategy to protect IPR (Intellectual Property Rights). It's required by the need for China to open wider to the outside world, to improve the investment environment and raise the capacity for independent innovation. The Chinese Government has a clear-cut position and firm determination on IPR protection. We have taken active actions with achievements witnessed by all. We will continue to improve the legal system, intensify law enforcement and strike against various infringements so as to protect the lawful rights and interests of IPR owners.

点评：

① 英译的第一个"it"引导的是主语从句，第二个"it"明显是指"保护知识产权"，因此翻译时最好是把这个主语译出来。如果用"it"，英语表达得不够清楚。
② "中国政府在保护知识产权方面态度是明确的，决心是坚定的，行动是积极的，成效也是有目共睹的。"这句汉语属于递进式的排比句，这种用法增强了语势，强烈地表达出中国政府为保护知识产权所做的一切努力。英译将这句话分成两句，虽然意思准确无误，但语势却荡然无存。另外，虽然这句话没有表明明确的时间，但实际上已经隐含了中国政府长期以来就是这样做的这层意思，所以英译时最好在时态或时间上有所变化。
③ 最后一句属于汉语的连动式，主句应该是"保护各国知识产权权利人在华合法权益"，因此翻译时也可以将这句中的动词译成整个句子的谓语，其他译成方式状语。

改译：

It is China's national strategy to protect IPR (Intellectual Property Rights) and that is required by the need for China to open wider to the outside world, to improve the investment environment and raise the capacity for independent innovation. For a long time has the Chinese Government been taking a clear-cut position and firm determination on IPR protection, and great results have been achieved through its active actions and witnessed by all. We will keep on protecting the lawful rights and interests of IPR owners in the future by improving the legal system, intensifying law enforcement and striking against various infringements.

学生译作分析

原文：

在经济全球化趋势深入发展的情况下，主张加强南南合作和南北对话，呼吁世界贸易组织重启"多哈回合"谈判，推动全球经济均衡、协调和可持续发展，实现各国共享成果、普遍发展、共同繁荣。

学生原译文：

Faced with the growing trend of economic globalization, we call for enhancing South-South cooperation and North-South dialogue and call on the World Trade Organization to resume the Doha Round of negotiations to promote balanced, coordinated and sustainable development of the global economy to enable all countries to share its benefits and realize common development and prosperity.

分析：

(1) 汉语"经济全球化趋势深入发展"中的"趋势"一词可以看成是范畴词，不一定非要翻译成英语中的"trend"或者"tendency"，就像"在……的情况下"不一定非要译成"under the condition"一样，因为这里的意思是"随着全球化深入发展"，这种发展本来就是一种趋势。

(2) 汉语"加强"译成英语"enhancing"显得非常抽象，因为后面跟的是两个动作名词"cooperation"和"dialogue"，"enhance cooperation"还勉强，但"enhance dialogue"就不太妥当。因此，可以考虑采用别的方法将意思译出。

(3) 汉语"推动"究竟是谁的动作，是中国政府所做出的努力还是"主张"和"呼吁"的结果或目的呢？原译文用英语的不定式将其译成表目的的状语，后面则省译"实现",用另一个不定式将整个句子连接起来。译成表结果的分句行吗?哪个更加准确?

(4) 译文中"share its benefits"中的"its"指代不明,究竟是指"多哈回合谈判"还是指"各个国家",因此改成"their"更好。

参考译文:

With the acceleration of economic globalization, China calls for more South-South cooperation and a better North-South dialogue and calls on the World Trade Organization to resume the Doha Round of negotiations, which will lead to balanced, coordinated and sustainable development of the global economy to enable all countries to share their benefits and realize common development and prosperity.

翻译技巧介绍

词语的选择

由于英语不是母语的缘故,中国学生在将汉语原文翻译成英语时,往往容易拘泥于原文中的词语,即:看到汉语的某个词,立即想出对应的英语同义词。而一旦找不到相对应的词,他们就会去查某本汉英词典或者文曲星之类的电子词典,直到找到对应的词语。这样做的结果是:英语译文的用词和句式基本上跟汉语原文相同。这样一来,译文要么读起来像"Chinese English",遣词造句毫无英语的味道;要么词不达意,老外根本无法读懂。例如:

原文:

文化产业是21世纪具有战略意义的**黄金产业**,但由于中国文化产业起步较晚,仍然处于**散乱弱小**的初级发展阶段,企业的规模与国际巨头相比差距甚大。

译文:

The **culture industry** is a **golden industry** with strategic significance in the 21st century. Since China's culture industry started up very late, it is still in a **weak and scattered** stage of elementary development, and its companies lag far behind foreign media giants in terms of scale.

对比原文和译文,我们不难发现,译者在翻译原文中的黑体字时,全部采用了对应的英语词语。但是,这些形式上对应的词语是否就能准确表达原文词语的意义呢?

(1) 首先,"文化产业"的定义究竟是什么?直到现在,我国对"文化产业"还没有形成统一的定义。而联合国教科文组织对文化产业的定义是:按照工业标准,生产、再生产、储存及分配文化产品和服务的一系列活动。那么，原文中的"文化产业"是否就能直接译成"culture industry"呢？也就是说，如果将其译成"culture industry"，英语读者是否能够明白它的含义呢？

Wikipedia 对"culture industry"的解释是："The term culture industry was coined by Theodor Adorno (1903 – 1969) and Max Horkheimer (1895 – 1973). They argued that popular culture is like a factory producing standardized cultural goods to manipulate the masses into passivity; the easy pleasures available through consumption of popular culture make people docile and content, no matter how difficult their economic circumstances."。由此看来，"culture industry"并不是给一个产业所下的定义，而是对"popular culture"的一种比喻。因此，如果直接将汉语原文中的"文化产业"翻译成"culture industry"，就可能无法使英语读者正确理解原文的含义。那么，"文化产业"究竟翻译成什么更加合适呢？根据上下文，这句话出自一篇关于中国维护知识产权、打击音像盗版的文章。由于音像制品在我国属于大众传媒，因此可以考虑将这里的"文化产业"翻译成"entertainment industry"。Wikipedia 对"entertainment industry"的解释是："The entertainment industry (much of which is informally known as show business or show biz) consists of a large number of sub-industries devoted to entertainment. However, the term is often used in the mass media to describe the mass media companies that control the distribution and manufacture of mass media entertainment."。英语读者不一定能理解"culture industry"，但一定能理解"entertainment industry"。

（2）"黄金产业"不能直接译成"golden industry"。虽然英语"golden"一词有"precious"、"marked by peace, prosperity"和"suggestive of gold, as in richness or splendor"的意思，也有"a golden era"（全盛时期）、"a golden opportunity"（千载难逢的机会）、"a golden generation"（前途光明的一代）的用法，但却没有汉语"黄金产业"所表达的"能带来巨大财富"的意思。因此，这里还是用英语的"cash cow/money spinner — a project that generates a continuous flow of money"（赚大钱的事业）更加合适。

（3）原文中的"散乱弱小"并不是"weak and scattered"的意思，而是指这个行业还"不成规模"，而且"不够强大"，也就是说仍有"做大做强"的潜力，因此译成"it remains uncompetitive in its infancy"。

参考译文：

As a cash cow in the 21st century, China's entertainment industry started up very late. It still remains uncompetitive in its infancy, and its companies lag far behind foreign media giants in terms of scale.

通过上面这个翻译句子的分析可以看出，很多译者总觉得汉语是自己的母语，理解是没有问题的，但实际上真正读懂读透原文也不是一件容易的事情。只要真正读懂原文，正确理解原文词语的含义，并尽量用符合英语表达习惯的词句来翻译，就能使译文表意清楚准确。

以下再举几个例子来加以说明。

原文1：

最近河南安阳火柴厂向铁道部发出**紧急报告**：我厂是全国最大的火柴生产厂家，担负着河南全省民用火柴供应的任务。由于木材短缺，现已濒临停产。**情况的确严重**。该厂近几个月产量大幅度下降，以至造成**火柴市场紧张**，城市黑市价格高出正常售价四倍多，农村、山区百姓出现**吃饭点灯难现象**。

译文1：

Recently the Anyang Match Factory of Henan Province sent an **urgent report** to the Ministry of Railroad: Our factory is the biggest match producing factory in the country, and is responsible for the task of supplying civil matches for the whole province. Because of shortage of timber, the factory is facing a closedown. **The situation is indeed serious.** Over the last few months, production dropped so sharply that it has caused **market tense.** In cities, the price of matches is four times its normal one, and in the countryside, there is even **the phenomenon of people's having difficulties in eating and lighting**.

译文2：

The Anyang Match Factory, a major match producer for domestic use in Henan Province and the biggest one in the country, recently sent **an SOS** to the Ministry of Railways, saying that the factory was running short of timber. **The message is not a false alarm.** The drastic cutbacks in the output of the factory have **caused an acute shortage of matches in the market** over the last few months. In the cities, a box of matches is now selling at four times its normal price on the black market; in the countryside, people **do not even have matches to light their cooking stoves and their oil lamps**.

原文2：

中国**具备着**在一个较长时期保持经济快速增长的潜力和条件：因为中国拥有巨大的**市场**需求，居民储蓄率**保持**较高水平，拥有丰富且**素质不断提高的**劳动力资源，改革开放将**增强**经济发展的内在活力。中国将坚持以人为本、全面协调的可持续发展的科学发展观，**统筹**城乡发展，统筹区域发展，统筹经济社会发展，统筹人与自然和谐发展，统筹国内发展和对外开放，**切实把经济社会发展转入**科学发展的轨道。

译文1：

China **has maintained** the potential and conditions of a rapid economic growth for a fairly long period: China has a huge market demand, and its savings rate **remained** at a high level. China also has rich and **constantly improved quality** of the labor resources, and reform and opening up will **enhance** the inherent vitality of economic development. China will adhere to people-centered, comprehensive, coordinated and sustainable development of the scientific development concept, **make overall planning for** urban and rural development, regional development, economic and social development, the harmonious development of man and nature, **coordinate** domestic development and opening to the outside world, and **effectively switch** economic and social development onto the track of scientific development.

译文 2:

China **has** the potential and conditions to maintain fast economic growth for a fairly long period in that China has huge market demand, **a relatively high residents' saving rate**, abundant labor resources **with ever-increasing quality**, and reform and opening-up will **invigorate** the inherent vitality of its economic development. China will uphold the scientific concept of development featuring people-oriented, comprehensive, harmonious and sustainable development, and **strike a proper balance between** urban and rural development, development among different regions, economic and social development, development of man and nature, and domestic development and opening up to the outside world, **earnestly gearing** economic and social progress onto a track of scientific development.

原文 3:

农村发展滞后和城乡**二元结构**，是制约中国现代化建设的**难点**。中国将**实行**工业**反哺**农业、城市支援农村、对农村和农民"**多予少取放活**"的方针，加快建立**统筹城乡发展**的体制机制，推进农村综合改革，**建设**现代农业，**加强**农村基础设施建设，**加快**农村社会事业发展，**促进**农业不断增效、农村**加快**发展、农民**持续增收**。

译文 1:

Lagging rural development and **urban-rural dual structure** is the **difficulty/sticking point** to restrain China's modernization drive. China will **implement** the policy of industry **nurturing** agriculture and cities supporting the countryside, the rural areas and farmers, "**giving more to the less**" so as to speed up the establishment of **an institutional mechanism to coordinate urban and rural development**, **promote** rural reform and modern agriculture, **strengthen the building** of rural infrastructure, **accelerate** the development of social undertakings in rural areas, **promote** the development of agriculture continued to **improve** efficiency, and **speed up** the development of rural areas to sustain increase in the income of peasants.

译文 2:

The lagging-behind rural development and **urban-rural dual economic structure are what impede** China's modernization drive. By **adopting** the policy of industry **back-feeding** agriculture, urban areas supporting rural areas and **giving more to**, **taking less from and allowing more flexibility** for the rural areas and farmers, China will **expedite** the building of **systems and mechanisms for balanced urban-rural development**, **promote** comprehensive rural reform,

develop modern agriculture, **reinforce** rural infrastructure so as to **drive** rural social undertakings, **enhance** agricultural efficiency and rural development and **boost** farmers' income.

上面的例句告诉我们，在将汉语译成英语时，一定要先理解汉语词语的意思，认真琢磨其内在的含义，真正理解之后，再用符合英语的词语或句子将意思表达出来，不仅要让英语读者能够理解，还要尽量让他们读起来感觉符合他们的习惯表达方式。

课堂翻译训练

1. 我们认为，中非之间有着良好的团结与合作传统，长期以来真诚相待、休戚与共；中非友谊经受住了时间和国际风云变幻的考验，历久弥坚，深入人心。
2. 中国人民生活仅在总体上达到小康水平。中国人民总体上刚刚解决温饱问题。居民收入和消费水平总体上还较低。
3. 中国将继续促进国际收支基本平衡，高度重视贸易顺差问题，不断扩大进口，努力减少贸易顺差，促进进出口基本平衡。
4. 中国对某些进口产品的要求偏低，一些二流甚至三流产品进入了国内市场，有很多还是被淘汰了的产品。随着经济的发展，中国逐渐跟国际接轨后，中国市场出现了很多替代产品，其品质和售后服务等并不亚于洋品牌。
5. 贫富差距不只是在中国，是在任何国家都存在的现象，既然贫富差距目前还不可改变，那么提高中低收入者的收入，让他们有能力消费，显然是一种比较好的做法。
6. 如果听任跨国公司的恶意并购自由发展，中国民族工业的自主品牌和创新能力将逐步消失，国内龙头企业的核心部分、关键技术和高附加值就可能完全被跨国公司所控制。如果大量利润和社会财富的控制权掌握在跨国公司手里，尽管 GDP 总量很大，而国家的利益却受到损害，广大人民也得不到实惠。
7. 20 年前黄金价格创下 800 美元天价的主要原因是美元贬值和美国经济滞胀，同时还伴随着其他国家盯住美元的固定汇率制解体。目前中国汇率改革刚刚开始，黄金价格的敏感变动也在情理之中。
8. 2006 年中国两次成品油价格上调使消费者的用车成本继续上升，奇瑞又提出的"给最省油的车以最省钱的价格"的理念来迎合当下消费者的胃口，使得奇瑞又在今年的中国汽车销售市场上取得了不俗的成绩。
9. 经贸利益是构筑中欧关系基础的重要因素。在贸易领域，2004 年，中欧贸易额已达 1 773 亿美元，占当年中国外贸总额的 15.4%，是 1975 年双方建交时的 74 倍；2005 年又猛增 22.6%，达 2 173 亿美元。2006 年 1—4 月，中欧贸易额达 786 亿美元，同比增长 20.5%。

欧盟是中国第一大贸易伙伴和累计最大的技术引进来源地，中国则是欧盟第二大贸易伙伴。

10. 中国应积极参与 WTO 新一轮农业谈判，建立能够约束发达国家农业补贴的新规则和新机制，形成公平竞争的国际农产品贸易环境。

课后练习

将下列短文译成英语，注意运用本单元所学的翻译技巧。

1.

你一口气提出了三个问题，实际上涉及到了中美贸易的方方面面。美国商务部长埃文斯目前正在中国访问，除了商务部的官员与他双边会谈外，温家宝总理也将予以会见。此访将有助于双方进一步就中美贸易中各方面的问题进行沟通，广泛交换意见，有助于增进双方的理解。

中美经贸是互惠互利、互补有无的。总的来说，两国贸易发展很快，情况是好的。2002年双方贸易额达到 971.8 亿美元，增长幅度较大。至于双方在一些问题上的不同看法，如贸易逆差问题，中方官员已多次向美方介绍了中方的观点。事实上，美方的逆差并没有那么大，双方对贸易额存在不同的统计方法。同时，我们还应该从历史的角度来看待这个问题，从 1972 年起，美国连续 21 年对中国都保持顺差，中国是逆差，中国只是在 1993 年以后才出现顺差，而且这种顺差也不是像美方有些人讲的那么大。中国的出口大多是美国不再生产的产品，所以美国民众从进口中国产品中也获得了很多好处。此外，中国对美贸易一半以上是由外资企业完成的，这就包括了许多美国或中美合资企业。中国愿意进一步增加从美国的进口，但我们也希望美国减少或者取消对中国出口的限制。

关于中国开放的速度问题，中国在加入世界贸易组织后严格按照中国所承诺的时间表履行了各项承诺，中方履约的态度是非常真诚的。

中方要发出的信息同样十分清楚：中国的市场是开放的，中国愿意进一步扩大从美国的进口，进一步发展同美国的经贸关系，中方愿意和美方共同努力，使中美关系在良好、健康的环境下发展。

2.

品牌常被认为是西方广告业发展的产物，然而，最早的"品牌"可追溯到中国和埃及的早期文明。数千年前中国制造的陶器上面就有陶器艺人留下的符号或印记，古埃及的壁画上也有身上印有标记的牲畜，这些可能就是历史上最初的"品牌"。

时过境迁，如今美国人有"卡迪拉克"，日本人有"丰田"，德国人有"奔驰"，他们都以自己拥有的优质名牌而骄傲。中国的民族品牌与世界级品牌相比相形失色，这就是我们不可否认、必须面对的现实。随着品牌全球化的到来，国际竞争国内化，洋品牌不断向中国的市场发起攻击。在这种情况下，我们必须回答的一个问题便是：中国品牌如何才能迎战洋品牌呢？

我国的许多企业一心只想抢滩国际市场，只顾迈向大都市，看似风光无限，其实很不明智。我们应该看到，中国已成为全球最大的开发市场，中国有13亿人口，占世界人口的20%，消费支出的增长速度比任何一个发达国家都快。我国的本土市场才是民族品牌发展的真正机会，尤其是拥有9亿人口的农村市场。也正因为如此，许多国外强势品牌都在千方百计围绕中国农村市场大做文章。

品质是品牌的生命，消费者总是以良好质量的产品为选择对象。中国企业的产品质量忽上忽下，国人难以建立信心，严重影响了品牌的塑造。因此，对于立志迎战洋品牌的民族品牌来说，当务之急就是提升自己的产品品质。企业必须清楚地认识到，产品1%的缺陷，对于买到产品的消费者来说，就是100%的损失。只有创造出超越洋品牌的产品品质，民族品牌才能在竞争中立于不败之地。

Unit 15

佳译赏析

广东玩具业：召回事件不是滑铁卢[1]
Back from the Brink

"产品召回年年都有，没想到今年这么厉害，'中国制造'受伤害很大。"谈及那场始料未及却又来势凶猛的产品召回事件，广东省东莞龙昌国际控股有限公司（Lung Cheong International Holdings Limited）董事总经理（Managing Director）梁钟铭（C. M. Leung）心情很是沉重[2]。

"We have recalls every year, but none can compare with this year," said C. M. Leung, Managing Director of Lung Cheong International Holdings Ltd.（Lung Cheong Holdings）, depressed by the dark clouds caused by the unexpected massive worldwide recalls of Chinese toys. "Made-in-China products have been deeply hurt." he said.

2007 年 9 月前后[3]，全球最大玩具企业美国美泰公司[4]在一个多月的时间内，连续三次召回共 2 100 多万件由中国企业代为加工制造的玩具产品。可后来美泰承认，这些产品中除了一小部分是中方原因（玩具涂料铅超标）外，大部分是由于美泰公司的产品设计出了问题，跟中方制造公司没任何关系[5]。然而，最终受损失的却是中方。

From August to the beginning of September this year, the largest toy company in the world—US-based Mattel, Inc.—issued three recalls of over 21 million toys produced by Chinese manufacturers in just one month. Later, Mattel admitted that the biggest contributor to the recalls was flawed design aspects of the products and that this wasn't the fault of the Chinese manufacturers. While lead paint recalls made up a sizeable proportion of the tainted toys, defectively designed toys were the larger proportion. However, the Chinese manufacturers suffered heavy losses.

2007年8月11日,美泰公司首次召回96万7千件涂料铅超标塑料玩具后的第9天,受牵连的中方公司[6]——广东省佛山市利达玩具有限公司副董事长张树鸿自杀。这个在当地有着良好声誉的企业立即陷入破产的边缘,2 500名员工也随之被遣散。事实上,美泰公司80%~90%的产品都来自中国,出事前,利达与美泰已愉快合作了15年,一直因高质高效得到美泰的好评和信任。

On August 11, nine days after Mattel's first recall of 967,000 plastic toys containing lead paint, Zhang Shuhong, Vice Chairman of Lee Der Industrial based in Foshan City, Guangdong Province, where the toys were manufactured, committed suicide. The company had enjoyed a good reputation around the city, but quickly was on the verge of bankruptcy, and 2,500 employees were laid off after the recall. Around 80 to 90 percent of Mattel products are manufactured in China. Mattel and Lee Der had cooperated over the last 15 years without any major difficulties. Lee Der had won the trust of the US partner because of its efficiency and the high quality of its products.

坏事变好事
A blessing in disguise

根据广东省海关提供的数据,受美泰玩具"召回"事件的影响,2007年9月,广东全省出口玩具7.1亿美元,比上个月下滑近578万美元,出现年内首次环比负增长[7]。此外,广东省对于欧盟的玩具出口增幅当月也出现了明显的放缓趋势。

Statistics from the Guangdong Customs Bureau show that in September, from the impact of the recalls, Guangdong toy manufacturers exported $710 million worth of toys, $5.78 million less than the month before. It was the first negative growth for Guangdong toy makers this year. Growth of Guangdong toy exports to the European Union also declined in September.

2007年9月21日,美泰公司全球业务的执行副总裁托马斯·狄鲍斯基最终在北京向中国道歉,公开承认召回的绝大多数产品是由于美泰公司在设计上的失误造成的,并表示愿为玩具召回事件负全面责任。狄鲍斯基的讲话虽然在一定程度上减轻了中国玩具制造商的压力,但造成的损失却无法挽回。[8]

On September 21, Mattel's executive vice-president of global operations, Thomas Debrowski, issued an apology in Beijing about the recall of the defectively designed toys, and said Mattel was willing to shoulder full responsibility for the recall of those toys. Debrowski's remarks somewhat lifted the burden of responsibility on China's toy manufacturers, but the damage had already been done.

从最新的事实和统计数据来看,广东玩具业已逐步走出产品召回事件的阴影,产品出口也随之出现了回升。据广东省黄埔海关最新公布的统计数据,受"玩具召回事件"影响,9月份出口受到了短暂影响,增幅下降到5.4%,10月份出口增幅即回升至27.6%。

Latest statistics indicate that Guangdong's toy industry has gradually shrugged off the negative impacts from the recalls and that exports are picking up again. Guangdong's toy exports in October grew 27.6 percent year on year; against a 5.4-percent increase in September following the recalls, according to the latest statistics from the Huangpu Customs.

但是,在广东省公平贸易局局长陈立鹏看来,"这次事件已严重损害了中国企业的声誉,令它们蒙受了很大的经济损失。一个简单的道歉是绝对不能补偿这些损失的。"为此,陈立鹏表示,他正在就此接洽中美律师,愿意帮助中国企业跨国起诉美泰。

Chen Lipeng, Director of the Guangdong Fair Trade Bureau, was discontent about Mattel's apology. "The incident has deeply hurt the reputation of Chinese companies and caused them huge economic losses," he said. "A simple apology won't help repair all the damages." Chen stated that he was in talks with both Chinese and American lawyers and was willing to help Chinese companies launch a transnational lawsuit against Mattel.

然而,业界目前关心的并不是要向美泰公司讨回公道,更多的是考虑自己以后的生存处境。据梁钟铭总经理介绍,在这次产品召回事件中,受冲击最厉害的大多是那些以代加工为主要业务的玩具企业,它们的共同特点是:成本低、利润薄、抗风险能力差。

However, the most pressing task for Guangdong's toy makers is not finding justice, but how to survive in the future. Leung said that contract original design manufacturers were hit hardest during the recalls. These contractors share common features: low cost, low profit, and poor risk aversion.

"这次产品召回事件将加速广东玩具业的转型和重组,一些落后的小企业被淘汰,生存下来的企业必须提高产品的科技含量,走自主创新的道路。这对行业规范化很有好处。"梁钟铭认为,对于那些真正专注发展玩具业,以及本身已重视质检的企业来说[9],可能是一个有利拓展市场空间的机会。"从这方面来讲,这次玩具召回事件也是坏事变好事。"梁钟铭说。

"On a positive note, the recalls will stimulate the transformation and restructuring of Guangdong's toy industry," Leung said. "Some small companies lagging behind will be wiped out, while the surviving companies must improve the technology of their products and carry out independent innovation. It is conducive to the industry." Leung said that companies that are truly attuned to the needs of the market and continue innovating and quality controlling will enjoy better development potential. "The recalls might not be a totally bad thing," Leung said.

恶性竞争
Vicious competition

上世纪70年代,香港工业起飞,人力资源成本高涨,这时恰逢中国内地实行对外开放政策。于是,在经营出现困难的情况下,一大批香港劳动力密集型制造企业转移到了与之毗邻的广东省珠三角地区。龙昌国际就是其中之一,如今它已发展成为在香港联交所[10]上市已整整10年的国际知名玩具企业。

In the 1970s, when Hong Kong's industries boomed, human resources costs also soared. It was then that the mainland began the process of reform and opening-up. Looking to cut its costs, many of Hong Kong's labor-intensive industries transferred over the border to the Zhujiang Delta area, Guangdong Province. Lung Cheong Holdings was one of those companies and has been an internationally recognized toy company listed in Hong Kong for the past 10 years.

龙昌国际所在的东莞市,距离香港不到100公里。如今,这里的玩具企业超过了2 000家,与玩具相关的企业更是高达四五千家,玩具业已成为东莞市的八大支柱产业之一。

Based in Dongguan City, Lung Cheong Holdings is situated less than 100 km from Hong Kong. The city has over 2,000 toy companies and enterprises related to them number over 5,000. The toy industry is one of the eight pillar industries for Dongguan.

据东莞市政府有关部门提供的一份调研报告显示,在东莞生产的玩具产品中,外销比重达90%以上。在中国占70%的全球玩具市场份额中,其中有30%是出自于东莞。东莞玩具企业主要以港资为主,约占80%。

About 90 percent of the toys produced in Dongguan are exported, according to a report from the city's administrative department. China manufacturers about 70 percent of the toys on the global market, and 30 percent of those come from Dongguan. Hong Kong-invested toy companies comprise 80 percent of all toy manufacturers in Dongguan.

在这些玩具企业中,大多数是以代为加工外资品牌,而且规模较小,利润率极低。据上文提到的调研报告显示,在2004年调查的649家玩具企业中,只有约占2%的企业拥有自己的品牌。"大部分中小企业的设备相对简单,创新不足,往往没有自己的核心技术。"

Most of the toy manufacturers process toys for foreign brands, meaning they are small in scale and low in profit. A Dongguan research report reveals that, only 2 percent of the 649 toy companies surveyed in 2004 had their own independent brands. "Most of them don't have their own core technologies" the report stated. "They lack innovation, and their equipment is old."

近年来，随着人民币升值、内地出台法律规范劳动力市场，以及技术工人供应出现短缺等多方面因素，玩具制造业成本普遍升高，这使得利润本已低到极限的玩具业难以承受。于是，东莞玩具业出现了向外迁移的迹象，主要是流向经济欠发达的内陆地区，以及印尼、越南等周边国家。

In recent years, the cost of manufacturing has risen due to the appreciating Renminbi, the Chinese currency, new regulations for the labor market and a shortage of skilled workers. Some toy companies, finding hard to sustain themselves, have moved to less-developed inland regions, as well as to neighboring countries such as Indonesia and Viet Nam.

在这种情况下，一些玩具企业为了拿到订单，尽量压低价格。"一些企业为了把成本降低，甚至采用对消费者健康不利的原料，也是导致玩具产品回收个案上升的原因之一。"梁钟铭说。

Under such circumstances, some toy companies cut their prices to the minimum in order to secure orders. "The low cost has forced some toy companies to choose unhealthy raw materials which will cause damage to consumers and this is also one of the reasons for the rising numbers of recalls," said Leung.

自主创新是唯一出路
Innovation is key

由于大多是做贴牌生产[11]，广东省玩具业的利润率低的只有1%～3%。而且，近年来，美欧等传统市场出台了一系列技术标准，这给整个行业带来了更大的压力。例如，欧盟不仅进一步严格限制了进口玩具六种有害物质（铅、汞、镉、六价铬、多溴联苯和多溴二苯醚）的含有指标[12]，而且规定玩具报废后，也必须由生产者和经销商回收处理，并为此付费。

Since most of the products are foreign branded, the profit ratio of Guangdong's toy industry floats at only around 1 – 3 percent. Moreover, increasing technical barriers from the United States and European Union have added pressure to the industry. For instance, the European Union has issued stricter standards covering six toxic ingredients including lead, hydrargyrum, cadmium, hexavalent chromium and PBDEs. It also ordered that after the toys are discarded, producers and distributors must recycle and pay for the disposal.

事实上，在这次产品召回事件中，已经出现了一个现象[13]：不少中小企业都在发愁如何拿到合格和齐备的检验报告，经营状况直线下跌，可与此同时，一些实力较强的大企业接的单子反而比出事前增长了50%以上，令其生产能力都跟不上[14]。

Significant changes have taken place within the toy industry when the recalls took place.

Many small and medium-sized companies are worried about how to obtain licenses and qualified inspection reports, leading to nose-diving revenue. However, the order sheets of some large companies have increased 50 percent compared to the period before the Mattel recalls, and they have to work day and night to fulfill the orders.

"这个现象让很多企业明白,已不能再打价格牌,玩具企业要想生存,必须不断自我创新,提高产品附加值[15],这才是长远之计。"梁钟铭表示。

"The changes have made many companies realize that price wars no longer work as they did before," Leung said. "If you want to survive, innovation and continuous efforts to increase added value are essential."

经过多年的发展,广东省玩具业的生产技术水平在很多方面已经达到了国际先进水平。从整体上来说,生产出来的玩具品质也是有保证的。据统计,2006年中国出口到美国的玩具约30万批左右,而同期召回的玩具案例只有约29起。

After years of development, the technology level of the Guangdong toy industry has reached the international standard in many aspects. Generally speaking, toy quality there can be guaranteed. Statistics show China exported 300,000 batches of toys to the United States in 2006, and of these, there were only 29 cases of recall.

面向未来市场
Eyeing the future

经历了"美泰召回事件",一些玩具企业得到了教训,一些地方政府也加快了推动玩具产业升级的步伐。据东莞松山湖科技产业园区(Dongguan SSL Sci. & Tech. Industry Park)政策研究室(Policy Research Office)的肖乃勇透露,东莞市政府正在对包括玩具业在内的制造业进行一次大范围调研,最后会形成一个转型报告,里面会涉及一系列推动玩具产业升级的政策。

The Mattel toy recall incident has taught many toy companies a lesson, and some local governments have begun efforts to upgrade these industries. Xiao Naixiong, a policy research officer of the Dongguan SSL Science & Technology Industry Park, said that the city government is conducting a survey among Dongguan's toy-manufacturing companies, and, based on this, it will issue a report involving policies encouraging the upgrade of the toy industry.

此外,为了推动玩具产业升级,东莞市政府正在努力搭建平台,为企业和研究机构合作开发新一代高科技智能玩具。广东电子工业研究院就是其中的一个平台。据该院副院长唐振初介绍,目前该院已经掌握了一套用于智能玩具的集成芯片技术,可以使原有智能玩具三四千元的价格降至几百元。

In order to do this, the Dongguan Government is striving to build sound platforms for companies and research institutions to develop a new generation of hi-tech toys. The Guangdong Electrics Industry Institute (GEI) is one such platform. Tang Zhenchu, Vice President of the GEI, said the institute has invented system-on-a-chip technology that can reduce the cost of intelligent toys from several thousand yuan to several hundred yuan.

龙昌国际起步于上世纪60年代初期的香港,当时是一家典型的家庭小作坊企业,承包玩具代加工业务。8年后,龙昌才购入第一台生产玩具的旧机器——塑料挤压机,用来生产圣诞树的树头。后来经过与Taiyo、Tomy等日本大型玩具商合作,在业内也逐渐有了知名度。

Lung Cheong Holdings started as a small workshop in Hong Kong in the 1960s and manufactured toys under other brands. Eight years later, the company bought second-hand plastic processing equipment to produce Christmas trees. Through cooperation with big Japanese toy companies like Taiyo and Tomy, Lung Cheong Holdings became recognizable in the industry.

上世纪70年代初,为了减轻成本,龙昌把生产车间从香港搬到了内地东莞市,香港总部负责前期研发和销售。1997年在香港联交所上市后,龙昌的资金更为充裕,便开始注重为玩具注入高科技元素。

In the early 1970s, Lung Cheong Holdings moved its factory to the mainland to cut costs, while the Hong Kong headquarters remained responsible for product research and marketing. Since its listing in Hong Kong in 1997, the company has enjoyed sufficient capital and has been able to direct more attention to hi-tech toys.

"传统玩具利润极低,而数码高科技玩具的利润率可以达到30%～40%,而且市场潜力也很大。"龙昌国际品质部高级经理陈育川解释说,"市场告诉我们,不往前走就没法生存。"

"The profitability of traditional toys is very low, while that of digital hi-tech toys can reach 30 to 40 percent and has a potential market," said Chen Yuchuan, a senior manager with Lung Cheong Holdings. "The market teaches us we must innovate in order to survive."

梁钟铭还介绍,在龙昌8亿元人民币的年销售额中,现在每年用于研发的经费占到3%～5%。目前龙昌国际共有员工约6 500人,其中研发人员有320多人,覆盖玩具生产的各个环节。

Leung said that 3 to 5 percent of the company's 800 million yuan in annual sales revenue will be dedicated to research and development. Currently, the company has about 6 500 employees and around 320 are engaged in research and development, covering every aspect of toy production.

目前，在龙昌国际的产品结构中，低端代加工（OEM）的玩具占 50%，自主设计制造（ODM）的占 25%，拥有自主品牌（OBM）的只有 15% 左右。"在未来的 5 年时间内，我们的目标是把 OBM 的比例提高到 50%。"梁钟铭表示。

In Leung's company, original equipment manufactured (OEM) toys account for 50 percent; original design manufactured (ODM) toys make up 25 percent; and original brand manufactured (OBM) toys take 15 percent. "Our goal is to increase our OBM to 50 percent in the next five years," Leung said.

Words and Expressions

召回	recall
坏事变好事	a blessing in disguise
欧盟	European Union
走出……阴影	to get rid of
回升	pick up
跨国	transnational
风险预防	risk aversion
转型	transformation
重组	restructure
淘汰	wipe out
专注	attune to
恶性竞争	vicious competition
指望	look to do sth.
劳动力密集型的	labor-intensive
上市	list
珠三角	the Zhujiang Delta
支柱产业	pillar industry
核心技术	core technology
升值	appreciate
贴牌	foreign branded or original equipment manufactured (OEM)
有害	toxic
铅	lead
汞	hydrargyrum
镉	cadmium
六价铬	hexavalent chromium

多溴联苯醚	PBDE (Polybrominated Biphenyl Ether)
报废	discard
价格（等）猛跌	nosedive
打价格战	price wars
附加值	added value
调研	survey
集成芯片	system-on-a-chip
小作坊	small workshop
代加工	manufacture ... under other brands
挤压机	processing equipment
自主设计制造	original design manufactured
自主品牌	original brand manufactured

Notes

1. ① 2007 年 8 月 2 日至 9 月 5 日，美国最大玩具商美泰公司宣布，由于玩具涂料含铅成分过高，在全球召回近 2 100 万件中国生产的问题玩具，引发了中国玩具出口乃至"中国制造"的信任危机。

   ② 滑铁卢在这里是个比喻，指"彻底失败"。将其意译成"back from the brink"，取其"悬崖勒马"之意，表示只要认真总结教训，加紧改革，是完全能够避免一败涂地的。

2. "心情很是沉重"直接译成"depressed"即可，而增加"dark clouds"正好与"始料未及却又来势凶猛的产品召回事件"相连，效果更好。

3. 汉语的"前后"译成英语应该是"about"或"around"，但这次召回事件实际上是从 8 月 2 日开始的，所以将"9 月前后"酌情译成"from August to the beginning of September this year"比"around this September"更准确。

4. 美国美泰公司

   Mattel, Inc. engages in the design, manufacture, and marketing of toys and family products worldwide. Its products include fashion dolls and accessories, vehicles and playsets, and games and puzzles.

5. "设计出了问题"译成"flawed design aspects/problems"很准确，"flawed"就是"有问题，有瑕疵"。另外，"跟中方制造公司没任何关系"不能译成"has nothing to do with the

Chinese manufacturers", 而应该译成 "this wasn't the fault of the Chinese manufacturers"。

6. "受牵连的中方公司"中的"受牵连"不可直接译成"the Chinese company involved",因为这样翻译很难让读者明白这家企业和美泰的关系,所以翻译成"where the toys were manufactured",读者一看就知道这是一家从事贴牌业务的中国厂商。

7. "出现年内首次环比负增长"中的"环比"在翻译时可以省略,因为前文"比上个月下滑"就是"报告期水平与前一时期水平之比,表明现象逐期的发展速度"。

8. 背景资料:美泰是中国价廉物美产品的受惠者。这家年收入50亿美元的玩具商,在中国开业25年,生产了数十亿件玩具。

9. "对于那些真正专注发展玩具业……"中的"专注发展玩具业"实际上指的是:企业应根据自身的情况进行调整,以便与玩具市场协调发展,因此译成"attuned to the needs of the market"更加合适。

10. 香港联交所,即香港联合交易所。

11. 贴牌生产 OEM
又叫定牌生产和贴牌生产,最早流行于欧美等发达国家,它是国际大公司寻找各自比较优势的一种游戏规则,能降低生产成本,提高品牌附加值。近年来,这种生产方式在国内家电行业比较流行,如TCL在苏州三星定牌生产洗衣机,长虹在宁波迪声定牌生产洗衣机等。
具体说来,A方看中B方的产品,让B方生产,用A方的商标,对A方来说,这叫OEM(Original Equipment Manufacture),即原始设备制造商。根据A方的设计进行改进,然后生产,然后冠以自己的品牌进行销售,这叫ODM(Original Design Manufacture),即原始设计制造商。生产商完全自行创立产品品牌,生产、销售拥有自主品牌的产品,这叫OBM(Original Brand Manufacture)。有观点认为,收购现有品牌、以特许经营方式获取品牌也可算为OBM的一环。

12. 2003年2月,欧盟议会和欧盟理事会以2002/95/EC号文正式公布:要求从2006年7月1日起进入欧盟的电气电子产品都应符合欧盟有毒有害物质禁用指令(Restriction of Hazardous Substances, RoHS),目前主要针对电子电气产品中的铅(Pb)、镉(Cd)、汞(Hg)、六价铬(Cr6+)、多溴联苯(PBBs)、多溴联苯醚(PBDEs)六种有害物质进行限制,禁止含有有害重金属及以多溴联苯、多溴联苯醚作阻燃剂的电子电气产品进入欧盟市场。

13. "事实上,在这次产品召回事件中,已经出现了一个现象"中的"现象"一词如果按汉语字面的意思直接翻译成英语"phenomenon",表意就不会很准确,因为英语"phenomenon"一词的含义是:"an occurrence, a circumstance, or a fact that is perceptible by the senses"(现象,事件:可以被感官知的现象、事件或事实)。因此,将其译成"changes"更加贴切。

14. "令其生产能力都跟不上"就是指订单太多,只好加班加点才能完成,所以翻译成"have to work day and night to fulfill the orders"。

15 "产品附加值":生产和流通过程中附加到生产要素上的价值,即产品总价值减去企业投入的生产要素价值后剩余的部分。将劳动力和资本等生产要素转移的价值定义为产品的"基本价值"(Basic Value)。这样,产品价值就可以分为"基本价值"和"附加值"两部分。

他山之石

原文:

在 2007 年年初中国国家开发银行(下称国开行)就传出即将展开商业化改革的消息,经过整整一年的酝酿,在 2007 年的最后一天中国人民银行宣布,经国务院批准,中国投资有限责任公司(下称中投公司)的子公司——中央汇金投资有限责任公司(下称汇金公司)和国开行在北京签署协议,确认即日起汇金公司向国开行注资 200 亿美元。获得注资后,国开行商业化方案有望在 2008 年正式实行。

译文 1:

Rumors had been swirling since the beginning of 2007 that China Development Bank (CDB) would set off on the path to become a commercial lender. After a lengthy wait, confirmation finally came from the People's Bank of China, the central bank, on the last day of 2007. With the approval of the State Council, the Central Huijin Investment Co. Ltd. (Central Huijin), a subsidiary of China Investment Corp. (CIC), sealed an agreement with CDB in Beijing. Accordingly, Central Huijin immediately injected $20 billion into CDB, creating high hopes for the implementation of its reform plan in 2008.

译文 2:

It was rumored at the beginning of 2007 that China Development Bank (CDB), a policy bank in China, would set out to be reorganized into a commercial bank. Having had prepared for a whole year, the People's Bank of China finally announced on the last day of 2007 that, with the approval of the State Council, the Central Huijin Investment Co. Ltd. (Central Huijin), a subsidiary of China Investment Corp. (CIC), had reached an agreement with CDB in Beijing for an immediate injection of $20 billion into CDB, thus advancing the latter's transformation in 2008.

点评:

① 翻译这段文字前,应该首先查找相关的资料,充分了解与所译材料相关联的信息。

背景：中国国家开发银行是一家非常特殊的政策性银行，它由财政部在1994年出资500亿元人民币设立。这家银行不能吸收存款，其信贷资金主要通过发行金融债的方式筹集，拥有主权级别的信用评级。类似这样的银行中国还有两家，分别是中国进出口银行和中国农业发展银行。

政策性银行指由政府创立、参股或保证的，不以营利为目的，专门为贯彻、配合政府社会经济政策或经济意图，在特定的业务领域内，直接或间接地从事政策性融资活动，充当政府发展经济、促进社会进步、进行宏观经济管理工具的金融和机构。

按照《中华人民共和国商业银行法》，商业银行主要业务是吸收公众存款、发放贷款、办理结算等业务。按照基本确定的方案设计，国家开发银行将全面商业化，从此告别政策性银行，并将遵照《中华人民共和国公司法》的要求成立股份公司，并以自身信誉为担保发行金融债融资。虽然最终定性有待确认，但银行名称不变。

② 译文2在翻译"中国国家开发银行"时增加了一个插入语"a policy bank in China"。这一增译虽然不是很起眼，但却很出彩，因为它说明了"中国国家开发银行"的性质，为后面"to be reorganized into a commercial bank"做了铺垫，否则英语读者就有可能感到不解：这家银行是什么银行？为什么不是一家商业银行？

③ 译文1将"商业化改革"翻译成"become a commercial lender"。这一翻译与原文隐含的"商业银行"有出入，因为英语"commercial lender"不能完全等同于"商业银行"。以下是Wikipedia关于两者的介绍。

- In much of the world and especially in the UK, the phrase *commercial lender* refers to a lender arranging commercial loans especially commercial mortgages. In the UK it is generally taken to refer to a lender who lends to businesses rather than individuals. ie. a lender to commerce.

- In the US *a commercial lender* offers loans backed by hard collateral. In most cases this is real estate, but it can also include factoring, non-conforming assets, or other sources of collateral. *Commercial lenders* include commercial banks, mutual companies, private lending institutions, hard money lenders and other financial groups. These lenders typically have widely varying standards on which they base their loan criteria and evaluate potential borrowers—but are often focused exclusively on the private market and have more lenient financial qualifications than banks.

④ 译文2没有像译文1一样将"方案有望在2008年正式实行"直译成"creating high hopes for the implementation of its reform plan in 2008"，而是将此句意译成"thus advancing the latter's transformation in 2008"，意思是：这一注资实际上将推动国开行在2008年实施商业化的计划。表面上看来，译文1在字面上更符合原文，但译文2却更加简洁明了。

学生译作分析

原文：

中国是世界上最大的发展中国家。中国具有发展中国家二元结构的典型特征。人口多、底子薄，自然地理条件差距和人口资源分布差距很大，城乡和区域发展差距也很大。

学生原译文：

China is the world's largest developing country. China has a dual structure typical of developing countries, overpopulation, a weak economic foundation, the gap between the natural and geographical conditions and great disparities in the distribution of population, resources, and regional development gap between urban and rural areas is also very large.

分析：

① 将"二元结构"翻译成"a dual structure"在没有上下文的情况下不够准确，因为事实上"二元结构"在文中是指"城乡二元经济结构"，准确的表达方法是"dual economy"。Wikipedia 对此词的解释是：

- Dual economy：**imbalance between economic sectors**, an economy in which different sectors are growing at different rates. Manufacturing and service industries or rural and urban areas may show significant differences in economic performance.
- Dual economy (sometimes also known as a "dualistic economy") is the existence of two separate economic systems within one region; common in the less developed countries, where one system is geared to local needs and another to the global export market. For example, a modern plantation or other commercial agricultural entity operating in the midst of traditional cropping systems. In this kind of economy, agriculture and industry survive together

因此，可以将"二元结构"翻译成"dual economy"或"the dual structure in urban and rural economy"，如："The dual structure in urban and rural economy has not yet been changed, the gap between regions is still widening and there are still quite a large number of impoverished people."（城乡二元经济结构还没有改变，地区差距扩大的趋势尚未扭转，贫困人口还为数不少。）

② 译文将第二句话译成了一句话，意思上虽然没有太大的问题，但整个句子过长，主次不够分明，读起来也比较费劲。因此，可以考虑将整个句子拆开，按不同的意思

分别翻译，这样效果会更好。

参考译文：

China is the largest developing country in the world. China has the typical feature of dual economy as a developing country. With a big population and a weak economic foundation, China is one of the countries having within it the widest gap of the natural and geographic conditions as well as the population and resources distribution in the world. It is also one of the countries with the sharpest discrepancy of development between the urban and rural areas and among different regions.

翻译技巧介绍

重复的处理

"重复"这一手段在汉英两种语言中都经常使用，但由于两种语言的结构和习惯用法不完全相同，所以运用这一手段的方法也就会出现不同的特点。在翻译商务文献和资料时，可以考虑通过以下方式来处理重复词语和重复结构。

一、省略

在翻译商务文献和资料时，可以省略或简化汉语中为了求得句子平衡或起强调作用而重复的一些词语和结构。

（1）有问题的**进口**产品都是从国外**进口**的产品，不属于假冒**进口**产品。

译文：The questionable imported products indeed were from foreign countries and were not fake or products of counterfeiting.

（2）企业很难预测远期**汇率**水平，承担的**汇率**风险很大。

译文：It is hard for the dealers to estimate the long-term currency exchange rate, and they will have to shoulder many risks.

（3）中国虽然并**不反对**人民币升值，但却**反对**人民币过快升值，**反对**超过极限的、不合理的升值，**反对**不符合国情的过快升值。

译文：China agrees that the yuan should appreciate, but opposes rapid, unlimited and irrational appreciation that does not fit with the country's national development situation.

（4）中国政策性银行入股国际管理水平高、历史悠久的国际大银行**有利于**提高自身的国际化意识，**有利于**更快地实现商业化转型。

译文：This will benefit the commercialization and globalization awareness of China's policy banks, as they can draw on the advanced management expertise of international banks with long histories.

（5）做出中断买卖的**决定**是因为市场变化太快，哪怕这个**决定**可能是赔本的。

译文：The reason for the suspension was the market is changing too fast. Even if the decision means a loss, we have to do it.

（6）不止是我们的**商标**，中国好多知名**商标**在海外被抢注了。

译文：A handful of renowned Chinese brands are also suffering infringements and we are not alone in such cases.

（7）随着中国企业品牌和产品在世界市场上的影响越来越大，海外企业以**抢注**中国的商标作为一种在世界市场上竞争的新武器，而商标一旦在国外被**抢注**，企业就得买回本该属于自己的商标或"改名换姓"，这两种方法都需要付出高昂的代价。

译文：With Chinese brands gaining a foothold in the global market, overseas competitors are vying for these brands to sharpen their competitive edge, and once preempted, they have to buy back their trademarks or rename their products, both of which can lead to substantial costs.

（8）"如果我不在办公室，就在**星巴克**。如果我不在**星巴克**，就在去**星巴克**的路上。"这句话曾经俨然成了都市白领的流行语。

译文："If I am not in my office, I am either at Starbucks or on the way to Starbucks" became a mantra among Beijing's white-collar employees.

（9）由于资源和环境约束，新目录**不再鼓励**外资进入传统制造业、**不再鼓励**外资投资重要矿产、**不再鼓励**出口导向型外资进入。

译文：The new catalog no longer encourages foreign investment in the traditional manufacturing industry, major mining projects and export-oriented industries in a bid to protect environment and save national resources.

二、替代

在翻译商务文献和资料时，可以用代词、名词和其他词或者词组替代汉语中重复的部分。

1. 用代词代替重复部分

（1）洋品牌又一次倒在了"质量门"前。今年1月18日上海市工商局对**知名品牌**服装的抽查结果显示，40种**知名品牌**服装的59个样品中不合格的有25个。被检出不合格的产品包括Zara、CHANEL、ARMANI、MaxMara、BURBERRY、MNG等**知**

名品牌，销售价格一般在千元以上，最高的达6万元。

译文：On January 18 this year foreign brands failed again after the Shanghai Administration of Industry and Commerce conducted a similar quality inspection. The result showed that 25 of 59 samples of 40 well-known foreign brands had quality problems, including Zara, Chanel, Armani, Max Mara, Burberry and Mango, **which** were mostly sold for between 1,000 yuan and 60,000 yuan.

(2) 人民币升值降低了造纸等行业的进口成本，由于其原料大量依赖进口就可能会从人民币升值中受惠，而对行业产生有利影响。

译文：The RMB appreciation has reduced import cost of industries such as paper making, and many raw materials in these industries are imported. **This** will cause a positive impact on these industries.

(3) 在资源、环境等瓶颈约束日益明显的条件下，要从经济社会发展的需要出发，创新**利用外资**方式，优化**利用外资**结构，实现**利用外资**稳定健康发展。

译文：Restricted by such factors as resources and environment, we should proceed from the real demand of the national economy and ensure foreign investments by encouraging, attracting and optimizing the **use of them**.

(4) 据麦肯锡公司调查分析，在中国，**家庭**年收入在4 300美元以上的中、高收入**家庭**大约有3 000万户，而其中4%，即120万户**家庭**拥有高达10万美元以上的存款。

译文：A survey by McKinsey & Company shows that there are 30 million middle-and high-income households in China, with annual incomes exceeding $4,300. Four percent of **them** have deposits of more than $100,000.

(5) 中国生产的**紫菜**质量并没有问题，因为中国、日本、韩国生产的**紫菜**属同类品种，三国对该类**紫菜**的养殖加工方式基本相同。而且，企业所使用的**紫菜**加工设备基本都是从日本引进的。

译文：Quality-wise Chinese laver was on a par with **that** from Japan and South Korea. The methods of growing and processing in the three countries were basically the same and the processing equipment all comes from Japan.

(6) 运用 **WTO** 规则，行使 **WTO** 赋予我们的权利应对各种各样的贸易壁垒，是我们为营造公平的国际贸易环境所必须迎接的挑战。

译文：In order to create a fair international trade environment, we should make use of rights given by the WTO and **its** rules to fight all kinds of trade barriers.

2. 用其他词替代汉语中重复的部分

(1) 尽管这样，中国的地方藩篱要在短时间内拆除仍然有很多困难。而且，国际贸易的**保护主义**其实就是扩大了的地方**保护主义**，它和地方**保护主义**具有同样性质的错误。中国追求公平贸易的环境，还有很长的路要走。

译文：However, there are still many difficulties to remove all regional obstacles in China. Besides, protectionism in international trade is actually regional protectionism on a larger scale and it has the same faults as **the latter.** There is a long way for China to seek a fair trade environment.

(2) 根据入世协议的规定，今后几年中国农产品市场将进一步开放，关税水平继续降低。2005年，中国**农产品关税水平**将降至15.35%，而世界**农产品关税平均水平**为62%。

译文：According to China's commitments made to the World Trade Organization (WTO), its agricultural products market is to be opened wider in the years ahead, with corresponding tariffs reduced continually. In 2005, tariffs will be reduced to 15.35 percent, compared with **the global average** of 62 percent.

(3) 近年来国际小麦价格基本和国内的价格差不多，但是进口**小麦**的质量和纯度都优于国产**小麦**，国产**小麦**在国内市场上将遇到的激烈竞争是可以想像的。

译文：In recent years, international and domestic wheat prices have been largely similar despite the better quality and purity of **imports.** As a result, competition in the domestic wheat market is likely to become much fiercer in the foreseeable future.

(4) 在农**产品**质量上，中国**产品规格化标准化程度低**，**产品**质量不高，**产品**安全问题突出。

译文：In terms of quality of the Chinese agricultural products, it is generally low, and **standardization and safety are issues** in China.

(5) 很多国家在进口上都卡得很严，层层把关，而我们国家在这方面就弱得多。这导致该出的出不去，不该**进**的却大量涌**进**来。

译文：Many countries are strict with imports, but China is relatively lax in this respect, which **poses an obstacle to export**, while at the same time it is an ineffective barrier to products **flooding** the Chinese market.

(6) 目前从数量上来说，外商直接投资主要还是制造业，但随着政策环境的完善，今后，**服务业**将成为吸引外资的重点，特别是金融**服务业**。

译文：The manufacturing sector still gets the largest infusion of foreign capital, but a loosening of investment policy is expected to direct more foreign capital into the service sector, the **financial sector** in particular.

(7) 国内外汇市场供求状况也是近期**人民币升值**的原因，一些国内金融机构大规模抛售外汇，促使**人民币升值**。

译文：The supply and demand in foreign exchange market was also part of the reason for renminbi **appreciation**. Some financial institutions have sold foreign exchange in large amounts, which propped up the renminbi's **value**.

(8) 专家认为相比受到数量限制而言，不稳定的贸易环境对中国企业的损害会更大，美国进口商**不敢**下单、中国企业**不敢**接单。

译文：Experts believe that more than quota limits, it was the unstable trade environment that harmed Chinese enterprises as **neither** the United States **nor** the Chinese side **dared** to place or accept orders.

(9) 要减少贫困，最重要的不是直接扶助，而是向**贫困人口**、**贫困阶层**、**贫困地区**提供依靠自我奋斗向上流动的机会。

译文：What is most important to poverty alleviation is not direct assistance but affording **the impoverished** with opportunities to pull themselves up by their bootstraps.

三、重复

如果汉语句子的用词和结构强调的意味很浓，英译时就应该采取重复的形式，尤其是翻译经济政策和商务法律法规时应特别注意这一点。

(1) 中国恢复关贸总协定缔约国地位和加入世贸组织已经走过了 **15 年**的历程。**15 年**的沧桑变化，已经深深印在中国人的记忆之中，并且也为每一位关心和支持中国现代化事业的外国朋友所见证。

译文：China has gone through a journey of **15 years** in order to first resume the contracting party status in GATT and later to enter the WTO. The twists and turns over the past **15 years** have been deeply embedded in the minds of the Chinese people and witnessed by each and every foreign friend who cares for and supports China's cause of modernization.

(2) 我们**呼吁**国际社会鼓励并支持非洲谋求和平与发展的努力，为非洲国家和平解决冲突和进行战后重建提供更大帮助，特别**呼吁**发达国家增加官方发展援助，切实兑现开放市场和减免债务等承诺，**呼吁**有关国际组织提供更多资金支持和技术援助，增强非洲减贫、减灾、防治荒漠化的能力，帮助非洲实现联合国千年发展目标。

译文：We **call on** the international community to encourage and support Africa's efforts to pursue peace and development and provide greater assistance to African countries in peaceful resolution of conflicts and post-war reconstruction. In particular, we **urge** the developed countries to increase official development assistance and honor their commitments to opening market and debt relief, and **call on** the related international organizations to provide more financial and technical assistance to enhance Africa's capacity in poverty and disaster reduction and prevention and control of desertification, and help Africa realize the UN Millennium Development Goals.

(3) 中国将解决人民群众最关心、最直接、最现实的利益问题。

译文：China will resolve the **most** practical problems that are of greatest concern and most directly affect their interests.

(4) 新的世纪充满着机遇和**挑战**，让我们共同合作，迎接**挑战**，使多边贸易体制得到巩固和加强，为世界经济贸易的稳定和发展不断做出贡献。

译文：The new century is full of opportunities and **challenges.** Let us work together to meet these **challenges**, and to consolidate and strengthen the multilateral trading system and to make continued contributions to the stability and development of world economy and trade.

(5) 第一阶层，是那些年收入在8万元以上的高收入者，**钱**已经不是问题，问题是**钱**该花在哪里。

译文：The first class represents high-income earners with annual income exceeding 80,000 yuan. **Money** is not a problem for them, and they only need to consider where to spend their **money**.

(6) 高收入支持的**消费**群体正处在从国内富裕型家庭向国际中等水平冲击、跨越的阶段，是国内**消费**水平、**消费**特点与国际**消费**衔接，并起示范作用的先导力量。

译文：The high-income class is trying to keep up with the international middle class level and playing a demonstration and leading role in connecting the level and characteristics of domestic **consumption** with those of international **consumption**.

(7) 截至7月底，深圳市全市有"零就业家庭"2 000多户。深圳市计划要在9月底前实现95%的"零就业家庭"中至少有1人实现就业，力争年底让这些"零就业家庭"全部"归零"。

译文：The Shenzhen municipal government said that at the end of July, there were 2,000 **jobless households.** It hopes that by September at least 95 percent of these **households** will have at least one employed family member, and bring the number of **jobless households down to zero** by the end of the year.

(8) 缺乏本土创新的成长使零售企业之间很难拉开档次，最终导致**同地域**、**同档次**、**同类型**的多家企业之间展开过度竞争。

译文：The lack of uniqueness and creativity results in undifferentiated market solutions, leading to over-competition among many retail companies of the **same** grade and the **same** style in the **same** region.

四、部分重复

翻译过程中有时也可根据情况保留汉语中某些重复的词和结构，合并或省去另一些重复部分。

(1) 经济全球化时代造就了全球化的利益和**问题**，客观上要求各个国家、社会各界广泛协调，以便解决**问题**。我们并不奢望世界经济论坛能够直接解决多少**问题**，但我们有理由期望，通过让来自众多国家和地区的社会各界人士共处一堂讨论**问题**，世界经济论坛能够有助于推动解决**问题**。

译文：Economic globalization has also brought along globalized interests and **problems**, which call for broad coordination of all countries and all sections of society. We do not expect the World Economic Forum to solve any **problems** directly, but we have reason to believe that the big gathering of worldwide representatives can make a difference to their solution.

(2) 中国国有商业银行、股份制商业银行等金融机构**存款准备金率**再次上调0.5个百分点，执行8.5%的**存款准备金率**。这是中国央行40天内第二次提高**存款准备金率**了。

译文：From August 15, the **required reserve ratio** of state-owned and joint-stock commercial banks with the central bank will be further increased by 0.5 percentage points to 8.5 percent, the People's Bank of China (PBC) announced on July 18. This is the second time the central bank will raise **the ratio** within 40 days.

五、合并

如果原文中重复的部分不是特别强调的语气，可以考虑按照英语表达的习惯将重复的部分全部合并或部分合并。

(1) 上世纪90年代末，中国又实行了医疗**改革**、教育**改革**、住房**改革**，使得老百姓看病、接受教育、住房由福利性的公费变为了自费。

译文：In the late 1990s, the Chinese Government launched **reforms** of health care, educational and housing systems, with expenses in these fields, which had been formerly covered by the government, now paid by individuals.

(2) 现在中国人很着急，总想**一夜之间**成就什么大事情，**一夜之间**就成为市值最大的什么什么公司，这种盲目求大心理很打击投资者的信心并损害上市公司。投资者一旦对市场失去了信心，对上市公司失去了信心，要想再恢复就很难了。

译文：Chinese companies have always been in a rush. They always wanted to accomplish everything or became the biggest listed company **overnight.** This heedless ambition could eventually damage investor confidence and the company. Once investors lose confidence in the stock market and the listed companies, it will be hard to repair.

(3) 不加限制地引入国外强势文化品牌，可能危及中国文化安全，全球化再怎么发展，也不能全世界**都是**迪斯尼，**都是**好莱坞。

   译文：The unrestricted introduction of foreign advantaged popular culture brands might threaten China's cultural security. No matter how globalization evolves, it is not good to have a world **full of** Disneyland parks and Hollywood movies.

(4) 虽然对文化产业的外资要依法予以规制，但我们要以开放心态来发展文化产业，吸收世界其他文明的优秀**文化**，结合中国特色**文化**，发展出先进**文化**。

   译文：While we should regulate foreign investment in the entertainment industry according to law, we must adopt an open mind in developing our entertainment industry, trying to absorb good elements of other **cultures** and mix them into an advanced **culture** with Chinese characteristics.

(5) 《财富》杂志在做全球50位商界女强人评比时，有这么一段话，定义出什么叫**权力**是很容易的事情，定义出**权力**有多重、有多大的**权力**是件困难的事情。人人有**权力**，很难比较出**权力**的大小。没有联想就没有我，不是我**特别强**，而是联想**特别强**。我幸运，因为我坐在了这个位置上。

   译文：When *Forbes* magazine evaluated the top 50 businesswomen in the world, it said that it was easy to give a certain definition to "**power**" but difficult to give a definition to the weight of "**power**", for everyone has it and it's hard to tell whose is greater. No Lenovo, no me. It's not me but Lenovo that is **strong**. I'm just lucky because I happen to hold this post at Lenovo.

(6) 2000年，她在**联想**一系列重大行动中表现出色。其中包括**联想**入主赢时通、**联想**与电讯盈科合作、**联想**的拆股、**联想**筹备风险投资基金，以及**联想**与AOL时代华纳达成战略联盟等等。

   译文：In 2000, she took a string of successful initiatives for **Lenovo**, including its stock split, arranging VentureCapitalFund, investing in Yestock Information Technology Co. Ltd., cooperating with telecommunications provider in Hong Kong PCCW and planning an alliance with AOL Time Warner.

(7) 如果说到业界的压力，美国的纺织服装业涉及几十万人的**就业**，而中国则涉及近2 000万人的**就业**，应该说，中方企业的诉求**更大**、**更强烈**。

   译文：On pressure from the domestic textile industry, the pressure on the Chinese Government was **stronger** as the textile sector **employs** nearly 20 million in China compared with several hundred thousand in the United States.

(8) 至少短时间内，个人从事外贸不会对我们这样的大公司有实质性的影响，因为国外公司看中的是这个公司的**信誉**，而不是某个业务员的**信誉**，一个有**信誉**的公司的客户，是不可能被一个个人轻易抢走的

译文：Individual traders will not affect big companies such as ours in the near future at least. Overseas clients recognize the fine **reputation** of the company, not its individual employees. Individual traders are unlikely to succeed in taking customers from a **renowned** company.

课堂翻译训练

1. 外贸依存度是指一个国家的进口和出口贸易总额在本国国内生产总值（GDP）中所占的比重。外贸依存度反映了一个国家经济对外贸的依赖程度和参与国际分工的程度，折射出其经济发展战略的许多构成要素，并对其国际关系产生重要的影响。
2. 人民币升值需遵循渐进性与可控性的原则。其中渐进性至关重要，因为一旦违背渐进性原则，一次性大幅升值，将有可能丧失货币调控的主动权。
3. 从 2003 年开始，各种个人理财产品在市场上层出不穷，银行个人理财业务蓬勃发展。特别是随着中国入世以来，对外资银行的开放，中外银行纷纷推出个人理财服务项目，个人理财产品竞争开始"白热化"。
4. 政府只要将财政更多地投入到公共领域，完善各种保障机制，并通过各项政策调整居民与居民、居民与政府间的收入分配格局，就有可能真正调动居民的消费热情，提升居民的消费潜力，从而促成居民消费更快地增长，从而也就可以改变中国目前主要依靠投资拉动的经济增长模式。
5. 中国政府曾预料到居民消费价格会有大的上涨，在 2007 年初的时候将全年居民消费价格的涨幅在 2006 年的基础上翻了一倍，定在 3%。现在看来，4.8% 的涨幅，远超出了中国政府的预期，这一涨幅是 1997 年以来居民消费价格的年度最高涨幅。
6. 展望 2008 年，连续多年宏观经济景气较旺，新增就业人数增加较多，居民收入增长较快，消费结构升级对消费仍然会保持较强的促进作用，这些基本因素决定了 2008 年我国消费品市场销售增长率仍将保持高位。
7. 到 2020 年实现国内生产总值比 2000 年翻两番，达到 4 万亿美元，人均国内生产总值达到 3 000 美元，使经济更加发展、民主更加健全、科教更加进步、文化更加繁荣、社会更加和谐、人民生活更加殷实。
8. 我们对于中小企业市场及新兴市场都极为关注。在这些市场上，高利润率并不意味着高价格，高利润率也不意味着非要提供高端产品。

课后练习

将下列短文译成英语，注意运用本单元所学的翻译技巧。

1.

当晚安置停妥，次日早饭后便往街上寻觅书店。寻了许久，始觅着一家小小书店，三间门面，半边卖纸张笔墨，半边卖书。遂走到卖书这边柜台外坐下，问问此地行销是些什么书籍。

那掌柜的道："我们这东昌府，文风最著名的。所管十县地方，俗名叫做'十美图'，无一县不是家家富足，户户弦歌。所有这十县用的书，皆是向小号来贩。小号店在这里，后边还有栈房，还有作坊。许多书都是本店里自雕板，不用到外路去贩买的。你老贵姓，来此有何贵干？"老残道："我姓铁，来此访个朋友的。你这里可有旧书吗？"掌柜的道："有，有，有。你老要什么罢？我们这儿多着呢！"

2.

中国是世界大家庭的成员，中国的发展离不开世界，世界的繁荣也需要中国。中国坚持走和平发展道路，中国的发展是和平的发展、开放的发展、合作的发展、和谐的发展。中国走和平发展道路，就是既充分利用世界和平发展自己，又以自身的发展促进世界和平。中国早就向世界宣布，中国不称霸，现在不称霸，将来强大了也永远不称霸。

综合测试 2

班级 _____　　　姓名 _____　　　时间：120 分钟

I. Translate the following sentences into English. (50)

1. 星巴克中国总部目前的重点是瞄准了中国的二线城市。很可能不久之后，星巴克将和麦当劳、肯德基一样，会在中国遍地开花。(5)
2. 中国能消费高档车的人群比例虽然不大，但绝对数量非常大。在高额利润的驱使下，中国高档车市场自然成为跨国汽车巨头眼中的一个"亮点"。(6)
3. 个人经营外贸，得承担起以往整个公司的风险。并且，个人外贸可能会进一步加剧在进出口贸易中的相互压价，导致恶性价格竞争。此外，个人如何结汇、开信用证，在报关、纳税、经商过程中如何保持诚信，都是需要解决的新问题。(9)
4. 开始创业时，兄弟们往往很团结，但在家族企业做大以后，矛盾就会显现。一家亲戚都在企业里面，一旦家族矛盾与管理矛盾搅和在一起，造成管理错位，加上利益、权力和发展思路的纷争，必然会出乱子。(8)
5. 异议：品质异议须于货到目的口岸之日起 30 天内提出，数量异议须于货到目的口岸之日起 15 天内提出，但均须提供经卖方同意的公证行的检验证明。如责任属于卖方者，卖方于收到异议 20 天内答复买方并提出处理意见。(13)
6. 我不觉得传统就面临着死亡，只能是日落，有日落就有日出。中国只有 20% 的家庭有相机，对于 80% 没有相机的家庭来说，我不相信他们会直接用数码。在中东、非洲、东南亚等开发中的市场，传统市场的潜力还是非常大。这是柯达（Kodak）将来要与乐凯（Lucky）共同开发的市场。(9)

II. Translate the following passage into English. (30)

　　不久前，中国国家主席胡锦涛发出呼吁，希望有关各方拿出更大的政治诚意，显示必要的灵活性，积极推动多哈发展回合谈判进程，力争在香港会议上取得实质性成果。这就是中国的立场和期待。我多次来香港，但从来没看到这么多部长一块儿来。香港是个山清、海碧、干净、方便的城市，而且不塞车，饭菜一流，并连续 11 年被评为全球最自由的经济体。相信大家不会辜负香港给予你们的这些优惠，在此做出有利于人类进步的决断。

III. Translate the following letter into English. (20)

……先生：

现随函附寄贷记账单985号一份，计95.00美元，用以全部偿付你方对订单105号项下的货物损失的索赔。我们十分清楚我们无法弥补给你方带来的不便，但在今后的交易中，我们一定尽力使你方满意。我们一直努力做到通过提供最佳服务，使我方装运货物的质量得到你方的信任，但是有时尽管我们严加防范，困难问题仍会出现。再次感谢你方的协作，并相信我们之间的友好关系将一如既往继续发展下去。

……谨上

参考文献

[1] 刘敏娟. 新剑桥商务英语. 北京：人民邮电出版社，2006.
[2] 段云礼. 新编商务英语翻译教程. 天津：南开大学出版社，2005.
[3] 孙万彪. 高级翻译教程. 3版. 上海：上海外语教育出版社，2005.
[4] 剑桥大学考试委员会. 剑桥BEC真题集：中级. 北京：人民邮电出版社，2005.
[5] 剑桥大学考试委员会. 剑桥BEC真题集：高级. 北京：人民邮电出版社，2005.
[6] 胡春兰. 新经济英语. 北京：清华大学出版社，2004.
[7] 李朝. 商务英语翻译教程. 上海：复旦大学出版社，2003.
[8] 张春柏. 英汉汉英翻译教程. 北京：高等教育出版社，2003.
[9] 张新红. 商务英语翻译. 北京：高等教育出版社，2003.
[10] 梅清豪. 市场营销管理. 2版. 北京：中国人民大学出版社，2001.
[11] 庄绎传. 英汉翻译教程. 北京：外语教学与研究出版社，1999.
[12] 毛荣贵. 走出翻译误区. 上海：上海交通大学出版社，1999.
[13] 毛荣贵. 翻译技巧111讲. 上海：上海交通大学出版社，1999.
[14] 胡裕树. 现代汉语. 上海：上海教育出版社，1995.
[15] 张梅岗. 实用翻译教程. 武汉：湖北科技出版社，1993.
[16] 吕瑞昌. 汉英翻译教程. 西安：陕西人民出版社，1983.
[17] 张培基. 英汉翻译教程. 上海：上海外语教育出版社，1983.